AF889469

Recommended by Teachers
Trusted by Toppers

All in One®

Artificial Intelligence

Code-417

CBSE Class 9

Focused Theory ▪ Practice Exercise ▪ Sample Papers

Author
Lalita Kaler *(MCA)*

arihant
SUCCESS AND NOTHING LESS

arihant
SUCCESS AND NOTHING LESS

ARIHANT PRAKASHAN
(School Division Series)

卐 *ADMINISTRATIVE & PRODUCTION OFFICES*
Regd. Office
'Ramchhaya' 4577/15, Agarwal Road, Darya Ganj, New Delhi -110002
Tele: 011- 47630600, 43518550; Fax: 011- 23280316
卐 *Head Office*
Kalindi, TP Nagar, Meerut (UP) - 250002, Tel: 0121-7156203, 7156204

卐 *SALES & SUPPORT OFFICES*
Agra, Ahmedabad, Bengaluru, Bareilly, Chennai, Delhi, Guwahati, Hyderabad, Jaipur, Jhansi, Kolkata, Lucknow, Nagpur & Pune.

PO No : TXT-XX-XXXXXXX-X-XX

Published By Arihant Publications (India) Ltd.

For further information about the books published by Arihant, log on to www.arihantbooks.com or e-mail at info@arihantbooks.com
Follow us on

卐 *PRICE* ₹340.00

PRODUCTION TEAM

Publishing Managers
Mahendra Singh Rawat & Keshav Mohan

Cover Designer
Rakesh Rawat

Inner Designer
Ankit Tyagi

Project Head
Shruti Aggarwal

Page Layouting
Ravindra Kumar

Proof Reader
Sumit

Index *cum* Study Planner

Studied | Revised | Exam ready

One Book- Endless Features

to Help you Succeed

Chapter Intro

A quick information about the coverage of the chapter to explain students about what they are going to study.

CHAPTER **01**

Introduction to Artificial Intelligence

Artificial Intelligence (AI) is a branch of computer science that's concerned with creating intelligent machines capable of tasks typically requiring human intelligence, like learning, problem-solving, and decision-making. These machines are powered by algorithms that process massive amounts of data to identify patterns and improve their performance over time. AI is already having a huge impact on our world, from self-driving cars to facial recognition software.

1.1 Intelligence

Intelligence in human beings is **the ability to learn from experiences, solve problems, think abstractly, and understand complex concepts.** It involves gathering information from the surrounding world, analyzing it, and using that knowledge to make decisions and adapt to new situations.

Intelligence involves being creative, learning from experiences, reasoning through problems, and being able to communicate effectively with others.

"The aggregate or global capacity of the individual to act purposefully, to think rationally and to deal effectively with his environment." *Psychologist David Wechsler*

Complete Theory in Each Chapter

Each chapter has Complete, Easy to Understand and Simplified theory covering latest syllabus and NCERT Textbook. Theory is developed in such a way that it perfectly rectifies the complexity of NCERT Text making it suitable for all types of learners.

Info Wall

McCarthy presented his definition of artificial intelligence at a conference on the campus of Dartmouth College, USA in the summer of 1956. This conference led to the beginning of research in the field of artificial intelligence. McCarthy also created LISP ("List Processing"), programming language that still continues to be commonly used for several applications of artificial intelligence.

Info Wall

Random and Important facts that enhance the Knowledge about particular topic.

Try These 1.1

1. What do you understand by the term "AI"?
2. The main aim of artificial intelligence is to make the machine think and act like ______.
3. Distinguish between narrow intelligence and general intelligence.
4. Give three advantages and disadvantages of artificial intelligence.

Try These

A set of 3-5 Questions given in between the text, helps students to remain connected with the text while studying. They can instantly assess themselves for their understanding.

One Book- Endless Features

to Help you Succeed

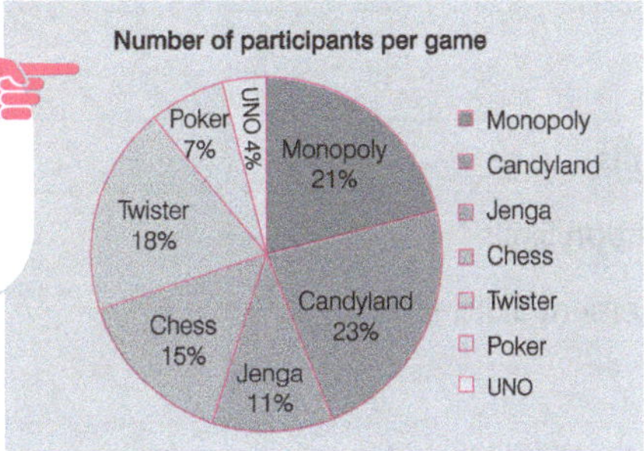

Illustrative Figures

To make the concepts completely visible, illustrative diagrams have been given at various place.

Review Exercise

Chapter exercise having all types of questions; MCQs, Assertion-Reason, Statement Based, VSA, SA, LA.

REVIEW EXERCISE Including Competency Based Questions

Part I

Multiple Choice Questions

1. Which of the following intelligence types have been implemented through Artificial Intelligence?
   (a) Ability to use language for conversing
   (b) Ability to recognise objects
   (c) Ability to learn from experience
   (d) All of the above
2. When was the term "Artificial Intelligence" first coined?

10. Which AI application assists in optimizing logistics and supply chain operations?
    (a) Healthcare (b) Agriculture
    (c) Retail (d) Transportation
11. Mr. Dinesh Patel, a computer science teacher at kendriya vidyalya, has developed an educational humanoid namely shalu, which can converse in 47 languages. Which AI technology helps shalu, the robot, converse with us humans? Competency Based Ques.

NCERT Folder

Complete explanations of all the questions of NCERT Exercises.

NCERT FOLDER Complete Explanations of all NCERT's Questions

A. Multiple Choice Questions

Q.1 Which one of the following is an application of AI?
(a) Remote controlled Drone
(b) Self-Driving Car
(c) Self-Service Kiosk
(d) Self-Watering Plant System

Q.2 This language is easy to learn and is one of the most popular languages for AI today
(a) C++ (b) Python
(c) Ruby (d) Java

- Education AI tutors can provide personalized learning experiences and identify skill gaps for students.
- Security AI can analyze threats and patterns to improve cybersecurity and disaster prediction.
- Efficiency AI can automate tasks, optimize processes, and reduce waste across industries.

Q.2 Can you list down a few applications in your smartphone that widely make use of computer vision?

Ans. Google Photos For image recognition and search.
Face ID (iPhone) For facial recognition and security.

Sample Question Papers

To make students practice of examination in real sense, there are 3 Sample Question Papers at the end. All these Sample Questions Papers are exactly prepared on the latest syllabus & pattern of examination.

Assessment Exercise

Complete Test of chapter in Exam format.

ASSESSMENT EXERCISE

Multiple Choice Questions

1. Which AI program defeated the world chess champion, Gary Kasparov, in a highly-publicized match?
   (a) Deep Blue (b) Watson
   (c) Kismet (d) ELIZA
2. Which AI-driven technology aims to simulate human-like conversation?
   (a) Machine Learning (ML) (b) Robotics
   (c) Virtual Reality (VR) (d) Chatbots
3. Which of the following is an application of AI used to process and understand human languages?
   (a) Predictive Analytics (b) Autonomous Vehicles
   (c) Natural Language Processing (NLP) (d) Facial Recognition

Sample Question Paper 1 (Solved)

Artificial Intelligence

Time : 2 hrs M.M. : 50

1. Please read the instructions carefully.
2. This Question Paper consists of 21 questions in two sections: Section A & Section B.
3. Section A has Objective type questions whereas Section B contains Subjective type questions.
4. Out of the given (5 + 16 =) 21 questions, a candidate has to answer (5 + 10 =) 15 questions in the allotted (maximum) time of 2 hours.
5. All questions of a particular section must be attempted in the correct order.
6. SECTION A - OBJECTIVE TYPE QUESTIONS (24 MARKS):
   i. This section has 05 questions.
   ii. Marks allotted are mentioned against each question/part.
   iii. There is no negative marking.
   iv. Do as per the instructions given.
7. SECTION B – SUBJECTIVE TYPE QUESTIONS (26 MARKS):
   i. This section has 16 questions.
   ii. A candidate has to do 10 questions.
   iii. Do as per the instructions given.
   iv. Marks allotted are mentioned against each question/part.

Section A : Objective Type Questions

1. Answer any 4 out of the given 6 questions on Employability Skills (1 × 4 = 4 Marks)
   (i) Physical exercise is used as a stress management technique because
   (a) it improves blood circulation
   (b) improves self-image
   (c) makes us feel better
   (d) All of the above

   (iv) It provides scheduling to each process to be run on.
   (a) Time sharing OS (b) Distributed OS
   (c) Real-time OS (d) Single-user OS

   (v) Visual communication among the people are dependent on ....
   (a) Signs, symbols and pictures
   (b) Text messages
   (c) Posture

Latest Course *Structure*

	UNITS	No. of Hours for Theory and Practical		Max. Marks for Theory and Practical
Part A	**Employability Skills**			
	Unit 1: Communication Skills-I	10		2
	Unit 2: Self-Management Skills-I	10		2
	Unit 3: ICT Skills-I	10		2
	Unit 4: Entrepreneurial Skills-I	15		2
	Unit 5: Green Skills-I	05		2
	Total	**50**		**10**
Part B	**Subject Specific Skills**	**Theory**	**Practical**	
	Unit 1: AI Reflection, Project Cycle and Ethics	30	25	10
	Unit 2: Data Literacy	22	28	10
	Unit 3: Math for AI (Statistics & Probability)	12	13	07
	Unit 4: Introduction to Generative AI	08	12	05
	Unit 5: Introduction to Python	01	09	08
	Total	**160**		**40**
Part C	**Practical Work:**			
	Unit 5: Introduction to Python **Practical File (minimum 15 programs)**			15
	Practical Examination • Simple programs using input and output function • Variables, Arithmetic Operators, Expressions, Data Types • Flow of control and conditions • Lists *** Any 3 programs based on the above topics**			15
	Viva Voce			5
	Total			**35**
Part D	Project Work / Field Visit / Student Portfolio * relate it to Sustainable Development Goals			15
	Total			**15**
	GRAND TOTAL	**210**		**100**

Detailed Curriculum / Topics

PART-A : EMPLOYABILITY SKILLS

S. No.	Units	Duration in Hours
1.	Unit 1: Communication Skills - I	10
2.	Unit 2: Self-Management Skills - I	10
3.	Unit 3: Information and Communication Technology Skills- I	10
4.	Unit 4: Entrepreneurial Skills - I	15
5.	Unit 5: Green Skills - I	05
	Total	**50**

PART-B : SUBJECT SPECIFIC SKILLS

UNIT 1 : AI REFLECTION, PROJECT CYCLE AND ETHICS

SUB-UNIT	LEARNING OUTCOMES	SESSION/ ACTIVITY/ PRACTICAL
AI Reflection	To identify and appreciate Artificial Intelligence and describe its applications in daily life.	**Session:** Introduction to AI and setting up the context of the curriculum • Recommended Activity: Make a statement about lighting and LUIS will interpret and adjust the house accordingly https://aidemos.microsoft.com/luis/demo
	To recognize, engage and relate with the three realms of AI: , Computer Vision, Data Statistics and Natural Language Processing.	Recommended Activity: The AI Game • Learners to participate in three games based on different AI domains. • Game 1: Rock, Paper and Scissors (based on data) https://next.rockpaperscissors.ai/ • Game 2: Semantris (based on Natural Language Processing-NLP) https://research.google.com/semantris/ • Game 3: Quick Draw (based on Computer Vision - CV) https://quickdraw.withgoogle.com/

SUB-UNIT	LEARNING OUTCOMES	SESSION/ ACTIVITY/ PRACTICAL
AI PROJECT CYCLE	Identify the AI Project Cycle framework.	**Session:** Introduction to AI Project Cycle • Problem Scoping • Data Acquisition • Data Exploration • Modeling • Evaluation • Deployment
	Learn problem scoping and ways to set goals for an AI project.	**Session:** Problem Scoping **Activity:** Brainstorm around the theme provided and set a goal for the AI project. • Discuss various topics within the given theme and select one. • Fill in the 4Ws problem canvas and a problem statement to learn more about the problem identified in the community/ society • List down/ Draw a mind map of problems related to the selected topic and choose one problem to be the goal for the project.
	Identify stakeholders involved in the problem scoped. Brainstorm on the ethical issues involved around the problem selected.	**Activity:** To set actions around the goal. • List down the stakeholders involved in the problem. • Search on the current actions taken to solve this problem. • Think around the ethics involved in the goal of your project.
	Understand the iterative nature of problem scoping for in the AI project cycle. Foresee the kind of data required and the kind of analysis to be done.	**Activity:** Data and Analysis • What are the data features needed? • How will the features collected affect the problem? • Where can you get the data? • How frequent do you have to collect the data? • What happens if you don't have enough data? • What kind of analysis needs to be done? • How will it be validated? • How does the analysis inform the action?
	Share what the students have discussed so far.	**Presentation:** Presenting the goal, actions and data. **Teamwork Activity:** • Brainstorming solutions for the problem statement.
	Identify data requirements and find reliable sources to obtain relevant data.	**Session:** Data Acquisition **Activity:** Introduction to data and its types. • Students work around the scenarios given to them and think of ways to acquire data. **Activity:** Data Features • Identifying the possible data features affecting the problem. **Activity:** System Maps • Creating system maps considering data features identified.

SUB-UNIT	LEARNING OUTCOMES	SESSION/ ACTIVITY/ PRACTICAL
	To understand the purpose of Data Visualisation	**Session:** Data Exploration/ Data Visualisation • Need of visualising data • Ways to visualise data using various types of graphical tools. Quiz Time
	Use various types of graphs to visualise acquired data.	Recommended Activities: Let's use Graphical Tools • Selecting an appropriate graphical format and presenting the graph sketched. • Understanding graphs using https://datavizcatalogue.com/ • Listing of newly learnt data visualization techniques. • Top 10 Song Prediction: Identify the data features, collect the data and convert into graphical representation. • Collect and store data in a spreadsheet and create some graphical representations to understand the data effectively.
	Understand modeling (Rule-based & Learning-based)	**Session:** Modeling • Introduction to modeling and types of models (Rule-based & Learning-based)
	Understand various evaluation techniques.	**Session:** Evaluation Learners will understand about new terms • True Positive • False Positive • True Negative • False Negative
	Challenge students to think about how they can apply their knowledge of deployment in future AI projects and encourage them to continue exploring different deployment methods.	**Session:** Deployment Recommended Case Study: Preventable Blindness. **Activity:** Implementation of AI project cycle to develop an AI Model for Personalized Education.
	To understand and reflect on the ethical issues around AI.	**Session:** Ethics Video Session: Discussing about AI Ethics Recommended Activity: Ethics Awareness • Students play the role of major stakeholders, and they have to decide what is ethical and what is not for a given scenario. • Students to explore Moral Machine (https://www.moralmachine.net/) to understand more about the impact of ethical concerns
	To gain awareness around AI bias and AI access.	**Session:** AI Bias and AI Access • Discussing about the possible bias in data collection • Discussing about the implications of AI technology

SUB-UNIT	LEARNING OUTCOMES	SESSION/ ACTIVITY/ PRACTICAL
	To let the students analyse the advantages and disadvantages of Artificial Intelligence.	Recommended Activity: Balloon Debate • Students divide in teams of 3 and 2 teams are given same theme. One team goes in affirmation to AI for their section while the other one goes against it. • They have to come up with their points as to why AI is beneficial/ harmful for the society.

UNIT 2 : DATA LITERACY

SUB-UNIT	LEARNING OUTCOMES	SESSION/ ACTIVITY/ PRACTICAL
Basics Of Data Literacy	• Define data literacy and recognize its importance Understand how data literacy enables informed decision-making and critical thinking • Apply the Data Literacy Process Framework to analyze and interpret data effectively • Differentiate between Data Privacy and Security • Identify potential risks associated with data breaches and unauthorized access. • Learn measures to protect data privacy and enhance data security	**Session:** Basics of data literacy • Introduction to Data Literacy • Impact of data Literacy • How to become Data Literate? • What are data security and privacy? • How are they related to AI? • Best Practices for Cyber Security Recommended Activity: Impact of News Articles Reference Videos: • https://www.youtube.com/watch?v=yhO_t-c3yJY • https://www.youtube.com/watch?v=aO858HyFbKI • https://www.cbse.gov.in/cbsenew/documents/Cyber%20Safety.pdf
Acquiring Data, Processing, and Interpreting Data	• Determine the best methods to acquire data. • Classify different types of data and enlist different methodologies to acquire it. • Define and describe data interpretation. • Enlist and explain the different methods of data interpretation. • Recognize the types of data interpretation. • Realize the importance of data interpretation	**Session:** Acquiring Data, Processing, and Interpreting Data • Types of data • Data Acquisition/Acquiring Data • Best Practices for Acquiring Data • Features of data and Data Preprocessing • Data Processing and Data Interpretation • Types of Data Interpretation • Importance of Data Interpretation Recommended Activities: • Trend analysis • Visualize and Interpret Data
Project Interactive Data Dashboard & Presentation	• Recognize the importance of data visualization • Discover different methods of data visualization	**Session:** Project Interactive Data Dashboard & Presentation • Data visualization Using Tableau Reference Links • https://public.tableau.com/en-us/s/download • https://www.datawrapper.de/ Video Links: • https://www.youtube.com/watch?v=NLCzpPRCc7U • https://www.youtube.com/watch?v=_M8BnosAD78

UNIT 3 : MATH FOR AI (Statistics & Probability)

SUB-UNIT	LEARNING OUTCOMES	SESSION/ ACTIVITY/ PRACTICAL
Importance of Math for AI	Analyzing the data in the form of numbers/images and find the relation/pattern between the them. Use of Math in AI.	**Session:** Importance of Math for AI • Finding Patterns in Numbers and images. • Uses of Math - ◆ Statistics ◆ Linear Algebra ◆ Probability ◆ Calculus
	Number Patterns Picture Analogy	**Activity:** • Observe the number pattern and find the missing number. • To find connections between sets of images and use that to solve problems,
Statistics	Understand the concept of Statistics in real life.	**Session :** • Definition of Statistics • Applications ◆ Disaster Management ◆ Sports ◆ Diseases Prediction ◆ Weather Forecast
	Application in various real life scenarios	**Activity:** Uses of Statistics in daily life • Students will explore the applications of statistics in real life .They collect data and can apply various statistical measures to analyze the data. **Activity:** Car Spotting and Tabulating Purpose:To implement the concept of data collection, analysis and interpretation. Activity Introduction: • In this activity, Students will be engaged in data collection and tabulation. • Data collection plays a key role in Artificial Intelligence as it forms the basis of statistics and interpretation by AI. • This activity will also require students to answer a set of questions based on the recorded data.
Probability	Understand the concept of Probability in real life and explore various types of events.	**Session:** Introduction to Probability • How to calculate the probability of an event • Types of events • Understand the concept of Probability using a relatable example. Exercise: Identify the type of event.
	Application in various real life scenarios	**Session:** Applications of Probability • Sports • Weather Forecast • Traffic Estimation Exercise: Revision time

UNIT 4: INTRODUCTION TO GENERATIVE AI:

LEARNING OUTCOMES	SESSION/ ACTIVITY/ PRACTICAL
Students will be able to define Generative AI & classify different kinds.	Recommended Activity: • Activity: Guess the Real Image vs. the AI-generated image
• Students will be able to explain how Generative AI works and recognize how it learns. • Applying Generative AI tools to create content. • Understanding the ethical considerations of using Generative AI.	Session: • Introduction to Generative AI • Generative AI vs Conventional AI
	Session: • Types of Generative AI • Examples of Generative AI
	Session: • Benefits of using Generative AI • Limitations of using Generative AI
	Recommended Activities: • Hands-on Activity: GAN Paint • Generative AI tools
	Session: • Ethical considerations of using Generative AI

UNIT 5: INTRODUCTION TO PYTHON

LEARNING OUTCOMES	SESSION/ ACTIVITY/ PRACTICAL
Learn basic programming skills through gamified platforms.	Recommended Activity: • Introduction to programming using Online Gaming portals like Code Combat.
Acquire introductory Python programming skills in a very user-friendly format.	Session: • Introduction to Python language • Introducing Python programming and its applications
	Theory + Practical: Python Basics • Students go through lessons on Python Basics (Variables, Arithmetic Operators, Expressions, Comparison Operators, logical operators, Assignment Operators, Data Types - integer, float, strings, type conversion, using print() and input()functions) • Students will try some simple problem-solving exercises on Python Compiler.
	Practical: Flow of control and conditions 1. Students go through lessons on conditional and iterative statements (if, for and while) 2. Students will try some basic problem-solving exercises using conditional and iterative statements on Python Compiler.
	Practical: Python Lists 3. Students go through lessons on Python Lists (Simple operations using list) 4. Students will try some basic problem-solving exercises using lists on Python Compiler.

PART-C: PRACTICAL WORK

UNIT 5: INTRODUCTION TO PYTHON: Suggested Program List

PRINT

- To print personal information like Name, Father's Name, Class, School Name.
- To print the following patterns using multiple print commands-

```
*                 * * * * *
* *               * * * *
* * *             * * *
* * * *           * *
* * * * *         *
```

- To find square of number 7
- To find the sum of two numbers 15 and 20.
- To convert length given in kilometers into meters.
- To print the table of 5 up to five terms.
- To calculate Simple Interest if the principle_amount = 2000 rate_of_interest = 4.5 time = 10

INPUT

- To calculate Area and Perimeter of a rectangle
- To calculate Area of a triangle with Base and Height
- To calculating average marks of 3 subjects
- To calculate discounted amount with discount %
- To calculate Surface Area and Volume of a Cuboid

LIST

- Create a list in Python of children selected for science quiz with following names- Arjun, Sonakshi, Vikram, Sandhya, Sonal, Isha, Kartik Perform the following tasks on the list in sequence-
  - Print the whole list
  - Delete the name "Vikram" from the list
  - Add the name "Jay" at the end
  - Remove the item which is at the second position.
- Create a list num=[23,12,5,9,65,44]
  - print the length of the list
  - print the elements from second to fourth position using positive indexing
  - print the elements from position third to fifth using negative indexing
- Create a list of first 10 even numbers, add 1 to each list item and print the final list.
- Create a list List_1=[10,20,30,40]. Add the elements [14,15,12] using extend function. Now sort the final list in ascending order and print it.

IF, FOR, WHILE

- Program to check if a person can vote
- To check the grade of a student
- Input a number and check if the number is positive, negative or zero and display an appropriate message
- To print first 10 natural numbers
- To print first 10 even numbers
- To print odd numbers from 1 to n
- To print sum of first 10 natural numbers
- Program to find the sum of all numbers stored in a list

Important Links	• https://cbseacademic.nic.in/web_material/Curriculum21/publication/secondary/Python_Content_Manual.pdf • https://drive.google.com/drive/folders/1qRAckDcuIA5i164OUFDIilxb8mT65MMb

PART-D: Project Work / Field Visit / Student Portfolio

*** relate it to Sustainable Development Goals**

Suggested Projects/ Field Visit / Portfolio (Any one has to be done)

Suggested Projects	1. Create an AI Model using tools like- • Teachable Machine (https://teachablemachine.withgoogle.com/) • Machine Learning For Kids (https://machinelearningforkids.co.uk/) 2. Choose an issue that pertains to the objectives of sustainable development and carry out the actions listed below. • To understand more about the problem identified, create a 4Ws problem canvas. • Identify the data features and create a system map to understand relationship between them • Visualize the data collected graphically (Spreadsheet software to be used store and visualize the data) • Suggest an AI enabled solution to it (Prototype/Research Work)
Suggested Field Visit	Visit to an industry or IT company or any other place that is creating or using AI applications and present the report for the same. Visit can be on physical or virtual mode.
Suggested Student Portfolio	Maintaining a record of all AI activities and projects (For Example Letter to Futureself, Smart Home Floor Plan, Future Job Advertisement, Research Work on AI for SDGs and AI in Different Sectors, 4Ws canvas, System Map). (Minimum 5 Activities)

Allinone®

COMPLETE STUDY | COMPLETE PRACTICE | COMPLETE ASSESSMENT

PART-A
Employability Skills

CHAPTER 01

Communication Skills-I

Communication is the process of exchanging information, thoughts, ideas, and feelings between people through speaking, writing, or body language. Good communication skills are crucial for success in various aspects of life. They help you to-build and maintain relationships, clearly express your thoughts and ideas and understand others' perspectives.

1.1 Introduction

Communication skills are those skills which are needed to speak and write properly. These are important for everyone, these teach us about how we can give and receive information and convey our ideas and opinions to those around us.

We must develop a variety of skills for both communicating to others and learning how to interpret the information received from others.

An effective speaker is the one who is able to speak appropriately whilst maintaining eye contact with the audience, uses different vocabulary and articulate speech to suit the need of audience.

Likewise, an effective writer should be able to use words in various style and techniques to communicate their message and ideas to the readers. Thus, good reading, writing, speaking and listening skills are essential for effective communication.

1.2 Communication

The word 'communication' derives from the Latin word 'Communicare', which means 'to share'. Communication is the 'sharing' of information between two or more individuals or within a group to reach a common understanding.

The information can be words, drawings, paintings, gestures, music or even sound also.

Communication involves at least two persons, i.e. a sender and a receiver. The sender develops and transmits a message to the receiver and the receiver, receives the message. It is successful only when there is a common understanding between the sender and receiver.

Importance of Communication

Ability to communicate clearly and share thoughts, feelings and ideas help us in all relationships. A good communication makes our personal as well as professional life smooth.

Some of the importance of communication skills are as follows:

I. **Inform** Communication is required to give facts or information to someone. i.e. Communicating the timetable of an exam to a friend.

II. **Influence** Communication is needed to influence or change a person in an indirect but usually important way. e.g. negotiating with a shopkeeper to reduce the price or helping a friend to overcome stress due to examination or any other reason.

III. **Express Feelings** Communication is needed to share and express our feelings to other in a healthy way. i.e. Sharing our excitement about doing well in our examination or sharing our feelings to parents and friends.

Elements of Communication

- Communication is a two-way exchange of information, i.e. giving and receiving.

- Speaking and writing to someone are examples of giving information.
- Reading and listening to someone are examples of receiving information.

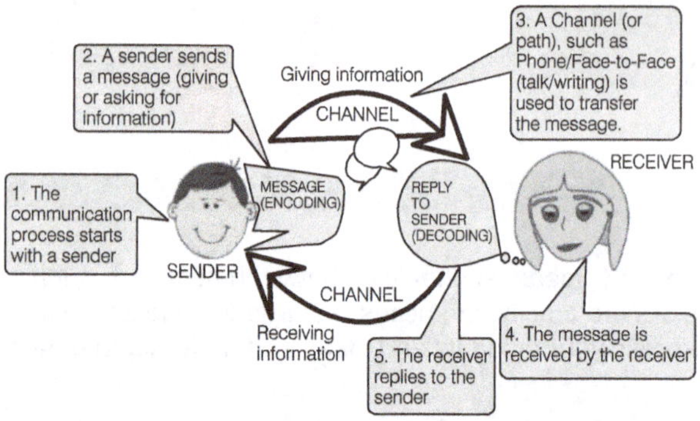

- **Sender** Sender is the person who is first in the process of communication. It decides what the message is, how it will be expressed and sent.
- **Ideas/Message** The message is the actual information that the sender wishes to convey to the receiver.
- **Channel/Medium** Channel is the means by which the message is sent. There can be various forms of media face-to-face communication, letters, radio, television and email etc.
- **Receiver** The person who received the message is called receiver.
- **Encoding** It means to change the message into a form suitable for sending.
- **Decoding** Decoding is the process in which the receiver interprets and understands the message.
- **Feedback** Feedback is the receiver's response to the message. Requesting classification is a part of a good feedback phase of communication cycle.

1.3 Perspectives in Communication

Perspectives are ideas, views, or fixed ways of thinking. These sometimes effect our communication. The perspective of communication is not only checks the way the message transmits information and influences the individual, it also examines the way that the message creates, sustains and changes cultures and communities.

The perspective of communication helps to explore the form, content, medium and pattern of the message and how it influences the way people interpret the meaning and take action.

It also helps to understand how messages are produced, how they are circulated among a group of people and how they are interpreted with an eye on the important consequences of the message.

Factors Affecting Perspectives in Communication

Sometimes, we are not able to communicate clearly because of some barriers that stop us from sharing and understanding messages.

Factor affecting perspectives in communication are as follows :

Language

The process of communication is both verbal and written. Language plays main role in all the types of communication. The same words can have very different meanings depending on how we interpret them.

In case of use of incorrect words, unfamiliar language and lack of detail, language can act as a barrier to communicate what one wishes to convey.

i.e. Language can act as a barrier when an Indian who knows only Hindi and a Chinese who has the knowledge of Mandarin only want to interact with each other.

Visual Perception

Visual perception is the ability to see and interpret (analyze and give meaning to) the visual information that surrounds us. Simply we can say that it is the brain's ability to make sense of what we see through our eyes.

For example, Completing partially drawn pictures with visual perception whereas they may be something else.

Past Experience

Sometime our past bitter experience stop us to communicate properly.

For example, "This shopkeeper cheated me last time. Let me be careful or I scored low marks in my maths exam, so I am scared to ask and answer question in class".

Prejudices

Prejudice means 'prejudgment'. It occurs when we take our past experiences with a person and assume that the same type of experience will happen with all people who are similar to the first. Prejudices are partly due to culture and partly due to personal preferences or experience.

It is used in reference to a preconceived judgment of someone due to their social class, gender, race, ethnicity, disability, age, gender and religion etc.

The problem with prejudices arises when they start to influence how or to whom we communicate.

Fixed ideas, such as thinking "No one in my class likes me" may stop a student from communicating openly in class.

Feelings

The process of communication becomes more affective when the sender shows enthusiasm and the receiver is receptive. The mood and feelings of both the parties, affect the process of communication. Our feelings and emotions, such as lack of interest or not trusting the other person, affect communication. i.e. "I am not feeling well, therefore, I don't want to talk".

So, when we are not feeling well and uncomfortable, we cannot pay attention to what other are saying.

Environment

There are many environmental factors that hamper the effectiveness of communication. Message may get blocked or misinterpreted due to environmental factors like location or situation where the communication takes place.

Noise or disturbance in the surroundings may make communication difficult.

For example, Talking to a friend in a function where there is loud music is being played by the Orchestra.

Personal Factors

Personal factors include our own feelings, habits and ways of thinking. For, example, Fear and low confidence may make communication difficult.

Culture

Signs which have a different meaning in different cultures, such as showing a thumb may mean 'good job' done for some people but may be insulting to others.

Effective Communication

Effective communication can happen if we follow the basic principles of professional communication skills. These can be abbreviated as 7 Cs, i.e., Clear, Concise, Concrete, Correct, Coherent, Complete and Courteous. These are further explained in the given below

- **Clear** The message should be clear and it must reflect what sender wants to say.
- **Concise** Use of simple words in communication and add only necessary words.
- **Concrete** Use exact words and facts.
- **Correct** The spelling and grammar should be flawless.
- **Coherent** Use sensible and related words to the topic.
- **Complete** Add all the information.
- **Courteous** Be respectful, friendly and honest.

Try These 1.1

1. **The content of the communication is called ....**
2. **Who is the person introducing a new thought?**
3. **What is encoding?**
4. **........... helps to understand how messages are produced.**
5. **What comes to our mind on seeing something in our perception?**
6. **Which factors includes our own feelings, habbits and way of thinking?**

1.4 Methods of Communication

There are different methods of communication, which include non-verbal, verbal and visual.

1. Verbal Communication

Verbal communication is the oldest means of communication. It is most commonly used as a medium for the exchange of information. Verbal communication is the sharing of information by using words.

Types of Verbal Communication

There are mainly two types of verbal communications, *viz*

(a) **Oral or Spoken Communication** In this communication, the exchange of information, ideas, and messages through spoken words.

For example, Face-to-Face conversation, group discussion, talking to family member at home, conversation with public through speeches, talking on phone and classroom teaching etc.

(b) **Written Communication** In this type of communication, the written signs or symbol are used to convey the message. We can say that, it is the communication which involves written or typed words.

For example, letters, notes, email, books, newspapers, SMS, documents and files etc.

Advantages of Verbal Communication

- Verbal communication is easy and quick.
- It is more reliable method of communication.
- It is cheaper way of communication and hence saves money.
- It promotes a secure exchange of ideas.

Disadvantages of Verbal Communication

- It has no legal validity and hence will lead to problems in certain situation.
- It has issues when communicating with distant people.
- Verbal communication is not effective due to cultural differences between the sender and receiver of the information.

- Verbal communication depends on words, sometimes the meaning become confusing and difficult to understand if the right words are not used.

> **Public Speaking** Public speaking means speaking infront of a large group. Often it makes people nervous. To get over the fear and become a confident and effective speaker we must use 3Ps, *viz*, prepare, practice and perform.
>
> - **Prepare** means think about the topic and prepare oneself in the best way to make one's listeners to understand the topic.
> - **Practice** means prior practices by oneself before public speaking.
> - **Perform** denotes start speaking confidently what one has preponed.

2. Non-Verbal Communication

Non-verbal communication is the message we send to others without using any words. It occurs without using any oral or written words.

We send signals and messages to others, through expressions, gestures and body postures.

Types of Non-Verbal Communication

There are some types of non-verbal communications as follows:

(a) **Facial Expression** Many a times, a facial expression shows the feelings of a person.
For example, when we are happy, we express it through a smile or when we are sad we show a gloomy face.

(b) **Posture** Postures are position of the body. They show our confidence and feelings.

For example, Straight body posture is seen as confidence. Holding your head may be taken as tiredness.

(c) **Gesture/Body Language** Gestures describe movements of parts of the body, especially hands or head, to express an idea or meaning. This includes waving, pointing and using our hands when speaking.

For example, Raising a hand may mean asking a question. Biting nails show nervousness.

(d) **Touch** We communicate a great deal through our touch, such as shaking hands and patting on the back.

For example, A firm handshake shows confidence. Sports coaches pat on the back of the players to encourage the players.

(e) **Space** The space between two persons while communicating, generally depends on the intimacy or closeness between them.

(f) **Eye Contact** Maintaining an eye contact with the person you are talking indicates interest, whereas, looking away can make the other person feel ignored.

(g) **Paralanguage** Paralanguage is the tone of our voice, speed and volume that makes a difference in the meaning of the communication. Speaking too fast may show excitement or nervousness. Speaking too slow may show seriousness, sadness or making a point.

Importance of Non-Verbal Communication

- Non-verbal communication makes our message stronger.
- Using the right gestures while speaking makes our message more effective.
- Non-verbal communication helps us understand our audience's reaction and adjust our behaviour or communication accordingly.
- It is helpful in communicating with illiterate people.
- Using the right gestures and postures helps us to be professional at work.
- If verbal message are blocked by noise or distance, etc, we can use hand movements to exchange our message.

Info Wall

Prof. Albert Mehrabian in 1970s proved that in personal communication, non-verbal communication is very important as it conveys 93% while verbal communication conveys only 7%. The exact breakup percentage he came up with is:

7% words	**Verbal communication**
38% tone of voice 55% body language	**Non-verbal communication**

3. Visual Communication

Visual communication involves sending and understanding messages only through images or picture. It is the transmission of ideas and information with the help of symbols and images.

Example of Visual Communication

Visual Communication: Exchanging Information through Images	
Traffic symbol which communicates not to blow horn.	
Sign for ladies and gents toilet.	

Sign for flammable substances.	
Sign used to pause a video or audio file in smartphone or computer.	
Traffic lights - Red for Stop; Yellow for Wait and Green for Go.	
Sign showing railway crossing.	
Sign for slippery surface.	
Sign which communicates that the area is a no smoking zone.	

Advantages of Visual Communication

- The main advantage of this type of communication is that we do not need to know any particular language for understanding it.
- It is simple, easy to understand and remains same across different places.
- The amount of time taken in understanding a visual communication is less as compared to other types of communication.

1.5 Writing Skills : Parts of Speech

In English, sentences are the basic framework of communication. They are important because unclear sentences create difficulty in understanding the meaning which is to be conveyed.

Sentence

A sentence is a group of words that communicate a complete thought. It always begins with a capital letter, and always ends with either a question mark, a full stop or an exclamation mark.

Phrase

A group of words, which does not make complete sense in itself is known as a phrase.

e.g., (i) Sushmita is a woman of **great intellect**.

(ii) The horse runs **at a good speed**.

In the given examples, the bold parts are phrases. They do not have any meaning of their own but they contribute to the meaning of the sentence as a whole.

Using Capitals

Capital letters are used at different places. The rules that suggest where a capital letter is to be used is given by MINTS. MINTS is a set of simple rules that helps an individual to capitalise words correctly. Each letter in the word MINTS refer to one capitalisation rules as given in the table below:

Alphabet	**M**	**I**	**N**	**T**	**S**
What it shows	Months	The letter 'I'	Names	Titles	Starting letter of sentences
Rule	Capitalise the first letter in all the names of months.	Capitalise the letter 'I' whenever it is used.	Capitalise the first letter in the names of people, places and days.	Capitalise the first letter in the titles used before people's name.	Capitalise the first letter in every sentence.
Example	I will go to college in June.	I play tennis with him every day.	This Tuesday, Vidya will be in Rajasthan.	Dr Shah and Mr Patel work together.	The cat ran out of the house.

Punctuation

Punctuation refers to the marks like comma, full stop, question mark etc., which help us in separating the parts of a sentence so that its meaning becomes clear. Knowledge of proper use of punctuation marks is necessary for writing and reading English correctly.

Some of the common punctuation marks and their use have been given below:

Punctuation name	Sign	Use	Examples
Full stop	.	Shows the end of a sentence. Also used to show short form of long words. e.g. 'doctor' can be shortened to 'Dr', when we use it as a title before a name.	This is a sentence. This is another sentence. Sanjay is a doctor. His patients call him Dr. Sanjay.
Comma	,	Sometimes, we use a comma to indicate a pause in the sentence. We can also use a comma to separate items when we are listing out more than two items.	After the waiter gave me a menu, I ordered food. I bought apples, oranges and grapes.
Question mark	?	We use a question mark at the end of a question.	What is your name? How old are you?
Exclamation mark	!	We use an exclamation mark at the end of a word or a sentence to indicate a strong feeling, such as surprise, shock or anger.	What a pleasant surprise! You are late!
Apostrophe	(')	We use an apostrophe followed by an s in a word to show that something belongs to someone. We also use an apostrophe to indicate the shortened form of some words in informal speech.	That is Divya's pen. Are these Abdul's books? Let's go. (Instead of Let us go.) He isn't here. (Instead of He is not here.)

Basic Parts of Speech

According to their function in a sentence, a word in the English language can be classified into eight basic parts of speech. These are as follows:

- Noun
- Verb
- Preposition
- Pronoun
- Adverb
- Interjection
- Adjective
- Conjunction

Main Parts of Speech

Main parts of speech indicates how a word functions in producing meaning in a sentence. These are the different types of words used in the sentence. The main parts of speech are given in the table below:

Part of Speech	What they do	Example sentence (Examples are underlined in the sentences)
Noun	Nouns are words that refer to a person, place, thing or idea. These are 'naming words'. They are sometimes used with an article (the, a, an).	<u>Rajiv</u> wrote a very long <u>letter</u>.
Pronoun	A pronoun is a word used in place of a noun.	<u>He</u> went to Rashid and told <u>him</u> the secret of his happiness.
Adjective	Adjectives are words that describe other words specifically nouns and pronouns.	The <u>young</u> boy is very <u>clever</u>.
Verbs	Verbs are words that show action.	Puja <u>wrote</u> a letter.
Adverbs	Adverbs are words that add meaning to verbs, adjectives or other adverbs. They answer the questions—How? How often? When? And Where?	She laughed <u>loudly</u>. Lucy is <u>very</u> tall.

Supporting Parts of Speech

Alongwith the main parts of speech, there are some other words that are required to make a sentence. These words are supporting words that join the main pairs of speech and add information to the sentences.

The four supporting parts of speech are given in the table below:

Supporting Parts of Speech	Use	Example sentences (examples are underlined in sentences)
Articles	The words 'a', 'an' and 'the' are known as articles. Articles are generally used before nouns. **An** is used before words with a vowel (a, e, i, o, u) sound. **A** is used before nouns with a consonant (all other alphabets) sound. **The** is used to refer to specific or particular words.	The car stopped suddenly because a cat ran in front of it. A book An apple An umbrella The sun
Conjunctions	Conjunctions are words that join two nouns, phrases or sentences. Some common conjunctions are 'and', 'or' and 'but'.	You can have either chocolate or vanilla icecream. Sheela and I went to the market.
Prepositions	Preposition connect one word with another to show the relation between them. They usually answer the questions 'where', 'when' and 'how'. Some common prepositions are 'on', 'at', 'in' etc.	The cat is on the roof. The shop is at the end of the market. Amit is standing under the tree. Raunak lives in Delhi.
Interjections	These words express strong emotions, such as happiness, surprise, anger or pain. They end with an exclamation mark.	Oh God! i don't know what to do in this horrible situation! Wow! it is magnificent.

1.6 Parts of a Sentence

Almost every sentence in English have two parts, i.e. a subject and a verb. Some sentences also contain a third part called an object.

- **Subject** A subject is a person or thing that does an action.
- **Verb** A verb describes the action performed.
- **Object** An object is a person or thing that receives the action or on which an action is performed.

For example, Dia and Sanjay broke the bottle.

In the given sentence, 'Dia and Sanjay' are the subject as they perform an action, 'broke' is the verb and 'the bottle' is the object as the action is performed on it.

Types of Objects

In a sentence, an object an either be direct or indirect.

- **Direct Object** Direct objects are the ones directly 'acted on' by the verb. In other words, direct object answers the question 'what?'

  For example, Ravi kicked the ball.

  In the given sentence, the action is directly performed on the 'ball'. Hence, 'the ball' is the direct object.
- **Indirect Object** Indirect object identifies the person or the thing for whom the action of the verb is performed. It answers questions such as 'to whom' and 'for whom'.

  For example, My mother bought a necklace for me.

  Or

  My mother bought me a necklace.

In the given sentences, 'necklace' is the direct object and 'me' is the indirect object.

Types of Sentences

Depending upon whether the subject of sentence performs or receivers an action, the sentences are of two types:

1. **Active Sentences** Active sentences are those sentences where the subject does an action.

   For example, She wrote a letter.

   He opened the door.
2. **Passive Sentences** Passive sentences are those sentences in which the subject receives an action.

   For example, A letter was written by her.

   The door was opened by him.

Depending upon the purpose of the sentence, sentences can be categorised into four types:

1. **Declarative Sentences** These sentences provides information or functions to state a fact. They are the most common type of sentences that always ends with a full stop '.'.

   For example, I completed my project.
2. **Interrogative Sentences** These sentences are used for asking questions. Therefore, they always end with a question mark '?'.

   For example, Did you complete project?
3. **Exclamatory Sentences** An exclamatory sentence expresses a strong emotion, such as joy, sadness, fear or wonder. It always ends with an exclamation mark '!'.

For example, I completed my project!

4. **Imperative Sentences** These sentences show an order, command, request or advice. It can end with a full stop or an exclamation mark ('.' or '!').

   For example, Complete your project.

Paragraphs

A paragraph is a group of sentences dealing with a particular topic. A paragraph must have one common idea. Rules for writing a paragraph:

- Give the paragraph unity
- Keep the paragraph short
- Make use of topic sentences
- Leave out unnecessary details
- Give the paragraph movement
- End the paragraph with a concluding sentence

For example, A paragraph on the 'value of trees' will be written as given below:

"Trees are our life line. We cannot live anywhere on the planet without trees. Trees give us food, oxygen and all the luxuries that we enjoy.

Trees are not only useful for mankind but also for nature. By producing fresh oxygen they make the environment pollution-free. They prevent soil erosion, droughts and flood.

So, man must stop cutting more and more trees, otherwise he will suffer greatly."

Try These 1.2

1. **............. communication is the sharing of information by using words?**
2. **What is the oldest means of communication?**
3. **Give one example of phrase.**
4. **What is the use of comma (,) as punctuation mark?**
5. **A/An ..... is a group of sentences dealing with a particular topic.**

1.7 Pronunciation Basic

Pronunciation

Pronunciation refers to the way in which a word or language is spoken, including the correct articulation, stress and intonation of sounds. It involves the manner in which individual sounds or phonemes are produced and combined to form words.

Correct pronunciation helps an individual to express his/her views in a clear and confident manner.

Speaking Correctly

In English, there are some words that have similar spellings but are pronounced differently. There also exists, words that have different spellings but they are pronounced in the same way. In such cases, the best way to learn the correct pronunciation of words, one must listen to a language expert carefully.

For example

Sun	Son	Sail	Sale	Tail	Tale

Phonetics

Each and every word that we speak is made up of one or more sounds. So, we put these sounds together to pronounce words. The study of these sounds that we make when we speak is called phonetics. For example, The word 'dog' is made up of three sounds d + o + g.

In English, there are 26 Alphabets and each of these alphabets are pronounced differently. However, there are more than 26 sounds in English.

For example, The letter 'a' can be pronounced in different ways in different words. Some of them are given in the table below:

Words	Pronunciation of the letter 'a'	Pronunciation in Hindi
cat, apple and back	ऐ	कैट, ऐपल, बैक
car, fast and park	आ	कार, फास्ट, पार्क
call, ball and saw	ऑ	कॉल, बॉल, सॉव्

Types of Sounds

All words in English are made of three basic types of sounds. These are as follows:

1. **Vowels** The English alphabet has 5 vowels - 'a', 'e', 'i', 'o' and 'u'. But there are 12 vowel sounds. This means that most vowels can be pronounced in different ways. We make a vowel sound when we read a vowel is a word.

   For example, The vowel 'i' is pronounced differently in 'bit' and 'bite' (बिट, बाइट).
2. **Diphthongs** When we combine the sound of two vowels, the sound produced is called a diphthong. A Diphthong starts as one vowel sound and go to another.

   For example, The sound of 'ou' n mouse (माउस).
3. **Consonants** All sounds except vowels and diphthongs are consonants sounds.

   For example, The sound of letters 'p' and 't' in the word 'pot'. (पॉट).

Some of the different sounds are given in the table below:

Vowel sounds	Examples
long 'ee' (ी) sound	Sleep (स्लीप)
	Feel (फील)
	Keep (कीप)
Short 'i' (ि) sound	Slip (स्लिप)
	Dip (डिप)
	Fill (फिल)
Short 'u' (ु) sound	Book (बुक)
	Put (पुट)
	Foot (फुट)
Long 'oo' (ू) sound	Boot (बूट)
	Group (ग्रूप)
	Two (टू)
Diphthong sounds	**Examples**
'ea' sound (ि + ा)	Near (नियर)
	Dear (डियर)
	Hear (हियर)
'ae' sound (े)	Late (लेट)
	Cake (केक)
	Game (गेम)
'oa' sound (ो)	Boat (बोट)
	Loan (लोन)
	Most (मोस्ट)
'ou' sound (ा + ु)	Mouth (माउथ)
	Cow (काउ)
	Cloud (क्लाउड)
Consonant sounds	**Examples**
'p' ('प') sound	Pen (पेन)
	Report (रिपोर्ट)
	Stop (स्टोप)
't' ('ट') sound	Train (ट्रेन)
	Story (स्टोरी)
	Put (पुट)
'k' ('क') sound	Book (बुक)
	Cold (कोल्ड)
	Music (म्यूसिक)
'l' ('ल') sound	Look (लुक)
	Place (प्लेस)
	School (स्कूल)

1.8 Greetings and Introductions

Greetings

Before starting a conversation with someone, we use words like 'Hello', 'Good Morning', 'Good Evening' etc. These words are called **greetings**. There are many ways in which an individual can greet a person. Generally, a greeting and the reply to a greeting depends upon who we are talking to and also according to the time of the day.

Types of Greetings

There are two types of greetings. They are described below:

- **Formal Greetings** Formal greetings are used when we address a stranger. It is also used to greet a senior, an elder or people with whom we have formal relations like teachers, boss etc. This type of greeting is mostly used in schools, colleges and offices.

  For example,

Greeting	Reply
Good Morning Everyone!	Good Morning, Sir!
Hello Mam. How are you?	I am doing well. Thank You!

- **Informal Greetings** These are used when we talk to our friends, family or a known person.

  For example,

Greeting	Reply
Hey!	Hello/Hi!
Hello. How's everything?	Hi. Everything is good. What about you?

- **Greetings according to time** Formal greeting can change according to the time of the day as show in the table:

Greeting	Reply
Good Morning	From early morning to 11 : 59 am
Good Afternoon	12 pm to 5 pm
Good Evening	5 pm to midnight

It is to be noted here that we do not greet people by saying 'Good night' even if it is night. 'Good night' is used at the end of the conversation.

Introducing Yourself and Others

When we tell others about ourselves using sentences that provide basic information about us like our name, our hobbies etc, it is known as **introduction**. We need to 'introduce' ourselves when we meet someone for the first time or when we want others to know about us. Introduction generally includes an individuals name, hometown, job, subjects as a student, interests, hobbies etc.

We should smile while introducing ourselves and look towards the other person.

For example, Good Morning. I am Aditi.

I am from Agra and I am a teacher.

I love reading books.

Sometimes we have to introduce someone to others. We can do this by telling their name, their job and how do we know them. We can also add some quality of their personality.

For example, This is my uncle Ramesh.

He is a doctor. He is also a very good guitarist.

Talking About Self

There are many occasions when we have to talk about ourselves. This is especially when we are meeting new people. Also, many a times we have to fill forms with information about ourselves.

Talking About Yourself

When we meet someone for the first time, they may want to know about us. So, we need to introduce ourselves.

Introduction definitely, starts with our name. Then we can tell them other things about us like our age, our interests, the place where we live, our likes, dislikes etc.

We can form these sentences using nouns and verbs.

For example,

- My name is Kavita. (Name)
- I live in Delhi. (Hometown)
- I study in class IX. (Class)
- My favourite subject is English. (Favourites)
- I like to play basketball. (Likes)
- I am a good team player. (Strength)
- I cannot manage my time properly. (Weakness)

Filling a Form

In many situations, we need to write about ourselves in a form. A form is a document, typed or printed with blank spaces to fill in the information.

We have different forms for different purposes. So we should carefully read a form before filling it. The form should be filled in a neat handwriting and with correct spellings. A general form usually asks for personal information as given in the table:

Name	Sometimes we might have to right first name, middle name and surname separately.
Date of birth	It is usually written in DD/MM/YYYY format.
Address	This is the postal address which includes your house number and the details of the street, area and the city.
PIN code	This is a group of numbers used by the post office to identify a region. It is an important part of an address.
Signature (or Sign)	This is your name or initials written by hand, in a specific way (which is difficult for anyone else to copy).

e.g. Harish Sethi was born on 5 December 1999. He lives in Agra, in a house named Sukh Nivas. His house number is 13 in Raja Nagar. His postal code is 282001. Harish filled a form asking for personal information like this.

First Name	Harish
Last Name	Sethi
Date of Birth	5 December 1999 (or 05-12-1999)
Address	Sukh Nivas, No. 13, Raja Nagar, Agra
Pin Code	282001

1.9 Asking Questions-I

Need for Asking Questions

A question is a request for any type of information. It could be an answer to a question in the textbook, information about a person or a place or about how to do a task.

For example, Where can I find a coffee shop?

Who is Rahul Dravid?

Asking questions is useful because it helps us to

- gain new knowledge, get information,
- ensure that what we know is correct,
- avoid doubts, confusion, misunderstanding and
- starting conversation with people by asking about them and their ideas.

How We Make Sure We Have Complete Information?

Asking right questions at the right time from the right person is very important. Incomplete or incorrect information will not help us to reach a place or do a certain task. We can follow the simple method of '5W + 1H' to make sure that we have all the information required to do a task. The 5W+1H method of asking questions is described in the table given below:

5W+1H Method for Asking Questions

Question Words	Usages	Examples
Who	'Who' is used to ask about people	Who is the new student in the class?
Where	'Where' is used to ask about a place	Where does she live?
When	'When' is used to ask about time	When did she join school?
What	'What' is used to ask about a thing, an idea or an action	What is her favourite subject?
Why	'Why' is used to find the reason	Why is she not talking to anyone in the class?
How	'How' is used to find the method	How can I help her make friends?

1.10 Asking Questions-II

A question is a sentence, phrase or word that can also be used to test someone's knowledge. We always use a question mark (?) at the end of a question.

We ask questions in our day-to-day conversations to get information. In order to get correct information we need to ask correct questions.

Types of Questions

There are two types of questions as discussed below

- **Close Ended Questions** Such questions are those which can be answered with a 'yes' or a 'no'. Their answers are limited to a 'yes' or a 'no' and no other detail is required.

  For example, Did he go to the temple?

  Yes.

- **Open Ended Questions** Those questions that requires answer in detail are open ended questions. The option of answers to such questions are unlimited.

  For example, What is your favourite memory from childhood.

The answer to such a question could be unlimited and will be described in detail.

Framing Close Ended Questions

Close ended questions are usually formed by beginning the question with auxiliary verbs like Be, Do and Have. Modal verbs like Can, Shall, May, Should, Could can also be used as these show possibility or necessity. One way to frame a close-ended question is to take a sentence without the above mentioned words and then adding any one of the words before the subject.

For example, The sentence 'I like it' can become "Do I like it?".

Or

'They talk on the phone everyday' will become "Do they talk on the phone everyday?"

It is important to note here that the helping verb, changes based upon the subject while the main verb remains unchanged.

Another way to frame close ended questions is to exchange the positions of the subject and the verb.

For example, "She can cook dinner." will change into "Can she cook dinner?"

Or

"They were cleaning the room." will become "Were they cleaning the room?".

Framing Open-Ended Questions

The answers to the open-ended questions are not limited or closed. They need to be answered with more information than a simple "yes" or "no". Open-ended questions can be formed by using the question words (5W+1H) like What, Why, Who, When, Where and How.

For example, the question is "What did you do?" an individual can answer anything relevant to the question such as "I went to the park", "I went to the market", "I went to the temple" etc.

Try These 1.3

1. .... is the way in which an individual says a word.
2. What is greeting?
3. A question is a request for any type of information. (T/F)
4. What symbol do we use at the end of a question?

Glossary

Communication It is the sharing of information between two or more individuals or within a group to reach a common understanding.

Visual Perception It is the ability to see and interpret (analyse and give meaning to) the visual information that Surrounds us.

Prejudices It means 'prejudgment'. It is used in reference to a perceived judgment of someone due to their social class, gender, race, ethnicity, disability, age, gender and religion etc.

Verbal Communication It is the sharing of information by using words.

Non Verbal Communication It is the message we send to others without using any words.

Visual Communication It involves sending and understanding messages only through images and picture.

Punctuation It refers to the marks like comma, full stop, question mark etc., which help us in separating the parts of a sentence so that its meaning becomes clear.

Pronunciation It refer to the way in which a word or language is spoken, including the correct articulation, stress and intonation of sounds.

Phonetics The study of these sounds that we make when we speak is called phonetics.

Close Ended Questions Those questions which can be answered with a 'yes' or a 'no'.

Open Ended Questions Those questions that requires answer in detail are open ended questions.

Let's Investigate

Activity 1

Role Play on Communication Process

Procedure

1. Form groups with three students in each group.
2. Assign roles within each group: one student as the salesperson and the other two as an old man and his wife.
3. Provide a scenario where the old couple visits a shop, and the salesperson needs to sell some items to them.
4. Encourage the groups to act out the conversation, focusing on effective communication skills.
5. After the role play, have a debriefing session where each group discusses what they learned from the activity, highlighting effective communication strategies, challenges faced, and areas for improvement.

Activity 2

Group Discussion on Factors Affecting Perspectives in Communication

Procedure

1. Form groups with three students in each group.
2. Assign each group to select one of the eight factors (Language, Visual Perception, Past Experiences, Prejudice, Feelings, Environment, Personal factors, Culture) that act as barriers to communication.
3. Have each group discuss how their chosen factor can impact perspectives in communication.
4. Encourage sharing of personal experiences or examples related to the chosen factor.
5. Each group should present a summary of their discussion to the class, emphasizing the importance of understanding and overcoming communication barriers.

Activity 3

7Cs of Effective Communication

Materials Required

Pen/pencil, Notebook

Procedure

1. Distribute notebooks to each student.
2. Have students write down examples of the 7Cs of communication in their notebooks.
3. Invite volunteers to share their examples for each of the 7Cs.
4. Encourage class discussion, with teacher guidance, to evaluate if the examples provided are correct or incorrect.
5. Emphasize the importance of clarity, coherence, and other 7Cs in effective communication.

Activity 4

Elements of Communication

Materials Required

Chart paper, Colors, Pencil

Procedure

1. Divide the students into small groups.
2. Assign each group to create a chart illustrating the elements of communication in the communication process cycle.
3. Provide materials like chart paper, colors, and pencils for the creative process.
4. Each group presents their chart to the class, explaining how the elements contribute to effective communication.
5. Encourage discussions and questions from the class to enhance understanding of communication elements.

Activity 5

Role Play of a Phone Conversation

Materials Required

Notebook, Pen

Procedure

1. Divide the class into groups of at least three students each.
2. Assign a scenario for a phone conversation to each group. For example, a conversation between a person

from the Call Centre and a customer discussing the delivery of a product to the customer's residence.

3. In each group, one student acts as the caller (representing the Call Centre), another as the receiver (customer), and the third student serves as an observer.
4. Write a script based on the assigned scenario, ensuring that it covers key aspects of communication between the caller and the receiver.
5. Students perform the role play by speaking the conversation aloud, following the script.
6. The observer provides feedback on the effectiveness of the communication, considering the 7Cs of communication (clearness, conciseness, concreteness, correctness, courtesy, coherence, and completeness).

Activity 6

Public Speaking

Materials Required

Notebook, Pen

Procedure

1. Form groups of three students each.
2. Within each group, collaboratively choose a topic for a short speech. Ensure that the topic is relevant and interesting.
3. Each student in the group uses the 3Ps method (Prepare, Practice, and Perform) to create and deliver a speech. Encourage the use of paragraphs for a well-organized presentation.
4. After each speech, the other group members provide constructive feedback on how effectively the speaker communicated the topic.
5. Rotate the speaker role within the group so that each student has an opportunity to give a speech.
6. As a culmination, one student volunteers to give a speech in front of the entire class, applying the feedback received during the group activities.
7. Encourage the class to provide feedback and create a supportive environment for public speaking.

Activity 7

Role Play with Non-Verbal Communication

Materials Required

Notebook, Pen

Procedure

1. Divide the class into groups of three students each.
2. Assign a scenario to each group, focusing on situations where non-verbal communication plays a crucial role. For example, a job interview, a negotiation, or a conflict resolution scenario.
3. Have each group prepare a script for the role play based on the given scenario.
4. In their respective groups, students should act out the role play, emphasizing non-verbal cues.
5. After the role play, one group volunteer from each group should perform the role play in front of the entire class.
6. Following the presentation, conduct a class discussion on how students utilized non-verbal communication in their role plays.

Activity 8

Dos and Don'ts for Effective Body Language

Materials Required

Notebook, Pen

Procedure

1. Have the same groups of three students from Activity 7 discuss and brainstorm a list of Dos and Don'ts for effective body language to avoid communication mistakes.
2. Each student in the group should compile a list of these Dos and Don'ts in their notebooks.
3. Encourage students to share their lists within their groups, discussing and refining the points to create a comprehensive set of guidelines.
4. After group discussions, open the floor for a class-wide discussion to compile a master list of Dos and Don'ts for effective body language.

Activity 9

Comparative Analysis of Communication Methods

Materials Required

Notebook, Pen

Procedure

1. Use the same groups from of three students to discuss the three primary methods of communication: Verbal, Non-verbal, and Visual.
2. In their groups, students should create lists highlighting the advantages and disadvantages of each communication method.

3. Encourage students to consider real-world examples to illustrate their points.
4. Groups will present their findings to the class, promoting class-wide discussion and comparison of the advantages and disadvantages of each communication method.
5. Conclude the activity with a class discussion on the importance of using a combination of communication methods for effective and well-rounded communication.

Activity 10

Identifying Parts of Speech

Materials required

Notebook, Pen

Procedure

Read aloud the paragraph given below.

"In the bustling city of Mumbai, I eagerly await my meeting with Professor Kapoor on Wednesday. My apartment is close to Mrs. Kapoor's bakery. I visited her establishment on Monday to purchase pastries. I selected chocolate éclairs, raspberry tarts, and a delightful cheesecake. Mrs. Kapoor is a warm-hearted woman. Did you get a chance to meet her?"

- This paragraph contains examples of the parts of speech you learned about in this lesson.
- Identify as many of these parts of speech as you can and mark them.
- Write the paragraph with proper punctuation and capitalization.

Activity 11

Constructing Sentences

Materials required

Notebook, Pen

Procedure

1. Pair up with a classmate.
2. Compile a list of five parts of speech you covered in the lesson.
3. Choose one part of speech from your list.
4. Each pair will create two simple sentences utilizing the selected part of speech.
5. Write down the sentences in your notebook.

Activity 12

Identify Name, Place, Animal, Thing

Materials required

Notepad, Pens

Procedure

1. Number yourselves within each group from 1 to 5.
2. Each member of the group will contribute a word that falls into one of the categories: name, place, animal, or thing. The fifth member will choose an action.
3. Groups have 30 seconds to brainstorm and decide on their words and action.
4. Record your words and action on the notepad.
5. Groups will take turns sharing their words and performing the action.

Activity 13

Sentence Structure Exploration

Materials required

Notebook, Pen

Procedure

1. Form pairs of students.
2. Write down three sentences, each containing a direct object.
3. Write down three additional sentences that include both direct and indirect objects.
4. Use different colors to mark the different parts of each sentence (Subject, Verb, Direct Object, Indirect Object).
5. One volunteer from each pair shares their sentences with the class, allowing for corrections and feedback.

Activity 14

Active and Passive Voice Exploration

Materials required

Notebook, Pen

Procedure

1. In the same pairs as Activity 13, write a paragraph on any topic.
2. Ensure the paragraph consists of at least two sentences in active voice and two sentences in passive voice.
3. One volunteer reads their paragraph aloud to the class.

4. The class provides feedback on the correct identification of active and passive voice usage.

Activity 15

Exploring Sentence Types

Materials required

Notebook, Pen

Procedure

1. With the same pairs as in the previous activities, create a list of at least eight sentences.
2. Ensure the list includes a minimum of two sentences for each type—declarative, interrogative, exclamatory, and imperative.
3. Different volunteers from each pair read out their sentences to the class.
4. The class provides feedback on the correctness of each sentence type.

Activity 16

Exploring Phonetics in the Classroom

Materials required

Notebook, Pen

Procedure

1. **Group Formation** Form groups of four students in each group.
2. **Classroom Exploration** Together as a group, create a list of five objects or items found in the classroom.
3. **Phonetic Analysis** Identify the vowels, diphthongs, and consonants in the listed words.
4. **Interactive Pronunciation** Each student takes turns pronouncing a word aloud within the group. The other group members provide feedback on the correctness of the pronunciation.

Activity 17

Collaborative Pronunciation Practice

Materials required

Notebook, Pen

Procedure

1. **Pair Formation** Form pairs of students.
2. **Word Pronunciation Practice** Your teacher will provide you with a list of words. Practice pronouncing these words aloud with your partner.
3. **Feedback Session** Your partner provides immediate feedback on the correctness of your pronunciation.
4. **Class wide Pronunciation Challenge** A volunteer from each pair reads out two words for the whole class. The class collectively provides feedback on the correctness of the pronunciation.

Activity 18

Formal and informal greetings

Materials required

Notebook, Pen

Procedure

1. Form pairs of students.
2. Each pair should write about two conversations—one with formal greetings and one with informal greetings and act it out.
3. One volunteer pair acts this out in front of the class.
4. The class says if the formal and informal greetings have been used correctly.

Activity 19

Introducing someone

Materials Required

Notebook, Pen

Procedure

1. Use same pairs of students as above.
2. Each pair should write a conversation to introduce someone to their friends and family and act it out.
3. One volunteer pair demonstrates it for the class.
4. The class says if the introductions have been made correctly.

Activity 20

Greetings

Materials required

Notebook, Pen

Procedure

1. Imagine that you are at home. The doorbell rings and you open the door. Write down.
2. What would you say when you see your uncle standing at the door?
3. What would you say when you see your friend standing at the door?

4. One volunteer acts it out in front of the class. The class (with teacher) discusses
5. What is the difference in the way you greet your friends and teachers?
6. Which method will be used in the following situations:
   (a) While talking to teacher in the classroom, and (b) While talking to your friends in the playground.
7. What are the different phrases used when greeting friends?
8. What are the phrases used when greeting elders, teachers, colleagues at work or in office?

Activity 21

Introducing Yourself and Form Filling Workshop

Materials required

Notebook, Pen, Sample forms

Procedure

1. Begin by providing each student with a sample form that they will use for this activity.
2. Instead of forming pairs, divide the class into small groups of three. This allows for more interactions and diverse perspectives.
3. Ask each student to introduce themselves to the group, providing the necessary details to fill out the form you provided.
4. Rotate the forms within the group, allowing each student to fill in the details for one of their peers.
5. Once the forms are filled, have the original owner review the information and add their signature if the details are correct.
6. Encourage group discussions to ensure everyone understands the importance of accurate information in forms.

Activity 22

Personal Introduction and Preferences Presentation

Materials required

Notebook, Pen, timer

Procedure

1. Form groups with three students in each group for a more dynamic interaction.
2. Instruct students to take turns introducing themselves and sharing their likes and dislikes with the group. Each person now has two minutes to talk about themselves.
3. Encourage the group to actively listen, ask questions, and provide constructive feedback during each presentation.
4. After each person's presentation, allow for group discussions and corrections.
5. At the end of the group presentations, select one representative from each group to present in front of the entire class.
6. The class will collectively provide feedback on what was presented, reinforcing positive aspects and offering suggestions for improvement.

Additional Instructions and Extensions:

1. **Diary and Progress** Encourage students to maintain a diary documenting their language learning journey. Regularly review and discuss their progress with the teacher.
2. **Social Interaction Challenge** In the next two days, challenge students to actively introduce themselves to new people, incorporating the learned expressions.
3. **Form Exploration** In the next 14 days, students should ask family members to share and explain forms they have filled in, gaining a broader understanding of form structures.
4. **Signature Creation** Task students with creating a unique and authentic signature for themselves.
5. **Form Creation and Peer Interaction** Over the next month, students should design a simple form, distribute copies to friends, and guide them in filling out the form as a practical application of their knowledge.

Activity 23

Interactive Questioning Session

Materials required

Notebook, Pen

Procedure

1. Divide the class into groups of four students each.
2. Introduce a hypothetical situation, using the 5W+1H method to provide key details.
3. In each group, students collaborate to formulate a list of questions aimed at gathering comprehensive information about the given situation.
4. A volunteer group presents their list of questions to the class.
5. The remaining students provide constructive feedback, evaluating the relevance and effectiveness of the questions posed.

Activity 24

Strategic Question Planning

Materials required

Notebook, Pen

Procedure

1. Pair up the students.
2. The teacher outlines a scenario for which students need to create plans.
3. Each pair compiles a list of questions they would ask in order to gather necessary information for planning. Additionally, they must articulate the purpose behind each question.
4. Partners share and discuss their question lists, providing insights into the effectiveness of each other's questions and the underlying purposes.

Activity 25

Guess the Personality Challenge

Procedure

1. Divide the class into five groups.
2. Each group selects a famous personality without revealing the identity to others.
3. Groups take turns asking indirect questions to other teams to guess the chosen personality.
4. Each group is allowed three questions initially. If the identity remains undisclosed, extend the questioning limit to five.
5. If needed, teams can provide a CLUE to help others in the guessing process.
6. Encourage creative and indirect questioning to make the activity more engaging.
7. The team that correctly identifies the other team's famous personality first, wins.

Activity 26

Framing Open-Ended and Closed-Ended Questions

Materials required

Notebook, Pen

Procedure

1. Form pairs of students.
2. Each pair generates five open-ended and five closed-ended questions, providing answers for all 10 questions.
3. After completing the questions, pairs exchange their lists with another pair for review.
4. One pair volunteers to share their questions and answers with the entire class.
5. The class collectively discusses and provides feedback on the framing of the questions, encouraging constructive criticism.

Activity 27

Group Practice - Effective Question Framing

Materials required

Notebook, Pen

Procedure

1. Form groups of four students each.
2. Collaboratively create a dialogue involving four people, incorporating at least six questions (both closed- and open-ended).
3. Act out the conversation within the group, ensuring each member participates in the discussion.
4. Volunteer groups present their dialogue to the entire class, focusing on the effective framing of questions.
5. Encourage the class to provide feedback on question quality, with an emphasis on constructive suggestions for improvement.
6. Rotate the groups, allowing different sets of students to showcase their dialogues and receive feedback.

NCERT FOLDER

Complete Explanations of all NCERT's Questions

A. Multiple Choice Questions

Q.1 What is the purpose of communication?

(a) Inform (tell someone about something)
(b) Influence (get someone to do something you want)
(c) Share thoughts, ideas, feelings
(d) All of the above

Q.2 Which of the following methods are used to receive information from the sender through a letter?

(a) Listening (b) Speaking
(c) Reading (d) Writing

Q.3 How do you receive information on phone?

(a) Listening (b) Speaking
(c) Reading (d) Writing

Q.4 Choose the correct example of oral communication.

(a) Reports
(b) Newspapers
(c) Face-to-face conversation
(d) Notes

Q.5 When we communicate verbally, we should use ....

(a) difficult words (b) simple words
(c) confusing words (d) abbreviations

Q.6 Why do we send emails?

(a) To reach on time.
(b) To share documents and files.
(c) To talk to each others.
(d) To meet each other.

Q.7 Which of these is a positive (good) facial expression?

(a) Staring hard
(b) Nodding while listening
(c) Wrinkled forehead
(d) Looking away from the speaker

Q.8 What does an upright (straight) body posture convey/show?

(a) Shyness (b) Fear
(c) Confidence (d) Intelligence

Q.9 Which of these is not an appropriate non-verbal communication at work?

(a) Putting arm around a coworker's shoulder.
(b) Shaking hands firmly.
(c) Looking at the speaker with a smile.
(d) Standing with an upright posture.

Q.10 When you are preparing for a presentation, you should ....

(a) focus on the objectives of the presentation.
(b) practice your speech in front of a mirror or friend.
(c) do rehearsals to time your presentation of slides.
(d) All of the above

Q.11 What is a sentence?

(a) A group of ideas that form a complete paragraph.
(b) A group of words that communicate a complete thought.
(c) A set of rules that we must follow to write correctly.
(d) A set of words that contains all the basic punctuation marks.

Q.12 Which of these sentences use uppercase letters correctly?

(a) I am Hungry.
(b) Divya and sunil are reading.
(c) The bucket is Full of water.
(d) She lives in Delhi.

Q.13 Which of these sentences are punctuated correctly?

(a) Where are you going.
(b) I have a pen a notebook and a pencil.
(c) I am so happy to see you!
(d) This is Abdul's house.

Q.14 Identify the subject in the sentence, "The children played football".

(a) The children (b) Children played
(c) Played (d) Football

Q.15 Identify the object in the sentence, "The children played football."

(a) The children (b) Children played
(c) Played (d) Football

Q.16 Which of these sentences has both indirect and direct objects?

(a) I am watching TV.
(b) She bought a blue pen.
(c) The girls played cricket.
(d) He wrote his sister a letter.

Q.17 Which of these sentences is in passive voice?

(a) They are watching a movie.
(b) The clock was repaired by Raju.
(c) He is sleeping in the room.
(d) My pet dog bit the postman.

Q.18 What is phonetics?

(a) It is the study of how we write words in English.

(b) It is the study of how people understand sentences.

(c) It is the study of how many words the English language has.

(d) It is the study of the sounds we make when we speak.

Q.19 What are the different types of sounds used in English pronunciation?

(a) Vowel sounds (b) Diphthong sounds

(c) Consonant sounds (d) All of these

Q.20 You say 'Good Morning' when it is ....

(a) 11 am (b) 9 am

(c) 8 am (d) All of these

Q.21 You may say 'Hi' when you meet ....

(a) your teacher in class (b) a senior in the office

(c) your Principal (d) your friends at a shop

Q.22 You say 'Good Afternoon' when it is ....

(a) 10 am (b) 11.59 am

(c) 6 pm (d) 1 pm

Q.23 You say 'Good Evening' when it is ....

(a) 11 am (b) 9 am

(c) 2 pm (d) 7 pm

Q.24 A postal code is ....

(a) a group of numbers or letters used to identify a government building.

(b) a code used to indicate the door number of a house.

(c) a group of numbers or letters used by the post office to identify a region.

(d) a code used to identify different post offices.

Q.25 Raju is the class monitor. He wants to know why Ramesh is coming late every day. Which of the following is a question that Raju can ask Ramesh?

(a) Do you come on time?

(b) Are you late?

(c) Why are you late every day?

(d) Will it not be easier to complete your work if you come on time?

Q.26 If you have not understood a task given to you, which question should you ask?

(a) Where are the reports of this task?

(b) Can you repeat the instructions for this task?

(c) Can you give me an example of this task?

(d) Why are you doing this task?

Q.27 Sheela does not have time so she decides to delay a task. Which question should she ask before ignoring the task?

(a) What is this task?

(b) When does this task need to be completed?

(c) Is this task important?

(d) No need to ask any question.

Q.28 Renuka is joining a new school. Which of the following questions will help her become comfortable with her new classmates?

(a) How along have you been studying here?

(b) Would you like to share my lunch?

(c) What do you all do in your free time?

(d) All the options are correct.

Q.29 What are close-ended questions?

(a) Questions that can have any answer.

(b) Questions that do not have answers.

(c) Questions with yes/no answers.

(d) Questions that have many answers.

Q.30 Which of these are open-ended questions?

(a) Where do you live?

(b) Are you hungry?

(c) How do you feel?

(d) Did you meet him?

Q.31 Which of these are question words?

(a) What (b) Want

(c) Which (d) How

Q.32 Which of these is the correct way to convert the sentence "You are studying" into a question?

(a) You are studying? (b) Studying you are?

(c) Are you studying? (d) Studying are you?

Answers

1. (d)	2. (c)	3. (a)	4. (c)	5. (b)
6. (b)	7. (b)	8. (c)	9. (a)	10. (d)
11. (b)	12. (b,d)	13. (c,d)	14. (a)	15. (d)
16. (d)	17. (b)	18. (d)	19. (d)	20. (d)
21. (d)	22. (d)	23. (d)	24. (c)	25. (c)
26. (b)	27. (b)	28. (d)	29. (c)	30. (a,c)
31. (a,c,d)		32. (c)		

B. Match the Column

Q.1 Match the following columns.

Column I (Communication Barriers)	Column II (Examples)
A. Language	1. Trying to read a book when somebody else is watching TV in the same room.
B. Emotional	2. In some cultures, wearing shoes and walking inside the kitchen is considered rude and disrespectful.
C. Environmental	3. Talking in Hindi when others know only Tamil.
D. Cultural	4. Parent is not talking to the child.

Ans. A → 3, B → 4, C → 1, D → 2,

C. Fill in the blank

Q.1 Fill correct nouns and verbs from the box to fill in the blanks given below.
girl, girls, boy, milk, dog, skipping, riding, running, studying, drinking, barking.

(a) The .... is ....

(b) The .... is ....

(c) The .... is ....

(d) The .... are ....

(e) Raju is ....

(f) The .... is ....

Ans. (a) The boy is running. (b) The girl is riding.
(c) The boy is studying. (d) The girls are skipping.
(e) Raju is drinking. (f) The dog is barking.

D. Subjective Type Questions

Q.1 Write down the seven factors affecting perspectives in communication.

Ans. Refer to text on page no. 4 (Factors affecting perspectives in communication).

Q.2 Give an example of the following :

(a) Clear communication
(b) Complete communication

Ans. Examples of Clear communication and Complete communication are given below:

(a) **Clear Communication** "Please Submit your homework by 3 PM tomorrow"
(b) **Complete Communication** "Please Submit your math homework by 3 PM tomorrow. You need to finish exercises 5 to 10 from chapter 3. Email your work to me at teacher@example.com".

Q.3 Write down the different types of verbal communication. Give an example for each type.

Ans. Refer to text on page no. 5 (Types of verbal communication).

Q.4 Put a ✗ mark against the actions below which are incorrect for demonstrating the use of non-verbal communication

(i) Laughing during formal communication.
(ii) Scratching head.
(iii) Smiling when speaking to a friend.
(iv) Nodding when you agree with something.
(v) Standing straight.
(vi) Yawning while listening.
(vii) Sitting straight.
(viii) Maintaining eye contact while speaking.
(ix) Biting nails.
(x) Firm handshake.
(xi) Clenching jaws.
(xii) Looking away when someone is speaking to you.
(xiii) Intense stare.

Ans. The incorrect (✗) for demonstrating the use of non-verbal communication are :
(i), (ii), (vi), (ix), (xi), (xii) and (xiii)

Q.5 Give examples of any four common signs used for visual communication.

Ans. Refer to text on page no 6 and 7 (Example of visual communication).

Q.6 Underline the noun, pronoun, adjective, verb and adverb in these sentences.

(a) Sanjay plays football everyday.
(b) Divya gave him new books.
(c) I opened the red box carefully.

Ans. (a) Sanjay (Noun) plays (Verb) football (Noun) everyday (Adverb).
(b) Divya (Noun) gave (Verb) him (Pronoun) new (Adjective) books (Noun).
(c) I (Pronoun) opened (Verb) the red box (Noun) carefully (Adverb).

Q.7 Identify the conjunctions and prepositions (Remember, conjunctions join two sentences while prepositions help answer the words 'where', 'when' and 'how'.). Choose the conjunctions and prepositions from the box given below and list in the correct box.

Under, And, In, At, Or, Up

Ans.

Conjunction	Preposition
And	Under
Or	In
	At
	Up

Q.8 **Write one sentence of each type—statement, question, exclamatory and order.**

Ans. **Statement** I live in Delhi.

Question Do you play cricket?

Exclamatory The birthday cake was so good!

Order Shut the door.

Q.9 **Which is your favourite festival? Write two paragraphs about your favourite festival. Each paragraph should have a minimum of four sentences. Make sure you follow all the rules about sentences and paragraphs you have learnt.**

Ans. My favourite festival is Holi. It is one of the most important festivals in India. Holi is the symbol of celebration of brotherhood. On this day, we all forget our enmities and get into the festival spirit. A day before, a ritual called 'Holika Dahan' is conducted. It symbolises the burning of evil powers. The next day people play with colours. They splash water colours on each other. Children play with water guns.

Holi spreads love and brotherhood. It brings happiness and harmony in the country. Holi symbolises the triumph of good over evil. This colourful festival unites people and removes all sorts of negativity from life. I eagerly wait for Holi every year.

Q.10 **Practice speaking correct sentences with your classmates. Try and find the parts of sentences which you use commonly.**

Ans. Do it yourself.

Q.11 **Write two to three lines to you would use to introduce yourself.**

Ans. My name is Ayushi.

I live in Agra.

I study in class IX.

Q.12 **Use the following words to complete the form given below.**
football and swimming, seven-years-old, Hassan, Yasmin, in Bengaluru.

(a) My first name is ....
(b) My surname is ....
(c) I am ....
(d) I live ....
(e) I like ....

Ans. (a) Yasmin (b) Hassan
(c) Seven-years old (d) in Bengaluru
(e) Football and swimming

Q.13 **Re-arrange the words to form questions.**

(a) she/like/sing?/Does/to

(b) waiting/What/are/you/for?

(c) play/like/football?/Do/you/to

(d) fighting?/they/are/Why

Ans. (a) Does she like to sing?
(b) What are you waiting for?
(c) Do you like to play football?
(d) Why are they fighting?

Q.14 **Make a note of five questions your friends asked you. How many were open-ended questions? Make a list of five close-ended questions you asked other people in one day.**

Ans. Five questions my friends asked me :

1. Why did you not come to school yesterday?
2. Did you take medicine?
3. How are you feeling now?
4. Will you be able to play?
5. Do you want to take rest?

Two of these were open-ended questions.
For example, 1, 3.

Close-ended questions

1. Have you completed your homework?
2. Do you play cricket?
3. Can you run 5 kilometres?
4. Is London the capital of England?
5. Did you enjoy the party?

REVIEW EXERCISE

Including Competency Based Questions

Part I

Multiple Choice Questions

1. Communication skills are those skills which are needed to

(a) Speak properly (b) Write properly
(c) Both (a) and (b) (d) None of these

2. The word 'Communication' came from the

(a) French word (b) Latin word
(c) Greek word (d) None of these

3. The information can be

(a) Drawings (b) Words
(c) Gestures (d) All of these

4. Communication involves

(a) Sender (b) Receiver
(c) Giver (d) Both (a) and (b)

5. Which of the following is the importance of communication skills?

(a) Inform (b) Influence
(c) Express feelings (d) All of these

6. .... means to change the message into a form suitable for sending.

(a) Decoding (b) Encoding
(c) Feedback (d) Receiver

7. Which of the following is the factor affecting perspectives in communication?

(a) Language
(b) Visual perceptions
(c) Past experience
(d) All of the above

8. Methods of communication includes

(a) Verbal Communication
(b) Non-verbal Communication
(c) Visual Communication
(d) All of the above

9. Face to face conversation, letters, notes, emails, books, newspapers, sms etc, are type of which method of communication? Competency Based Ques.

(a) Verbal Communication
(b) Non-verbal Communication
(c) Visual Communication
(d) All of the above

10. Facial expression, posture, gesture/body language, touch, space etc are types of which method of communication? Competency Based Ques.

(a) Verbal Communication
(b) Non-verbal Communication
(c) Visual Communication
(d) None of the above

11. What is a phrase?

(a) A group of ideas that form a complete paragraph.
(b) A group of words which does not make complete sense in itself.
(c) A group of words that communicate a complete thought.
(d) A group of words that contains all the punctuation marks.

12. Which of these is a phrase?

(a) I came late.
(b) Reena is singing a song.
(c) In the dark.
(d) The horse runs.

13. Identify the subject in the sentence. "The girls are singing a song".

(a) The girls (b) Girls are singing
(c) A song (d) Singing a song

14. Which of these sentences has both indirect and direct objects?

(a) I am playing football. (b) Mother is cooking food.
(c) He gave him a pen. (d) She came home on time.

15. When do we say 'Good Night'?

(a) 11:00 am
(b) 8 p.m
(c) At the end of the conversation in the evening
(d) 6 p.m.

16. At 4 p.m, we say

(a) Good Morning (b) Good Afternoon
(c) Good Evening (d) Good Night

17. If you want to know the address of a person, which question should you ask?

(a) Where do you live?
(b) Is this your house?
(c) Can you take me to your house?
(d) How can I reach your house?

18. Which of these is the correct way to convert the sentence "It was a beautiful dress", into a question? Competency Based Ques.

(a) It was a beautiful dress?
(b) What a beautiful dress it was?
(c) A beautiful dress was it?
(d) Was it a beautiful dress?

19. Which of these is a close-ended question?

(a) Where do you live?
(b) Did you have breakfast?
(c) What are your hobbies?
(d) Which is your favourite film?

20. "Get out of the class". This is a/an

(a) Question (b) Exclamatory sentence
(c) Statement (d) Order

21. Raju needs to get out of a building. Which of the following questions will help him? Competency Based Ques.

(a) How many floors does this building have?
(b) Where is the exit?
(c) How many exit gates are there in this building?
(d) How do you people go out of this building?

22. Correct arrangement of following words to form a question is this/a/dress/new/is

(a) Is this dress new? (b) This is a new dress?
(c) Is this a new dress? (d) A new dress is this?

23. You may say 'Hello' when you meet

(a) Your elders (b) Your boss
(c) Your seniors in office (d) All of these

24. Combination vowel sounds are also called

(a) Consonant (b) Vowel
(c) Diphthongs (d) None of these

25. 'Pen' is an example of

(a) Vowel sound (b) Consonant sound
(c) Diphthong sound (d) None of these

26. Which of these sentences is in Active Voice?

(a) The letter delivered by the postman.
(b) The song was sung by her.
(c) They are playing cricket.
(d) The plants are being watered by the gardener.

27. Identify the object in the sentence, "The girls are singing a song."

(a) The Girls (b) Are Singing
(c) A song (d) Singing a song

28. In the context of communication, which of the following are considered types of communication? Competency Based Ques.

I. Verbal Communication
II. Nonverbal Communication
III. Written Communication
IV. Emotional Communication

(a) I and II (b) II and III
(c) I, II, and III (d) I, II, III, and IV

29. Identify the parts of speech in the sentence: "The energetic puppy quickly chased its tail around the backyard." Competency Based Ques.

I. Noun II. Verb
III. Adjective IV. Adverb

(a) I and II (b) II and III
(c) I, III, and IV (d) I, II, III, and IV

30. Which methods can be considered as forms of communication? Competency Based Ques.

I. Speech II. Body language
III. Written messages IV. Morse code

(a) I and II (b) II and III
(c) I, II, and III (d) I, III, and IV

31. When discussing perspective in communication, which factors contribute to shaping one's perspective? Competency Based Ques.

I. Cultural background
II. Personal experiences
III. Social environment
IV. Genetic makeup

(a) I and II (b) II and III
(c) I, II, and III (d) II, III, and IV

32. Which of the following are parts of speech in writing skills? Competency Based Ques.

I. Noun
II. Verb
III. Conjunction
IV. Pronoun

(a) I and II (b) II and III
(c) I, II, and IV (d) III and IV

Answers

1. (c)	2. (b)	3. (d)	4. (d)	5. (d)
6. (b)	7. (d)	8. (d)	9. (a)	10. (b)
11. (b)	12. (c)	13. (a)	14. (c)	15. (c)
16. (b)	17. (a)	18. (d)	19. (b)	20. (d)
21. (b)	22. (c)	23. (d)	24. (c)	25. (b)
26. (c)	27. (c)	28. (c)	29. (d)	30. (c)
31. (c)	32. (c)			

Statement Based Questions

1. Statement 1 Written communication is formal and rigid.

Statement 2 The method of communication involves only verbal expressions.

(a) Both Statement 1 and Statement 2 are correct
(b) Both Statement 1 and Statement 2 are incorrect
(c) Statement 1 is correct but Statement 2 is incorrect
(d) Statement 2 is correct but Statement 1 is incorrect

2. **Statement 1: Nouns and verbs are parts of speech.**

   Statement 2: A sentence must always begin with a subject.
   (a) Both Statement 1 and Statement 2 are correct
   (b) Both Statement 1 and Statement 2 are incorrect
   (c) Statement 1 is correct but Statement 2 is incorrect
   (d) Statement 2 is correct but Statement 1 is incorrect

3. **Statement 1: Nouns are words that represent people, places, things, or ideas.**

   Statement 2: Conjunctions are used to express action or a state of being.
   (a) Both Statement 1 and Statement 2 are correct
   (b) Both Statement 1 and Statement 2 are incorrect
   (c) Statement 1 is correct but Statement 2 is incorrect
   (d) Statement 2 is correct but Statement 1 is incorrect

4. **Statement 1: The basic elements of a sentence include subject, predicate, and object.**

   Statement 2: Pronouns are used to replace only proper nouns in sentences.
   (a) Both Statement 1 and Statement 2 are correct
   (b) Both Statement 1 and Statement 2 are incorrect
   (c) Statement 1 is correct but Statement 2 is incorrect
   (d) Statement 2 is correct but Statement 1 is incorrect

5. **Statement 1: Basic greetings are universal and do not vary across cultures.**

   Statement 2: Introductions should always include personal details like age and address.
   (a) Both Statement 1 and Statement 2 are correct
   (b) Both Statement 1 and Statement 2 are incorrect
   (c) Statement 1 is correct but Statement 2 is incorrect
   (d) Statement 2 is correct but Statement 1 is incorrect

Answers

1. (c) **2.** (a) **3.** (c) **4.** (c) **5.** (c)

Assertion and Reason Based Questions

1. **Assertion: Non-verbal communication is an essential method of communication.**

   Reason: Non-verbal cues such as facial expressions and body language can convey messages more effectively than words alone.
   (a) Both Assertion and Reason are true, and Reason is the correct explanation of Assertion.
   (b) Both Assertion and Reason are true, but Reason is not the correct explanation of Assertion.
   (c) Assertion is true, but Reason is false.
   (d) Assertion is false, but Reason is true.

2. **Assertion: Effective communication is a two-way process.**

   Reason: It involves both sending and receiving messages, ensuring mutual understanding.
   (a) Both Assertion and Reason are true, and Reason is the correct explanation of Assertion.
   (b) Both Assertion and Reason are true, but Reason is not the correct explanation of Assertion.
   (c) Assertion is true, but Reason is false.
   (d) Assertion is false, but Reason is true.

3. **Assertion: Pronunciation plays a significant role in effective communication.**

   Reason: Clear and accurate pronunciation enhances the clarity of the message and reduces the chances of miscommunication.
   (a) Both Assertion and Reason are true, and Reason is the correct explanation of Assertion.
   (b) Both Assertion and Reason are true, but Reason is not the correct explanation of Assertion.
   (c) Assertion is true, but Reason is false.
   (d) Assertion is false, but Reason is true.

4. **Assertion: Understanding the parts of speech is crucial for improving writing skills.**

   Reason: Parts of speech help in constructing grammatically correct and coherent sentences.
   (a) Both Assertion and Reason are true, and Reason is the correct explanation of Assertion.
   (b) Both Assertion and Reason are true, but Reason is not the correct explanation of Assertion.
   (c) Assertion is true, but Reason is false.
   (d) Assertion is false, but Reason is true.

5. **Assertion: Perspective in communication refers to the way an individual sees and interprets information.**

   Reason: Different perspectives can lead to misunderstandings in communication.
   (a) Both Assertion and Reason are true, and Reason is the correct explanation of Assertion.
   (b) Both Assertion and Reason are true, but Reason is not the correct explanation of Assertion.
   (c) Assertion is true, but Reason is false.
   (d) Assertion is false, but Reason is true.

6. **Assertion: Effective communication is essential for success in both personal and professional life.**

   Reason: Communication helps in expressing thoughts, ideas, and emotions, leading to better understanding and cooperation.
   (a) Both Assertion and Reason are true, and Reason is the correct explanation of Assertion.
   (b) Both Assertion and Reason are true, but Reason is not the correct explanation of Assertion.
   (c) Assertion is true, but Reason is false.
   (d) Assertion is false, but Reason is true.

Answers

1. (a) **2.** (a) **3.** (a) **4.** (a) **5.** (a)
6. (b)

Part II

Very Short Answer Type questions

1. What is the key to effective communication?

Ans. Clarity and conciseness enhance understanding, fostering effective communication.

2. How does active listening improve communication?

Ans. Active listening shows respect, promotes understanding, and strengthens interpersonal connections.

3. Why is non verbal communication important?

Ans. Non verbal cues convey emotions and intentions, adding depth and nuance to verbal messages.

4. What is the impact of body language on communication?

Ans. Body language influences perceptions, conveying confidence or uncertainty, and contributes significantly to effective communication.

5. How does effective communication contribute to teamwork?

Ans. Clear communication enhances collaboration, reduces misunderstandings, and strengthens team dynamics for better overall performance.

6. What is the significance of listening skills?

Ans. Listening skills enhance understanding, build connection and promote effective communication by attentively receiving and comprehending spoken information.

7. Explain the importance of written communication.

Ans. Written communication ensures clarity, documentation, and a lasting record of information exchange through letters, emails, or reports.

8. Define visual communication.

Ans. Visual communication uses images, charts, graphs, and other visual aids to convey information quickly and effectively.

9. How can cultural awareness enhance communication skills?

Ans. Cultural awareness ensures sensitivity to diverse communication styles, norms, and values, promoting effective cross-cultural interactions and understanding.

Short Answer Type Questions

1. Who is an effective speaker?

Ans. An effective speaker is the one who is able to speak appropriately whilst maintaining eye contact with the audience, uses different vocabulary and articulate speech to suit the need of audience.

2. Who is an effective writer?

Ans. An effective writer is the one who is able to use written words in various style and techniques to communicate their message and ideas to the readers.

3. State any two importance of communication skill.

Ans. Two importance of communication skills are as follows :

1. **Inform** Communication is required to give fact or information to someone, viz. communicating the timetable about an exam to a friend.
2. **Influence** Communication is needed to influence or change a person in an indirect way and usually important way.

4. What do you understand by feedback in communication?

Ans. Feedback in communication is the receiver's response to the message. Requesting classification is a part of a good feedback phase of communication cycle.

5. State any two advantages and two disadvantages of verbal communication.

Ans. **Two advantages of verbal communication :**

- Verbal communication is easy and quick.
- It is more reliable method of communication.

Two disadvantages of verbal communication :

- Verbal communication has no legal validity and hence, will lead to problems in certain situation.
- It has issues when communicating with distant people.

6. Write a paragraph on the things you like about your school. The paragraph must contain at least 8 lines and should follow all the rules of punctuation.

Competency Based Ques.

Ans. The school is the place that prepares us for a better future. I love my school because it is one of the best schools in the city. The classrooms are wide, large and airy. My school has a very large playground where we play sports. There is a computer lab, science lab and a big library in my school. All of the teachers of my school are kind and cooperative. My school also takes part in various activities like sports, quiz competition, speeches etc. We celebrate all national events with great zeal. My school also offers annual picnics to senior students. I feel greatly honoured and happy to study in such a good school.

7. Introduce your friend in 5 lines.

Ans.

- This is my friend Rajni.
- She is 16-years old.
- She stays at Kalkaji.
- She is a very good dancer.
- She likes to eat Rajma-Chawal.

8. Write three sentences using conjunctions 'and', 'but', 'or' respectively.

Ans. (i) Ramesh saw the dog **and** ran into the house.

(ii) He is poor **but** honest.

(iii) You study hard for the exam **or** you will fail.

ASSESSMENT EXERCISE

Multiple Type Questions

1. Which of the following sentences does not have an object?
   (a) She came home early. (b) Geeta is reading a book.
   (c) Rajesh is watching television. (d) He is cleaning.
2. Which of these is an open-ended question?
   (a) Can you dance? (b) Did you go to the party?
   (c) Where do you live? (d) Do you like chocolates?
3. "What a beautiful picture!" This is an example of
   (a) Exclamatory sentence (b) Question
   (c) Statement (d) Order
4. 'Game' is an example of
   (a) Vowel Sound (b) Diphthong sound
   (c) Consonant sound (d) None of these
5. Which of these is the correct way to convert the sentence "It is a remarkable sight", into a question?
   (a) It it a remarkable sight? (b) What remarkable sight it is?
   (c) What a remarkable sight is it? (d) A remarkable sight it is?
6. 'Quickly' in an example of
   (a) Verb (b) Adjective
   (c) Adverb (d) Conjunction
7. This shows the end of a sentence.
   (a) Comma (b) Full stop
   (c) Question mark (d) Exclamation mark

Very Short Answer Type Questions

8. Define Communication.
9. What do you understand by Pronunciation?
10. Write the disadvantages of verbal communication.
11. What are the methods of communication?

Short Answer Type Questions

12. Write a paragraph describing your mother. The paragraph must contain at least 8 lines and should follow all the rules of punctuation.
13. Introduce yourself in 8 lines.
14. Write three sentences using prepositions 'on', 'of' and 'at' respectively.

Self Management Skills-I

CHAPTER 02

Self-management skills are the tools you use to be in charge of your own life. This means planning your time, setting goals, and motivating yourself to achieve them. It also involves managing your emotions, stress, and staying organized. With good self-management, you can be more productive, reach your goals, and live a healthier, happier life.

2.1 Self Management

Self-Management is referred to as 'Self-control' or 'Self-regulation'. It is considered as the ability to regulate one's emotions, thoughts and behaviour effectively in various situations. It includes managing stress and motivating oneself and setting and working towards personal and academic goals. Self-Management involves understanding person's ownself, understanding his interests and abilities, having a positive attitude and grooming oneself in order to develop self-confidence.

Self-Management can help in

- overcoming all challenges and difficulties.
- overcoming bad habits.
- developing good habits.
- reaching your goals.

When individual can manage himself, it helps him to avoid stress and provides opportunities to get involved in fun activities.

Positive Results of Self-Management

Parents, teachers and guardians are not always along the child to guide him/ her. In that case principles of self-management guide the individual day in and day out, on how to respond to the environmental forces. These environmental forces for students can be the class schedule, assignments, competitions, exams, different students and their behavior etc. Students can sail through various situations in life comfortable by taking following benefits from self-management

- It guides individuals to self-monitor their conduct and behavior

  Students, once become aware that they are responsible for their behavior, they become pro-active.

  - Prepares individual to complete the task independently.
  - Instills ownership to the task and the consequences amongst individuals.

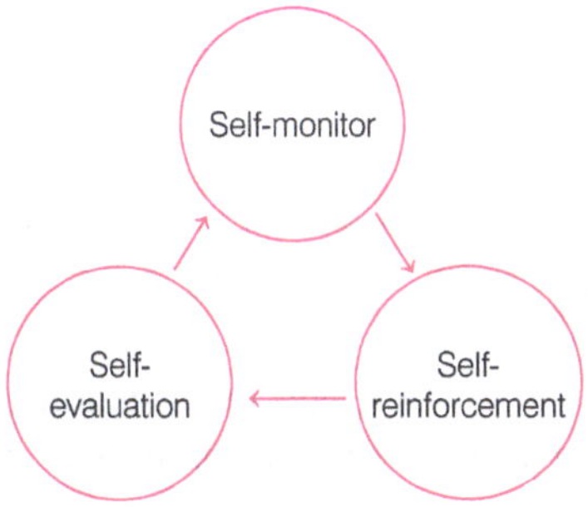

- It helps in self-evaluation

  Self-management makes individuals realize that they need to do course correction by themselves if they do not get desired goals. Once the goals are achieved as desired, it also motivates individuals.

  - Helps in setting individual goals
  - Directs evaluation of performance, objective resetting and enhances self-esteem.

- It leads to self – reinforcement of positive behavior Self-management reinforces appropriate behavior of students as per the time, situation and people involved. It motivates individuals to take up right things and refrains from getting indulged into negative things, keeping long term consequences in focus.
  - Enforces self-learning for goal achievement
  - Self-reliance is enhanced and which reinforces the behavior.

2.2 Self Management Skills

Self management skills boost your productivity and performance at work, which helps in achieving professional goals. It is a soft skill that increases your employability and gives you more control over your career path. These skills are essential to showcase that you will be a reliable employee.

For example, Students with strong self-management skill are able to do different activities effectively, including managing their timelines, focusing on their tasks, cooperating with others in school and at home and perform better in their studies. It helps in future studies, work and life.

Various Factors of Self-Management Skills

Self-management skills include the following factors

- **Self-Awareness** Its means knowing yourself as an individual – your values, likes, dislikes, strengths and weaknesses.
- **Self-Control** It is the ability to control your behaviour, discipline etc.
- **Self-Confidence** It means believing in yourself that you can do any task that is given to you and not scared of taking risks.
- **Problem-Solving** Its means understanding a problem and finding a solution using step-by-step method.
- **Self-Motivation** Its mean doing tasks on your own without any external motivation.
- **Personal Hygiene and Grooming** Its mean keeping oneself clean, healthy and smart.
- **Positive Thinking** It means expressing certainty or affirmation even in tough situations.
- **Team Work** It means working together with people to accomplish shared goals.
- **Time Management** It means achieving tasks on time and according to the plan.
- **Goal Setting** It means planning concrete goals to be accomplished within a set of time frame.

2.3 Strength and Weakness Analysis

Knowing yourself i.e. what you can do well and what not so well helps you in converting the weakness into strength and strength into an exceptional performance. Strength and weakness analysis begins with knowing yourself.

Knowing Yourself

Knowing yourself means understanding who you are, what you like or dislike, what are your beliefs, what are your opinions, what is your background, what you can do well or not etc. It is very important to know what you are, because only then you can measure your strengths and weaknesses.

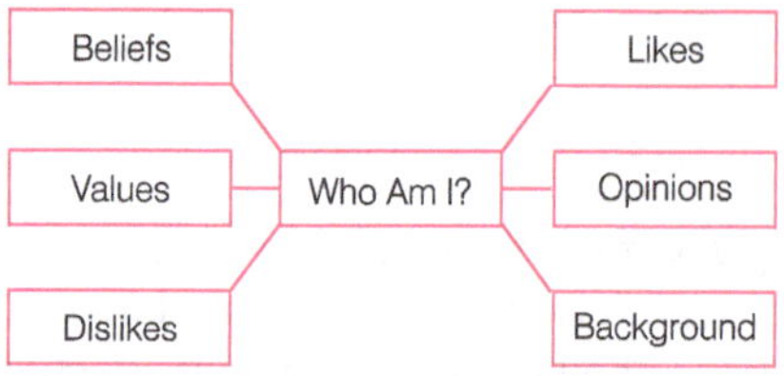

Strength and Weakness Analysis

Being self aware ('Who am I?') means looking outside our usual characteristics like name, qualification, relationship etc. It actually means knowing our inner-strength, hidden talents, skills and even weakness.

Strength

Strengths are what we do well and are good at. Everyone has some strengths.

Examples of Strength

- I play cricket very well.
- I help my parents in household chores.
- I am good at understanding other people's emotion.
- I am confident in dealing with strangers while keeping myself safe from any harm.

Identifying Strengths

You can identify your strengths by following some steps. These include

- Take time to think about what you do well.
- Think of anything that you are always good at.
- Think about what others appreciate about you.

Weakness

Weaknesses are known as 'areas of improvement'. These are what we do not do well and are not good at. Everyone has some weaknesses also.

Examples of Weakness

- I would like to learn more about computers and its application.
- I am unable to resist myself from junk food when my friends suggest.

Identifying Weakness

You have to identify your weakness by following steps. These include

- Point out the areas where you struggle and identify what you find difficult to do.
- Look at the feedback of others that you receive.
- Be open to feedback and accept your weakness without feeling bad. Consider it as an area of improvement.

How to Overcome Weakness

There are mainly three steps to overcome weakness

(i) By understanding ourselves we can know what we can and what we cannot do.

(ii) Based on that information, we can plan how to improve ourselves.

(iii) By improving our weakness, we will feel confident about ourselves.

Difference Between Interests and Abilities

Interests are the things that we enjoy doing. These may include

- Activities you like to do at school in your free time which make you happy.
- Activities that make you curious about and you would do even no one asked you to do.
- Activities you want to learn or like to do in the future.

Ability is an acquired or natural capacity that enables an individual to perform a particular job or task with considerable proficiency.

Sometimes interests may not match abilities. In those cases, you can either improve abilities or follow other path. For example, someone may like cricket which is his interest, but he may not be able to play the game due to the absence of his necessary power or skill (ability) required for the game. Thus, it is not necessary to try to become a cricketer in this case.

Try These 2.1

1 **Name two factors of self-management skill.**

2 **What is time management as factor of self-management skill?**

3 **Give one example of strength.**

4 **Give one difference between interests and abilities.**

2.4 Self-Confidence

Self-confidence is a sense of trusting own's abilities and self. If a person being intelligent, hardworking and talented, but lacks confidence and avoids taking initiative, then it may be difficult for others to recognise his talent.

Self-confidence can be developed through changes in **attitude** and **practice**.

Self-confidence is regarded as a quality which we build when we believe in our strength to succeed in anything we do in our life.

People who are confident believe that they can do anything given to them in any situation.

Qualities of self-confident people are discussed below

(i) **Self-Belief** It is confidence in our own abilities or judgment.

For example, Thomas Edison made thousands of prototypes of the bulbs, before he could finally invent the bulb. Inspite of struggling with repeated failures, his resilience (the capacity to recover quickly from the difficulties) and self-belief gave the world 'the bulb', an amazing product.

(ii) **Hard Work** Hard work is a great deal of effort done by a person.

For example, Dipa Karmakar, inspite of having a flat foot, worked hard and became the first Indian female gymnast in the Olympic.

(iii) **Positive Attitude** Positive attitude is nothing but focusing on the positives even in the time of adversity. It is a mental attitude that focuses on the bright side of life.

For example, The situation of losing a game can be perceived as losing something or as an opportunity to review the game strategies and improve to win in the future.

(iv) **Commitment** Commitment is the state or quality of being dedicated to a cause, activity etc.

For example, Mahatma Gandhi was highly committed to the cause of making India free from the British Raj by apply his non-violent civil disobedience method.

Factors That Help in Building Self-Confidence

Social

Interactions with family and social environment, like friends, relatives, teachers and media influences self-confidence of individuals. Development of confidence on self is a process which results from the experiences of individuals while interacting with others.

Cultural

Cultural factors comprise of values, beliefs and customs. Indians give higher importance to family values, believe in the philosophy of "Vasudhev Kutumbhkam" and follow custom of celebrating Diwali.

Conforming to cultural values, beliefs and customs enhances self-confidence.

Physical

Physical self-efficacy, physical activity and social physique anxiety are found to be influencing self-confidence of individuals. Physical activity is found to be directly related to self-confidence.

Physical self-efficacy refers to physical potential to complete a given task. Social physique anxiety is a concern amongst individuals about perceived evaluation of one's physical self by the society.

Building Self-Confidence

Three steps to building self-confidence are as follows

(i) **Appreciate Achievement and Accept Failure** The player celebrates the achievements when the team wins a competition and articulates learning when the team loses a competition.

(ii) **Have a Goal and Take Steps Towards** If a player have won bronze at an event, set the goal to win gold medal next time and take action for it.

(iii) **Always Look at the Good Side and be Happy** If a player has lost a match, he celebrates the efforts of those team members who performed well. He will talk to people who are confident and try to gain.

Self-Confidence Building Tips

- **Getting rid of negative thoughts** Going away from negative thoughts takes individuals closer to a peaceful positive mind. To travel away from negative thoughts, individuals need to involve themselves in an activity – take a walk, draw, sing, dance, chat, watch, read or talk.
- **Thinking positively** Positive thinking brings brain to a peaceful stance and increases productivity and performance. When individuals start thinking positively, they feel happy from within and their self-confidence boosts up.
- **Staying happy with small things** An individual who is full of gratitude for every small blessing in his life feels contended. Being thankful towards people and the world, instills confidence in individuals.
- **Staying clean, hygienic and smart** Personal hygiene is the first key to a confident person. Keeping hair, teeth, fingers, body and skin clean and well maintained is an easy and effective way to be at best.
- **Chatting with positive people** Interacting with positive people brings forth a fresh and progressive perspective to life.

  People in similar stages of life go through similar issues. Some positively handle these situations, and interacting with them shall help boost confidence.

Factors that decreases or influences our Self-Confidence

- When we are surrounded by people having negative attitude and their attitude is reflected in their speech.
- When we expect our success at the very first attempt itself and are reluctant to try it again.
- When we do not take lesson from our past mistake, only feel bad about it and keep thinking of it.
- When we think we cannot do a particular work.

2.5 Positive Thinking

Positive thinking is a positive approach that looks toward's life's challenges with a positive outlook or finds positivity in everything around us.

A person's attitude may be 'positive' or 'negative'. Positive thinking makes a person to look at the good in things, observe, understand and work towards improving the thing further. But negative attitude makes a person to worry and look for the bad elements in things.

The Importance of Positive Thinking

If an individual has a positive attitude toward's life and its challanges, can overcome them and grow positively in life and work. The benefits of having positive attitude are follows

- It helps to overcome challenges.
- It makes a person an energetic individual who can do well.
- It helps the person to improve his work.
- It makes the person and people around him happy.

How to Keep Persons Thinking Positive?

There are few simple steps to given below to cultivate a positive attitude in life. Let us understand this with the help of the abbreviation 'SMILE'.

S → **Start Your Day in a Positive Way**

For example, exercising, reading or watching something motivating, talking to people who are positive and make you smile.

M → **Manage Time to Relax**

For example, sit in a relaxed position and just feel how you are breathing. You can do yoga, meditation or listen to music for relaxation and calmness.

I → **Imagine the Best in Any Situation**

For example avoid thinking of bad things and instead think how you can make things better.

L → **Learn to Take Feedback in a Positive Way**

For example, if someone gives you feedback, objectively think how it will help you to improve and start working on it.

E → **Express Gratitude**

For example, be thankful for all the good things you have, to people who have helped you or pat your back for the good things you have done.

2.6 Personal Hygiene

Personal hygiene is the habit or practice of keeping ourselves clean. Cleanliness helps us to maintain our well-being and health. Being healthy helps us to attend school, college and office regularly. We have to maintain our personal hygiene. For example a beautician takes special care of his dental health as he works closely with customer. He must not have a bad breath which disturbs his customer. A receptionist at a four-star hotel make sure that his clothes are always clean with no sweat or food stains.

Importance of Personal Hygiene

Personal hygiene is very important as it helps us to

- Stay healthy.
- Create a good image of ourselves.
- Avoid feeling ashamed in public due to our bad breath, body odour etc.

Three Steps to Personal Hygiene

The three main steps of personal hygiene include :

Care

- Brush your teeth daily.
- Rub oil/cream to take care of your skin.
- Keep your hair free of dandruff.
- Cut your nails every week.
- Change your toothbrush as soon as it deshapes.

Wash

- Take proper bath everyday.
- Wash your hands frequently.
- Wash your hair atleast every second day.
- Wash your face, feet often.
- Wash your clothes regularly.

Avoid

- Keep your feet dry and change socks regularly
- Always blow nose/cough into a handkerchief to avoid spreading germs.

Essential Steps of Hand Washing

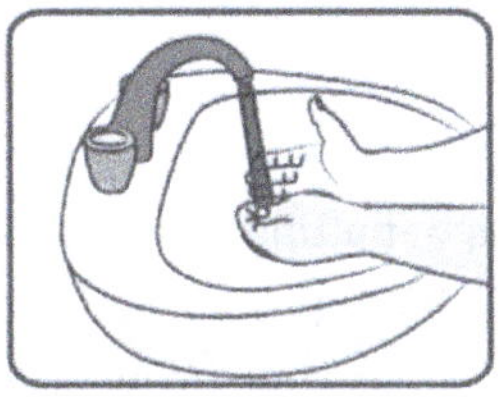

Wet hands with water

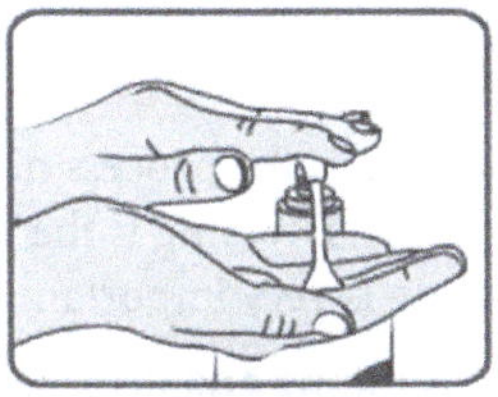

Apply enough soap to cover all hand surfaces

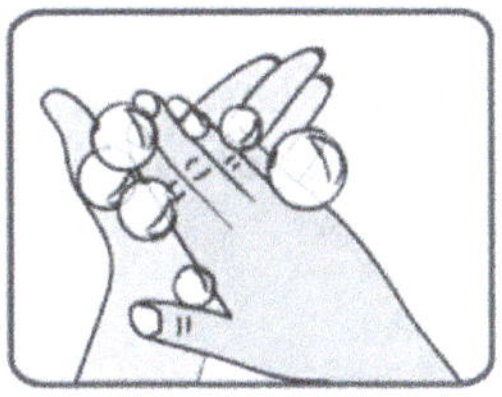

Rub hands palm to palm

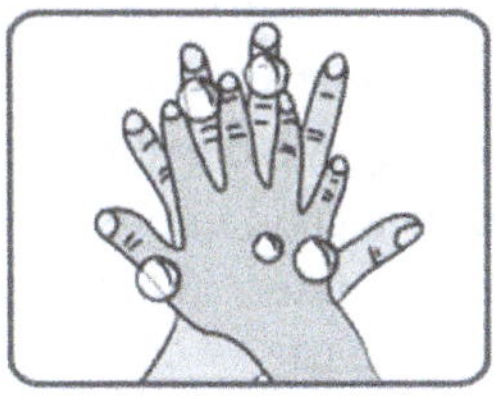

Right palm over left dorsum and vice versa

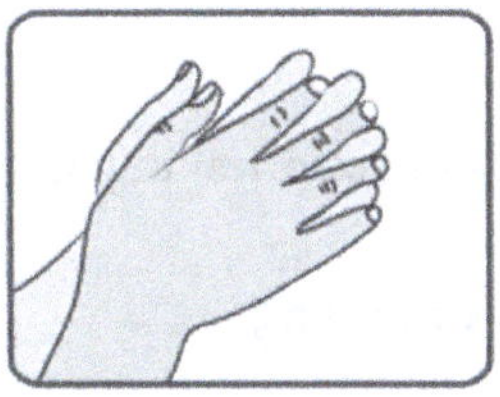

Palm to palm with fingers interlaced

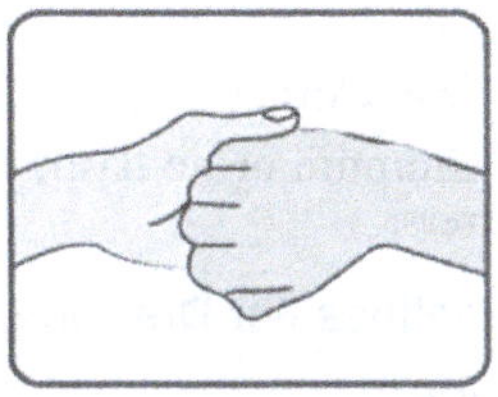

Back of fingers to opposing palms with fingers interlocked

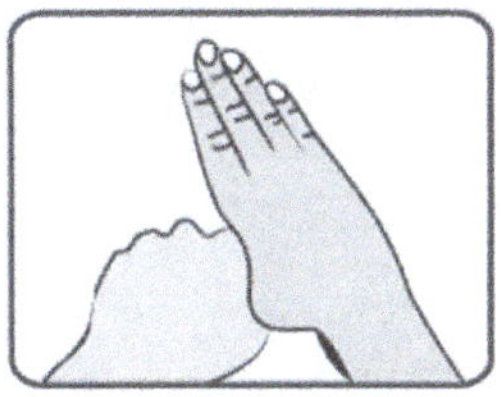

Rotational rubbing of left thumb clasped in right palm and vice versa

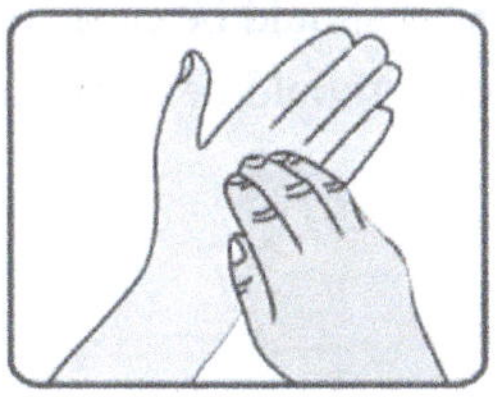

Rub inner surface of palms

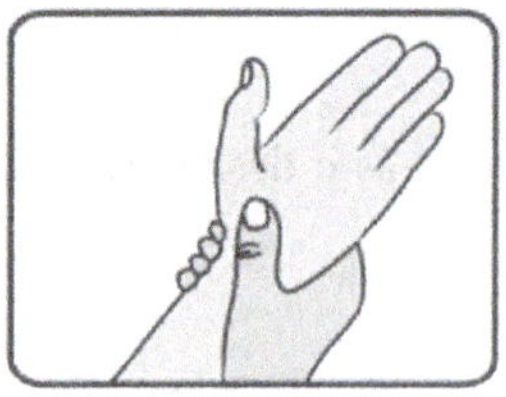

Rub inner surface using the thumb

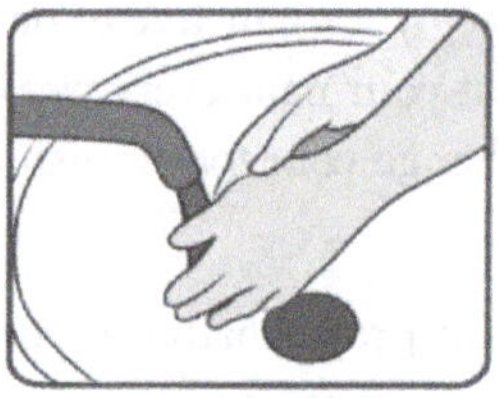

Rinse hands thoroughly with water

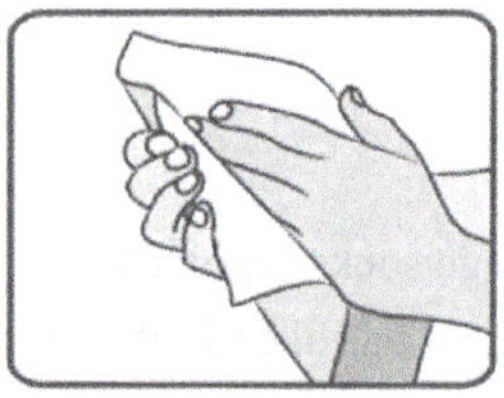

Use towel to dry

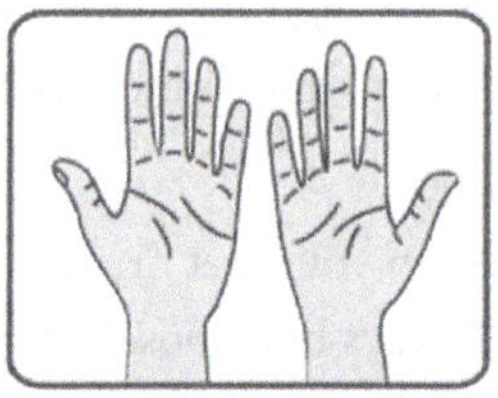

Your hands are now clean.

2.7 Grooming

Grooming is the process of making yourself look neat, tidy and smart. Dressing is the action of putting on clothes. Dressing is very important for grooming.

The grooming and dressing can either send the message that you are confident, smart and sincere or possess opposite qualities.

The Importance of Grooming and Dressing

Grooming and dressing are important because they help us

- make a good impression of ourselves
- feel confident about ourselves
- look smart

Examples of Good Dressing and Grooming

- Clean face, short hair for boys and neatly tied hair for girls.
- Clean clothes
- Minimum or no flashy things (accessories) in your dress.

Guidelines For Dressing and Grooming

Clothes

- Clothes should be neat, clean and ironed.
- Shoes should be clean and polished.
- Socks should be clean and changed everyday.
- Keep simple accessories like, belts, jewellery etc.
- In certain jobs display of bodily tatoos and piercing is not allowed.

Hair

- Simple hair styles and well combed hair are preferred as these give a smart look.
- Hair should be washed regularly to keep clean.

Face

- Shave regularly, it gives a clean look face.
- Moustache should be neatly trimmed.
- Brush the teeth twice a day to maintain dental hygiene.
- Teeth should be kept clean, without any stains and smell.
- Avoid eating paan or chewing betel leaves.

Try These 2.2

1. **What is self-belief?**
2. **Give one example of positive thinking.**
3. **Name the steps to personal hygiene.**
4. **What is mean by dressing?**

Glossary

Self-management skills include self-awareness, self-control, self-confidence, problem-solving, self-motivation, personal hygiene and grooming, positive thinking, team work, time-management and goal setting.

Our **strengths** are what we do well and are good at.

Weakness are known as 'areas of improvement'.

Interests are the things that we enjoy doing.

Ability is an acquired or natural capacity that enables an individual to perform a particular job or task with proficiency.

Self-confidence is a sense of trusting own's abilities and self. It can be developed through change in attitude and practice.

Positive thinking is a positive approach that looks towards life's challenges with a positive outlook.

Personal hygiene is the habit or practice of keeping ourselves clean.

Let's Investigate

Activity 1

Enhancing Self-Management Skills

Materials required

Student textbooks, pen

Procedure

1. Begin by reading the following paragraph to the class. "Manish got admission to a new school. His clothes were not clean, shoes were not polished, and laces were not tied. He did not smile at anyone and looked sad. He did not look confident. What are the qualities of self-management that you think are missing in Manish?"
2. Instruct students to individually write down their thoughts on the missing self-management qualities in Manish. Encourage them to think about aspects such as personal appearance, behavior, and attitude.
3. Choose one volunteer to share what they wrote, and open the discussion to the rest of the class. Encourage students to express their opinions on the self-management skills they believe Manish is lacking.

Activity 2

Assessing Self-Awareness

Materials required

Student textbooks, pen

Procedure

1. Form pairs of students who are friends or know each other well.
2. Provide each pair with the following table:
3. Instruct students to rate each other on the scale of 'Good,' 'OK,' or 'Bad' for each self-management skill mentioned in the table.

My name		My friend's name
Self management skills	My rating to my ability	My friend's rating to my ability
1. Confidence (self confidence)		
2. Positive and cheerful (Positive and Thinking)		
3. Neat and Clean (Personal Hygiene and Glooming)		
4. On- Time(Punctuality)		

4. After both students have rated each other, encourage them to discuss their ratings. This can lead to self-reflection and insights into areas for improvement.
5. Conclude the activity by having a brief class discussion, allowing students to share their experiences and thoughts on self-awareness and the importance of self-management skills.

Activity 3

Aim in life

Materials required

Pen/pencil, notepad or sheets of paper

Procedure

1. Form pairs of students. Make a list of tasks/activities you can do well.
2. Write your main aim in life.
3. Share your notes with your partner and discuss your personal characteristics.
4. Fill in the table given below

List what you believe as a person by starting the sentences with 'I am' (I am a sensitive person).	
List all you can do well by starting the sentences with 'I can' (I can identify safety aspects and seek support when witnessing or experiencing violence and abuse).	
List what you plan to do by starting the sentences with 'I will' (I will train myself in yoga).	
State your aim in life. Start the sentence with 'My aim is' (My aim is to become an accomplished sportsperson).	

Activity 4

Community Engagement and Positive Impact

Procedure

1. Reflect on the positive impact of social work on personal well-being.
2. Identify a situation in your neighborhood that needs attention (e.g., dirty streets, a hungry animal, a road hazard).
3. Take action to address the situation and document your efforts.
4. Write about your experience in your notebook and submit it for review in the next class.

Worksheet 1: What are my interests?

Group 1

S.No	Interests	Yes	No
1.	I enjoy working with a group of people.		
2.	I love to make new friends.		
3.	I feel comfortable around new people.		
4.	I like listening to people who have thoughts different than mine.		
5.	I like to report the problems in my locality to the Municipality/Panchayat.		
6.	I like responding to people enthusiastically.		
7.	I like organising events.		
8.	I want to resolve conflicts between people.		

Group 2

S.No	Interests	Yes	No
1.	I like working with tools.		
2.	I enjoy making things with my own hands.		
3.	I like to move around a lot.		
4.	I like to use gestures and non-verbal cues when I communicate.		
5.	I like to learn by doing.		
6.	I like playing sports every day.		
7.	I like assembling parts of instruments or machine using instructions.		

Group 3

S.No	Interests	Yes	No
1.	I enjoy learning about numbers.		
2.	I like to do experiments at home.		
3.	I want my things to be organised.		
4.	I like to see a pattern or logic in things that happen around me.		
5.	I like to save out of my pocket money.		
6.	I enjoy collecting coins/stamps.		
7.	I like to make and follow a plan.		

Group 4

S.No	Interests	Yes	No
1.	I like giving directions to people.		
2.	I want to learn new concepts and express my ideas visually.		
3.	I enjoy creating new product designs.		
4.	I prefer pictures over text in a magazine.		
5.	I enjoy drawing.		
6.	I like solving jigsaw/visual puzzles.		
7.	I like redecorating the room for fun.		
8.	I enjoy working with different colours.		

Worksheet 2: What are my abilities?

Group 1

S.No	Abilities	Yes	No
1.	I can resolve problems between friends.		
2.	People seek my advice.		
3.	I am good at organising events.		
4.	People call me a good listener.		
5.	I make new friends easily.		
6.	I can work with a group of people.		

Group 2

S.No	Abilities	Yes	No
1.	I am good at athletics/sports.		
2.	I am physically active.		
3.	I learn better by doing.		
4.	I have a sense of balance and coordination.		
5.	I can assemble parts of an instrument or machine by following instructions.		
6.	I work well with tools.		
7.	I use a lot of gestures and non-verbal cues to communicate.		
8.	I can make things using my hands.		
9.	I move around a lot.		

Group 3

S.No	Abilities	Yes	No
1.	I plan my activities for the day.		
2.	I keep my things in an order.		
3.	I see logic in things that happen around me.		
4.	I save some percentage of my pocket money.		
5.	I conduct a variety of experiments at home.		
6.	I can quickly calculate the total of a list.		
7.	I follow a step-by-step approach to solve problems.		

Group 4

S.No	Abilities	Yes	No
1.	I am good at solving jigsaw/visual puzzles.		
2.	I can give clear and precise directions.		
3.	I draw well.		
4.	I look at pictures in the magazine than reading the text.		
5.	I learn concepts and express my ideas visually.		
6.	I can arrange a room for various occasions.		
7.	I can make models.		

Activity 5

Role-Play - Building Self-Confidence

Materials required

Pen/pencil, Notepad or sheets of paper

Procedure

1. Form groups of four students in each group.
2. Choose from one of the given situations or create new scenarios to make it more relatable:
   - You are tasked with organizing a school event, and you need to pitch your ideas to the school administration.
   - You have to interview for a part-time job that requires strong communication skills.
   - You need to confront a friend who has been spreading rumors about you.
3. List the steps you would take to handle the situation confidently, focusing on communication, preparation, and self-assurance.
4. One group volunteers to present their role-play in front of the class.
5. Discuss and ensure that the steps for handling the situation confidently are followed.

Activity 6

Building Confidence through Positive Words

Materials required

Pen/pencil , Notepad or sheets of paper

Procedure

Make a list of feel-good sentences that you will say to yourself every day when you wake up in the morning and before you go to bed.

- Share positive affirmations with your peers and discuss how these affirmations contribute to building confidence.
- Encourage each student to create a personalized list based on their achievements, compliments, and reflections on failures.

Activity 7

Practice Activity - Self-Reflection on Confidence and Goals

Materials required

Pen/pencil, Note pad or sheets of paper

Procedure

1. Write down three qualities about yourself, your goals in life, and your plan to achieve them.
   - Encourage students to choose qualities and goals that are personally meaningful to them.
   - Provide examples such as academic achievements, personal strengths, and long-term aspirations.
2. My qualities:
   - For example, I am a good listener and empathetic.
3. My goals:
   - For example, I want to excel in my chosen field of study and contribute to a community project.
4. My plans:
   - For example, I will prioritize my time, seek mentorship, and engage in relevant extracurricular activities to enhance my skills.
   - Discuss the importance of setting realistic goals and developing actionable plans to build confidence and work towards achieving those goals.

Activity 8

Storytelling and Positive Attitude Reflection:

Procedure

1. Gather in a circle for a discussion with the teacher.
2. Share a story related to positive attitude.
3. Discuss the connection between the story and positive attitude.
4. Reflect on the role of attitude in our lives.
5. Share personal approaches and attitudes towards similar situations.
6. Discuss strategies for maintaining a positive approach in challenging situations.

Activity 9

Class Rules Role-Play and Analysis:

Materials

Pen/pencil, notepad or sheets of paper.

Procedure

1. Form groups of three students.
2. Each group prepares a role-play based on the given situation.
3. Two students act out the role-play, and the third observes and takes notes.
4. Analyze the positive aspects of dealing with the situation and identify areas for improvement.
5. A volunteer group presents their role-play to the class, followed by a group discussion.

Activity 10

Positive Language Transformation:

Materials

Pen/pencil, notepad or sheets of paper.

Procedure

1. Use the same groups from Activity 9.
2. Transform the following statements using positive words/thinking.
   (a) "I cannot give a speech in the school assembly."
   (b) "I made a lot of errors in my computer work."
   (c) "I did not like the school project."
3. Discuss the positive transformations within the group.

Activity 11

Self-reflection on how you will follow positive attitude practices

Materials required

Pen/pencil

Procedure

Make a list of things you will do from today to start thinking positively in your daily life.

Start your day in a positive way	
Make time to relax	
Imagine the best in any situation	
Learn to take criticism in a healthy way	
Express gratitude	

Activity 12

Role-play on Personal Hygiene

Materials required

Pen/pencil, notepad or sheets of paper

Procedure

1. Form groups of three.
2. Each group chooses one of the following situations.
3. Within each group, two members act out the situation, and the third member observes and makes notes on what went well, what could have been better, and what parts of CARE, WASH, and AVOID were displayed in the role-play.

Situations

(a) One of your classmates often gets left out from activities and games in school.
He/she has body odour (bad smell) issues, so other classmates avoid including him/her in classroom activities and games. You have decided to help by talking to him/her about personal hygiene and grooming.

(b) You have recently gone through the lesson on personal hygiene and sanitation and have understood its importance.
You have a neighbor who often throws garbage in public areas, and you decide to educate him/her about the importance of health, hygiene, and sanitation.

(c) You are the class monitor. One of your classmates is very sick and sometimes ends up spreading germs in the class. You have to talk to your classmate about his/her personal hygiene and cleanliness practices.

Activity 13

Personal Hygiene Practices

Materials required

Pen/pencil, writing/notepad

Procedure

1. Answer the statements with 'Yes' or 'No'.
2. If your answer is 'Yes', you are already following personal hygiene standards. If your answer is 'No', then you have to start following the personal hygiene standard immediately.
3. Write your plan for improvement for all the 'No' answers in the table provided.

Situations

Statements	Yes/No	My plan for improvement
I wash my hands with soap every time I use the toilet.		
I do not bite my nails. They are always clean and clipped.		
I cover my mouth every time I cough or sneeze in public places.		
I regularly take a bath to avoid body odour.		
I do not have dandruff or dirt in my hair.		
I never wear dirty clothes.		
My feet are smooth and not dry.		
My hair is clean, non-greasy/not oily, and it smells fresh all the time.		

Activity 14

Role-play on Dressing and Grooming Standards

Materials Required

Pen/pencil, Notepad or sheets of paper

Procedure

1. Form groups of three within your class.
2. Choose one of the following situations for your role-play.
3. Two members of each group will act out the situation, while the third member observes and takes notes on dressing and grooming standards.
4. After the role-play, discuss what went well, what could be improved, and the overall dressing and grooming displayed in the scenario.

Situations

(a) Interschool Debate Competition: Creating a Good First Impression

Scenario You have to participate in an interschool debate competition. Discuss with your friend what all will you do to create a good first impression.

Guidelines for Role-play

- Focus on preparing for the debate and the steps you take to present yourself professionally.
- Consider aspects such as clothing choice, grooming, and body language.
- The observer should note positive and negative aspects related to dressing and grooming.

(b) Educating a Classmate on Dressing and Grooming Standards

Scenario You have noticed that your classmate does not wear appropriate clothes to school. You have to educate him about the dressing and grooming standards.

Guidelines for Role-play

- Act out a conversation where you approach your classmate with sensitivity and respect.
- Address the importance of dressing appropriately for the school environment.
- Provide constructive suggestions for improvement.
- The observer should note how effectively the message is communicated and the classmate's response.

Debriefing

- After each role-play, discuss the observations made by the observer.
- Share insights on what worked well and what could be improved in terms of dressing and grooming.
- Discuss the importance of creating a positive and professional image in different situations.
- This activity aims to enhance communication skills, awareness of dressing and grooming standards, and the ability to provide constructive feedback.

Activity 15

Self-reflection on Dressing and Grooming Well

Materials required

Pen/pencil, notebook

Procedure

Answer the statements with a 'Yes' or a 'No'. If your answer is 'Yes', you are already following the desired norms of grooming. If your answer is 'No', then you have to start working on the various aspects of personal grooming.

Statements	Yes/No	My plan for improvement
Wear clothes that fit you		
Make sure your clothes are neat and ironed		
Hair is clean and always combed		
Teeth are always clean and brushed every day		
Wear shoes that are clean and polished		

Plan for Improvement

1. **Wear clothes that fit you**
   - Identify clothing items that do not fit well.
   - Set aside time to go through your wardrobe and donate or replace ill-fitting clothes.
   - Invest in clothes that complement your body shape.
2. **Make sure your clothes are neat and ironed**
   - Establish a routine for ironing clothes before wearing them.
   - Check clothes for wrinkles before leaving the house.
   - Consider organizing your wardrobe to make it easier to select and maintain well-kept clothes.
3. **Hair is clean and always combed**
   - Schedule regular hair washing based on your hair type.
   - Invest in a good quality comb or brush.
   - Learn simple hairstyling techniques for a polished look.
4. **Teeth are always clean and brushed every day**
   - Set a consistent time for brushing teeth, such as morning and night.
   - Carry a travel toothbrush and toothpaste for on-the-go oral care.
   - Consider incorporating flossing into your routine for comprehensive dental care.
5. **Wear shoes that are clean and polished**
   - Develop a habit of cleaning shoes after each use.
   - Invest in shoe cleaning supplies and polish.
   - Rotate between different pairs of shoes to prolong their lifespan and maintain cleanliness.

Note Consistency is key to improvement. Create a schedule or set reminders to help establish and reinforce these grooming habits. Regular self-assessment will ensure progress and adherence to desired grooming norms.

NCERT FOLDER

Complete Explanations of all NCERT's Questions

A. Multiple Choice Questions

Q.1 Which of the following is not a self-management skill?

(a) Problem solving (b) Bargaining
(c) Understanding self (d) Confidence building

Q.2 Grooming is a term associated with

(a) time management
(b) problem solving
(c) neat and clean appearance
(d) self-management

Q.3 What steps should one take to build confidence?

(a) Set goals in life.
(b) Appreciate oneself for all the achievements.
(c) Always think positively.
(d) Talk to people who are confident.

Q.4 Which of the following is a quality of a self-confident person?

(a) Patient
(b) Compassionate
(c) Committed
(d) Passionate

Q.5 What is the best way to start our day positively?

(a) Think about all that can go wrong.
(b) Think about the difficult test you will face during the day.
(c) Think about all your accomplishment so far and feel good about it.
(d) Think about the traffic on the road and feel stressed.

Q.6 Rahul gets feedback on his project work from his class teacher. Which of these options demonstrates positive attitude in this situation?

(a) Rahul ignores the feedback.
(b) Rahul takes the feedback but does not use it.
(c) Rahul tells others that the teacher is wrong.
(d) Rahul learns from the feedback and makes his project work better.

Q.7 What can you do to get rid of negative thoughts or feelings?

(a) Meditate to calm down and feel positive.
(b) Ignore them and move on in life.
(c) Act based on the negative thoughts or feelings.
(d) Talk to a friend and share all your negative feelings.

Q.8 **Do you think people living in hill stations can skip taking a bath for many days?**

(a) No, irrespective of the climate, one should take a bath regularly.

(b) Yes, not taking bath for many days is acceptable for people staying in cold climate.

(c) Yes, if they wipe themselves with a wet cloth, then it is fine.

(d) None of the above

Q.9 **Radha wants to grow her hair and she applies a lot of hair oil. She does not wash her hair for days and sometimes it smells bad too. What would be your suggestion to her?**

(a) She can leave the oil in her hair, after all it helps her hair to grow.

(b) She can leave it on at night and wash her hair every day before leaving home.

(c) She should not apply the oil at all.

(d) She can apply the oil and pour a little water on her hair before leaving home to reduce the smell.

Q.10 **Dressing and grooming are important because they helps us to look ....**

(a) Smart

(b) Untidy

(c) Shabby

(d) All of the above

Q.11 **The following image is an example of .... shirt.**

(a) Informal (b) Formal

(c) Both of the above (d) None of these

Q.12 **The following image is an example of .... T-shirt.**

(a) Informal (b) Formal

(c) Both of the above (d) None of these

Answers

1. (b)	**2.** (c)	**3.** (a,b,c,d)		**4.** (c)
5. (c)	**6.** (d)	**7.** (a)	**8.** (a)	**9.** (b)
10. (a)	**11.** (b)	**12.** (a)		

B. Subjective Type Questions

Q.1 **Write a short note on the factors influencing self management.**

Ans. Refer to text on page no. 30 (Various factors of self-management skills).

Q.2 **List any five self-management skills.**

Ans. Self-management skill are the abilities that allow people to control thoughts, feelings and actions.

Five self-management skills are :

(i) **Self-Awareness** Knowing yourself as an individual. Know your values, likes, dislikes, strengths and weakness.

(ii) **Self-Control** Ability to control your behaviour, discipline etc.

(iii) **Self-Confidence** Believing in yourself that you can do all the tasks given to you and not scared of taking risks.

(iv) **Problem Solving** Understanding a problem and finding a solution using step-by-step method.

(v) **Self-Motivation** Doing tasks on your own without any external motivation.

Q.3 **What are the factors that affect self-confidence?**

Ans. There are some factors that affect or decrease our self-confidence. These one as follows

(i) When we think we can not do a particular work, it affects our self-confidence.

(ii) When we do not take lesson from our past mistake, but keep thinking about it and feeling bad about it. All these disturb our self-confidence.

(iii) When we expect to be successful at the very first attempt itself and do not try again, this attitude affects our self-confidence.

(iv) When we are surrounded by people having negative attitude and negativity in their speech, it affects our self-confidence.

Q.4 **List three things you will do for personal hygiene in each of care, wash and avoid to keep clean.**

Ans. Refer to text on page no. 33 (Three steps to personal hygiene).

REVIEW EXERCISE

Including Competency Based Questions

Part I

Multiple Choice Questions

1. Which of the following is not a self-management skill?
(a) Self motivation (b) Problem solving
(c) Team work (d) Drawing pictures

2. Believing in yourself that you can do any task that is given to you is ....
(a) Self-control (b) Self-awareness
(c) Self-confidence (d) Positive thinking

3. Ability to control your behaviour, discipline etc is regarded as
(a) Self-control (b) Self-awareness
(c) Self-confidence (d) Problem solving

4. Expressing certainty or affirmation even in tough situation is known as ....
(a) Self-motivation (b) Positive thinking
(c) Self-awareness (d) Self-confidence

5. What is self-management?
(a) Self-regulation (b) Self-awareness
(c) Self perseverance (d) Both (a) and (b)

6. Which type of people can easily convince others?
(a) Rich people (b) Self-confident people
(c) Talkative people (d) Influential people

7. Which of the following statements about positive thinking is correct?
(a) Positive thinking results in positive circumstances.
(b) Positive thinking helps in focusing on the bright side of an individual's life.
(c) Positive people can easily overcome problems and achieve success.
(d) All of the above

8. Suggest the following factor which helps in building self-confidence.
(a) Geographical factors (b) Climate factors
(c) Social factors (d) None of these

9. What makes us strong and determined?
(a) Experience (b) Positive thinking
(c) Present environment (d) None of these

10. I have the power to make my dreams true is an example of
(a) Self-awareness (b) Self-confidence
(c) Positive thinking (d) Self-control

11. Planning concrete goals to be accomplished within a set timeframe is known as
(a) Time management (b) Goal setting
(c) Problem solving (d) None of these

12. Despite having a flat foot, Dipa Karmakar became the first Indian female gymnast who took part in the Olympics. It is an example of her .... Competency Based Ques.
(a) Time management (b) Self awareness
(c) Hard work (Self-confidence)
(d) None of the above

13. What is an example of time management?
(a) The skill of completing a work previously, so as to have leisure time.
(b) The skill of planning and organising time to manage all activities.
(c) The skill of finishing work within 24 hours.
(d) None of the above

14. Personal hygiene is important because it help us
(a) Stay healthy (b) Create good images
(c) Avoid self control (d) Both (a) and (b)

15. Arrange serially the essential steps of hand washing. Competency Based Ques.
(i) Apply enough soap to cover the hand.
(ii) Wet hands with water.
(iii) Rinse hands thoroughly with water.
(iv) Rub inner surface of palms.
(a) (ii), (i), (iv), (iii) (b) (i), (iii), (ii), (iv)
(c) (ii), (iii), (iv), (i) (d) (i), (iv), (iii), (ii)

16. Which of the followings is correct to maintain positivity?
(a) Make time to relax.
(b) Find out the best in any situation.
(c) Criticise the negative things.
(d) Both (a) and (b)

17. After losing a game a player considers to improve the standard of the team for next time – it is an example of Competency Based Ques.
(a) Self-control (b) Self-awareness
(c) Problem solving (d) Positive thinking

18. Proper dressing helps a person
(a) to make good impression of himself.
(b) to feel confident about himself.
(c) to become famous.
(d) Both (a) and (b)

19. When it comes to personal hygiene and grooming, which practices contribute to maintaining a healthy and presentable appearance? **Competency Based Ques.**
I. Regular handwashing
II. Neglecting dental care
III. Wearing clean and well-fitted clothes
IV. Ignoring body odor
(a) Only I and III (b) Only II and IV
(c) Both I and III (d) Both II and IV

20. In the context of self-management skills, which of the following are considered essential components for personal development? **Competency Based Ques.**
I. Goal setting
II. Time management
III. Emotional intelligence
IV. Social media expertise
(a) I and II (b) II and III
(c) I, II, and III (d) I, III, and IV

Answers

1. (d)	2. (c)	3. (a)	4. (b)	5. (d)
6. (b)	7. (d)	8. (c)	9. (b)	10. (b)
11. (a)	12. (c)	13. (b)	14. (d)	15. (a)
16. (d)	17. (d)	18. (d)	19. (a)	20. (c)

Statement Based Questions

1. Statement 1: Self-management does not involve the ability to prioritize tasks effectively.
Statement 2: Self-management skills include the capacity to organize and manage time efficiently.
(a) Both Statement 1 and Statement 2 are correct
(b) Both Statement 1 and Statement 2 are incorrect
(c) Statement 1 is correct but Statement 2 is incorrect
(d) Statement 2 is correct but Statement 1 is incorrect

2. Statement 1: Strength and weakness analysis helps in understanding personal capabilities.
Statement 2: Identifying strengths and weaknesses is a crucial step in self-improvement.
(a) Both Statement 1 and Statement 2 are correct
(b) Both Statement 1 and Statement 2 are incorrect
(c) Statement 1 is correct but Statement 2 is incorrect
(d) Statement 2 is correct but Statement 1 is incorrect

3. Statement 1: Personal hygiene is essential for maintaining good health.
Statement 2: Grooming includes practices related to personal appearance and cleanliness.
(a) Both Statement 1 and Statement 2 are correct
(b) Both Statement 1 and Statement 2 are incorrect
(c) Statement 1 is correct but Statement 2 is incorrect
(d) Statement 2 is correct but Statement 1 is incorrect

4. Statement 1: Self-confidence is built through positive thinking and overcoming challenges.
Statement 2: People who are confident believe that they can do anything given to them in any situation.
(a) Both Statement 1 and Statement 2 are correct
(b) Both Statement 1 and Statement 2 are incorrect
(c) Statement 1 is correct but Statement 2 is incorrect
(d) Statement 2 is correct but Statement 1 is incorrect

5. Statement 1: Self-management involves setting goals and planning how to achieve them.
Statement 2: Positive thinking should be ignore in self-management.
(a) Both Statement 1 and Statement 2 are correct
(b) Both Statement 1 and Statement 2 are incorrect
(c) Statement 1 is correct but Statement 2 is incorrect
(d) Statement 2 is correct but Statement 1 is incorrect

6. Statement 1: Self-management skills include time management and organization.
Statement 2: Grooming is a part of self-confidence development.
(a) Both Statement 1 and Statement 2 are correct
(b) Both Statement 1 and Statement 2 are incorrect
(c) Statement 1 is correct but Statement 2 is incorrect
(d) Statement 2 is correct but Statement 1 is incorrect

Answers

1. (d)	2. (a)	3. (a)	4. (a)	5. (c)	6. (a)

Assertion and Reason Based Questions

1. Assertion: Self-management skills are essential for personal and academic success.
Reason: They help individuals organize their time, set goals, and prioritize tasks effectively.
(a) Both Assertion and Reason are true, and Reason is the correct explanation of Assertion.
(b) Both Assertion and Reason are true, but Reason is not the correct explanation of Assertion.
(c) Assertion is true, but Reason is false.
(d) Both Assertion and Reason are false.

2. Assertion: Personal hygiene and grooming are important aspects of self-confidence.
Reason: Maintaining good personal hygiene and grooming enhances an individual's self-esteem and how others perceive them.
(a) Both Assertion and Reason are true, and Reason is the correct explanation of Assertion.
(b) Both Assertion and Reason are true, but Reason is not the correct explanation of Assertion.
(c) Assertion is true, but Reason is false.
(d) Both Assertion and Reason are false.

3. Assertion: Interest in a particular activity may not necessarily indicate the ability to perform it proficiently.

Reason: For instance, one may like cricket but may lack the necessary power or skill required to play the game, showcasing a misalignment between interest and ability.

(a) Both assertion and reason are true, and the reason is the correct explanation of the assertion.
(b) Both assertion and reason are true, but the reason is not the correct explanation of the assertion.
(c) Assertion is true, but the reason is false.
(d) Assertion is false, but the reason is true.

Answers

1. (a) **2.** (a) **3.** (a)

Part II

Very Short Answer Type Questions

1. What does team work involve in self-management?

Ans. Collaborating with others to achieve shared goals and objectives.

2. How does self-management contribute to stress avoidance?

Ans. By developing good habits, overcoming challenges, and engaging in enjoyable activities.

3. How can you identify your strengths?

Ans. Reflect on what you do well, consider others' feedback, and recognize areas where you consistently excel.

4. Why is self-confidence crucial in recognizing talent?

Ans. Lack of confidence can hinder talent recognition; building self-confidence involves attitude changes and practice.

5. How does positive thinking impact personal growth?

Ans. Positive thinking fosters resilience, overcoming challenges, enhancing work performance, and promoting happiness in oneself and others.

6. What does 'SMILE' stand for in cultivating a positive attitude?

Ans. 'SMILE' stands for Stay positive, Manage stress, Inspire others, Learn continuously, and Express gratitude.

7. What does dressing and grooming help achieve?

Ans. Dressing and grooming help look smart, feel confident, and make a favorable impression on others.

8. How can positive thinking be maintained?

Ans. Maintain positive thinking by staying optimistic, understanding situations, and working towards improvement instead of dwelling on negatives.

Short Answer Type Questions

1. Write any five impacts of self-management skills.

Ans. Self management is considered as the ability to regulate one's emotions, thoughts and behaviour effectively in various situations. Some important impacts of self-management skills are

(i) It helps us have control over negative emotions, behaviours and habits.
(ii) It helps us have control over our actions, so that we do not act in impulse and develop good habits.
(iii) It helps us to be organised.
(iv) It helps us to develop positive attitude.
(v) It helps us to overcome challenges and difficulties.

2. How do we identify our weakness?

Ans. Weaknesses are areas of improvement, where we need to develop and build ourselves. We can identify our weakness in the following ways :

(i) We must look at the feedback we received from others.
(ii) We must point out areas of our difficulty.
(iii) We should open to feedback of others and accept our weakness without feeling bad about it.

3. What is self-confidence? Suggest any two qualities of a self-confident person.

Ans. Self-confidence is a sense of trusting in one's own abilities and self. It tells what we are made up of and how we feel about ourselves.

Two qualities of a self-confident person are :

(i) **Self-Belief** It is confidence in our own abilities or judgment. People learn from their own mistake and achieve success.
(ii) **Positive Attitude** It is focusing an on the positive side of an event in the time of adversily. The situation of losing a game can be perceived as an opportunity to review the game.

4. What do you mean by positive thinking? Write about the importance positive thinking.

Ans. Positive thinking helps in creating a real values in our lives. It requires a person to look at the good in things, observe, understand and works for improving them.

The importance of positive thinking are

(i) It overcomes challenges.
(ii) It makes us do well by making us energetic.
(iii) It help us better at work.
(iv) It make us and people around us happy.

ASSESSMENT EXERCISE

Multiple Type Questions

1. Which of the following is a self-management skill?
   (a) Self-control (b) Self-awareness
   (c) Self-motivation (d) All of these
2. 'I am unable to resist junk food when someone offers me', is an example of
   (a) Weakness (b) Self-control
   (c) Positive attitude (d) None of these
3. Which type of hairstyle is giving a smart look?
   (a) Trendy hairstyle (b) Simple hairstyle
   (c) Well combed hair (d) Both (b) and (c)
4. Which way of fashion is not allowed in certain jobs?
   (a) Wearing Sandals (b) Wearing informal dress
   (c) Displaying bodily tatoos and piercing (d) All of these
5. In the context of self-management skills, which of the following are considered aspects of positive thinking?
   I. Visualizing success
   II. Focusing on limitations
   III. Embracing challenges
   IV. Dwelling on past mistakes
   (a) Only I and III (b) Only II and IV
   (c) Both I and III (d) Both II and IV

Very Short Answer Type Questions

6. Name two benefits of self-management.
7. Why is self-awareness important in strength and weakness analysis
8. Why is personal hygiene important?

Short Answer Type Questions

9. What is self-management? Suggest atleast two self-management skills.
10. What are strengths and weakness? Why it is important to know our own strengths and weakness?
11. What are interests and abilities? Why is it important for a person to know his interests and abilities?
12. What is self-confidence? Suggest three steps for building self-confidence.
13. Why positive thinking is very important for us?
14. What is personal hygiene? Elucidate any four basic habits to maintain personal hygiene.
15. What do you mean by grooming and dressing? Write about the importance of dressing and grooming.

Basic ICT Skills-I

CHAPTER 03

ICT skills are the abilities you need to use technology effectively. This includes using common software programs, searching the web for information, and communicating online. It also involves understanding how to use technology safely and responsibly. In today's world, ICT skills are essential for success in many fields.

3.1 Introduction

ICT stands for Information and Communication Technology. It includes a diverse set of technological tools and resources used to communicate, create, disseminate, store and manage information.

ICT includes computers, Internet, broadcasting technologies and telephony. People use technology every day at home and at workplace.

ICT tools enable anytime, anywhere access to information and resources. The various ICT tools that are used include computes we use at work, smartphone through which we talk, Internet for getting information, communicating with others through E-mail and social networks, watching movies etc.

For example, to find a job you may have to search the Internet for job openings, create a resume on a computer, use E-mail to send the resume, send messages through your phone to communicate appear for telephonic interview and get your offer letter through E-mail.

ICT skills help us to communicate, run our business and stay connected with our family and friends. Hence, every person needs to acquire ICT skills and build them to stay updated with the latest softwares and applications (apps).

The basic ICT skills that you need are knowing how to

- Operate computers.
- Browse the Internet for collecting, storing and disseminating information.

3.2 ICT at Workplace

ICT has become part of our workplace in all sectors of economy, money transactions through online banking system, development of research papers in educational institutions etc.

At workplace, we used different computer softwares and applications to complete different tasks like making documents, calculations, tables, graphs etc. We can also use applications to do every day work, like buying things, booking train or bus tickets, Internet banking and making online payments.

Modern ICT employs a variety of media forms which includes text, graphics, animation, audio and video. It also involves creating, curating, managing images and documents; gathering and processing data and presenting them; working with audio and video tools to create media rich communications.

3.3 ICT at Home

These days most of the people use television for entertainment. New devices, such as smartphones with an Internet connection are now being used to stay connected with family and friends on a regular basis through social media networks, such as Facebook, Instagram and Twitter. We use computers and mobile phones for talking to each other, sending and receiving information, watching videos and news, listening to music and playing games.

You can visit the following sites and know about the ICT activities:

Sector	ICT used for	Website
Agriculture	Various activities related to research, development and training in agriculture and allied fields	http://dare.nic.in/ https://bit.ly/2H3DJfU
Retail	Training programmes in the retail sector	http://rasci.in/
Beauty and Wellness	Training programmes in beauty and wellness sector	http://www.bwssc.in/
Banking and Finance	Training programmes in banking, financial services and insurance sector	http://www.bfsissc.com/
Apparel	Training programmes in Apparel sector	http://sscamh.com/indexHome.php
Logistics	Training programmes in Logistics sector	http://Isc-india.com/
Healthcare	Training programmes in Healthcare sector	http://www.healthcare-ssc.in

3.4 ICT Tools : Smartphones and Tablets

Smartphones and tablets are becoming more and more important as most people carry them around and use them in daily activities like sending E-mails and messages, sharing pictures etc.

The spreading of an idea or news occurring some where in the world is now possible through social sites on the Internet. Smartphones are now being used to stay connected with social media and exchange information.

Smartphones

Mobile phones are ICT tools for talking to people but smartphones are more advanced. With a simple mobile phone you can only make phone calls and receive calls. With a smartphone, you can make calls and do things that you normally do using a computer, such as browsing the web, sending E-mails, making video calls, playing games, listening to music, watching movies and much more.

Smartphones do not need a telephone line. They use wireless (mobile) networks to make calls and to connect to the Internet. Some of the popular operating systems for smartphones are Android, Apple iOS and Windows Mobile.

Tablets

For some activities, such as reading a book for a longtime, the screen of a mobile may be too small. For such activities, we can use a tablet. A tablet is a mini computer with input, output and processing functions that are all combined into one touchscreen, where you can do various tasks just by touching its screen. It is bigger than a smartphone and you can perform all the functions that one can perform on a computer or a smartphone.

TV and Radio

TV and Radio are being used as an ICT tool since a long time. Radio is used to broadcast audio while TV is used to broadcast audio-visual information to many people. You can hear news, songs, stories, speeches, cricket commentary etc on radio, while TV is used for watching movies, news, weather forcasting, songs, cartoons and educational lectures.

Applications or Apps

Smartphones perform so many functions with the help of software applications (Apps). On the screen of smartphone or Tablet, you see a lot of small pictures (or icons). If you touch these, they start programs or functions required for watching movies, playing games, using camera etc.

Apps are software programs that perform different functions. Some of the apps are already present on the phone or tablet. These are called default apps.

Besides, there are hundreds of other apps that can be purchased or downloaded free of cost from online stores. There are several online stores, including Google Play Store for Android phone and Apple App Store for Apple phone.

Commonly found Applications

Some of the default apps installed on all smartphones/mobiles are given below:

- **Phone** This app is used to make calls. It also stores the contacts and call history.
- **Calendar** It shows a calendar and you can also enter appointments, remainders etc in it.
- **Camera** It is used to take photos and videos.
- **Mail** This app is used to send and receive E-mails using your E-mail account in G-mail, Yahoo, Outlook etc.
- **Gallery** It helps you to store all photos and videos and arrange them into albums.
- **Maps** This app helps you to find directions where you want to go. It uses GPS (Global Positioning System).
- **Browser** It allows you to open a browser to search and visit different websites.
- **Clock** This app shows the time and also sets alarm, timers etc.

- **Messages** This app is used to send and receive SMS messages.
- **Music** This app allows you to play songs and music.

Try These 3.1

1 TV and Radio are being used as an ICT tool. (True/False)
2 Commonly found application(s) on phone is/are
   (a) Gallery (b) Browser (c) Clock (d) All of these
3 Write any use of ICT at workplace.
4 What is app?

3.5 Mobile Device Layout

Some of the basic controls you see on mobile device are as follows:

- **Power button** This is used to start and shut down a mobile device.
- **Screen** A screen on which we perform functions by touching with our fingers.
- **Back button** This is used to go back to the previous screen in an application.
- **Microphone** This is present at the bottom of the mobile and used when we talk to someone.
- **Menu button** This is used to show the options available in a particular app. This may not be present in all mobile devices.
- **Home button** This brings you back to the home screen.
- **Earpiece** This helps you to listen to voice calls.
- **Volume buttons** This helps you to increase or reduce the sound of your mobile.

Basic Features of a Mobile Device

Some of the basic features present in all mobile devices are given below:

- **Bluetooth** It is a short range wireless technology which helps you to connect with other devices. Other device should be within 30 feet of where you are. Once connected, you can share photos, songs etc.
- **Chargeable battery** It is a portable power pack which can be recharged. It allows you to use the mobile device anywhere.
- **Wi-Fi** It is a wireless network technology that helps you connect to the local area network. This is used to connect to the Internet.
- **Cellular network connectivity** It provides the network through which you can make calls.
- **Global Positioning System (GPS)** It is a navigation (direction finding) system that helps you to navigate, find direction and maps to specific locations.

Home Screen of a Mobile Device

The home screen is the first (start) screen of a mobile device. There are three main parts of the home screen as:

(i) **Top** The top part of the screen is called the status bar. It displays icons to show the network signal, battery life, Wi-Fi and Bluetooth connectivity, 3G/4G status etc.

(ii) **Middle** This is the main part of the screen that consists of icons/shortcuts to the applications. These icons can be placed anywhere you want.

(iii) **Bottom** This is the lower part of the screen which is called the Dock. The apps in this area can always been seen even if we move to a different pages.

Basic Gestures Used

Gestures are used to interact with the touchscreen of your mobile device. For example, instead of clicking a mouse to open an App, you tap on the touchscreen.

Some of the gestures are as follows:

- **Tap** Touch the screen with your finger, once, to click.
- **Tap and hold** This is similar to right clicking your mouse.
- **Drag** To tap, hold and move your finger across the screen.
- **Swipe** To slide finger to the right, left, up or down of the screen like turning a page.
- **Double tap** To tap twice quickly-this is to zoom out (increase the size) of something.
- **Pinch** To bring thumb and finger together on the screen to zoom in (reduce the size). e.g. to make a picture appear smaller.

Try These 3.2

1 ...... helps you to listen to voice calls.
   (a) Earpiece (b) Microphone
   (c) Mic (d) Speaker
2 A/An ...... on which we perform function by touching with our fingers on phone.
3 What is the use of bluetooth?
4 Define pinch the basic gesture of mobile device.

3.6 Computer System

A computer system is a programmable machine designed to store and retrieve information and perform arithmetic and logical operations to produce meaningful results in desired format. The term computer is derived from the Latin word 'Computare' which means 'to calculate'.

The basic functions of a computer system are to accept the input, process the input, display the output and to store data.

Note *The I/O devices that are attached externally to the computer machine are called peripheral devices.*

Parts of Computer System

Parts of a computer are as follows:

(i) Input Devices (Unit)

(ii) Output Devices (Unit)

(iii) Central Processing Unit (CPU)

(iv) Memory Unit

1. Input Devices

An input device is a hardware device that sends data into the computer system. These devices are used to input (or enter) data and instructions into the computer system. All instructions are accepted by the CPU through electrical pulses from various kind of input devices.

Some of the input devices are Keyboard, Pointing Devices, Scanner, MICR, OCR, OMR, Barcode Reader, Microphone (Mic), Web Camera, Digital Camera, Biometric Sensor, Smart Card Reader, which described below:

I. Keyboard

It is the most commonly used input device which uses an arrangement of buttons and keys. Both data and program can be entered into the computer through the keyboard. It is an essential device for interactive processing because the user can easily issue commands to receive the data response immediately on the computer screen.

Layout of a Keyboard

Types of Keys on Keyboard

- **Function keys** Keys labelled from F1 to F12 are function keys. You use them to perform functions. Their functions differ from program to program. The function key F1 in most programs is to get help on that program.
- **Control keys** Keys such as Ctrl, Alt, Shift, Tab are special control keys that perform special functions depending on when and where they are used.
- **Enter key** The label on this key can be either Enter or Return depending on the brand of computer that you are using. You use them to move the cursor to the beginning of a new line. In some programs, it is used to send commands and to confirm a task on a computer.
- **Punctuation keys** These include keys for punctuation marks such as colon (:), semicolon (;), question mark (?), single quotation mark (' '), double quotation mark (" ") etc.
- **Navigation keys** Some keys such as the arrow keys, Home, End, PageUp and PageDown are navigation keys. The Home and End keys move the cursor to the left and right end of a line of text, respectively. The PageUp and PageDown keys are used to move one page up and one page down, respectively.
- **Command keys** Some keys such as Insert, Delete and Backspace are command keys. When the Insert key is turned ON, it helps you overwrite characters to the right of the cursor. The Delete key and Backspace key are used to remove typed characters and other objects on the right and left side of the cursor respectively.
- **Windows key** It opens the Start menu.

II. Pointing Devices

A pointing device is used to communicate with the computer by pointing to the locations on the monitor.

It can also be used for

- sending command signals to the computer.
- selecting items on the screen.
- selecting commands from command menu.
- drawing graphics, sketches, etc.

Some commonly used pointing devices are mouse, joystick, light pen, graphics tablet, touch screen and trackball, which described below :

(i) **Mouse** It is a pointing device that allows to control the movement of pointer (also known as **mouse pointer**) on screen. Mouse performs various functions by detecting two-dimensional motion relatively to its supporting surface. Generally, a mouse has two buttons-right button and left button.

Wired Mouse

Wireless Mouse

Mouse also includes a scroll wheel between these two buttons to scroll down the application window and their contents also. These are three types of mouse as – Wireless mouse, Mechanical mouse, Optical mouse. Some actions or functions of mouse are as follows:

- **Roll over/hover** Some actions can be done by simply rolling over or hovering an object. When you bring the mouse over a file, it will show the details of that file.
- **Point and click** As you move the mouse on your desk, a pointer moves correspondingly on your computer's screen. The mouse allows you to select an item on the screen. When you click a particular file, it gets selected.
- **Drag and drop** To move an item, you need to click it, and then holding the mouse button down, move the item to a new location. After you move the item to the new location, you release the mouse button. This is called drag and drop.
- **Double click** It means to quickly click the left mouse button twice. When we double click the file icon, it will open the file.

(ii) **Joystick** It is a pointing device that moves in all directions and controls the movement of the cursor. A joystick is similar to a mouse excepts that the movement of cursor on screen stops working as soon as user stop moving the mouse. But with a joystick, the pointer continuous moving in the previously pointing direction.

Joystick

Commonly, joysticks are used for playing computer games like flight simulators but occasionally used for CAD/CAM systems and other applications.

(iii) **Light Pen** It is a handheld electro-optical pointing device, which is used for making drawings, graphics and for menu selection. It senses the light from the screen when it becomes closer and generates a pulse. Light pen is used especially in Personal Digital Assistants (PDA). It is very useful in identifying a specific location on the screen.

Light Pen

(iv) **Graphics Tablet** A graphics tablet (or digitisers, digitising tablet, or simply tablet) is an input device that consists of an electronic writing area and a special pen that works with it.

It allows artists to create hand-made images and graphical images with motion and action, similar to the way a person draws images with pencil and paper. When user draws anything on the tablet with the special pen, the drawing appears on the screen.

Graphics Tablet

Graphics tablet may also be used to capture data or handwritten signatures.

(v) **Touchscreen** It is an electronic visual display that can detect the presence and location of a touch within the display area. The term touch screen generally refers to touching the display of the device with a finger or hand.

The touchscreen sends a signal to the computer. This signal gives the location on the screen, which has been touched. Touchscreen is quick and simple to use. Generally, smartphones have a high-resolution capacitive touch screen. There are different types of touchscreens available with electronic devices like capacitive touchscreen, resistive touchscreen and gorilla glass touchscreen, etc.

Touch Screen

(vi) **Trackball** It is designed for computers, generally serves as mouse replacement. It is primarily used to move the cursor on the screen. The trackball has a ball on its top. Trackball can be rolled with fingers and the internal rollers sense the motion, which is transmitted to the computer. Trackballs are common on CAD workstations and sometimes seen on computerised special purpose work stations, such as the radar consoles in an air-traffic control room or sonar equipment on a ship or submarine.

Trackball

III. Scanner

It is an input device that makes copies and reproduces text and images and convert it into a digital file, allowing the computer to read or display the scanned object. Scanners can be used for storing the documents in their original form that can be modified and manipulated later on. It is mainly used to convert a scanned document in a digital format.

Scanner

Scanners come in a variety of sizes from hand held models to desktop models as Handheld scanners, Flatbed scanners and Drum scanners.

IV. MICR (Magnetic Ink Character Recognition)

It is a character recognition technology which is primarily used by the banking industry to facilitate the processing of cheques. This technology allows the computer to read information (such as account numbers) on printed documents. MICR can read upto 2400 documents/min. The MICR coding system contains 14 characters (4 special symbols and 10 decimal digits). So, it can recognise these 14 characters only. The type font E-13 B, a standard typographical style, is used to print the characters or identification marks.

V. OCR (Optical Character Recognition)

It is used to translate scanned images of handwritten, type-written, printed text or special type font printed on conventional paper with conventional ink into machine-encoded text. OCR is widely used to convert books and documents into electronic files, to computerise a record-keeping system in an office or to publish the text on a website.

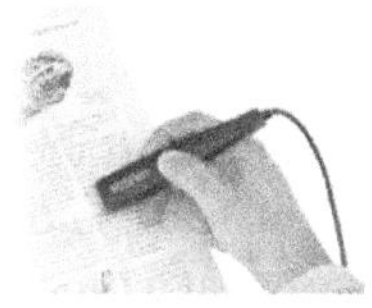
OCR

An optical reader uses photoelectric devices to scan the characters being read and convert the reflected light patterns of the data into binary data suitable for computer input. The normal speed of an OCR is 1500 to 3000 characters per second.

The technology is being developed for greater accurate recognition and is also known as Intelligent Character Recognition (ICR).

VI. OMR (Optical Mark Reader)

OMR is the process of detecting the presence of intended marked responses. OMR is mainly used to detect marks on a paper. It uses a beam of light that is reflected on the paper with marks, to capture presence and absence of data (Marks).

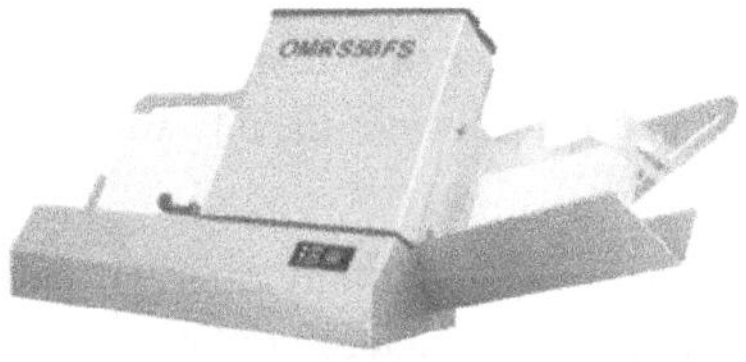
OMR

The OMR reader interprets the patterns of marks into a data record and sends this to the computer for storing, analysing and reporting. OMR is widely used to read the answer of objective type tests, voting applications and other evaluations studies.

VII. Barcode Reader

It is an input device used for reading printed bar codes (Universal Product Code) available on product to be sold. A barcode reader emits a beam of light, which reflects off the barcode image.

A light sensitive detector in the barcode reader identifies the barcode image by recognising special bars at both the ends of the image.

Once code is identified, it is converted into a numeric code. A perfect example of a barcode reader is its use in a super market where barcode scanner reads the price of a product.

A barcode is a machine readable representation of information in the form of stripes of dark and light ink.

Barcode Reader

VIII. Microphone (Mic)

We can send sound to the computer through a special manual input device called microphone or mic. A mic converts the received sound into computer's format, which is called Digitised Sound or Digital Audio. To convert a voice into digital form, an additional hardware is always needed which is known as Sound Card.

Sound is used most often in multimedia, where user can make his/her presentation more attractive using recorded narration, music or sound effects.

A microphone can be attached to a computer to record sound. Now-a-days, microphones are also being used with speech recognition software. This means that you do not have to type the document, rather just have to speak and the spoken words appear in your document.

Microphone

IX. Web Camera (Webcam)

Webcam is a digital camera attached to computers and can be used for video conferencing or online chatting, etc. It is a video capturing device.

Webcams are able to capture full motion videos as well.
A webcam connected to a computer allows the user to view either a still picture or motion video of a user or other object.

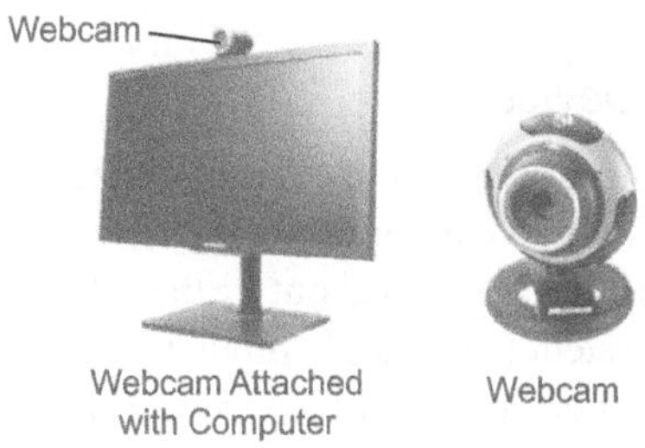

Web Camera

Now-a-days, webcams are either embedded into the display with laptops or connected *via* USB or firewire port or Wi-Fi to the computer system. After connecting webcam to a computer, you need to install a required software or drivers.

X. Digital Camera (Digicam)

It is an input device that stores the pictures or videos in an electronic format instead of film. There are several features that make digital camera a popular choice, when compared to film cameras. Most enjoyable feature is the LCD display on the digital camera.

Digital Cameras

This display allows users to view and save photos or videos after the picture or video has been taken, that means, if you take a picture and don't like the results, you can delete it, or if you like the picture, you can save it and easily show it to other people.

XI. Biometric Sensor

It is a device which recognises physical or behavioural traits of an individual. Biometric sensors are mainly used marking attendance of employees/students in organisations/institutions. Biometric sensors are working with accuracy, so these can be widely used in security purpose.

XII. Smart Card Reader

It is a device which is used to access the microprocessor of a smart card. There are two kinds of smart cards.

Memory cards the cards which contain only non-volatile memory storage components and some specific security logic. Microprocessor cards contain volatile memory and microprocessor components. The card is made-up of plastic generally PVC. Smart cards are used in large companies and organisation for strong security authentication.

2. Output Devices

An output device is a part of computer hardware equipment, used to communicate the results of data processing which are carried out by the information processing system (such as a computer), to the outside world. Output devices carry the results of various operations performed by the user. Output device makes it possible to view or print data.

Some of the devices, which are used to display the processed result or output are Monitor, Printer, Plotter, Speaker, Headphone, Projector, Speech synthesizer which explained as below :

I. Monitor/VDU

A monitor (called a Visual Display Unit, VDU) is an electronic visual device used to display the output. The rectangular area of the monitor, its refresh rate and dot pitch, all directly affect the resolution of the display.

A monitor is of two kinds : Monochrome display monitor and Color display monitor.

A monochrome display monitor uses only one color to display text and color display monitor can display 256 colors at a time.

An image on the monitor is created by a configuration of dots, also known as pixels.

The clarity of image depends on three factors :

- **Resolution of Screen** Resolution refers to the number of pixels in horizontal and vertical directions. The resolution of monitor is higher when the pixels are closer together.
- **Dot Pitch** It refers to the diagonal distance between two colored pixels. The smaller the dot pitch, the better the resolution.
- **Refresh Rate** The refresh rate of a monitor is the maximum number of times the image on screen can be drawn or refreshed per second.

II. Printer

It is an output device which produces a hard copy of documents that are stored in an electronic form on physical print media such as paper or transparencies. So, printers are the primary output devices used to prepare permanent documents.

The speed of a printer is normally rated either by Pages Per Minute (PPM) or by Characters Per Second (CPS). Printer resolution is a numerical measure of print quality that is measured in Dots Per Inch (DPI).

Printers can be classified into two broad categories as follows :

(i) **Impact Printers** These printers rely on a forcible impact to transfer ink to the print media, similar to the action of a typewriter. There is a mechanical contact between the paper and the print head.

(ii) **Non-impact Printers** These printers are much quieter than impact printers as their printing heads do not strike on the paper.

These printers are comparatively faster and produce high quality output. They can be used for printing text and graphics both in black & white and colored.

III. Plotter

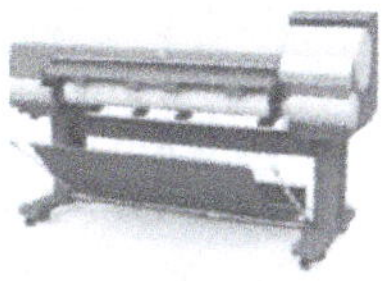
Plotter

It is an output device similar to a printer that uses a pen, pencil, marker or other writing tools to make a design. Plotters are generally used to generate the map of building and shopping malls. A plotter is a computer printing device for printing vector graphics. In the past, plotters were widely used in applications such as Computer Aided Design (CAD) and other printing jobs. Though, they have generally been replaced with wide-format conventional printers.

IV. Speaker

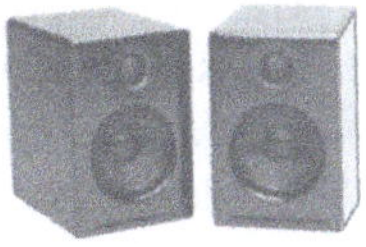
Speaker

It is an output device that receives the sound in the form of electric current from the sound card and convert it into sound format. Speakers are used for listening music. Computer speakers (multimedia speakers) are the speakers, which are attached internally or externally to a computer system.

V. Headphones

Headphones

These are a pair of small loudspeakers or less commonly a single speaker, held close to a user's ears and connected to a signal source such as an audio amplifier, radio, CD player or portable media player. They are also known as stereo phones, headsets or cans.

VI. Projector

It is an output device which is used to project information from a computer onto a large screen, so it can be viewed by a large group of people simultaneously. Projectors are widely used for classroom training or conference holes with a large audience. It provides a temporary output display.

VII. Speech Synthesizer

It is used to produce sound from a text and can be implemented in software and hardware. A text-to-speech system converts normal language text into speech.

3. Central Processing Unit (CPU)

It is the part of a computer system that carries out the instructions of a computer program, to perform the basic arithmetical, logical and input/output operations of the system. The CPU is also known as the **brain of the computer**. The speed of CPU depends upon the type of microprocessor used and it is measured in MegaHertz (MHz). Two typical components of a CPU are Arithmetic Logic Unit and Control Unit.

I. Arithmetic Logic Unit

In computing, an Arithmetic Logic Unit (ALU) is a digital circuit that performs arithmetic and logical operations. The ALU is a fundamental building block of the central processing unit of a computer. ALU uses registers to hold the data that is being processed. Most ALUs can perform the following operations :

- Logical Operations (AND, NOT, OR)
- Arithmetic Operations (addition, subtraction, multiplication and division)
- Bit-shifting Operations (shifting or rotating a word by a specified number of bits to the left or right, with or without sign extension)
- Comparison Operations (= =, <, <=, >, >=)

- **Register** It is the internal part of CPU which gives special purpose location to arithmetic logic unit and control unit. These are used to store intermediate results obtained during the execution of instructions.
- **Microprocessor** It is fabricated on a single IC (Integrated Circuit). IC is a piece of silicon, composed by thousands of transistors.
- **Motherboard** The main circuit board contained in any computer is called a motherboard. It is also known as the main board or logic board or system board or planar board. All the other electronic devices and circuits of computer system are attached to this board like, CPU, ROM, RAM, expansion slots, PCI slots and USB ports. It also includes controllers for devices like the hard drive, DVD drive, keyboard and mouse. In other words, motherboard makes everything in a computer work together.

II. Control Unit

It coordinates the input and output devices of a computer system. Control Unit (CU) fetches the instructions which are given in the form of micro-programs. It directs the operation of other units by providing timing and control signals.

In general, CU is a central part of the computer that controls its operations and entire processing. The control unit is the circuit that controls the flow of data through the processor and coordinates the activities of the other units within it. Control unit acts like human nerves system, which does not process data but behaves as a central unit for other data manipulating components.

4. Computer Memory

The computer memory is one of the most important elements in a computer system.
It is the internal or external storage area, which holds the data and instructions during processing in the form of binary numbers.

Memory also relates to many devices and components that are responsible for storing data and applications on a temporary or a permanent basis. Computer memory can be classified into two types— Primary memory and Secondary memory/Storage device.

I. Primary Memory

It is also known as main memory. It is the internal memory used by computer to hold data and instructions. The primary memory has limited storage capacity.

It holds the data and programs needed at that instant by CPU. Primary memory is volatile in nature i.e. it requires constant power supply to motion the current information.

There are two types of primary memory i.e. RAM and ROM.

(i) **RAM** (Random Access Memory) It is the internal memory that can be read from as well as written to. This memory is often associated with volatile types of memory. It can hold data only on temporary basis because it requires a continuous flow of electrical current. If current is interrupted, data is lost.

RAM

(ii) **ROM** (Read Only Memory) In ROM, information once stored remain fixed, i.e. it can not be changed. So, ROM can only be read and used. The contents of ROM remain stored even if power is turned OFF.
This memory is often associated with non-volatile types of memory. ROM cannot be altered once the chip has been made.

ROM

> **Cache Memory**
>
> It is a storage buffer that stores the data that is used more often, temporarily and makes them available to CPU at a fast rate.
>
> The data and instructions that are required during the processing of data are brought from the secondary storage devices and stored in the RAM.
>
> Cache memory is a very high speed memory placed in between RAM and CPU. Cache memory increases the speed of processing.
>
> Cache memory is very expensive, so it is smaller in size. Generally, computers have cache memory of sized 256KB to 2MB.

II. Secondary Memory/Storage Device

Secondary memory, also known as Secondary Storage or Auxiliary Memory, is the slower and cheaper form of memory. It is a permanent storage device. CPU does not access the secondary memory directly. The content in it must first be copied into the RAM to be processed. Secondary memory is non-volatile in nature, i.e. the information does not get erased even when the power is switched OFF and data will not be destructed until and unless the user erases it.

Secondary Memory Devices include

Magnetic Disks	Optical Discs	Solid State
Floppy Disk	CD	Pen/Flash Drive
Hard Disk Drive	DVD	
Magnetic Tape	Blu-ray Disc	

(i) **Floppy Disk** (Diskette) A Floppy Disk Drive (FDD) is a computer disk drive that enables a user to save data on removable diskettes. This portable storage device is a rewritable media and can be reused a number of times. It is made of plastic with magnetic coating on it. It is round in shape and is covered by square plastic jacket. Floppy disks are commonly used to move files between different computers. Although 8" disk drives made available in 1971 were the first real disk drives, the first widely used floppy disk drives 4", $5\frac{1}{4}$", which were later replaced with $3\frac{1}{2}$" floppy disk drive. However, today these drives are replaced with CD-R and other writable disk drives and flash drives.

(ii) **Hard Disk Drive** A Hard Disk Drive (HDD) is a non-volatile and random access digital data storage device. It is a data storage device used for storing and retrieving digital information using rotating disks (platters) coated with magnetic material. All programs of a computer are installed in hard disk within a particular drive.

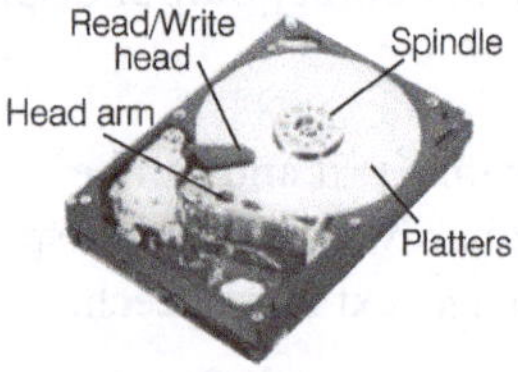

Hard Disk Drive

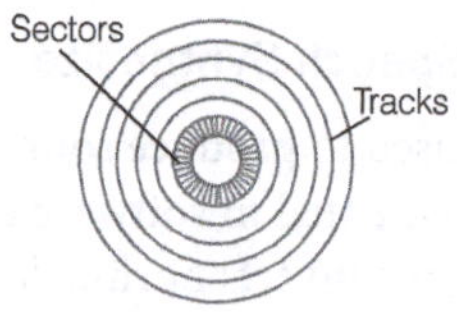

Tracks and Sectors

It consists of a spindle that hold non- magnetic flat circular disks, called platters, which hold the recorded data.
Each platter requires two read/write heads, that is used to write and read the information from a platter. All the read/write heads are attached to a single access arm so that they cannot move independently.

The information is recorded in bands, each band of information is called a track. Each platter has the same number of tracks and a track location that cuts across all platters is called a cylinder. The tracks are divided into pie-shaped sections known as sectors.

Note Floppy disk were a popular storage medium from the 1970s to the early 2000s but their use has declined significantly since then.

(iii) **Magnetic Tape** It is a medium of data storage, made up of a magnetic material. It is a storage medium on a large open reel or in a smaller cartridge or cassette (like a music cassette). It is used for those applications that are based on sequential data processing i.e. it is a sequential data access medium.
Due to this (sequential data access) nature, these tapes are not suitable for data files that need to be revised or
updated often. They are generally used to store backup data or that type of data, which is not frequently used or to transfer data from one system to another.

(iv) **Compact Disc (CD)** It is an optical media that is used to store digital data. It is relatively cheap, small, portable and round in shape storage medium which is made up of molded polymer. It consists of a circular disc, which is coated with a thin metal that is highly reflective. Laser beam technology is used for recording/reading of data on the disc. It is also known as laser disc or optical laser disc, due to the use of laser beam technology. CD provides random access medium for high capacity secondary storage. The diameter of the CD ranges from 10cms to 30cms. One CD can store 600 MB to 750 MB.

(v) **Digital Video Disc (DVD)** It is also known as Super Density (SD) disc. A DVD is an optical disc storage media manufactured for the first time by Philips, Sony, Toshiba and Panasonic in 1995. DVDs offer higher storage capacity than compact discs while having the same dimensions.
Depending upon the disk type, DVD can store several Gigabytes of data (4.7 GB-17.08 GB). DVDs are primarily used to store music or movies and can be played back on your television or on the computer too. They are not rewritable media.

(vi) **Blu-ray Disc (BD)** It is an optical disc storage medium designed to recapture the data normally in DVD format. Blu-ray discs contain 25 GB (23.31 GB) per layer space. The name blu-ray disc refers to the blue laser used to read the disc, which allows information to be stored at a greater density. Blu-ray can hold almost 5 times more data than a single layer DVD.

(vii) **Pen/Flash/Thumb Drive** A flash drive is a data storage device that consists of flash memory (USB memory/key memory) with an integrated, Universal Serial Bus (USB) interface.
USB flash drives are typically removable, rewritable and physically much smaller than a floppy disk. A USB flash drive, thumb drive or pen drive is a portable drive that is same as the size of your thumb that connects to the computer USB port. Today, flash drives are available in various storage capacities as 256 MB, 512 MB, 1 GB, 4 GB, 16 GB, 64 GB, etc. Flash drives are widely used as an easy and small medium to transfer and store the information from the computers.

Pen Drive

(viii) **Memory Stick** It is USB-based flash memory drive. A family of flash memory cards from Sony designed for digital storage in cameras, camcorders and other handheld devices. Capacity of memory stick varies from 4 MB to 256 MB.

Memory Stick

Basic Units of Measurement

When user uses a RAM, ROM, Floppy disk or Hard disk, the data is measured using some units. In computer terminology, they are called Nibble, Bit, Byte, Kilobyte, Gigabyte etc.

Units of Computer Memory Measurements

- **Bit** (Binary digit) The smallest unit of data. It is either 0 or 1.
- **Nibble** A group of 4 bits or half a byte.
- **Byte** A group of 8 bits. A byte can represent 256 (2^8) distinct values, such as the integers from 0 to 255. Each keyboard character is represented through atleast 1 byte.
- **Kilobyte** (KB) It is actually 2^{10} bytes or 1 KB = 1024 bytes.
- **Megabyte** (MB) It is actually 2^{20} bytes or 1 MB = 1024 KB.
- **Gigabyte** (GB) It is actually 2^{30} bytes or 1 GB = 1024 MB.
- **Terabyte** (TB) It is actually 2^{40} bytes or 1 TB = 1024 GB.
- **Petabyte** (PB) It is actually 2^{50} bytes or 1 PB = 1024 TB.
- **Exabyte** (EB) It is actually 2^{60} bytes or 1 EB = 1024 PB.
- **Zettabyte** (ZB) It is actually 2^{70} bytes or 1 ZB = 1024 EB.
- **Yottabyte** (YB) It is actually 2^{80} bytes or 1 YB = 1024 ZB.
- **Brontobyte** It is actually 2^{90} bytes or 1 Brontobyte = 1024 YB
- **Geopbyte** It is actually 2^{100} bytes or 1 Geopbyte = 1024 Brontobyte. Geopbyte is the highest and bit is the smallest memory measurement unit.

Try These 3.3

1 1GB equals to

(a) 1024 MB (b) 1024 KB

(c) 1024 Byte (d) 1024 TB

2 MICR stands for ....

3 Name the types of printer.

4 Give any one difference between RAM and ROM.

3.7 Ports and Connections

The slots or channels into which we connect the mouse/keyboard/external hard disk wires are called ports. Thus, ports help us to connect input, output and storage devices in a computer system.

There are several types of ports that you can use to connect a computer to an external devices and networks.These are

- **Universal Serial Bus (USB) port** generally connects peripheral devices, such as a mouse or a keyboard or a printer to a computer using the cable.
- **Display port** connects the monitor or any display unit to the computer using the cable. These can be of different types, like Video Graphics Array (VGA) and High Definition Multimedia Interface (HDMI), depending on the requirement.
- **Audio ports** help to connect microphone, speakers and headphones to a computer system. Often, the speaker and headphone port is called the line out port, i.e. it is meant for sound output.
- **Ethernet port** is used for connecting the system to high speed Internet cable.
- **Power port** is used for connecting the computer system to the power supply.

3.8 Basic Computer Operations

Computer Hardware and Software

A computer system consists of two main parts Hardware and Software. The physical parts that we can see and touch are called the hardware. It is the machinery of a computer. e.g. Keyboard, Mouse, Monitor, CPU etc.

The software that we cannot see and makes the hardware work the way we want. It is a collection of computer programs, procedures and related data that provide the instructions for telling a computer what to do and how to do it.

e.g. The monitor is a hardware. When we start a program, it is displayed on the monitor. This is done by the software which displays things on monitor. Hardware would not be of any use without the software.

The most important software in any computer is the Operating System (OS). This is the software that starts working as soon as we switch ON a computer. It displays the desktop on the monitor.

Some of the most commonly used operating systems for laptops and desktop are Ubuntu, Microsoft Windows, Mac OS etc.

Mobile devices also have operating system that helps them perform their functions. Some of the mobile operating systems are Apple iOS and Google Android.

Starting a Computer

When a computer is switched ON, it performs some basic processes or functions, before it is ready to take instructions from the user.

To start a computer, press the Power [⏻] button on the CPU. This will start the Windows operating system and display the windows desktop on the monitor.

Basic Functions Performed when a Computer Starts

A computer automatically runs a basic program called BIOS (Basic Input/Output System) as soon as it is switched ON or the power button is pushed ON.

The BIOS first does a self test. If the self-test shows that the system is fine, the BIOS will load the operating system. This means that the computer's operating system, is now ready to take inputs from the user.

Login and Logout

When multiple users use the same computer, each user has his/her own files and applications. To make sure that nobody else sees other's work, each user should have login-IDs and passwords. A login and password is like a key to lock which allows them to use the computer.

When user login to the computer with his/her logic-ID and password, the computer knows that they are an authorized user and allows them to work on applications in the computer.

Once they finish working, they must log out or sign out so that no one else can see their work.

Shutting Down a Computer

In Ubuntu operating system, user can shut down the computer by clicking "Systems" at the top right and then click on Shut Down option.

When user clicks Shut Down, the operating system will close all the applications and turn off the computer.

Need to perform basic file operations

Information on a computer is stored in electronic files, which can be put into separate folders. It is easier to manage the electronic files as they can be simply copied, moved, renamed or even deleted.

3.9 Files and Folders

All information stored in a computer is kept in files. Different types of files store different types of information. Each file is given a file name and has a file name extension that identifies the file type.

The file name and file name extension are separated by a period or a dot (.).

For example, a document created using Notepad will have extension .txt.

There are other types like .doc, .xls, etc. An image file usually has an extension .jpg, while a sound file usually has .mp3. A folder is a location where a group of files can be stored. A folder within a folder is called sub folder.

Creating a File (Using a Text Editor in Ubuntu)

Let us create a new file using a text editor in Ubuntu :

- To open a text editor, type 'editor' in the search dialog box. Then double click the text editor option. This will open a blank document.

Note In Windows, you can open the Notepad and type in the text.

- Here you can add text.
- To save the file click Save. In Save As dialog box, browse to the Desktop folder, type the name and click Save button.

Try These 3.4

1. **Name any two port.**
2. **Some commonly used OS is/are**
   (a) Ubuntu **(b) Windows**
   (c) Mac OS **(d) All of these**
3. **A computer consists of two main parts are ....**
4. **To start a computer, press the Power button. (True/False)**

3.10 Communication and Networking

Basics of Internet

The Internet is a huge network of computers around the world. Using the Internet you can get any information that is stored in a web page on the World Wide Web. With the help of the Internet, you can gather a lot of knowledge which is available on it. The knowledge is stored in a big library/storehouse, called the World Wide Web (WWW) or the web.

WWW is a collection of different websites that you can view if you are connected to the Internet. You can also use these websites to buy something, watch movies, read books, learn new skills, educate yourself, find the best colleges to study further etc.

Uses of the Internet

There is no limit to what you can do online,but some of the most common uses of Internet are as follows:

(i) **Search Information** You can get the latest information about anything that is uploaded on the web, whether it is result of any exam, news, a cricket match, election details and many more.

(ii) **Entertainment** You can listen to music, play games, watch movies, share images or videos etc using Internet.

(iii) **E-mail and Chatting** You can receive and send messages to others all around the world in quick and easy manner. G-mail, Outlook etc are used for E-mailing while Facebook messenger, Whatsapp etc are used for chatting.

(iv) **Social Networking** You can share your interests, knowledge and stories with your family, friends, relatives etc around the world. e.g. Facebook, Twitter etc.

(v) **Online Shopping** You can buy and sell things such as books, electronic goods, clothes, shoes etc over the Internet. You can also pay for these things *via* digital modes of payments such as wallets, plastic cards or through e-Banking etc.

(vi) **Online Booking** You can book movie tickets, hotels, bus/train/plane tickets etc using Internet.

(vii) **Online Learning** There is a number of courses available online-some are free while others are paid.

(viii) **Online Banking** You can do banking operations, like checking details of your bank account or transferring money from one account to another through mobile banking/NEFT/RTGS.

Connecting to the Internet

To connect to the Internet, there is need following:

(a) A device, such as a computer, laptop or mobile.

(b) A connecting device, i.e. a modem.

Info Wall

Internet Service Provider (ISP) is a company which provides the Internet connectivity using the phone lines or a wireless network.

Types of Connections

There is two types of Internet connection as:

(a) **Wired connections** When our computer is connected to the Internet using a wire or cable, it is called a wired connection. We use Ethernet cables (cables used for connecting to the Internet) to connect to the modem which connects to the ISP using a phone line.

(b) **Wireless connections** Computers can also be connected to the Internet using wireless technology. Laptops need a wireless Internet card to connect to a modem with using any cables. Wi-Fi, WiMAX are the ways to connect the Internet wirelessly.

Bandwidth

It is the amount of data that can be transmitted over a network in a certain amount of time.

e.g, The amount of water flowing through a pipe depends on its thickness.

Similarly, the amount of data that your network can receive or send depends on its bandwidth. In case of digital devices, the bandwidth is usually expressed in bits per second (bps) or bytes per second.

In case of analog devices, the bandwidth is expressed in cycles per second or Hertz (Hz).

Data transfer speed over the networks is calculated in terms of bits per second.

1 Kbps (Kilobits per second) = 1000 bits per second

1 Mbps (Mega bits per second) = 1000 kilobits per second

1 Gbps (Giga bits per second) = 1000 mega bits per second

World Wide Web

The World Wide Web (WWW) or simply the web is a huge collection of information. It was introduced on 13th March 1989. It is a vast network of linked hypertext files, stored on computers throughout the world that can provide a computer user with information on a huge variety of subjects.

Thus, it serves as a platform through which users can use or share information.

It is made up of

- A web page
- A website
- A web browser
- A system to transfer information between the web browsers and the web pages.

Web Page

A web page is a document present on a computer that is connected to the Internet. There are hundreds of web pages. Each web page has a unique address/location like to the address of a house. We can use the address to see a particular web page. To view a web page, you need a web browser on your computer.

Website

A group of web pages that follow the same theme and are connected together with hyperlinks is called a website.

Websites and web pages are written in a coding language that makes it possible to add pictures, sound and interactivity to plain old text, making people's reading experience more exciting. The very first page of a website is called home page of that website.

e.g. http://www.carwale.com is a website while http://www.carwale.com/new/ is a web page.

Internet Browser/Web Browser

To see the information on the various websites, you need an Internet browser. Internet browser or web browser (Commonly referred to as browser) is an application or an application software program on your computer, laptop or mobile which helps to visit the various websites. It is an application for using and sharing information on the World Wide Web.

The most popular web browsers that are used today as Mozilla Firefox, Google Chrome, Internet Explorer, Apple Safari, Opera etc.

Searching for Information

Follow the below steps to search for information on Internet:

Step 1 Open the browser, e.g. Google Chrome.

Step 2 Type the topic about which you want information in the search box and press Enter key.

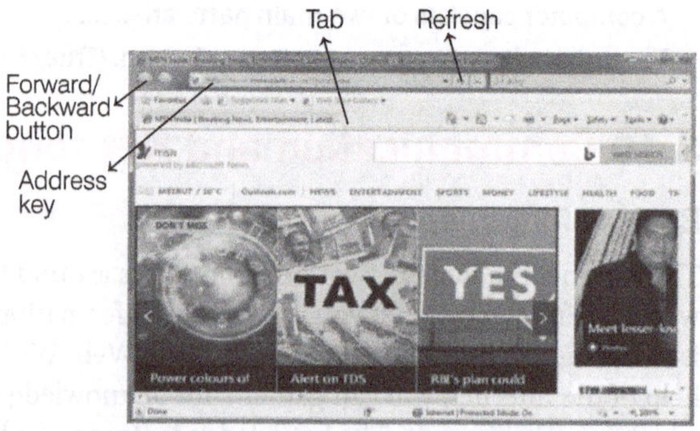

Step 3 The search results having the required information will be displayed.

In Ubuntu

- In Ubuntu operation system, click the Firefox icon from side menu bar to open the Firefox Mozilla browser.
- Search the information which you want.

> **Hyperlinks**
> There are hyperlinks present on web pages of browser. If you click a hyperlink, it will take you to another part on the same page or to a different page.

Important Parts of a Web Browser

(i) **Address bar** (Alt+d) You can type the address/URL of a website in the bar and press Enter. The browser will display the page linked to that URL.

(ii) **Tabbed browsing** (Ctrl+T) Tabbed browsing allows a user to view multiple pages in the same window. So, if you want to compare two types of computers for example mainframe and micro, you can open the two different tabs in same window.

(iii) **Backward and forward buttons** (Alt + Left or Right arrow) These buttons allow to go back to the last page viewed or go forward to the next page viewed.

(iv) **Refresh button** (F5) Sometimes, you do not see the complete page correctly. You can reload the page by clicking the Refresh button.

Try These 3.5

1 **Use(s) of the Internet**

(a) Entertainment (b) E-mail chatting

(c) Search information (d) All of these

2 **What is the use of online learning?**

3 **Define bandwidth in one line.**

4 **To reload a page, shortcut key ...... is used.**

3.11 Introduction to E-mail

Electronic mail or E-mail is a quick way of sending messages to people using Internet. Electronic mail is a message sent over the Internet from one person to another. It consists of lines of text and images. The invention of E-mail has influenced our lives and they have become a popular means of communication.

Files containing videos, documents, spreadsheets etc., can be sent along with the E-mail as attachments. E-mail is fast and easy to use. It can be sent to multiple people at the same time.

Comparing between Postal mail and E-mail

	Postal mail	E-mail
Address	Postal mail address is a street, city etc., of a geographical location.	An E-mail address is a digital location on a mail computer where you can send or receive an electronic message.
Written on	Postal mail is written with paper and pen.	An E-mail is written on a computer or mobile device.
Sent *via*	Postal mail is sent by bus, air, train.	An E-mail travels in a digital format over an Internet connection.
Received in	Postal mail is brought by the postman and dropped into the letterbox outside our house.	E-mail comes into inbox of the receiver's E-mail account.

E-mail ID or Address

An E-mail address is composed of two separate parts :

1. Your personal identity or account name (user name) on that mail server.
2. The domain name of the mail server computer on which you have an E-mail account.

An E-mail address is generally in the form of username@domain name. Some examples of E-mail address are – arihant@gmail.com, webmaster@yahoo.com, etc.

In E-mail address, symbol '@' is used as an separator. It separates your account name and domain name.

Advantages of E-Mail

1. The delivery of messages is very fast.
2. The cost of E-mailing is almost free as it involves negligible amount of telephone and Internet Service Provider (ISP) charges.
3. Multiple copies of the same messages can be sent to a group of people at the same time and can be sent as easily to a single person.
4. Pictures, documents and other files can also be attached to messages.

Disadvantages of E-Mail

1. Viruses attached with an E-mail could seriously affect recipient's computer.
2. E-mails cannot really be used for official business documents. They may be lost and you cannot find them.
3. E-mails may be intercepted by hackers as E-mail, before it is delivered to the recipient, 'bounces' between servers located in different parts of the world.

4. If an E-mail is too long or not drafted properly by the sender, the reader may lose interest to read the mail till the end.

Creating an E-mail Account

There are various web-portals (websites), which allow you to create free E-mail account. e.g. www.gmail.com, www.yahoo.com, www.hotmail.com, www.rediffmail.com, www.msn.com, etc.

Some steps for opening an E-mail account are as follows :

Step 1 Enter the URL address as www.gmail. com. Gmail Homepage will appear.

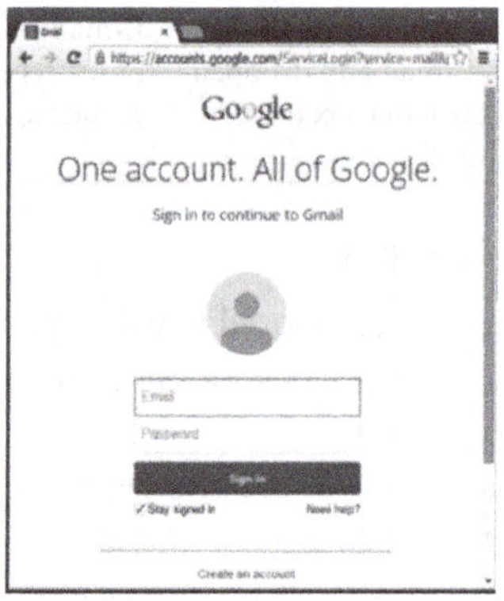

Step 2 Click on Create an account hyperlink. The Registration Form will appear.

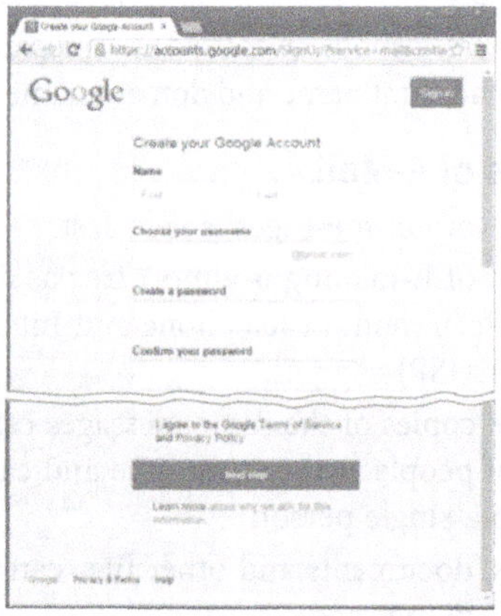

Step 3 Fill those details which are mandatory. You can also skip some of the personal details.

Step 4 After completing the registration form, click on Next step button.

Step 5 Create your public Google+ profile page will appear. If you want to create a profile, click on Create your profile button otherwise click on No thanks button.

Step 6 After the creation of an E-mail account, the confirmation information will be given to the user and web page will display on the browser.

Writing an E-mail

After login, if a user wants to create an E-mail click on COMPOSE button and New Message window will display on the screen.

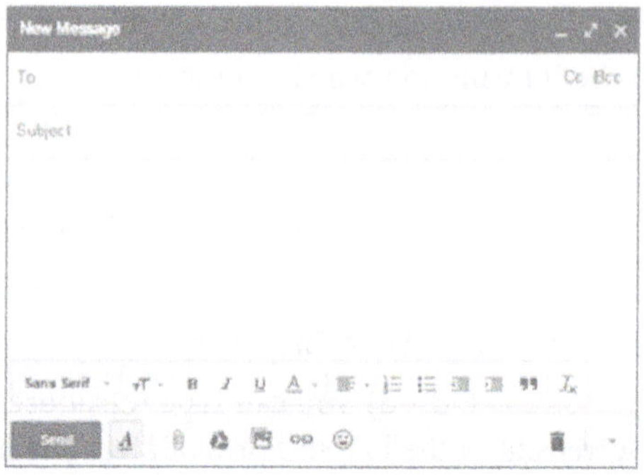

In this window, **To** text box carries the E-mail address of the recipient, **Subject** carries the heading for E-mail or subject of the E-mail and the **whole body** of text matter comes within the Body option.

For sending an E-mail, click on Send button. E-mail delivers to the recipient's end instantly.

Instead of this, if a user wants to send a file (.doc, .pdf, .jpg, etc.) then click on Attach files for the attachment of files.

There are various options which are accessible within an E-mail like Text Formatting, Cc (Carbon Copy), Bcc (Blind Carbon Copy) etc.

Some of these are as follows :

- **Cc** (Carbon copy) This allows an E-mail to be send to a large number of people by writing their respective addresses separated by commas.
- **Bcc** (Blind carbon copy) This is Cc, except that the recipient does not see the list of people in the Bcc field.
- **Signature** This is one of the basic elements of an E-mail message. By this, you are often able to set a signature, meaning a few lines of text which will be added to the end of the document.

Attaching a file to an E-mail

An attachment is a type of file such as a photo or document that you can send along with your E-mail.

To send a soft copy in the form of attachment, follow these steps :

Step 1 Click on COMPOSE button on Gmail account window. New Message box will display on the screen.

Step 2 Type the E-mail address of the recipient in To: line or you can also select E-mail address from your address book.

Step 3 Type the subject of the E-mail in the subject line.

Step 4 To attach any soft copy, click on Attach files button ( ) and the Open dialog box will display on the screen.

Step 5 Select the file which you want to attach. After selecting the file, click on Open button.

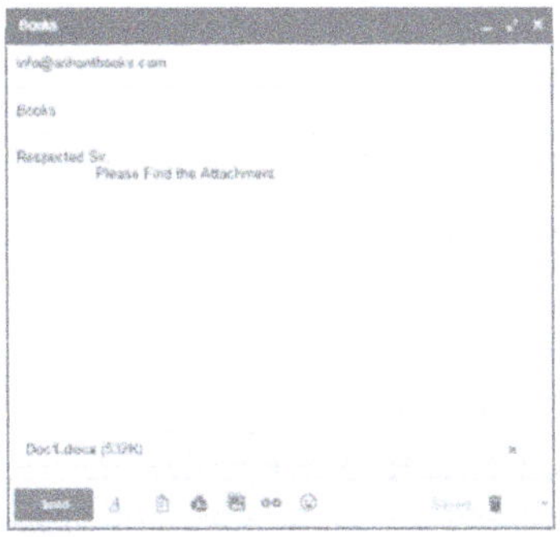

Step 6 When the file gets attached to E-mail, click on Send button.

Managing Folders

There are different folders that could help you manage and organise your E-mails, which describe below:

- **Inbox** A place where E-mail messages are received. The inbox is the default location for all incoming mails unless rules have been setup to forward messages to another program or folder.
- **Outbox** A term used to describe the location or folder where E-mail is stored before being sent. It gives the opportunity to the user to review, edit and delete messages before they are sent.
- **Drafts** This folder contains items that have not yet been sent. An E-mail is saved to the drafts folder when a user composes an E-mail and then click the Save and Close button.
- **Sent Items** This folder contains all items that have been sent but not deleted. It saves all the messages that were successfully sent.
- **Junk/Spam** This folder holds e-mails that may not be useful.
- **Trash** This folder holds E-mails that you no longer need and have deleted. To delete an E-mail, you select an E-mail and then click on the Delete button for it to be moved from inbox to trash folder.

Receiving an E-mail

Receiving mails will appear in inbox. It shows the name of the sender, subject and a title of the main message. It will remain bold till you open it.

Step 1 Click on the mail to open it.

Step 2 Once you have read the E-mail, you can reply, forward or delete the mail.

Step 3 If the message was sent to many people, you get another option, i.e. Reply to All. When you click this, the reply will be sent to all the people who received a copy of this mail.

Replying to an E-mail Message

For replying to an E-mail message, follow these steps :

Step 1 Open the E-mail which you have to answer.

Step 2 Click on Reply option.

Step 3 Click on Reply to all option for answering the all recipients of To and Cc boxes.

Forwarding an E-mail Message

To forward an E-mail message, follow these steps :

Step 1 Open the E-mail which a user wants to forward.

Step 2 Click on Forward option.

Step 3 Enter the names of the recipients in To, Cc and Bcc boxes.

Step 4 Click on Send button.

Forward is used to send a copy of received E-mail to someone else.

Deleting an E-mail

E-mail can be delete by clicking on delete icon. This will remove the E-mail from inbox and move it to the Trash folder. It will remain there for a few days before it is removed from the system.

Try These 3.6

1. **Name any two attachments that can be sent through E-mail.**
2. **Write any two disadvantages of E-mail.**
3. **Bcc stands for ....**

Glossary

Gestures are used to interact with the touchscreen of your mobile device.

An **input device** is a hardware device that sends data into the computer system.

Output devices carry the results of various operations performed by the user.

The **CPU** is also known as the brain of the computer. The speed of CPU depends upon type of microprocessor used.

The **Internet** is a huge network of computers around the world.

A **web page** is a document present on a computer that is connected to the Internet.

Electronic mail is a message sent over the Internet from one person to another.

Let's Investigate

Activity 1

Evolution of ICT

Materials required

Diagrams or models of basic computer components, illustrations of peripheral devices, chart sheets, sketch pens, and pencils.

Procedure

1. Form groups of five students each.
2. Divide the chart paper into three columns representing the past, present, and future.
3. Choose a topic related to the evolution of ICT for each time period.

- **Past** Explore the early developments and key milestones in the history of ICT.
- **Present** Focus on current technologies, trends, and their impact on society.
- **Future** Speculate on potential advancements and innovations in ICT.

Activity 2

Transformative Impact of ICT

Materials required

Poster board, newspapers cuttings, pens, etc.

Procedure

1. Form groups of three students.
2. Discuss the role and significance of ICT in personal life and the workplace.
3. List at least five points for each area.
4. Prepare a poster depicting five ways each in which ICT is transforming: (a) Personal life (b) Workplace
5. Include an activity using ICT, the corresponding technology, its impact, and how it was conducted before. Example: Online shopping - technology (e-commerce platforms), impact (convenience), pre-technology (in-store shopping).
6. Use newspaper cuttings or other materials to visually enhance the poster.

Activity 3

Exploring Mobile Devices

Materials required

Pen, Notebook, Various mobile devices (smartphones and tablets)

Procedure

1. Divide the class into groups, ensuring each group has access to at least one mobile device. Adjust the group size based on the number and types of devices available.
2. Each group member powers on the assigned device and explores the home screen, noting down the names of icons visible in the status bar and on the home screen.
3. After exploration, one volunteer from each group presents the icons they've noted to the class.
4. Following each presentation, engage the class in a discussion about the functionalities of the icons identified.
5. Rotate the groups so that each member gets a chance to explore a different device.
6. Conclude the activity with a summary discussion highlighting common features across different devices and any unique functionalities observed.

Activity 4

Exploring Mobile Device Features

Materials Required

Pen, Notebook, Smartphone or Tablet for each participant

Procedure

1. Begin by forming small groups based on the number of mobile devices available. Ideally, each group should have one mobile device. If you have a mix of smartphones and tablets, ensure a diverse distribution among the groups.
2. Assign each group a mobile device (smartphone or tablet).
3. Instruct each member of the group to turn on the assigned device and take note of the names of icons in the status bar and the dock.

4. Once everyone in the group has observed and recorded the icons, select one volunteer from each group to come to the front of the class.
5. The volunteers will share and read aloud the names of the icons they noted on their respective devices.
6. Open the floor for a class discussion where students can share their observations and discuss the various features of the icons.
7. Encourage students to ask questions and exchange insights about the different icons and their functions.
8. After the discussion, provide additional information or tips on specific icons, ensuring that students have a clear understanding of the basic features of mobile devices.
9. Conclude the activity by summarizing the key takeaways and reinforcing the importance of understanding the icons for efficient use of mobile devices.

Activity 5

Exploring Computer Basics

Materials required

Pen/pencil, notebook, computer

Procedure

1. Divide the class into groups based on the number of available computers.
2. In each group, assign different roles to students:
   - **Student A** Start the computer and log in.
   - **Student B** Identify and label the keys on the keyboard.
   - **Student C** Demonstrate various mouse functions, such as hover, click, double-click, etc.
3. Rotate the roles within the group so that each student gets a chance to experience different aspects.
4. Encourage communication and collaboration among group members during the activities.
5. After all students have had the opportunity to participate, gather the groups for a debrief session.
6. During the debrief, have each group discuss what went well and any challenges faced during the activities.
7. Open the floor for feedback from other groups. Students can share their observations on what was done correctly and offer suggestions for improvement.
8. As a class, compile a list of best practices for computer use based on the feedback and observations.
9. Conclude the activity by discussing the importance of these basic computer skills in today's digital age and how they can be applied in various aspects of life.

Activity 6

Keyboard Proficiency Practice

Materials Required

- Computers with text editors (Ubuntu with 'editor' or Windows with Notepad)

Procedure

1. **Group Formation** Organize students into groups based on the number of available computers.
2. **Open Text Editor** On Ubuntu, open a text editor by typing 'editor' in the search bar and selecting Text Editor.

   On Windows, open Notepad by typing "Notepad" in the Windows Search bar and selecting it from the search results.
3. **Home Row Practice** Position your hands on the keyboard following the guidelines in Figure.

   Type the given letters and words in the text editor.
   - **Letters in the home row** asdf; lkjhj; asdfgf; lkjhj;
   - **Letters in the top row** qwerty poiuy trewq yuiop
   - **Letters in the bottom row** zxcvb nm,./bvcxz.,mn

   Rotate through the students in the group to ensure everyone gets a chance to practice.
4. **Word Typing Exercise** Each student types five words using the keyboard. Encourage creativity and variety.

   Example words: add, all, ask, sad, gas, dad, lad, had, hall, fall, row, tow, top, out, pot, rot, wire, tire, type, write, cab, nab, man, can, van, ban.

   Ensure that all students in the group have an opportunity to practice.
5. **Review and Feedback** Facilitate a brief discussion within each group to share experiences and challenges.

   Provide constructive feedback on hand positioning, typing speed, and accuracy.
6. **Optional Extension** Challenge students to create their own list of words and share them with the group for additional practice.

   Introduce timed typing exercises to enhance speed and accuracy.

Activity 7

Exploring Computer Components

Materials required

Pen/pencil, notebook, whiteboard or flip chart paper, markers

Procedure

1. Divide the class into groups of 4-5 students each.
2. In each group, brainstorm and list the basic input and output devices needed in a computer in your notebooks.
3. Collaboratively draw a diagram of a computer system on the whiteboard or flip chart paper, illustrating all the devices connected to it. Label the diagram and mention the uses of the various devices.
4. Discuss within the group to ensure everyone understands the functions of each device.
5. Select one volunteer from each group to present the illustration to the class, explaining the functions of the devices.
6. Encourage questions and discussions from the class.

Activity 8

Hands-On Device Connection

Materials required

Pen/pencil, notebook, computer, various computer peripherals (printer, monitor, keyboard, mouse, speakers), connecting cables

Procedure

1. Form groups of 4-5 students each.
2. Distribute computer peripherals and cables to each group.
3. Assign each member of the group to connect one part of the computer (printer, monitor, keyboard, mouse, speakers) to the central processing unit (CPU).
4. Instruct students to fit the cables into the correct ports as explained in class.
5. Emphasize proper cable handling and connection procedures to avoid damage.
6. Have each group check if each device is working properly by performing simple tasks, such as printing a document, moving the mouse, and checking the display and sound.
7. Encourage troubleshooting and problem-solving within the groups.
8. Rotate roles within the groups to ensure everyone gets hands-on experience with different devices.
9. Discuss any challenges faced during the activity as a class and share solutions.

Activity 9

Creating a File

Materials required

Pen/pencil, Notebook, Computer

Procedure

1. Form groups based on the number of available computers. Each group member will create a file, while others in the group can observe and provide feedback.
2. Open a text editor on the computer. Use Ubuntu's text editor or Notepad on Windows.
3. Type details such as name, class, address, parent's name, etc., for a student.
4. Save the file on the desktop.

   Keyboard Shortcuts to Study:
   - CTRL+Z: Undo
   - CTRL+Y: Redo
   - CTRL+A: Select all
   - CTRL+X: Cut
   - CTRL+C: Copy
   - CTRL+V: Paste
   - CTRL+P: Print
   - CTRL+S: Save

   Interaction The first group will ask questions to other groups, such as:
   - What does CTRL+Z do?
   - What is the shortcut for Copy?

Activity 10

Exploring the Uses of the Internet

Materials required

Pen/pencil, Notebook, Access to the Internet (if available, but not mandatory for this particular activity)

Procedure

1. Divide the class into small groups, depending on the number of computers available. If computers are not available, the activity can still proceed with groups discussing and presenting orally.

2. Each group member should contribute by listing one use of the Internet and briefly describing what they would do using an Internet connection. Encourage creativity and a wide range of uses. Examples could include research, communication, entertainment, online learning, etc.
3. After each member presents their idea, the rest of the group should provide feedback. This feedback could include whether the proposed use is accurate, practical, and how it aligns with the actual uses of the Internet. This helps to enhance understanding and correct any misconceptions.
4. Select one group to volunteer and present their list of uses and activities to the entire class. This group can explain each use in more detail.
5. Open the floor for feedback from the rest of the class. Encourage students to share their thoughts, ask questions, and provide additional insights. This promotes active engagement and a deeper understanding of the various uses of the Internet.
6. As part of the feedback session, discuss the importance of responsible and ethical Internet use. Emphasize the need for critical thinking and fact-checking, especially in the age of information overload.

Activity 11

Planning a Trip Using Web Browsing

Materials required

Pen/pencil, Notebook, Computer with an Internet connection

Procedure

1. Form Groups Divide the participants into groups based on the number of available computers. Each group should ideally have access to a computer with an internet connection.
2. Observer and Participant Roles Assign roles within each group. One member will actively perform the steps outlined below, while the other member will act as an observer, providing feedback on the process.
3. Researching Train Information
   (a) **Visit IRCTC Website** Open a web browser and navigate to the official IRCTC website (https://www.irctc.co.in/).
   (b) **Search for Trains** Use the search feature on the website to find trains from your current location to your relative's city. Enter the necessary details such as source, destination, and date of travel.
   (c) **Note Train Timings and Fare** Look for information on train timings and ticket fares for the chosen trains. Note down the relevant details in your notebook.
4. Exploring Cities and Places
   (a) **City 1 Information** Use the internet to gather information about the first city you plan to visit. Explore tourism websites, city guides, or travel blogs to find interesting places to visit.
   (b) **City 2 Information** Similarly, gather information about the second city, including tourist attractions, landmarks, and any other points of interest.
5. Researching Connecting Trains
   (a) **Use IRCTC to Find Connecting Trains** Return to the IRCTC website and search for trains connecting the two cities you plan to visit. Look for available timings and ticket fares for these connecting trains.
   (b) **Note Down Details** Record relevant information about the connecting trains, such as timings and fares, in your notebook.
6. Feedback and Discussion
   (a) **Switch Roles** Rotate roles within the group. The observer becomes the active participant, and vice versa.
   (b) **Feedback Session** Discuss the process with your partner. Provide feedback on what was done correctly and suggest improvements or alternatives if needed.

Activity 12

Advantages of Using E-mail

Materials required

Pen/pencil, Notebook

Procedure

1. Formation of Groups Divide the class into groups of 5 students each.
2. Introduction Start by briefly explaining the purpose of the activity, which is to discuss the advantages of using e-mail compared to sending a letter through postal mail.
3. Discussion Encourage each group to engage in a discussion about the topic.
   Ask each student to express their preference for either sending an e-mail or posting a letter and provide reasons for their choice.

4. **Note-Taking** In their notebooks, students should jot down key points discussed within their group.
5. **Group Discussion** After allowing sufficient time for group discussions, bring the focus back to the whole class.

   Ask each group to share their main points and reasons for their preferences.
6. **Compile Advantages** Facilitate a class discussion where students collectively compile a list of advantages of using e-mail over sending a letter through postal mail.

   Encourage critical thinking and consider aspects such as speed, cost, convenience, and environmental impact.
7. **Notebook Reflection** In their individual notebooks, have each student reflect on the discussion and note down any new insights gained or perspectives changed during the activity.
8. **Class Summary** Summarize the main advantages of using e-mail based on the group discussions and individual reflections.

   Encourage students to consider real-world applications where e-mail is particularly advantageous.

Activity 13

Creating an Email Account

Materials required

Pen/pencil, Notebook, Computer with Internet connection

Procedure

1. Depending on the number of computers available, organize students into groups.
2. Individual tasks within groups:

   (a) **Create an e-mail account** Each student takes turns to create an email account using Gmail.com or any other free email service. It's important to emphasize the need to make careful note of the email address and password. This step involves the following:

   Visit the chosen email service provider's website (e.g., gmail.com).

   - Click on the "Sign up" or "Create account" button.
   - Fill in the required information such as name, desired email address, password, and other details.
   - Follow the prompts to complete the account creation process.
   - Take note of the created email address and password in their notebooks.

   (b) **Sign out and sign in** After creating the email account, students should practice signing out and signing back into the account. This step ensures that they understand the login process and can successfully access their newly created email accounts. Emphasize the importance of not sharing
3. Depending on the number of students and computers, rotate students so that each person in the group has the opportunity to create an email account and practice signing in and out.
4. At the end of the activity, conduct a brief review session to address any questions or concerns. Ensure that students are comfortable with the basic functions of creating, signing in, and signing out of an email account.

Activity 14

Writing an E-mail

Materials Required

Pen/pencil, Notebook, Computer with an Internet connection

Procedure

1. Divide the students into groups based on the number of available computers. Ideally, each group should have access to at least one computer.
2. Instruct each student to create a new e-mail address for themselves. This could be a temporary or student-specific e-mail address, ensuring privacy and security.
3. Choose a specific future festival as the theme for the e-mails. This could be a cultural, religious, or seasonal festival depending on the context of the classroom.
4. **Writing E-mails** Ask each student to write an e-mail to two other members of their group, using the newly created e-mail address.

   The content of the e-mail should include warm wishes for the chosen future festival. Encourage students to be creative and thoughtful in their messages.
5. **Peer Review and Guidance** While one student is writing the e-mail, the other group members should watch and provide guidance.

   Encourage constructive feedback on the content, tone, and language used in the e-mail.

Emphasize positive aspects and suggest improvements.

6. Rotate the roles so that each student in the group has the opportunity to write an e-mail and receive feedback.
7. After the activity, gather the groups for a discussion. Allow students to share their experiences, challenges faced, and lessons learned during the activity.

Activity 15

Receiving and replying to an e-mail

Materials required

Pen/pencil, Notebook, Computer with an Internet connection

Procedure

1. Depending on the number of computers available, form groups with each group having access to at least one computer.
2. The teacher sends an e-mail to a student in each group informing them about a group dance competition. The e-mail should contain all necessary details such as the date, time, venue, rules, and any other relevant information regarding the competition.
3. The designated leader of each group reads the e-mail received from the teacher.
4. The group leader forwards the e-mail to all members of the group to ensure everyone is informed about the details of the dance competition.
5. The group leader initiates a discussion within the group regarding their interest in participating in the dance competition. They consider factors such as availability, willingness to participate, preparation time required, etc.
6. After discussing with the group members, the leader drafts a reply to the teacher's e-mail. The reply should indicate whether the group intends to participate in the dance competition or not. If they decide to participate, they may also include any questions or clarifications they may have regarding the competition.
7. Once the reply is finalized, the group leader sends it to the teacher as a response to the original e-mail.

NCERT FOLDER

Complete Explanations of all NCERT's Questions

A. Multiple Choice Questions

Q.1 What is a short-range wireless communication technology called?

(a) Wi-Fi (b) Internet
(c) Bluetooth (d) PS

Q.2 Which part of the home screen is visible on all pages?

(a) Status bar (b) Main icon area
(c) Dock (d) Clock

Q.3 What does GPS stand for?

(a) Global Positioning System
(b) Global Payment System
(c) Global Program System
(d) Global Pointing System

Q.4 Which of the following units make up the CPU? Choose and tick all the correct options.

(a) Processing Unit (b) Input Unit
(c) Memory Unit (d) Control Unit
(e) Output Unit

Q.5 Which of the following are names of ports in a computer? Choose and tick all the correct options.

(a) HDMI (b) Input
(c) VGA (d) USB
(e) Ethernet

Q.6 There is a talent contest in your town. For participating in the audition, you have to send a recording of a song. What would you connect to your computer to record you song?

(a) Keyboard (b) Microphone
(c) Scanner (d) Mouse

Q.7 Which of the following functions are performed using a mouse. Choose and tick all the correct options.

(a) Turn on computer (b) Typing
(c) Right click (d) Drag and drop an icon

Q.8 What is the term used when you press and hold the left mouse key and move the mouse around?

(a) Highlighting (b) Dragging
(c) Selecting (d) Moving

Q.9 **Which one of the following shortcut key is used to paste a file? Tick mark the correct answer.**

(a) Ctrl + C (b) Ctrl + P (c) Ctrl + V (d) Ctrl + X

Q.10 **Which of the following is a valid file extension for Notepad file? Tick mark the correct answer.**

(a) .jpg (b) .doc (c) .text (d) .txt

Q.11 **Which key do you use to copy something? Tick mark the correct answer.**

(a) Ctrl + X (b) Ctrl + C (c) Ctrl + Z (d) Ctrl + T

Q.12 **To connect to the Internet, the computer has to be connected to the**

(a) Internet Society (b) Internet Architecture

(c) Internet Service Provider

(d) Large Area Network

Q.13 **What is the Internet?**

(a) Phone connections

(b) Collection of computer networks

(c) Network of computers in an office

(d) None of the above

Q.14 **What do I need to get information from the World Wide Web?**

(a) Computer (b) Browser

(c) Internet Connection (d) All of these

Q.15 **Which of the following is a web browser?**

(a) Internet (b) Chrome

(c) Windows (d) None of these

Q.16 **Here are the steps to sign in to your Gmail account.**

(i) Type username (ii) Go to www.gmail.com

(iii) Click Sign in (iv) Type password

Choose the option with the correct order.

(a) (i) > (ii) > (iv) > (iii) (b) (ii) > (i) > (iii) > (iv)

(c) (ii) > (i) > (iv) > (iii) (d) (ii) > (iii) > (i) > (iv)

Q.17 **Which one of the following statement is false?**

(a) You need to create an account before you can send an E-mail.

(b) You should sign out of your account when you are not using the computer.

(c) You do not need an Internet connection to use your Gmail account.

(d) You must not share your password with others.

Q.18 **Which of the following in an e-mail service?**

(a) WhatsApp (b) WeChat

(c) Gmail (d) Facebook

Q.19 **What do you type of the "To" field?**

(a) The topic of the E-mail

(b) The main message of the E-mail

(c) E-mail address of the person to whom you want to send a copy of the E-mail

(d) E-mail address of the person you are sending the mail to

Q.20 **You want to send an e-mail message to your friend Sushil. In which order will you perform the given steps to write and send an E-mail to him?**

(i) Type Sushil's E-mail address, subject and message

(ii) Click on the Compose button

(iii) Click Send

(iv) Open your E-mail account.

(a) (iv)>(ii)>(i)>(iii) (b) (iv)>(i)>(ii)>(iii)

(c) (iv)>(i)>(iii)>(ii) (d) (iii)>(i)>(ii)>(iv)

Answers

1. (c)	2. (c)	3. (a)	4. (a,c,d)	5. (a,c,d,e)
6. (b)	7. (c,d)	8. (b)	9. (c)	10. (d)
11. (b)	12. (c)	13. (b)	14. (d)	15. (b)
16. (c)	17. (c)	18. (c)	19. (d)	20. (a)

B. State whether True or False

Q.1 **The full form of ICT is Information Commuting Technology.**

Ans. False; The full form of ICT is Information and Communication Technology.

Q.2 **Live sports and news can only be shown using ICT.**

Ans. True

Q.3 **E-mail cannot be sent to more than one person at a time.**

Ans. False; E-mail can be sent to large number of people by writing their respective addresses separated by commas.

Q.4 **E-mail is an electronic message sent over the Internet or a computer network.**

Ans. True

Q.5 **Pictures, videos, audio files, and spreadsheet files cannot be attached with an E-mail.**

Ans. False; Attachment such as picture, video, etc. can send along with your Email.

Q.6 **By choosing the "Reply" option, the E-mail address of the sender of the original message will appear in the "To" field.**

Ans. True

Q.7 **E-mail is an electronic message transmitted over the Internet or computer network from one user to another.**

Ans. True

Q.8 **You can forward the e-mail by clicking on the delete icon.**

Ans. False; Delete icon is used to delete the Email.

C. Fill in the blanks

Q.1 **In "To :" section .... is typed for sending a message through E-mail.**

Ans. E-mail id of the receiver

Q.2 The Attach button in E-mail often has a .... as its symbol.

Ans. Paperclip

Q.3 In the .... section of the E-mail, the topic of the mail is written.

Ans. Subject

Q.4 After typing the message in the main body of the E-mail, you need to click on .... button to send the E-mail.

Ans. Send

D. Subjective Type Questions

Q.1 Give any two uses of ICT at home.

Ans. Two uses of ICT at home are as follows:

(i) People uses television for entertainment.

(ii) We use computers and mobile phones for talking to each other, sending and receiving information, watching videos, playing games etc.

Q.2 What are the emerging skills in ICT?

Ans. Emerging skills in ICT are:

(i) Develop knowledge and skills to plan.

(ii) Implement and manage ICT solutions to support emergency response.

Q.3 What are the key skills one should possess to use ICT?

Ans. The basic ICT skills that you need are:

(i) Knowing how to operate computers.

(ii) Knowing how to browse the Internet for collecting, storing and disseminating information.

Q.4 Identify the following symbols and write the name in the blank space.

(a)  ....

(b) 

....

(c)  ....

(d)  ....

(e)  ....

(f)  ....

Ans. (a) Phone (b) Calendar (c) Music (d) Gallery (e) Clock (f) Messages

Q.5 Write any two differences between a smartphone and a tablet.

Ans. Differences between smartphone and tablet are:

Smartphone	Tablet
Comes with different storage capacity.	Usually have higher storage capacity.
Watching a movie or making changes to a picture is difficult.	Watching videos and making changes to a photo is better and easier due to bigger screen size.

Q.6 Write the purpose of the I/O devices

(a) Mic/Microphone **(b) Scanner**
(c) Camera **(d) Barcode Reader**
(e) Printer **(f) Speaker**

Ans. (a) **Microphone** is used to record voice on the computer.

(b) **Scanner** is used to scan/capture a paper image, document and converts it to digital file on computer.

(c) **Camera** stores the pictures or videos in an electronic format.

(d) **Barcode Reader** is an input device used for reading printed bar codes available on product to be sold.

(e) **Printer** helps to printout the visual output on the paper.

(f) **Speaker** plays back all the sound based output.

Q.7 Rearrange the steps for starting a computer in the correct sequence.

(a) Desktop appears after login

(b) Login screen appears

(c) Power on Self-Test (POST) starts

(d) Operating system starts

(e) Welcome screen appears

Ans. Correct sequence is (d), (c), (e), (b), (a)

Q.8 Describe the functions of at least 5 types of keys.

Ans. Functions of different types of keys:

(i) **Control Keys** They perform special functions depending on when and where they are used.

(ii) **Enter Key** It is used to move the cursor to the beginning of a new line.

(iii) **Navigation Keys** These are used to move up and down, right and left in a document.

(iv) **Windows Key** It is used to open the Start menu.

(v) **Punctuation Keys** These are used for punctuation marks.

Q.9 Describe the functions of a mouse.

Ans. Refer to text on page no. 49. (Mouse)

Q.10 Write a short note on the uses of Internet.

Ans. Refer to text on page no. 57. (Use of the Internet)

Q.11 List the steps to search for information using a web browser.

Ans. Refer to text on page no. 58 and 59. (Searching for information)

Q.12 What characters should the password have in E-mail address, to make it more secure?

Ans. In E-mail, a password should be at least 8 characters long and contain letters, numbers and special characters. This will make it more secure.

REVIEW EXERCISE

Including Competency Based Questions

Part I

Multiple Choice Questions

1. .... includes computers, Internet, broadcasting technologies and telephony.
(a) ICT (b) Browser
(c) IT (d) None of these

2. With a .... you can only make calls and receive calls.
(a) Smartphone (b) Android phone
(c) Simple phone (d) Tablet

3. This is used to enter appointments, remainders etc.
(a) Mail (b) Calendar
(c) Phone (d) Clock

4. Which of the following is/are features of mobile device?
(a) Bluetooth (b) Wi-Fi
(c) Camera (d) All of these

5. The top part of the screen is called the ....
(a) Status bar (b) Main part
(c) Dock (d) All of these

6. Which of the following device is used to enter information into the computer?
(a) Output (b) Input
(c) Computer (d) Memory

7. It is used to record voice on the computer.
(a) Projector (b) Speakers
(c) Microphone (d) Scanner

8. Which of the following is a brain of computer?
(a) RAM (b) ROM
(c) ALU (d) CPU

9. The bandwidth is usually expressed in
(a) bits per second (b) bytes per second
(c) Both (a) and (b) (d) None of these

10. .... is a document present on a computer that is connected to the Internet.
(a) Web page (b) Website
(c) Browser (d) Server

11. World Wide Web is made up of
(a) web page
(b) web browser
(c) a system to transfer information
(d) All of the above

12. When working with files and folders on a computer, what does the term "directory" commonly refer to? **Competency Based Ques.**
I. A storage device
II. A type of file format
III. A container for organizing files
IV. A computer program
(a) Only I (b) Both II and IV
(c) Only III (d) None of these

13. In the context of basic computer operations, what is the primary function of the "Copy" operation? **Competency Based Ques.**
I. To permanently delete a file
II. To duplicate a file in the same location
III. To move a file to a different location
IV. To open a file for viewing
(a) Only II (b) Both I and III
(c) Only IV (d) None of these

14. When considering Ports and Connections on a computer system, what does a USB port typically allow for? **Competency Based Ques.**
I. Audio output II. Peripheral devices
III. Internet connectivity IV. Display connection
(a) Only I (b) Both II and III
(c) Only IV (d) Only II

Answers

1. (a)	**2.** (c)	**3.** (b)	**4.** (d)	**5.** (a)
6. (b)	**7.** (c)	**8.** (d)	**9.** (a)	**10.** (a)
11. (d)	**12.** (c)	**13.** (a)	**14.** (d)	

Statement Based Questions

1. Statement 1: Files and folders are used to organize and store data on a computer.
Statement 2: The primary purpose of folders is to display information on the computer desktop.
(a) Both Statement 1 and Statement 2 are correct
(b) Both Statement 1 and Statement 2 are incorrect
(c) Statement 1 is correct but Statement 2 is incorrect
(d) Statement 2 is correct but Statement 1 is incorrect

2. Statement 1: Mobile device layout includes hardware components such as the screen, buttons, and speakers.

2. **Statement 1: Mobile device layout includes hardware components such as the screen, buttons, and speakers.**

Statement 2: Basic computer operations involve complex tasks that require advanced technical knowledge.

(a) Both Statement 1 and Statement 2 are correct
(b) Both Statement 1 and Statement 2 are incorrect
(c) Statement 1 is correct but Statement 2 is incorrect
(d) Statement 2 is correct but Statement 1 is incorrect

3. **Statement 1: ICT tools, such as smartphones and tablets, play a significant role in communication and productivity.**

Statement 2: Introduction to email is a fundamental aspect of ICT at the workplace.

(a) Both Statement 1 and Statement 2 are correct
(b) Both Statement 1 and Statement 2 are incorrect
(c) Statement 1 is correct but Statement 2 is incorrect
(d) Statement 2 is correct but Statement 1 is incorrect

4. **Statement 1: Ports and connections are used to connect peripherals to a computer.**

Statement 2: USB (Universal Serial Bus) is a common type of port used for connecting devices.

(a) Both Statement 1 and Statement 2 are correct
(b) Both Statement 1 and Statement 2 are incorrect
(c) Statement 1 is correct but Statement 2 is incorrect
(d) Statement 2 is correct but Statement 1 is incorrect

5. **Statement 1: Computer systems consist of hardware and software components.**

Statement 2: ICT at home involves the use of technology for various domestic activities.

(a) Both Statement 1 and Statement 2 are correct
(b) Both Statement 1 and Statement 2 are incorrect
(c) Statement 1 is correct but Statement 2 is incorrect
(d) Statement 2 is correct but Statement 1 is incorrect

6. **Statement 1: Email is a common method of electronic communication.**

Statement 2: Attachments in emails allow users to send and receive files.

(a) Both Statement 1 and Statement 2 are correct
(b) Both Statement 1 and Statement 2 are incorrect
(c) Statement 1 is correct but Statement 2 is incorrect
(d) Statement 2 is correct but Statement 1 is incorrect

Answers

1. (c) **2.** (c) **3.** (a) **4.** (a) **5.** (a) **6.** (a)

Assertion and Reason based Questions

1. **Assertion: Mobile device layout is designed to provide an intuitive and user-friendly experience for individuals using smartphones and tablets.**

Reason: The layout includes touchscreens, icons, and gestures that make navigation easy for users.

(a) Both Assertion and Reason are true, and Reason is the correct explanation for Assertion.
(b) Both Assertion and Reason are true, but Reason is not the correct explanation for Assertion.
(c) Assertion is true, but Reason is false.
(d) Both Assertion and Reason are false.

2. **Assertion: Ports and connections are crucial components of a computer system.**

Reason: They enable the connection of external devices such as printers, USB drives, and monitors to the computer.

(a) Both Assertion and Reason are true, and Reason is the correct explanation for Assertion.
(b) Both Assertion and Reason are true, but Reason is not the correct explanation for Assertion.
(c) Assertion is true, but Reason is false.
(d) Both Assertion and Reason are false.

3. **Assertion: In Email address, (.) is used as an separator.**

Reason: Email allows users to send and receive messages, attachments, and documents without internet.

(a) Both Assertion and Reason are true, and Reason is the correct explanation for Assertion.
(b) Both Assertion and Reason are true, but Reason is not the correct explanation for Assertion.
(c) Assertion is true, but Reason is false.
(d) Both Assertion and Reason are false.

4. **Assertion: Notepad has .doc file extension.**

Reason: Notepad is used to send email.

(a) Both Assertion and Reason are true, and Reason is the correct explanation for Assertion.
(b) Both Assertion and Reason are true, but Reason is not the correct explanation for Assertion.
(c) Assertion is true, but Reason is false.
(d) Both Assertion and Reason are false.

5. **Assertion: Email can be sent to multiple people at the same time.**

Reason: Email is only used for professional communication.

(a) Both Assertion and Reason are true, and Reason is the correct explanation for Assertion.
(b) Both Assertion and Reason are true, but Reason is not the correct explanation for Assertion.
(c) Assertion is true, but Reason is false.
(d) Both Assertion and Reason are false.

6. **Assertion: ICT tools like smartphones and tablets have become essential in the workplace for communication and productivity.**

Reason: These devices allow employees to access emails, collaborate on documents, and stay connected with colleagues even while on the move.

(a) Both Assertion and Reason are true, and Reason is the correct explanation for Assertion.

(b) Both Assertion and Reason are true, but Reason is not the correct explanation for Assertion.

(c) Assertion is true, but Reason is false.

(d) Both Assertion and Reason are false.

7. Assertion: Basic computer operations involve input, processing, storage, and output.

Reason: These operations are fundamental to the functioning of a computer system, allowing it to perform tasks and solve problems.

(a) Both Assertion and Reason are true, and Reason is the correct explanation for Assertion.

(b) Both Assertion and Reason are true, but Reason is not the correct explanation for Assertion.

(c) Assertion is true, but Reason is false.

(d) Both Assertion and Reason are false.

8. Assertion: Files and folders are used to organize and manage data on a computer.

Reason: Folders can contain multiple files, and organizing data in this way makes it easier to locate and access information.

(a) Both Assertion and Reason are true, and Reason is the correct explanation for Assertion.

(b) Both Assertion and Reason are true, but Reason is not the correct explanation for Assertion.

(c) Assertion is true, but Reason is false.

(d) Both Assertion and Reason are false.

Answers

1. (a)	2. (a)	3. (d)	4. (d)	5. (c)
6. (a)	7. (a)	8. (a)		

Part II

Very Short Answer Type Questions

1. Define ICT in the workplace.

Ans. Information and Communication Technology (ICT) enhances work processes using digital tools for communication and data management.

2. How does ICT benefit home life?

Ans. ICT at home improves efficiency and connectivity through smart devices, making daily tasks convenient and accessible.

3. Name two ICT tools for communication.

Ans. Smartphones and tablets are common ICT tools facilitating seamless communication through calls, messages, and social media.

4. Explain mobile device layout.

Ans. Mobile device layout comprises a touchscreen interface with icons, apps, and settings, promoting user-friendly navigation and functionality.

5. What is a computer system?

Ans. A computer system integrates hardware and software components to process data and execute tasks, facilitating various applications.

6. Identify common computer ports.

Ans. USB, HDMI, and Ethernet ports are examples of connectors used for data transfer, display, and network connectivity.

7. Define basic computer operations.

Ans. Basic computer operations include input, processing, output, and storage, forming the fundamental steps in information processing.

8. How are files and folders organized?

Ans. Files and folders are organized hierarchically, creating a systematic structure for storing, accessing, and managing digital information.

9. What is the significance of communication in ICT?

Ans. Communication in ICT promotes collaboration and connectivity, facilitating information exchange and teamwork through various digital channels.

10. Explain networking in ICT.

Ans. Networking in ICT involves connecting devices to share resources and information, fostering efficient communication and collaboration within a system.

11. What is the purpose of email?

Ans. Email serves as a digital communication tool, allowing users to send and receive messages, documents, and multimedia content.

12. How do smartphones enhance workplace productivity?

Ans. Smartphones boost workplace productivity by providing instant access to emails, calendars, and business applications, streamlining communication and tasks.

13. Name two input devices.

Ans. Keyboards and mice are common input devices allowing users to interact with and input data into a computer system.

Short Answer Type Questions

1. What do you mean by tablet?

Ans. A tablet is a mini computer with input, output and processing functions that are all combined into one touchscreen, where you can do various tasks just by touching its screen.

2. Name any four apps which installed on smartphones by default.

Ans. Phone, Calendar, Camera, Mail

3. What is the difference TV and radio?

Ans. Radio is used to broadcast audio while TV is used to broadcast audio visual information to many people.

4. Name the online stores including for Android phone and Apple phone.

Ans. Google Play Store for Android phone

Apple App Store for Apple phone

5. What is the use of Maps app in phone?

Ans. Maps app helps you find directions to where you want to go.

6. Define the following.
(i) Wi-Fi (ii) Chargeable battery

Ans. (i) **Wi-Fi** is a wireless network technology that helps you connect to the local area network.

(ii) **Chargeable battery** is a portable power pack which can be recharged. It allows you to use the device anywhere.

7. What is peripheral? Name any two peripheral devices.

Ans. Input and output devices are also called peripherals. Two peripheral devices are keyboard and monitor.

8. Define motherboard.

Ans. Motherboard also referred to as a system board, is the main circuit board inside a computer. It connects input, processing and output devices. It also includes controllers for devices like the hard drive, DVD drive, keyboard and mouse.

9. List any two ports that can use to connect to a computer.

Ans. (i) **Display port** It connects the monitor or any display unit to the computer using cable.

(ii) **Audio port** It helps to connect microphone, speakers and headphones to a computer system.

10. How to create a new file using a text editor in Ubuntu?

Ans. To create a new file using a text editor in ubuntu, you need

- To open a text editor, type 'editor' in the search dialog box. Then, double click the text editor option. This will open a blank document.
- Where you can add text.

11. What do you need to connect to the Internet?

Ans. To connect to the Internet, you need

- A device, such as a computer, laptop or mobile.
- A connection device, i.e. a modem.

12. Explain file and folder.

Ans. **Files** These are the collection of data stored on auxiliary storage media. The name given to a file or document by the user is called **file name.** Each file has a specific filename and has a file extension that identifies the file type.

Folders These are containers that you can use to store files. Folders can also store other folders, i.e. sub-folders. You can create any number of sub-folders and each can hold any number of files and additional sub-folders.

13. List any two important parts of a web browser.

Ans. (i) **Address bar** You can type the address/URL of a web page in this box and press Enter. The browser will display the page linked to that URL.

(ii) **Tabbed browsing** It allows a user to view multiple pages in the same window.

14. How can the E-mail be delete?

Ans. Refer to text on page no. 61. (Deleting an E-mail)

15. Explain the difference between a smartphone and a tablet.

Ans. Differences between a smartphone and a tablet are as follows:

Smartphone	Tablet
Used as a phone but with some additional features such as camera.	Used as a wireless portable personal computer with a touchscreen interface which makes it more useful than notebook computer.
Screen size is small.	Has a big screen.
Watching a movie or making changes to a picture is difficult.	Watching videos and making changes to a photo is better and easier due to bigger screen size.
Comes with different storage capacities.	Usually have higher storage capacity.

ASSESSMENT EXERCISE

Multiple Choice Questions

1. Smartphones can work on following operating system(s)?

(a) Android (b) Apple iOS (c) Windows (d) All of these

2. Which of the following basic controls help you to listen to voice calls?

(a) Earpiece (b) Volume button (c) Mic (d) Microphone

3. Which of the following is an input device?

(a) Printer (b) Plotter (c) Scanner (d) Projector

4. Which memory depands on voltage?

(a) RAM (b) ROM (c) Hard disk (d) CD

5. It serves as a platform through which users can use or share information.

(a) Website (b) Web page (c) WWW (d) Browser

6. E-mails can be sent to multiple users along with the

(a) procedure (b) attachments (c) subjects (d) accounts

7. What type of ICT tool is a Smartphone primarily considered as?

I. Input device
II. Output device
III. Processing device
IV. Communication device

(a) Only I (b) Only IV (c) Both II and IV (d) Both III and IV

8. How does email contribute to communication and networking?

I. Enables instant messaging
II. Facilitates sharing of physical documents
III. Allows for asynchronous communication
IV. Provides real-time video calls

(a) Only I (b) Both II and III (c) Only IV (d) Only III

Very Short Answer Type Questions

9. Name two type of primary memory.

10. Write the two advantages of E-mail.

11. Name the parts of computer system.

12. Expand the terms MICR and OCR.

Short Answer Type Questions

13. What are the uses of ICT?

14. Write any two sectors where ICT used for.

15. Give any two differences between input device and output device.

16. List any two storage devices.

17. Write the steps to forward the E-mail.

CHAPTER 04

Entrepreneurship Skills-I

Entrepreneurial skills are the tools and personality traits that help people turn ideas into successful businesses. These skills include things like creativity, risk-taking, and problem-solving, but also communication, financial management, and the ability to build a strong team. In short, it's what it takes to get a great idea off the ground and keep it growing.

4.1 Introduction

Business is an economic activity related with continuous and regular production and distribution of goods and services for satisfying human needs.

Businesses can be for profit entities or non-profit entity or organisation. Profit entities is one whose main goal is to make money. Non-profit entity or organisation usually have other non business goals, such as helping the community.

But sometimes, there is a gap between what is needed and what is available. This gap is used by some people as an opportunity by providing necessary products and services. Such people are called entrepreneur.

In other words, an entrepreneur is a person who is self-employed, is willing to take a calculated risk and brings in a new idea or method to start a business.

But, all self employed person are not entrepreneurs. A shopkeeper cannot be called an entrepreneur unless he uses a new idea or method in the business.

4.2 Types of Business Activities

Broadly a business can belong to one of the following categories:

(a) **Product Business** A business where a seller and buyer exchange an item, which can be seen and touched, is called a product based business. For example, A sports shop.

(b) **Service Business** A business where a seller helps the buyer to finish some work. For example, A cricket coaching centre.

(c) **Hybrid Business** A business in which both product and services are sold is referred as Hybrid business. For example, Restaurants where the food itself is the product sold and the catering is the service provided.

Differences between Product and Service Business

The key differences between product and service business activities can be summarised as follows:

Categories	Product Business	Service Business
Seen and touched	Product can be seen and touched. Customer pays for physical exchange of thing under this business.	Service cannot be seen or touched. Customer pays for an experience under this business.
Stored	Product can be made and stored.	A service cannot be stored.
Mode and transported	Product can be made at home or factory. It can be transported.	A service cannot be made or transported.
Same quantity and quality	The quality and quantity of the product will be same every time.	The quality and quantity of a service can be different at different times under this business.

Types of Product Based Business

There are two types of product based business:

(a) **Manufacturing Businesses** In manufacturing businesses, products are first made in factories and then sold in market.

(b) **Trade Businesses** In trade businesses, products are transported from factory to warehouses and shops near to customers where trade businesses buy and sell a product. Examples of these business include wholesalers, distributors and retail shops.

Types of Businesses in Our Community

Based on size

- **Micro Enterprise** A micro enterprise is a business enterprise where the investment in plant and machinery or equipment is not more than INR 1 crore and turnover does not exceed INR 5 crores.
- **Small Enterprise** A small enterprise is a business enterprise where the investment in plant and machinery or equipment is not more than INR 10 crore and turnover does not exceed INR 50 crores.
- **Medium Enterprise** A medium enterprise is a business enterprise where the investment in plant and machinery or equipment is not more than INR 50 crore and turnover does not exceed INR 250 crores.

Based on legal form

- **Sole Proprietorship** In a sole proprietorship, the ownership and control of the business is with one single person, and the liability of the owner is not separate from the entity.
- **One Person Company** A One Person company also has only one person as a member, who acts in the capacity of both, a shareholder and a director, but an OPC is legally separate from its owners. There is no threat on the owner's personal property in case of unmet liabilities.
- **Partnership** Partnership is a legal form, where at least two people, or more start a business as co-founders or co-owners and divide the share as per agreement. The partners are personally liable for an unlimited amount of liabilities.
- **Limited Liability Partnership** In a Limited Liability Partnership, there are two or more partners. In this, no one single partner or owner is individually responsible for any other partner's or member's negligence or misconduct or liability.
- **Company** A company is defined as a legal entity formed to get engaged in business, by a group of individuals. Usually, these individuals have limited liability, and the capital in units of equal value of a company are called 'shares'. Company can be public or private.

Based on sector

- **Primary Sector** This sector includes businesses that involve extraction, retrieval, harvest and production of raw materials using natural products from the earth. For example, some raw materials include coal, wood, grains, iron, corn etc. Thus, some primary sectors include mining, agriculture, fishing, horticulture etc.
- **Secondary Sector** The main activity of businesses in this sector is transformation of raw materials into finished goods. It takes products from primary sector and organizes all factors of production to make utility as well as luxury products.
- **Tertiary Sector** This sector is defined by provision of services to businesses and customers. It is completely based on a service and there is no production of goods involved.

Try These 4.1

1. Name any two business activities.
2. Give the example of hybrid business.
3. How many types of product based business are there?
4. Name one sector of primary, secondary and tertiary.

4.3 Entrepreneurship

The process of developing a business plan, launching and running a business using innovation to meet customer needs and to make profit is known as entrepreneurship.

Ideas created by an entrepreneur can be of many kinds; new types of products, new services e.g. home delivery, credit services, new marketing ideas, cost reduction ideas, etc.

An **enterprise** is a project or undertaking that is bold and fulfills need and wants of the society which no longer has ever addressed.

Entrepreneurship Development

It involves enabling entrepreneurs through institution-building learing & development programs and structured training. Largely, the objective of these programs is to empower budding entrepreneurs to start and run their business effectively and efficiently. These programs cover aspects of entrepreneurial skills, business planning, fundraising, setting up of a new venture and growth & development strategies.

Role of Entrepreneurship

- **Capital Formation** Entrepreneurship leads to value addition and creation of wealth, because entrepreneurs promote capital formation by mobilising the idle savings of public.
- **Employment Generation** There is potential for increase in large-scale employment opportunities with increase in entrepreneurial activity. As more enterprises, offices,

factories, businesses, trading entities etc. are set up, numerous job opportunities are created for skilled, unskilled and unemployed people, especially in developing countries.

- **Balanced Regional Development** Entrepreneurship helps to remove regional disparities through setting up of industries in less developed and backward areas. Micro businesses and cottage industries also play a role in increasing entrepreneurial activity in many specific cultural regions.
- **Value Creation** Value creation occurs when the worth of products and services increases for a customer base and a business earns profit by selling the product or service to fulfil customer needs and wants. Value is created when outputs are more valuable than inputs. Value creation is the foundation of every entrepreneurial activity or business.
- **Wealth Distribution** Wealth and income are distribution across people and geographies due to entrepreneurship and transaction-based activities. Employees are paid salaries, vendors are paid for their supplies, goods are sold in multiple markets, services are provided at large scale etc. This stimulates distribution of wealth to larger sections of society.
- **Industrialization and Development** Establishment of even a single enterprise can lead to beginning of a new industry. In a specific region, if a business is set up and seen to be a profitable opportunity, it is likely that others will get motivated to set up similar businesses. Additionally a business might require certain inputs, which leads to setting up of businesses that can supply those inputs. Hence, entrepreneurship catalyses industrialization in almost a chain reaction form, which in turn contributes positively to economic and infrastructural development.

Rewards of Entrepreneurship

- **Economic Development** Some features of economic development include optimal use of resources, creation of new ideas, wealth generation, continuous flow of money, skill building etc. All these factors are enabled due to entrepreneurship and are essential for economic development of a nation.
- **Enterprise and Business Creation** Business creation is a direct result of entrepreneurship. Many types of enterprises can be created by coordinating and combining different types of resources such as physical, financial, human, intellectual and entrepreneurial skills such as risk taking, innovation, leadership, resource planning etc.
- **Capacity Building** Skilled development and training is a significant reward of entrepreneurship as an entrepreneur invests in training employees and building their managerial capabilities. Similarly, an entrepreneur also develops his/her own capabilities by solving problems, making decisions, embracing failures, experimenting with alternative approaches etc.
- **Improved Standard of Living** With entrepreneurship, customers have many options of choosing from different products and services to solve the same purpose. This variety and availability of improved goods and services offered by enterprises leads to higher standards of living.

Qualities of a Successful Entrepreneur

An entrepreneur needs to have the following set of qualitites:

(a) **Patience** Success may not be achieved quickly. It is important for an entrepreneur to have patience while running the business.

(b) **Positivity** When people starts a business, they may face lots of difficulties and failure. An entrepreneur should stay positive and continue to work hard to achieve this goal.

(c) **Hardworking** Every new business goes through failures and therefore, an entrepreneur needs to work hard till he becomes successful.

(d) **Never Giving up and Perseverance** It is necessary for an entrepreneur to continuously work hard towards his own and company's goals. The entrepreneur must not give up even he/she suffers failure. He/she must demonstrate perseverance and work hard to achieve his/her goal.

(e) **Confidence** An entrepreneur needs to be very confident while taking decisions about his business. He/she also needs to communicate confidently with the customers.

(f) **Open to Trial and Error** Entrepreneur needs to be open to new ideas and try them without fear of failure. Entrepreneur will have to use trial and error method while starting a business. He/she should also experiment with different ideas in order to become successful.

(g) **Creativity and Innovation** An entrepreneur should come up with original and creative solution to a problem after analysing it with various prospective. They should also be able to recognise an opportunity in a problem and find an innovative solution.

(h) **Risk Bearing** An entrepreneur should be willing to take a calculated risk and is always open to new idea to make his/her business grow.

4.4 Distinguishing Characteristics of Entrepreneurship and Wage Employment

Entrepreneurship means, organising, developing and managing a business venture along with any of its risks in order to make profit.

- **Profit** The profit earned is the excess of earning. It is calculated by deducting all expenses from earning.
- **Risk** A risk is situation where result is unknown and may lead to a loss in future. Entrepreneurship is not without risks but entrepreneurs are not afraid of taking calculated risks. Risk may result in failure, however, entrepreneurs continue their courses of action till they succeed.

Characteristics of Entrepreneurship

Some of the distinguishing characteristics of entrepreneurship are:

- Risks taking nature.
- Believe in hard work and discipline.
- Entrepreneurs show adaptability and flexibility in achieving the goals and customer satisfaction.
- Knowledge of the product and services as per demand in market.
- Financially literate and has money management skills.
- Effective planner and executes efficiency.

Wage Employment

Wage employment is always consist of two parties. One is known as the employer and other is the employee. The continuity of the service in case of wage, employment depends on the terms and conditions laid down in the contract between these two parties. Continuity of service also depends upon the relationship between these two parties.

Difference between Entrepreneurship and Wage Employment

- An entrepreneur is the business owner and an employee is the worker and get a salary.
- An entrepreneurs are self-employed while the employees are wage earner.
- An entrepreneur work for self but wage earners work for others and get a salary for his work.
- The wage employment does not involve too much risk but entrepreneurship involves taking certain amount of calculated risks.

A Comparison between Entrepreneurship and Employment

Activities	In Entrepreneurship	In Employment
Allows a person to make money.	Yes	Yes
Finding solutions for a community problem by himself/herself.	Yes	No
The job done by the person is decided by himself/herself.	Yes	No
Use personal knowledge and interest to make money for oneself.	Yes	No
Use innovation and creativity to attract clients.	Yes	No
Keep most of the money, i.e., profit made for a product/service.	Yes	No
Take risk to make profit.	Yes	No

Benefits of Entrepreneurship

The various benefits include the following:

(a) **Do What You Are Interested In** Entrepreneurship allows to start something according to choice. These choice depend upon hobbies and skills of entrepreneur.

(b) **Work for Yourself, and Not for Other** Entrepreneur work for own and not for someone else. An entrepreneur decide the kind of work and how to do it.

(c) **Make Profits for Yourself** The principle focus of entrepreneurship is earning money. An entrepreneur decide how much money to earn and how to earn.

(d) **More Risk, More Profit** There are risks in entrepreneurship. It allows entrepreneur to decide how much risk to take. Usually, the larger the risk, the bigger could be profit.

4.5 Entrepreneurship Development Process

It is the process of enhancing the knowledge and skills of entrepreneurs with help of various training programme. Entrepreneurship development process can take place through formal and informal learning system.

- **Formal Learning System** In the formal learning system, training programmes are conducted to bring about awareness, knowledge and skill related to entrepreneurship.
- **Informal Learning System** It is a spontaneous process of learning through conversation, exploration and enlargement of the experience.

Steps of Starting a Business

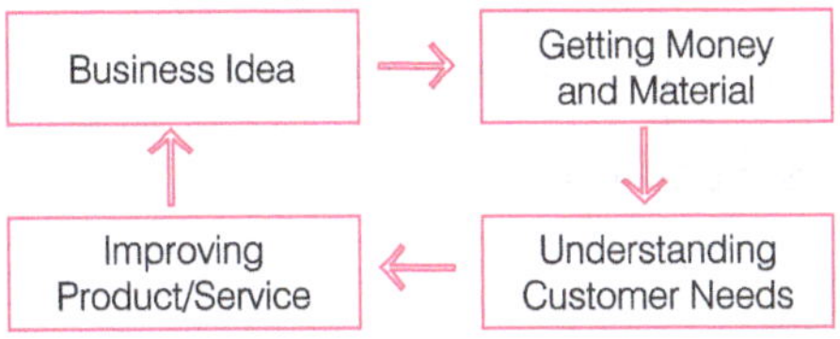

1. **Business Idea** The first step while starting a business is to come up with an idea. A business idea is based on (a) Interest of individual, (b) Market need
2. **Getting Money and material** Second steps of starting business is the use of idea to start on a small scale with some money. It helps in buying basic material.
3. **Understanding Customer Need** Once entrepreneur starts selling, he/she will find out the likes and wants and also dislikes of customers.
4. **Improving Product/Service** He/she can use this knowledge of what your customer likes and does not likes to improve their product.

Try These 4.2

1. **What is enterprise?**
2. **Write the role of entrepreneurship as wealth distribution.**
3. **Wage employment is always consists of how many parties?**
4. **What is the importance of patience for successful Entrepreneur?**

Glossary

An **entrepreneur** is a person, who is self-employed, is willing to take a calculated risk and brings a new idea to start a business.

Entrepreneurship means organising, developing and managing a business venture alongwith any of its risks in order to make profit.

Wage employment consists of employer and employee.

Generally, **business activities** are of three types, *viz*, product business, service business and hybrid business.

There are mainly two types of **product based business**, i.e. manufacturing business and trade business.

Entrepreneurship development process can take place through formal learning system and informal learning system.

There are mainly four steps for **starting a business**, *viz*, business idea, getting money and material, understanding customer need and improving product and services.

Let's Investigate

Activity 1

Exploring Diverse Business Models

Procedure

1. The class will be organized into three teams—Product Business Team, Service Business Team, and Hybrid Business Team.
2. Each team will be given approximately 15 minutes to brainstorm and identify a variety of examples across product, service, and hybrid-based businesses. The objective is to think creatively and consider different types of businesses rather than focusing solely on different companies within the same category.
3. Teams are required to fill the following table with their generated examples. The team presenting the most diverse and innovative range of examples will be declared the winner.

Table: Types of Business

Type of Business	Product Business	Service Business	Hybrid Business
Large Businesses	1.	1.	1.
	2.	2.	2.
	3.	3.	3.

Activity 2

Exploring Business Ventures

Materials Required

Pens, chart paper, markers, magazines/newspapers, glue, scissors, etc.

Procedure

1. Divide the class into three groups of students.
2. Each group will brainstorm and compile a list of potential business ventures, categorizing them into Product, Service, or Hybrid models.
3. Using the provided materials, each group will create a visually appealing poster showcasing their selected business ideas. They can use drawings, magazine/newspaper cut-outs, and colorful markers to enhance their posters.
4. Once the posters are complete, each group will take turns presenting their ideas to the rest of the class, explaining the nature of their business ventures and the reasoning behind their choices.
5. After all presentations, encourage discussion and feedback among students regarding the feasibility and creativity of the proposed business ideas.
6. Conclude the activity by emphasizing the importance of innovation and critical thinking in entrepreneurship.

Activity 3

Entrepreneurial Observation and Innovation

Materials Required

Notebook, pen

Procedure

1. Divide the class into teams of 5 students each. If there are 30 students, create 6 teams.
2. Choose a leader for each team who will facilitate the activity.
3. Each team member will:
   - Observe and make a list of individuals seen while commuting to school, noting their activities.
   - Compile two lists: one comprising individuals working for themselves and another of those employed by others.
   - Identify various types of businesses in the local area.
   - Reflect on products or services not readily available in the neighborhood, requiring people to travel elsewhere for purchase.
   - Consider if these gaps present opportunities for potential business ideas.
   - Brainstorm innovative ways to address these unmet needs and fill the identified gaps.
4. Each team will engage in a group discussion to share and refine their ideas.
5. Encourage teams to present their most promising business ideas to the class, fostering creativity and critical thinking.

Activity 4

Exploring the Impact of Entrepreneurs

Materials Required

None

Procedure

1. Divide the class into groups of 4-5 students each.
2. Instruct each group to brainstorm and identify entrepreneurs who have had a significant impact on society or individuals.
3. Once each group has chosen an entrepreneur, instruct them to imagine a scenario where this entrepreneur and their business never existed.
4. Discuss within the group how their lives and the world in general would be affected if the chosen entrepreneur's contributions were absent.
5. Each group should prepare a brief presentation outlining the key contributions of their chosen entrepreneur and the potential consequences if they were not part of the picture.
6. Select one volunteer from each group to present their findings to the class.
7. As the presentations are delivered, encourage the rest of the class to ask questions and provide additional insights.
8. A designated student can record the examples shared by each group on the board.
9. After all presentations, initiate a class discussion on the importance of entrepreneurs in shaping our world, driving innovation, and fostering economic development.
10. Summarize the key points and encourage students to reflect on how entrepreneurs contribute to societal progress.

Activity 5

A Successful Entrepreneur's Journey

Procedure

1. Form pairs of students. One student will take on the role of a successful entrepreneur, envisioning

themselves in their thriving business about 10 years into the future.

2. The other student will act as an interviewer representing a prominent business magazine, tasked with interviewing the successful entrepreneur.
3. The interviewer will ask questions provided in the table below and record the answers.
4. Following the interview, one volunteer pair will present their questions and answers to the class.

S.No.	Questions	Your Answer
1.	Describe your thriving business. What industry are you in?	
2.	Share the inspiration behind starting your own business instead of pursuing a job in a company.	
3.	How did the initial idea for your business come to you, and how did you develop it?	
4.	Reflect on the challenges you faced when starting your business. Were you initially successful?	
5.	Identify the most significant obstacle you encountered and explain how you overcame it.	
6.	Entrepreneurship often involves failures. Can you share a notable failure from your journey and the lessons learned?	
7.	Based on your experience, what advice would you offer to aspiring entrepreneurs looking to start their own business?	

Activity 6

Local Entrepreneurial Insights

Procedure

Engage with the entrepreneurial spirit in your community by exploring and understanding the qualities of local business owners. Connect with business owners in your neighborhood, discuss their experiences, and identify the attributes that contribute to their success. Record your findings in the table provided below.

Business Owner's Name	Qualities	Impact on Business	Entrepreneurial Status
[Owner's Name]	[List Qualities]	[Describe Impact]	Yes/No
[Owner's Name]	[List Qualities]	[Describe Impact]	Yes/No
[Owner's Name]	[List Qualities]	[Describe Impact]	Yes/No

Activity 7

Exploring Enterprise Characteristics

Procedure

1. Divide the class into groups of 5 students each. If there are 30 students, create 6 groups, and designate a leader for each group who will facilitate the activity.
2. Provide each group with a table containing the following information, and ask them to fill it up with either "Yes" or "No."

Type of Business	Is it making money?	Does it sell something for profit?	Does it use what it has or knows best?	Does it take a risk?
Stationery Shop				
Local Milk Dairy				
Plumbing Shop				

3. After the groups have completed the table, one group can volunteer to explain their answers to the class. The other groups should provide feedback, indicating whether the answers are correct or incorrect. Additionally, they should check their answers against the correct ones to ensure accuracy.

Activity 8

Exploring the Advantages of Entrepreneurship

Procedure

1. Divide the class into groups of 5 students each. For example, if there are 30 students in the class, there will be 6 groups.
2. Within each group, designate a leader.
3. Each group will brainstorm and discuss the advantages of entrepreneurship over wage employment.
4. Using available resources (paper, markers, digital tools), each group will create a visual representation (such as a poster or infographic) showcasing the advantages they identified.
5. Two groups will volunteer to present their visual representations to the class.
6. After each presentation, the other groups will provide constructive feedback on the content, clarity, and creativity of the presentation.
7. Following the feedback, the class can engage in a brief Q&A session where students can ask questions

to clarify any points or seek further information from the presenting groups.

Activity 9

Sustainable Entrepreneurship Workshop

Materials Required

1. Recyclable materials such as old newspapers, tins, glasses, etc.
2. Glue, scissors, markers, and any other crafting supplies.

Procedure

1. Form groups of 4 or 5 participants in each group.
2. Each group brainstorms and develops an eco-friendly product idea using recyclable materials. The product should be designed for the benefit of the environment.
3. Follow the four steps of sustainable entrepreneurship listed below: (a) Identify a problem related to environmental sustainability. (b) Devise a solution in the form of a product using recyclable materials. (c) Plan the production process, considering the environmental impact. (d) Develop a strategy for presenting and marketing the product.
4. Craft the product using recyclable materials collected from home, etc. If time is limited, students can create the product after the session and bring it to the next meeting.
5. Each team presents their sustainable product, highlighting how they incorporated the four steps of sustainable entrepreneurship.
6. Teams attempt to "sell" their eco-friendly products to classmates.
7. Other teams provide feedback, expressing their preferences and suggesting improvements. They also state the amount of "virtual eco-coins" (instead of real money) they would be willing to exchange for the products.
8. Each student reflects on the experience by answering the following questions in their notebook:
   - As a creator, what inspired your choice of an eco-friendly business idea? Why did you select this idea?
   - Did you make any adjustments to your idea based on feedback from your peers? If so, what changes did you make?
   - As a potential buyer, were you interested in purchasing any of the eco-friendly products presented? If yes, which product and why?
   - Did you anticipate receiving virtual eco-coins for your sustainable business idea? Why?
   - As a potential buyer, were you willing to exchange virtual eco-coins for products made by your peers? Why or why not?
   - What insights did you gain about sustainable entrepreneurship through this activity?

NCERT FOLDER

Complete Explanations of all NCERT's Questions

A. Multiple Choice Questions

Q.1 Business is a (an) .... activity.

(a) social (b) economic
(c) hazardous (d) selling

Q.2 What is the aim of entrepreneurship?

(a) Earn a profit
(b) Solve customers' need innovatively
(c) Both of the above
(d) None of the above

Answers

1. (b) 2. (c)

B. Fill in the Blank

Q.1 State whether the person engaged in the activity mentioned below is an Entrepreneur or an Employee.

(a) Rahul starts a shop to sell Chaat and special Paani Puri. He is an ....

(b) Shahid becomes the manager of a dealership selling food products. He is an ....

(c) Ritu leaves the company she worked for and starts catering food for marriage programmes. She is an ....

Ans. (a) Entrepreneur (b) Employee (c) Entrepreneur

Q.2 **Arun bakery, which makes and sells bread to people. ....**

Ans. Product business

Q.3 **Ram's repair shop, which repairs motorcycle. ....**

Ans. Service business

Q.4 **Hari's hair-salon, where he cuts hair for women and men. ....**

Ans. Service business

Q.5 **Write P-Product, S-Service and H-Hybrid for the following businesses.**

(a) **Ice-cream seller: ....**
(b) **Restaurant/Cafeteria owner: ....**
(c) **Car-driving/School owner: ....**

Ans. (a) P-Product (b) H-Hybrid (c) S-Service

C. Match the Following

Q.1 **Match the following columns.**

	Column A		Column B
1.	Business idea	A.	Arun goes to the bank to get loan for the shop.
2.	Get money	B.	Arun and Shyam are thinking about selling tea in front of their school.
3.	Customer needs	C.	Arun and Shyam decide to sell tea along with free biscuits.
4.	Attract customers	D.	Shyam takes his tea samples to customers to understand their taste preferences.

Ans. 1 → B, 2 → A, 3 → D, 4 → C,

D. Subjective Type Questions

Q.1 **List three businesses seen around you. Share details of what the business does and how they run it?**

Ans. Three businesses I have seen in my locality are:

(a) **Dolma Aunty, The Momo Seller** One aged lady, Dolma Aunty from Manipur has a small stall in our locality. She is making vegetarian and chicken momos which she sells from 12 noon to 8 pm at night. Her momos are very popular among young generation. By selling momo, she is surviving in Delhi.

(b) **Naresh, The Burgerwala** A young man, named Naresh has a small stall nearby a park, where he sells fresh aloo tikki burger. As his food is very tasty, everybody likes it. He sells burger from 4 pm to 9 pm at night and earns a good amount of money.

(c) **Pooja, The Beautician** Pooja is an enterprising girl who has taken a beautician course and also has marked for sometimes in a beauty parlour. Now, she is doing the business independently. She has good contacts with her customers and charges less than the beauty parlour. Her service is satisfactory to like customers, thus she is doing well in her business.

2. **Read the following statement and write 'Yes' or 'No' as to whether the person is an entrepreneur or not.**

	Statement	Yes/No
1.	Ravi made tea for his friends in the office. Everyone liked the tea very much and told him that he is very good at making tea.	
2.	Savita, a house wife, needs extra money for her kids' tuition. She notices that in the afternoon, the children coming out of a nearby college look tired and hungry. She makes refreshing *Neembu Pani* and *samosas* and sells them to the students.	
3.	Rahul loves dogs. He plays with dogs of his friends' family. One day when they were going out-of-station, they asked Rahul to take care of their dog. Rahul thought that this was a good idea, 'taking care of dogs when the owner is traveling'. He started his own company which is like a 'hotel for dogs'. When the dog-owners travel, they leave their dogs at this hotel and pay the company money for each day, they take care of the dog. Is Rahul an entrepreneur?	
4.	Monica noticed that her neighbours used to face a problem. They had to leave their young baby behind when they went for work. Monica started going to this house in the evening to take care of the baby for them. Her neighbours were very happy and used to give her chocolates for doing that.	

Ans. 1. No, 2. Yes, 3. Yes, 4. No

Q.3 **Gulab lives in a small village in Rajasthan. She noticed that all the women in her village were good at making paintings and handicraft product. She collected money and started a business. Gulab would help the women to get material from cities and support them in making latest designs. She would then arrange for these paintings and handicraft products to be sold in big cities. How do you think Gulab, is helping her society as an entrepreneur?**

Ans. Gulab helps like poor women in her village by supply them raw material and modern designs. She has made arrangement for selling of this product. This helps the women to be economically independent. By helping the women, he directly helps the community. In this way, by his business idea, she has helped her society a lot.

Q.4 **Give examples of three entrepreneurs you know who live around you. Write how they are helping your city?**

Ans. Do it yourself.

Q.5 Identify qualities of the following entrepreneurs. Also write why you think this person has this quality or the qualities.

(a) **Anil wanted to do something very different and something no one has thought of before. He decided to start a special travel services for old people/senior citizens.**

(b) **Rakesh loves playing outdoors. He used to spend his evenings with his friends, playing games. But, he had seen that many of his friends didn't like playing outdoors because they didn't feel safe. He decided to open a playground for children of all ages, with proper security. He found an unused playground, got permission to use it and asked his friends to help him clean it. He hired a security guard for the playground. He charged a small fee for people who wanted to play. Both parents and children liked his idea, and started playing there regularly. His business helped children who would not play outdoor before.**

(c) **Radhika was a cook in a small restaurant in her area. She made enough money to support her husband and children. She decided to start her own food stall to sell Punjabi food. She would make special parathas. A few days after starting her business, the police came and told her that she was not allowed to run her stall in the area. Radhika did not give up. She started a Tiffin service through which she would deliver fresh food to people.**

Ans. (a) Anil has decided to start a special travel services for senior citizens. There are lots of travelling agencies who entertained general people, but none of them has realised the need of senior citizens.

Anil thought some special facilities like special travel discounts, specified medical facilities, healthy and light foods etc. are to be given by his travelling agency. Thus, Anil has the quality of an entrepreneur who thinks different.

(b) Rakesh is a sport person. He has changed his passion into business.

He has knowledge of outdoor games. With this knowledge he has made the effective planning and extended it. Thus, he is a real entrepreneur.

(c) Radhika has started food service as she has like special attitude for cooking and ambition to do something big in life.

She is a true entrepreneur as she does something she is interested in. By applying her cooking skill she has started the new business, i.e. tiffin service through which she would deliver fresh food to people.

Q.6 Do you think you have the qualities of an entrepreneur in you? If yes, give examples when you have shown these qualities.

Ans. Do it yourself.

Q.7 Read the story of Sushma, the toy maker once again and fill in the boxes mentioning the various qualities that Sushma might have possessed as an entrepreneur.

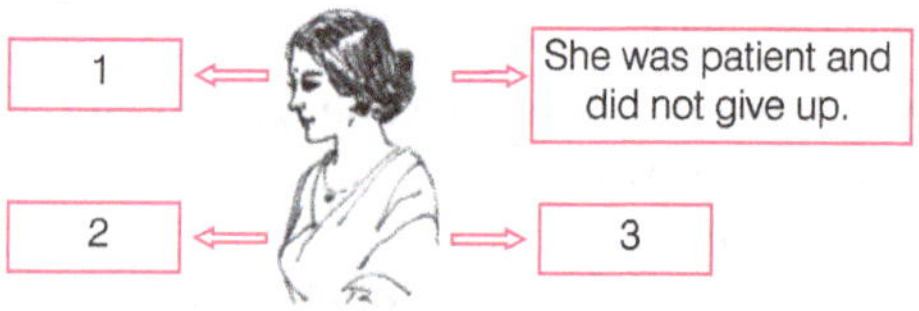

Ans. 1. She made huge efforts to persuade her customers to buy her toys.

2. She was thinking positively and improved her product.

3. She became partner with different toy shops and created a website to sell online.

Q.8 List any four characteristics of entrepreneurship.

Ans. Four characteristics of entrepreneurship are

(i) Risks taking nature.

(ii) Believe in hard work and discipline.

(iii) Financially literate and has money management skills.

(iv) Effective planner and executes efficiency.

Q.9 List any two characteristics of wage employment.

Ans. Two characteristics of wage employment are

1. Allows a person to make money (get a salary).
2. Wage employment work for others.

Q.10 Name any one factors that is common to both entrepreneurship and wage employment on contract basis.

Ans. Aim of earning money is common to both entrepreneurship and wage employment on contract basis.

Q.11 What are the three types of business activities? Explain with examples?

Ans. The three types of business activities are

- **Product Business** A business where a seller and buyer exchange an item, which can be seen and touched, is called a product-based business. For example, A Sports Shop.
- **Service Business** A business where a seller helps the buyer to finish some work. For example, A cricket coaching center.
- **Hybrid Business** A hybrid is the one where the business is doing both selling product and selling services. For example, Rahul starting a sports academy for coaching and selling sports equipment.

Q.12 What are the key differences between product and service-based businesses?

Ans. Key differences between product and service-based businesses are as follows

Product Business	Service Business
Product can be seen and touched. Customer pays for physical exchange of things.	Service cannot be seen or touched. Customer here pays for an experience.
A product can be made and stored in a shop or a warehouse (usually).	A service, for example, cutting hair, cannot be stored. Service is provided when a customer asks for it.

Q.13 If you had a choice to start a business of your own, which business will you start (include in your reply the product or service that you would like to take up)? Why do you want to start this type of business?

Ans. If I have a choice to start my own business then I will start a cricket sports academy for coaching and selling. The business will follow the hybrid type of business model, where both selling products (sports item) and services (coaching) will be provided. I love to play cricket. I have participated in many state level matches. I have enough experience of playing cricket. Applying my experience and passion, I want to start this business.

Q.14 What is the meaning of manufacturing and trading based business?

Ans. Manufacturing businesses are the businesses that make a product and sell it. Products are usually made in factories. Trading based businesses buy a product and sell it. They transport the product from the factory to warehouse and then wholesalers, distributors and retail shops.

Q.15 My customers are not buying my food product because they do not like the flavour of it. What step of the business should I follow next?

Ans. If my customers are not buying food products due to its flavour, I will try to improve the product/services in next steps. I will try to know their preferred taste and flavour and make product accordingly.

Q.16 Write the four steps of entrepreneurship development. Give one example.

Ans. Four steps of entrepreneurship development are

1. Business idea
2. Getting money and material
3. Understanding customer needs
4. Improving product/service.

For example,

Rakesh wants to open a small food stall near a railway station. He asked his father and uncle for a small loan to set up the stall. After establishing the stall he found that his customers like tasty and cheap foods.

By applying his experience in a South Indian food stall, Rakesh has started to make Dosas and Idlis for his customers, which are both pocket friendly and delicious.

REVIEW EXERCISE

Including Competency Based Questions

Part I

Multiple Choice Questions

1. Businesses cater to the need of the

(a) area
(b) society
(c) market
(d) village

2. An entrepreneur is a self employed person and is willing to take a

(a) product and service
(b) satisfying human need
(c) calculated risk
(d) regular production

3. The role and benefits of entrepreneurship are

(a) Social development
(b) Improved standard of living
(c) Optimal use of resources
(d) All of the above

4. Entrepreneurs uses optimal ways of using the resources to

(a) reduce cost (b) increase profit
(c) Both of these (d) None of these

5. Qualities of entrepreneurs are

(a) hardworking (b) never giving up
(c) perseverance (d) All of these

6. Experiment with different idea is the quality related to
(a) perseverance (b) confidence
(c) trial and error (d) creativity

7. The quality of creativity and innovation of entrepreneurs is related to
(a) patience (b) positivity
(c) hardworking (d) solution

8. Ability to take up risks is a
(a) role of entrepreneur
(b) quality of entrepreneur
(c) characteristics of entrepreneurship
(d) None of the above

9. The employees are
(a) self employed (b) wage-earner
(c) take risk (d) self job decider

10. A risk may lead to a
(a) excess of earning (b) loss in future
(c) human needs (d) growth

11. Wage employment is always consists of
(a) one party (b) two parties
(c) three parties (d) four parties

12. The wage employment does not involve too much
(a) salary (b) opportunity
(c) innovation (d) risk

13. The principle focus of entrepreneurship is
(a) more risk (b) more work
(c) more profit (d) more job

14. Product and services both are sold in
(a) Product business (b) Service business
(c) Hybrid business (d) General business

15. Product can be seen and touched in
(a) Product business (b) Service business
(c) Hybrid business (d) General business

16. Manufacturing businesses are the types of
(a) Trade businesses (b) Product based business
(c) Hybrid based business (d) Service based business

17. Which one is not steps of starting a business?
(a) Business idea
(b) Getting money and material
(c) Understanding customer needs
(d) Trade services

18. What is entrepreneurship? **Competency Based Ques.**
i. The process of developing a business plan and running a business
ii. The act of being self-employed and earning a steady source of income
iii. Launching and running a business using innovation to meet customer needs
iv. The continuous production and distribution of goods and services
(a) Both i and ii (b) Only iii
(c) Both i and iii (d) Only iv

19. Which factor is crucial for economic development in the context of entrepreneurship? **Competency Based Ques.**
i. Increased competition in the market
ii. Entrepreneurial creation of jobs
iii. Optimal use of renewable resources
iv. Lower prices of products and services
(a) Only i and ii (b) Only ii and iii
(c) Only ii and iv (d) All of these

20. What is the primary role of an entrepreneur in improving the standard of living? **Competency Based Ques.**
i. Creating new business opportunities
ii. Selling products at competitive prices
iii. Providing better and cheaper products and services
iv. Introducing innovative marketing ideas
(a) Only i (b) Only ii
(c) Only iii (d) Both ii and iii

21. Which quality is essential for a successful entrepreneur? **Competency Based Ques.**
i. Patience ii. Positivity
iii. Hardworking and perseverance
iv. Open to trial and error
(a) Only i, ii, and iii (b) Only ii, iii, and iv
(c) Only i, iii, and iv (d) All of these

22. What distinguishes a self-employed person from an entrepreneur? **Competency Based Ques.**
i. Willingness to take a calculated risk
ii. Running the business solely for a steady income
iii. Being open to new ideas and innovation
iv. Engaging in continuous production and distribution
(a) Only i and ii (b) Only ii and iii
(c) Only i and iii (d) All of these

Answers

1. (b)	2. (c)	3. (d)	4. (c)	5. (d)
6. (c)	7. (d)	8. (c)	9. (b)	10. (b)
11. (b)	12. (d)	13. (c)	14. (c)	15. (a)
16. (b)	17. (d)	18. (c)	19. (a)	20. (c)
21. (d)	22. (c)			

Statement Based Questions

1. Statement 1: Entrepreneurship is the process of developing a business plan, launching, and running a business using innovation to meet customer needs and to make a profit.
Statement 2: Enterprise is a project or undertaking that is bold and fulfills a need of the society which no one has ever addressed.

(a) Both Statement 1 and Statement 2 are correct
(b) Both Statement 1 and Statement 2 are incorrect
(c) Statement 1 is correct but Statement 2 is incorrect
(d) Statement 2 is correct but Statement 1 is incorrect

2. Statement 1: Entrepreneurs create value by making available better and cheaper products and services for customers.

Statement 2: Entrepreneurs grow their businesses, and as they do, investors put money into their businesses expecting good returns.

(a) Both Statement 1 and Statement 2 are correct
(b) Both Statement 1 and Statement 2 are incorrect
(c) Statement 1 is correct but Statement 2 is incorrect
(d) Statement 2 is correct but Statement 1 is incorrect

3. Statement 1: Improved Standard of Living—More things available to live a comfortable life.

Statement 2: Entrepreneurs compete in the market, leading to lower prices of products.

(a) Both Statement 1 and Statement 2 are correct
(b) Both Statement 1 and Statement 2 are incorrect
(c) Statement 1 is correct but Statement 2 is incorrect
(d) Statement 2 is correct but Statement 1 is incorrect

4. Statement 1: Entrepreneurship involves taking calculated risks.

Statement 2: Wage employment involves too much risk.

(a) Both Statement 1 and Statement 2 are correct
(b) Both Statement 1 and Statement 2 are incorrect
(c) Statement 1 is correct but Statement 2 is incorrect
(d) Statement 2 is correct but Statement 1 is incorrect

5. Statement 1: Financial literacy and money management skills are characteristics of entrepreneurship.

Statement 2: In wage employment, the continuity of service depends on the terms and conditions laid down in the contract.

(a) Both Statement 1 and Statement 2 are correct
(b) Both Statement 1 and Statement 2 are incorrect
(c) Statement 1 is correct but Statement 2 is incorrect
(d) Statement 2 is correct but Statement 1 is incorrect

Answers

1. (a) 2. (a) 3. (a) 4. (c) 5. (a)

Assertion and Reason Based Questions

1. Assertion: Entrepreneurship involves the continuous production and distribution of goods and services to fulfill societal needs.

Reason: Entrepreneurs take calculated risks to bridge the gap between demand and supply by introducing new ideas and methods.

(a) Both assertion and reason are true, and reason is the correct explanation of the assertion.
(b) Both assertion and reason are true, but reason is not the correct explanation of the assertion.
(c) Assertion is true, but the reason is false.
(d) Assertion is false, but the reason is true.

2. Assertion: A business where a seller helps the buyer to finish some work.

Reason: The example of this business is a sports shop.

(a) Both assertion and reason are true, and reason is the correct explanation of the assertion.
(b) Both assertion and reason are true, but reason is not the correct explanation of the assertion.
(c) Assertion is true, but the reason is false.
(d) Assertion is false, but the reason is true.

3. Assertion: Entrepreneurship leads only self development by generating employment opportunities.

Reason: As entrepreneurs scale their businesses, they create more job opportunities, contributing to higher employment rates.

(a) Both assertion and reason are true, and reason is the correct explanation of the assertion.
(b) Both assertion and reason are true, but reason is not the correct explanation of the assertion.
(c) Assertion is true, but the reason is false.
(d) Assertion is false, but the reason is true.

4. Assertion: Entrepreneurs contribute to improving the standard of living by providing innovative solutions to societal problems.

Reason: Through creativity and innovation, entrepreneurs introduce products and services that enhance people's quality of life.

(a) Both assertion and reason are true, and reason is the correct explanation of the assertion.
(b) Both assertion and reason are true, but reason is not the correct explanation of the assertion.
(c) Assertion is true, but the reason is false.
(d) Assertion is false, but the reason is true.

5. Assertion: Entrepreneurship involves taking calculated risks.

Reason: Entrepreneurs are afraid of failure and hesitate to continue their course of action until they succeed.

(a) Both assertion and reason are true, and the reason is the correct explanation of the assertion.
(b) Both assertion and reason are true, but the reason is not the correct explanation of the assertion.
(c) Assertion is true, but the reason is false.
(d) Assertion is false, but the reason is true.

6. Assertion: In wage employment, continuity of service depends on terms laid down in the contract.

Reason: Continuity of service does not depend upon the relationship between two parties.

(a) Both assertion and reason are true, and the reason is the correct explanation of the assertion.

(b) Both assertion and reason are true, but the reason is not the correct explanation of the assertion.

(c) Assertion is true, but the reason is false.

(d) Assertion is false, but the reason is true

Answers

1. (a) 2. (c) 3. (d) 4. (a) 5. (c) 6. (c)

Part II

Very Short Answer Type Questions

1. What is the primary purpose of entrepreneurship?

Ans. Entrepreneurship involves continuous production and distribution of goods and services, fulfilling societal needs through innovative ideas.

2. How does entrepreneurship contribute to economic development?

Ans. Entrepreneurs create value, attract investment, and generate jobs, leading to economic growth and improved standards of living.

3. What defines a successful entrepreneur's qualities?

Ans. Successful entrepreneurs exhibit qualities such as patience, positivity, hard work, confidence, openness to trial and error, and creativity.

4. Why is the optimal use of resources crucial for entrepreneurs?

Ans. Entrepreneurs aim to reduce costs and increase profits by finding optimal ways to use natural resources, both renewable and non-renewable.

5. How does entrepreneurship benefit society through competitive prices?

Ans. Entrepreneurs, through market competition, lower product prices, making goods and services more affordable and accessible to the public.

6. What is a characteristic of entrepreneurship?

Ans. Ability to take calculated risks, embracing failure but persisting until success is achieved.

7. What is a benefit of entrepreneurship?

Ans. Freedom to pursue interests, work for oneself, decide earnings, and the potential for higher profits with calculated risks.

Short Answer Type Questions

1. What are the key differences between entrepreneurship and enterprise?

Ans. The process of developing a business plan, launching and running a business and also using innovation to meet customer needs for making profit is known as entrepreneurship.

An enterprise is a project or undertaking that is bold and fulfills a need and wants of the society. The need previously unfulfilled.

2. What are the key differences between patience and Hardworking?

Ans. Success may not be achieved quickly. It is important for an entrepreneur to have patience while running the business. Every new business goes through failures and therefore, an entrepreneur needs to work hard till it becomes successful. It is necessary for an entrepreneur to continuously work hard to achieve his company's goal.

3. List any two difference between entrepreneurship and wage employment.

Ans. The two differences between entrepreneurship and wage employment are

(a) An entrepreneur is the business owner and an employee is the worker and get a salary.

(b) The wage employment does not involve too much risk but entrepreneurship involves taking certain amount of calculated risks.

4. List any two comparison of activities between entrepreneurship and employment.

Ans. Two comparison of activities between entrepreneurship and employment are

(a) The job done by the person is decided by himself or herself. But in employment, the job done by the is decided by employer.

(b) Use personal knowledge and interest to make money for oneself is possible in entrepreneurship not in employment.

5. Explain any two steps of entrepreneurship development.

Ans. Two steps of entrepreneurship development are

(a) **Business Idea**

The first step while starting a business is to come up with an idea. A business idea is based on

- Interest of individual
- Market need.

(b) **Getting money and material**

Second steps of starting business is the use of idea to start on a small scale with some money. It helps in buying basic material.

ASSESSMENT EXERCISE

Multiple Type Questions

1. A shopkeeper cannot be called an entrepreneur unless he uses a new
   (a) risk (b) idea (c) project (d) customer
2. Prices of products come down when the entrepreneurs complete in the
   (a) economy (b) resources (c) market (d) method
3. It is necessary for an entrepreneur to continuously work
   (a) deal (b) idea (c) use (d) hard
4. An entrepreneur is always open to new idea to make his/her business
   (a) grow (b) method (c) duration (d) risk
5. Profit is calculated by deducting all expenses from
   (a) earning (b) future (c) risk (d) method
6. Business is an activity for satisfying
   (a) entrepreneur (b) owner (c) new idea (d) human needs
7. Creation of more job by entrepreneur is
   (a) Economic development (b) Social development
   (c) Living standard development (d) Service development
8. Entrepreneurship allows to start something according to
   (a) market (b) choice (c) need (d) innovation

Very Short Answer Type Questions

9. What is entrepreneurship?
10. Define profit in entrepreneurship.
11. Describe wage employment.

Short Answer Type Questions

12. What are the key differences between creativity and Innovation?
13. Give Distinguished characteristics of entrepreneurship and wage employment.
14. List any two benefits of entrepreneurship.
15. List any two difference between Manufacturing businesses and Trade businesses.
16. What are the rewards of entrepreneurship?
17. How is entrepreneurship and employment different in terms of roles?

CHAPTER 05

Green Skills-I

Green skills are basically the tools we need to build a sustainable future. They encompass knowledge about the environment, along with the abilities to use green technologies and make eco-friendly decisions. These skills are both technical, like working with renewable energy, and behavioral, like understanding resource efficiency. By developing green skills, we can create a society that thrives while protecting our planet.

5.1 Introduction to Environment

Everything around us forms our environment. It affects all aspects of our life, likewise our day to day activities also affect the environment.

We depend on different environmental resources, like; Forests, Grasslands, Rivers, Plants etc for our food and other needs.

Over the years with economic development there has been an increase in environmental pollution that threatens the stability of environment. We need to plan the maintenance of the environment in a sustainable manner, so that we can enjoy the good environment, it may be sustainable agriculture, developing eco-fashion design, manufacturing of solar panel, etc.

Relationship Between Society and Environment

The society constitutes of group of people living together in a community, a village, a city, a town, a states or a country. It is these group of people with their own set of ideologies and beliefs that affects the environment. If a group of people believe that rivers are sacred, then all people belonging to that group will resonate the practices that support their belief.

If a group of people believe that killing of animals is a heinous crime, the people in that community will reflect it in their behaviour shaping their relationship. But, if a group of people is greedy and is concerned to accumulate wealth, their actions will echo their mind-set and will have adverse effect on the environment.

As said every action have an equal and opposite reaction. So, is this true in case of the Society and Environment. To fulfil our greed, we are exploiting the resources nature has given us, while nature has its own way to show its fury.

Issues like Global Warming, Climate change, other man-made disasters are a few that have a directly implication of man's activities.

Natural Disasters like earthquakes have a direct impact on the economy hence affecting the society. Hence, it may be concluded that both society and environment are interdependent and cannot exist in isolation.

5.2 Natural Resources

A resource is any natural or artificial substance, energy or organism which is used by humans for its welfare.

Natural resources are the resources that are available freely in nature such as water, land, soil, rocks, forests, animals, fossil fuels and minerals. They are the basis of life and all life forms depend on them. Natural resources are used to survive and to function properly.

Natural resources can be consumed directly or indirectly. Humans depend on forest directly for food, biomass, health, recreation etc. Indirectly forests help in climate regulation, prevention of floods, storm protection etc.

Natural resource can be in solid, liquid or gas form. They can be organic, inorganic, metallic or non-metallic.

Different forms of natural resources are given below:

(i) Land Resource

Land as a resource is used for food production, for residence and recreation. It is a finite (limited) resource, used for agriculture and non-agriculture such as developing infrastructure.

(ii) Forest Resource

A forest is a natural, self sustaining community characterised by the presence of trees. Wood from forest is used in making furniture, tool handles, railway sleepers, matches, ploughs, bridges, boats etc. Wood is also used as an energy source for cooking and keeping warm.

Flora and fauna of forests provide other resources like tannins, gums, drugs, spices, waxes, honey, horns, musk, ivory, hides etc.

(iii) Water Resource

Water covers about three quarter of Earth's surface which includes water in rivers, lakes, oceans, underground aquifers etc. It is a necessary element for life and vital in agriculture, industry, household, recreation (activities like swimming, fishing) and in environmental activities.

(iv) Mineral Resource

Mineral deposit is a concentration of naturally occurring solid, liquid or gaseous material. They are present in or on the Earth's crust in such form that their extraction and conversion into useful materials are profitable now or in future. Minerals are non-renewable. They can be metals like iron, copper, aluminium or non-metals like salt, gypsum, clay, sand phosphates. Some minerals consist of a single element such as gold, silver, diamond, sulphur etc.

(v) Food Resources

Resources that are used as food or provide food for organisms are called food resources, e.g. plants. Agriculture is main source of plant food for human. Plants serve as food resource for herbivores and omnivores. They are eaten by animals and birds who become the food for carnivores and omnivores.

(vi) Energy Resources

Resources that produce heat, power that can be used as energy to produce electricity or to move objects are called energy resources.

Different types of energy resources are given below:

- Nuclear fusion e.g. solar energy.
- Gravity generated by Sun and Moon.
- Nuclear fission (atomic energy).
- Energy in the interior of the Earth.
- Energy stored in chemical bonds, e.g. fossil fuels. Because fossil fuels provide huge amount of energy but they have harmful effects on the environment. They are also non-renewable.

Artificial Resources

Resources developed by humans during the growth of civilisation are called artificial resources. For example, biogas, thermal electricity, plastics etc.

Categories of Natural Resources

Natural resources can be categorised as follows

- **Inexhaustible Resources** The resources which cannot be exhausted by human consumption are called inexhaustible resources, e.g. solar radiation, wind power, water power, tidal power etc.
- **Exhaustible Resources** Resources that are available in limited quantities and are going to be exhausted due to continuous use are called exhaustible resources e.g. stock of coal. It is in limited quantity and it's continuous use will exhaust this resource.
- **Renewable Resources** Resources that are constantly available (like water) or can be replaced or recovered (like vegetative land) are called renewable resource. Some resource can be replaced but the process may take many years. They are not counted as renewable.

  Some exhaustible resources are naturally regenerated, e.g. forest trees and plants. They are renewable. But if the forest is totally cut down to get land for construction of buildings, then the forest cover is lost forever.

- **Renewable Energy Systems** Renewable resources that are constantly replaced and are less polluting, are used to produce energy such as hydropower (energy from moving water), solar, wind, geothermal (energy from the heat inside the Earth).
- **Non-Renewable Resources** The resources that cannot be easily replaced once they are destroyed or used up are called non-renewable resource, e.g. fossil fuels, minerals. It takes thousands of years for minerals to form again in a process called rock cycle, so it is a non-renewable resource.

  Some non-renewable resources are called **Inorganic Resources** as they come from non-living things like minerals, they come from rocks, land, soil etc.

Non-Renewable and Renewable Resources

Non-renewable Resources	Uses	Renewable Resource	Uses
Coal (Cheapest source of fuel)	Cooking, heating, used as fuel in power houses and factories	Water (2.5% fresh water on Earth)	Hydroelectricity from river water, sea tides and ocean tides
Petroleum (Petrol, diesel, mineral oil)	Run motor vehicles, furnaces and power houses	Sun	Solar energy in calculators, light street lamps, room heaters, water heaters
LPG (Liquified Petroleum Gas)	Cooking and running vehicles	Wind	Wind energy for running wind mills, grinding grains, pumping water
CNG (Compressed Natural Gas)	Running vehicles	Biomass (produced from plant and animal wastes)	Produce electricity and heat for cooking, lighting
Minerals	Gold, bauxite, mica, iron-ore, etc. have lot of uses	Soil	Provide shelter, agriculture
Nuclear Plants	Source of electricity	Forests	Preserve ecological balance, give clean air and forest products like wood, fuel, medicines

5.3 Ecosystem and Factors Causing Imbalance

Ecological imbalance is caused when natural or a man-made disturbance disrupts the natural balance of an ecosystem. Human activities have direct implication in causing ecological imbalance.

Following are the man-made disruption that causes ecological imbalance:

Over Exploitation

It takes place when harvesting of resources is more than their reproduction or replenishment (recovery). It means that a particular species or a resource is used up or taken away much faster than its natural population can recover or replace it.

For example, Removal of wild medicinal plant at a much faster rate than it can be replaced naturally. Over hunting, over fishing also makes a species extinct. Excessive grazing, destruction of forests, water acquifers and natural habitats are overexploitation of natural resources.

Mining

Mining takes place when mines are dug below the Earth's surface to get ores. The ores are then refined to extract valuable elements like metals, gems, minerals.

The environmental impacts of mining are erosion, formation of sinkholes and loss of biodiversity. Chemicals from the mines also cause contamination of soil, ground water and surface water.

Deforestation

Clearance of forest or stand of trees to convert that land to non-forest use for agriculture, construction etc. is deforestation. It causes loss of habitat for plant and animal species living in the forest and may lead to their extinction.

Pollution

The word is derived from the Latin word 'Polluere' meaning 'to soil' or 'defile (contaminate)'. Pollution is caused by pollutants which are unwanted solid, liquid or gaseous in nature.

Pollutants are produced due to human activity. They bring undesirable changes in our surroundings that have harmful effects on plants, animals and human beings.

For example, Factories release harmful chemicals in air, land and water thus contaminating the atmosphere and causing water pollution.

Fossil fuel emissions pollute the air as they emit carbon dioxide, methane and nitrous oxide on burning.

Types of Pollution

	Land Pollution	Water Pollution	Air Pollution
Definition	Damage to land due to presence of harmful substances on it.	Addition of harmful substances, disease causing germs to water bodies like rivers, lakes, sea, ocean.	Addition of harmful gases, particles, smoke in air.
Effects	• Diseases-dysentry, Cholera, Typhoid. • Contamination of land. • Less availability of land for agriculture, forest and houses.	• Diseases-dysentry, Diarrhoea, Jaundice, Typhoid • Less availability of clean drinking water. • Loss of local earning opportunities like fishing, tourism etc.	• Heart and breathing problems, cancers. • Lack of clean air. • Climate change, droughts, famines, floods.
Cause	• Deforestation, mining. • Use of excessive chemicals, (pesticides, fertilisers) in agriculture. • Release of sewage, toilet waste, waste from factories/houses • Dumping of chemical wastes, plastics.	• Release or leakage of sewage from sewer lines. • Throwing human waste/household waste in water. • Dumping of chemical wastes from factories and farms. • Dumping of plastics like water bottles. • Accidental oil leakage from ships.	• Burning of fossil fuels from vehicles, factories that include emissions like CO_2, methane, nitrous oxide, CFCs etc. • Burning crop residue and wastes. • Smoke from factories. • Dust from construction. • Emissions from pesticides and fertilisers.
Prevention	• Reduce waste. • Segregate (separate) waste before dumping. • Use more biodegradable products. • Adopt natural and organic methods of farming. • Plant trees.	• Do not throw waste, chemical into water bodies. • Do not throw chemicals, medicines, oils in drain. • Avoid use of pesticides, fertilisers. • Ensure proper treatment of sewage and factory waste. • Use water wisely.	• Use renewable sources of energy. • Avoid fuels and vehicles that create lot of pollution. • Stop people from burning wastes, crop residues. • Avoid pesticides, fertitisers that release harmful gases.

Types of Pollutants

	Biodegradable Pollutants	Non-Biodegradable Pollutants
Definition	Pollutants that can be broken down into simpler, harmless substances naturally by the action of moisture and bacteria.	Pollutants that cannot be broken down into simpler, harmless substances.
Examples	Vegetable/Fruit waste, sewage waste, paper, wood, cattle dung, agricultural waste from organic farms.	Plastics, insecticides, pesticides, chemicals like mercury or lead, aluminium, glass

5.4 Effects of Environmental Imbalances

Environmental degradation disrupts the delicate balance in nature. It changes the Earth in many ways. The ill-effects of environmental imbalances are described below :

Climate Change

Frequent changes in climate is the result of global warming and green house effect.

Global Warming

Global warming is the heating up of the Earth. This happen when the burning of fossil fuels like coal, petrol, diesel produce gases that trap and prevent Earth's heat from escaping.

Green House Effect

The Earth becomes hotter due to global warming which is caused by emission of gases that trap heat. This is called the **green house effect.**

Forest convert carbondioxide into carbon and oxygen. But the loss of forest cover and increasing release of green house gases through industrialsation contributes to green house effect.

Green House Gases

Green house gases occur naturally through decomposition of organic matter and through human activity like agriculture, burning of fossil fuels. These gases are water vapour, Carbondioxide (CO_2), Methane (CH_4), Nitrous Oxide (N_2O) and Ozone (O_3).

Some green house gases have no natural sources but are side products of industrial processes or specially manufactured for various purposes such as clearing agents, refrigerants and electrical insulators.

These are fluorinated gas : Chlorofluorocarbons (CFCs), Hydro Chlorofluorocarbons (HCFCs), Hydrofluorocarbons (HCFCs). These gases causes snow to melt very fast.

arbondioxide gas has increased by 31% since pre-industrial times. It causes more heat to be trapped in the lower atmosphere resulting in frequent floods, changes in climate, damage to crops and animal life.

Harmful Radiation

The atmosphere protects us from the harmful radiations from the Sun. It is done by the Ozone layer, a layer of gas all around the Earth in the atmosphere.

Cleaning chemicals, coolants in refrigerators and air-conditioners release substances such as chlorofluorocarbons that deplete the ozone layer. These chemicals destroy the ozone layer by making holes in it through which harmful radiations reach earth. The radiations cause increased incidence of health disorders such as skin cancer.

Natural Disasters

These include floods, earthquakes, landslides, storms etc. Human actions in exploiting natural resources for making dams, buildings aggravates the impact of natural calamities and disasters.

5.5 Saving the Environment : What can you do?

For saving the environment, there is need to educate people. Education gives people the knowledge and skills that they need to perform.

Educating people about the environment, through the environment and for the environment will enlighten them in utilising their knowledge and skills for saving the environment.

Education help in saving the environment in three ways :

1. Learning About The Environment

Learning about the environment focuses mainly on acquisition of knowledge and understanding of our surroundings and related issues.

2. Learning Through The Environment

It refers to the processes of learning while being engaged with environment inside and outside the classroom. Learning processes like observation, hands on experience, learning by doing, problem solving are focussed here. Direct contact with environment, helps in acquiring knowledge, skills, aesthetic appreciation (admiring nature) and practical experience of learning.

Damage to the environment can be reduced by developing skills and knowledge needed for efficient resource utilisation, green processes and technologies. Integrating this knowledge into businesses and daily activities reduce damage to environment.

3. Learning For the Environment

It aims at the development of an informed response and responsibility towards the environment.

Try These 5.1

1. **Name the artificial resources.**
2. **What is inorganic resource?**
3. **Earthquakes, landslides etc are which type of disasters?**
4. **Which type of gases deplete the ozone layer?**

5.6 Reduce, Reuse, Recycle

Three Rs can be applied for saving the environment. They are Reduce, Reuse and Recycle. It is a modern waste management concept.

Reduce

It refers to 'do not use what you do not need'. Reduction at source will have lesser chances of waste generation. This will reduce the pressure on our natural resources also.

People can reduce the use of unnecessary items while shopping, buy items with minimum packaging, avoid buying disposable items and avoid asking for plastic carry bags. Using reusable cloth or jute bag is better than plastic bags.

Reuse

It refers to reuse the materials for other purposes such as making pillow covers or rags out of used shirts or ladies suits.

Recycling

It refers to reusing some components of the waste that may have some economic value. Recycling helps in conservation of resources, reduction in energy used for manufacturing and reducing pollution. Metals, paper, glass, plastics are recyclable. Aluminium and steel can be recycled many times. Wet waste from kitchen (fruit, vegetable peels) are also recyclable as it can be utilised to make compost and used as an organic fertiliser. For this, every house should segregate (separate) waste into dry and wet garbage.

Kitchen waste are wet garbages that can be turned into vermicompost. Dry garbages are also mostly recyclable. Break through technologies have developed recently to recover useful materials from industrial wastes.

Non-toxic solid waste should also be segregated. They should be properly disposed in **landfills** that are sealed to avoid any leakage and contamination of surrounding land and groundwater.

Example of Reduce, Reuse, Recycle

Material	Reduce : Use less things	Reuse : Use things for longer time	Recycle : Use things in new/different ways
Paper	• Reduce wastage of paper. • Do not leave too much spaces while writing.	• Use both sides of paper for writing. • Give old books/ notebooks to someone needy.	• Recycle to make paper again. • Make papier mache products by using paper pulp, glue, starch or wall paper paste.

This will help in reducing cutting of trees from which paper is made.

Actions for Saving The Environment

	Avoid	Prefer
Air pollution	• Burning material, e.g. wheat, rice straw in farms.	• To use natural ventilation or fans instead of AC.
Energy Use	• Leaving electrical lights or appliances on when not in use.	• To use public transport like bus, metro and cycles instead of cars. • To use solar and wind energy.
Water pollution	• Throwing wastes in rivers and lakes.	• Using recycled water or water harvested through rains wherever possible, e.g. watering garden plants.
Waste	• Using plastic bags.	• To segregate waste before throwing to separate biodegradable waste.
Chemicals in food	• Using chemical pesticides and fertilisers.	• To use and promote organic foods and farming methods.
Forest plants	• Avoid over use of paper.	• Reuse paper wherever possible.
Water	• Avoid over use of water.	• Reduce water usage, e.g. bathing by using bucket filled with water instead of shower.

5.7 Conserving Natural Resources

Conservation

It refers to the proper management of natural resources to prevent their exploitation, destruction or degradation.

Conservation is the sum total of activities where natural resources are used efficiently to derive benefits but at the same time preventing their excessive use to avoid any destruction, degradation or wastage.

To conserve a resource, first step is resource audit which examines the way of consumption of resources, then to take conservation measures accordingly is the next step.

Example

1. For energy use audit, examine the use of AC system, ventilation system, light system and entry of sunlight into the room/building.
2. Plan energy saving measures by cleaning dust from tubelights for better lighting, regular servicing and maintenance of home appliances. Switching off lights, fans, devices when not in use.

This helps to conserve energy which ultimately saves money and fossil fuels.

Conservation of the natural resources are described below

Soil Conservation

It refers to adopting various methods to check soil erosion and to improve soil fertility. Soil conservation can be done by the following ways :

- **Maintenance of Soil Fertility** Fertility can be maintained by adding manures and fertilisers regularly and by crop rotation (growing of different crops in succession).
- **Control on Grazing** Grazing uproots the grasses therefore it should be allowed in specific areas only.
- **Reforestation** Planting of trees and increasing vegetation cover to reduce soil erosion.
- **Terracing** A farming practised in hilly areas. It is done by dividing a hill slope into several flat fields. This controls rapid run of water.
- **Contour Ploughing** Ploughing at right angles of the natural slopes. This allows the furrows to trap water and check soil erosion caused by rain water.

Water Conservation

Water conservation and its management is essential for the survival of mankind, plants and animals. This can be done by following ways:

- **Growing Vegetation** Vegetation in the catchment areas (land areas from which water flows into river) help in holding water in the soil. The water then percolates into deeper layers and forms or increases ground water.
- **Construction of Dams and Reservoirs** This helps in two ways– regulate water supply to the fields and enables the generation of hydroelectricity.
- **Sewage Treatment** Treating of sewage water and then releasing the clear water into the rivers.
- **Prevent Water Pollution** By treating industrial wastes (effluents) prevents chemicals from entering water sources. Thermal pollution of fresh water should also be prevented.
- **Rainwater Harvesting** This should be done by storing rainwater and recharging groundwater.
- **Watershed Management** Watershed is a single unit of land with its water drainage system. Its management includes soil and water management which increases vegetative cover in the area.

Energy Conservation

Human use a lot of non-renewable sources of energy for their needs. Since these resources are limited, their conservation is essential. Energy conservation refers to efficient use of the energy sources and save them wherever possible. Some of the ways of conserving energy are as follows:

- Switch off lights, fans, TV, electrical items when not in use.
- Use tube lights and energy efficient bulbs that save energy.
- Remove dust from tubes and bulbs and keep them clean to improve lighting levels by 10-20%.
- Some electric items like AC, geysers, heaters, dryers use lot of electrical power, use them when necessary.
- Use pressure cooker and keep vessels covered while cooking to save energy and for faster cooking.
- Do not keep the door of refrigerator open for a long time and cool down the hot foods before putting in refrigerator.
- Use cooking methods that use less energy like use a pressure cooker or solar cooker.
- Travelling in a bus or in a group in a carpool also saves energy.

Food Conservation

Conserving food and its storage have been practiced by people to feed mankind during shortage. Food is stored in warehouses to feed people on large scale. At home food is stored in refrigerators. There are various other ways of food preservation to prevent its spoilage from harmful bacteria and other micro-organisms.

Forest Conservation

It refers to the retention of existing forest or the creation of new forest at the levels prescribed by the state or local authority.

For this, forest conservation programs are initiated but participation of the local community living in and around the forest is important for their success.

5.8 Sustainable Development and Green Economy

The current way of economic development is using up resources of the world rapidly. The future generation would have to face serious environmental problems that are much worse than present situation.

The increase in population and income has increased the consumption of goods. This has led to rise in production for which natural resources are used rapidly.

This is unsustainable so the society must change its development strategy to a form which will not destroy the environment. This new form of sustainable development can be brought if people practice a sustainable life style and ensure judicious utilisation of resources.

5.9 Biodiversity

Biological diversity is variety and richness of different plants and animal species found locally in a region, in the country and the world. It exists in different type of ecosystems-both terrestrial (land) and aquatic.

Biodiversity is essential for the following purposes:

- Preserving ecological processes such as fixing, recycling of nutrients
- Soil formation
- Circulation and cleansing of air and water
- In maintaining global life support systems such as plants giving out O_2 and absorbing CO_2
- Maintaining the water balance within ecosystems
- Watershed protection
- Maintaining stream and river flows throughout the year
- Erosion control
- Local flood reduction

5.10 What is Sustainable Development?

As per World Commission on Environment and Development, 1987, Sustainable development is defined as 'development that meets the needs of the present without compromising the ability of future generations to meet their own needs'.

It guarantees the balance between economic growth, care for the environment and social well-being.

The concept appeared for the first time in 1987 with the publication of the Brundtland Report. The report warned about negative environmental consequences of economic growth and globalisation. Sustainable development includes the following:

- Reducing excessive use of resources and enhancing resource conservation.
- Recycling and reuse of waste material.
- Scientific management of renewable resources, especially bio-resources.
- Planting more trees.
- Planting green grassy patches between concrete buildings.
- Using more environment friendly material or biodegradable material.
- Use of environment friendly technologies that are based on efficient use of resources.

Sustainable Development Goals

Sustainable Development Goals (SDGs) also known as Global Goals are a universal call to action to end poverty, protect the planet and ensure that all people enjoy peace and prosperity.

They were launched at the United Nations Sustainable Development Summit held in New York in September 2015, forming the 2030 agenda for sustainable development. The agenda with its 17 SDGs was adopted by world leaders in 2015. Main idea is to develop a roadmap for progress that is sustainable and leaves no one behind.

Objectives For Making SDGs

The SDGs are framed with the objective to address vital issues facing businesses, governments and society about poverty, gender equality, water use, energy, climate change and biodiversity. Aim is to provide secure, affordable and sustainable economy for which countries are framing policies and regulations.

5.11 Green Growth

It refers to the aims for achieving economic growth that is socially inclusive and environmentally sustainable. The **Ministry of Environment, Forest and Climate Change**, Government of India recognised green growth in its vision, wherein 'poverty eradication' along with green growth is important for green economy.

As per the **Finance Commission of India**, green growth is "rethinking growth strategies with regard to their impacts on the environmental sustainability and the environmental resources available to poor and vulnerable groups". Extent of economy to grow green is on two things—ability to reduce the quantity of resources required and support economic growth that leads to social equality and job creation.

For sustainable development, any activity for economic growth must also consider its environmental impacts. e.g. Vehicles on road that leads to traffic jam, waste of time for commuters, emission of harmful gases should be slowly replaced with an efficient public transport system.

5.12 Green Economy

Green economy was coined in 1989 in a report titled 'Blue Print for a Green Economy' made for the Government of United Kingdom by leading environmental economists.

According to United Nations Environment Program (UNEP) 2011, "green economy is one that results in improved human well-being and social equity, while significantly reducing environmental risks and ecological scarcities". It is low in carbon, resource efficient and socially inclusive.

Importance of Green Economy

A green economy is a system which helps in economic growth at the same time, taking care of the environment. It is beneficial from three aspects which are shown in the figure below

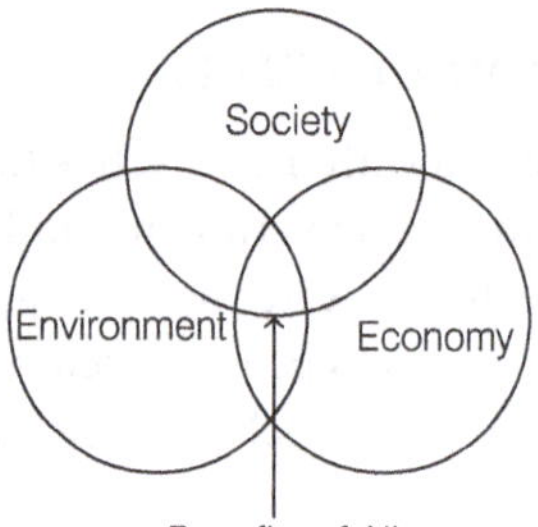

The figure shows that green economy is beneficial for all, i.e., **environment, economy** and **society**.

Building factories, using chemicals for more crops harm the environment. But if farmers do not use fertilisers, then it will harm the economy of the farmers.

But both, the environment and economy are part of society. As people become aware of serious health hazards caused by fertilisers and pesticides in their food, they will put pressure on farmers to reduce the use of chemicals.

People will use more of green products made by ecosensitive industries and products that cause severe damage to the environment may not be used. In this way green economy is beneficial from three aspects, i.e. environment, economy and society.

Green Consumer

A green consumer is very concerned about the environment and therefore only purchases products that are environment friendly and eco-friendly. Eco-friendly products are those that have very little packaging, made from natural ingredients and their making do not causes pollution.

Components of a Green Economy

Green economy uses less resources, causes less pollution and provides growth for everyone. The components are as follows:

Renewable Energy

- Energy from renewable sources like wind, water, Sun, Earth, biomass etc. These are available in large quantities and cause less pollution.
- India is amongst the top 10 countries for production of renewable energy through solar, wind and biomass.

Green Building

- Buildings that cause minimum damage to the environment during their construction and operation.
- Green buildings use energy, water and other resources wisely with minimum waste.

Well-Managed (Sustainable) Transport

- Sustainable means what is good for the economy as well as the future of the environment.
- Sustainable transport cause less or no damage to the environment.
- It costs less and help more people move quickly.

Water Management

- Need to avoid wastage of water.
- Need to reduce water pollution.
- Need to recycle water for various purposes.

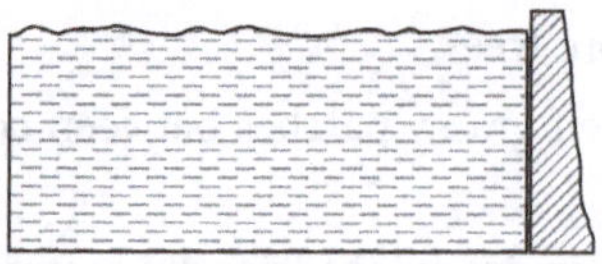

Waste Management

- Waste materials increase land, water and air pollution and causes loss of resources for cleaning the waste.

- Waste can be managed by separating it before throwing.
- Using 3R-Reduce, Reuse and Recycle will help in waste management.

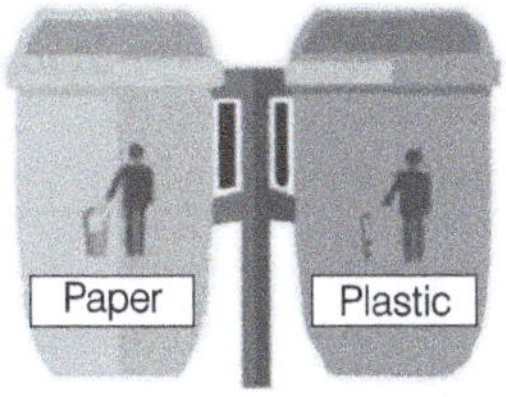

Land Management

- Land is needed for many purposes like farming, forests, factories, homes, roads etc.
- Land management is when land is used in a way that it meets the requirements of people without causing damage to the environment.

5.13 Skill Development For Green Economy

India is facing a major challenge of expanding access to food, energy, water, essential goods and services to its growing population. Therefore, it needs to work towards the objective of alleviating poverty and facilitating sustainable development.

Skill development for a green economy ensures an efficient transition from unsustainable to a green economy. This is done by matching supply with the demands needed for skill development.

For example, An organic farmer needs to have knowledge and skills for growing organically certified crops. Similarly, solar technicians or engineers should possess the knowledge and skills for design, installation and maintenance of solar panels and appliances. Green job can be with business, non-profit organisations, government or education.

Some green jobs may not require specific skills.

For example, A graphic designer or a cashier working for a green organisation will not require specific skill development.

But they will be contributing to the development of green growth and economy.

5.14 Green Skills

Green skills are skills used to promote green economy. They are needed in areas similar to renewable energy, sewage water treatment, developing climate resilient cities, green construction, solid waste management etc. Green skills are also known as skills for sustainability.

According to **Green Skills Agreement**, "skills for sustainability, also known as green skills, are the technical skills, knowledge, values and attitudes needed in the workforce to develop and support sustainable social, economic and environmental outcomes in business, industry and the community".

Info Wall

Green skills are those skills required to adapt processes, services and products to climate change and the environmental rules and necessities related to it. They embrace the information, abilities, values and attitudes required to live in, develop and support a sustainable and resource-efficient society.

Areas of Green Skills

Some of the areas in which green skills contribute to the sustainable development are as follows:

- Using renewable energy (e.g. solar power, wind energy)
- Water and waste management
- Rain water harvesting
- Conserving energy
- Reducing pollution

Importance of Green Skills

Green skills are crucial for making a transition from an economy based on energy and emissions to cleaner and greener production and services. It prepares people for green jobs that contribute to preserving or restoring the quality of the environment, while improving human well-being and social equality. For this, technologies to make use of solar energy such as solar lights, solar cooker, solar water heaters etc. are developed.

Green skills contribute to preserving or restoring environmental quality for sustainable future. Therefore, it include jobs that protect ecosystems and biodiversity, reduce energy and minimise waste and pollution. In future green skills are going to be more important as all countries will move towards a greener economy.

National Skill Development Mission

The mission was officially launched by Government of India in 2015. It is developed to create convergence across sectors and states in terms of skill training activities including green skills. The knowledge and skills needed for managing resources and supporting efficiency are as follows:

Purpose	Knowledge and Skills Needed For Green Economy
Manage natural resources	• To assess environmental impact. • To design and adopt technologies to reduce consumption of natural resources. • To understand legislation and guidelines for sustainable use of natural resources.
Support climate resilience	• To develop models for interpreting climate change projections. • To develop risk management strategies for future resource availability. • To adopt technologies that improve resilience (flexibility) to climate change.
Support resource efficiency	• To develop business models that are resource efficient. • To develop and adopt technologies that maximises resource utilisation and reduce wastage.
Support low-carbon industry	• To develop technologies that promote renewable energy sources. • To design and adopt technologies and products that minimise carbon emission.

Green Skill Development Programme

The Ministry of Environment, Forest and Climate Change has taken the initiative for skill development in environment and forest sector. It enables India's youth to get gainful employment and/or self-employment. This program is called Green Skill Development Programme. The programme aims to develop green skilled workers having technical knowledge and commitment to sustainable development to attain the sustainable development goals.

Green skills thus aim to balance economic development with environmental conservation, so that needs of the society, economy and environment are efficiently met with minimum damage to the environment.

Green Consumer Day

The Green Consumer Day is celebrated globally on 28th September of every year. On this day people celebrate Earth by bringing about awareness on how small actions can help Earth to remain green and clean.

People wear the colour green to express to the world their feelings regarding the universe and mother nature. People tend to recycle more than usual on that day.

5.15 What are Green Jobs?

Green job is employment in any industry that contributes to preserving or restoring environmental quality in that sector and allowing for sustainable development. The jobs that help protect ecosystems and biodiversity as well as aim to reduce energy, materials and water usage are included in green jobs. They can be in any sectors such as agriculture, manufacturing, research and development activities etc. They can bring transition from high carbon to low carbon economy by promoting environment friendly technologies. Sectors with potential to green jobs are as follows:

Sectors With Potential to Green Jobs

Sector	Areas/Field	Green Jobs
Agriculture	• Organic farming • Watershed management • Rain water harvesting	• Water quality technician • Rain water harvesting professional and technician • Solar pump technician • Greenhouse or polyhouse professional and technician
Construction	• Planning, design and manufacturing of energy efficient lighting appliances and equipments • Planning, design and construction of green buildings • Increasing efficiency of existing buildings through energy audits • Green plumbing, using sensor based equipments	• Green builders • Green design professionals • Green workers

Sector	Areas/Field	Green Jobs
Energy	• Research, construction and monitoring of power plant including plant efficiency and carbon sequestration (removal of carbon) • Increased power plant efficiency	• Solar cell technicians and engineers • Wind energy professionals • Wind energy workers • Wave energy producers • Biofuel professionals
Forestry	• Reforestation and afforestation projects • Agroforestry and vertical farming (growing crops on vertical stacks/layers)	• Natural scientists
Manufacturing	• Pollution control • Energy efficiency • Recycling waste materials	• Recyclers
Retail	• Greener products and specially targeted green stores	• Green salesperson • Accountants • Cashiers • Sales associates
Automotive and transport	• Research and design on more fuel efficient vehicles and on public transport systems • Manufacture of alternatively fuelled vehicles	• Clean car engineers
Tourism and hospitality	• Eco-friendly practices such as centralised lighting and air conditioning systems for saving electricity • Eco-tour guides	• Eco-tour guides • Green tour guides
Education	• Research and development activities for promoting green growth and economy • Teaching environmental education • Research and development in conservation of natural resources	• Teachers teaching environmental education • Green scientist • Conservation biologists

5.16 Green Projects

Green projects are implemented by people and organisations concerned and motivated to do something for saving the environment. Green projects are implemented in areas like waste management, energy conservation, green sanitation, biofuel use, green buildings etc.

Examples of Green Projects

1. **Solid Waste Management by 'Swachh Cooperative'** Swachh cooperative is in Pune and is wholly owned by waste pickers. These people are engaged in door step collection of waste. The cooperative has successfully integrated informal waste picking with Pune city's solid waste management system.

   They now work with dignity and ensure efficient disposal of wastes. Wet waste is used for regeneration of biogas and solid waste is recycled.

2. **Modern Chulha of Society of Development and Environment Protection** In this project, modern chulhas are developed which are energy efficient cooking stoves.

   These stoves help the movement of air through it, so that wood burns easily and efficiently. Chulha uses biomass that reduces consumption of wood by 50% and reduction in smoke by 80%. The chulhas are developed by the society of development and environment protection and named as 'Modern DEEP (Development and Environment Protection).

   This project trains masons and welders to produce these chulhas thereby increasing employment and entrepreneurship opportunities. Project was first started in 1995 in 35000 households of solan district in Himachal Pradesh.

3. **Bio-toilet by 'Green Solution Foundation'** Bio-toilet project is initiated by Green Solution Foundation (GSF). It provides hygienic sanitation in villages and slums of cities that lack in sewage systems. This eco-friendly toilet has a biodigester tank that uses aerobic bacteria and converts human waste into environment standard compatible water. This can be used for flushing and irrigation.

   The GSF provides training on toilet use and servicing, which increases employment and entrepreneurship opportunities. The bio-toilets are funded by users and donors.

   Benefits of Bio-toilets

   - Efficient sewage system
   - Water conservation due to less flushing
   - Decrease in soil and water contamination
   - Decrease in diseases due to hygienic sanitation

Try These 5.2

1. What is energy conservation?
2. When does green consumer day celebrate?
3. Give two benefits of Bio-toilets.
4. Give two examples of green skills that you can start learning from now.

Glossary

Natural resources are available freely in nature like land, forest, water, mineral, food and energy resources.

Three 'R'– **Reduce**, **Reuse** and **Recycle** are three ways of saving the environment.

Components of green economy includes developing more of renewable energy, green buildings, sustainable transport, water management, waste and land management.

Skill development for a green economy ensures sustainability alongwith development.

Green skills are the technical knowledge, values and attitude needed to support sustainable and resource efficient society.

National Skill Development Mission was launched in 2015 and the initiative for skill development is taken by Ministry of Government, Forest and Climate.

Green job is employment in any industry that contributes to preserving or restoring environmental quality in that sector such as agriculture, construction, etc.

Green projects are for saving the environment and implemented in areas like waste management, energy conservation etc.

Let's Investigate

Activity 1

Understanding Environmental Impact and Plastic Usage

Materials required

Pen and Notebook, Internet access for research (optional)

Procedure

1. Form groups of three students.
2. Research and compile a list of factors (things or actions) that significantly influence the environment.
3. Discuss the impact of plastic on the environment and answer the following questions: (a) Research and explain the process of how plastic is made. (b) Identify and list common plastic articles used in daily life. (c) Investigate and discuss the environmental effects of plastic usage. (d) Brainstorm and propose practical ways to reduce individual and collective plastic consumption. (e) Explore the life cycle of plastic, from disposal to its environmental impact.
4. Each group presents their findings and insights to the rest of the class.
5. Encourage class-wide discussion and feedback on the presented information.
6. Conclude with a collective reflection on the importance of individual and collective actions in mitigating environmental impact.

Activity 2

Steps to Promote Environmental Conservation

Materials required

Pen, Notebook

Procedure

1. Utilize the same groups as in the previous activity.
2. Reflect on your daily routine from the moment you wake up to when you go to sleep. Identify actions you can take during this time to contribute to environmental conservation.
3. Write a note detailing the actions you would take at home or at school to accomplish the following objectives:
   (a) Collecting waste paper and repurposing reusable materials (for crafts, papier-mâché, creating rough books, etc.).
   (b) Advocating for the use of both sides of paper.
   (c) Discouraging unnecessary consumption and casual use of paper, pencils, etc.
   (d) Employing notebooks responsibly and avoiding tearing out pages.
   (e) Discouraging the use of disposable pens and promoting the use of refillable items.
   (f) Creating rough pads using blank sheets from old notebooks.

Activity 3

Promoting Sustainable Practices

Materials Required

Pen, notebook, chart paper, colors, crayons, etc.

Procedure

1. Form groups with four students in each group.
2. Identify and list the various energy and natural resources utilized throughout a typical day, such as transportation fuels, electricity, water, etc.
3. Brainstorm and devise strategies to reduce the consumption of these resources at each step.
4. Create an informative poster on 'Sustainable Living'. Include short notes on the following topics:
   (a) Rainwater Harvesting
   (b) Household Composting
   (c) Rooftop Gardening
   (d) Organic Farming
   (e) Efficient Water Use (e.g., Drip Irrigation)

Encourage students to think holistically about resource conservation and sustainable practices in their daily lives.

Activity 4

Promoting Sustainable Practices

Procedure

1. Form groups of 3–4 people in each group.
2. Within your group, discuss various sustainable practices and their significance in fostering environmental responsibility.
3. Each group selects a spokesperson to present the identified sustainable practices and their impact to the rest of the class.

Activity 5

Promoting Sustainable Practices

Materials required

Pen ,Chart paper, Colors, Crayons, Magazines, Newspapers, Glue

Procedure

1. Maintain the same group as in the previous activity.
2. Create an informative poster highlighting the importance of adopting sustainable practices. Utilize the key points discussed in your previous conversation.
3. Encourage creativity by incorporating visuals from magazines and newspapers. Cut out relevant images and texts to enhance your poster.
4. Emphasize the significance of a sustainable lifestyle, including aspects such as eco-friendly habits, renewable energy, waste reduction, and conservation of natural resources.
5. Each group member should actively participate in the creation of the poster, expressing their individual understanding of the importance of sustainability.
6. Display the completed posters in the classroom or a common area to raise awareness among peers about the significance of a sustainable and green economy.

NCERT FOLDER

Complete Explanations of all NCERT's Questions

A. Multiple Choice Questions

Q.1 What are some of the environmental changes caused due to modern methods of agriculture?

(a) Chemical pollution due to fertilisers
(b) Improvement in the environment
(c) Lower air pollution due to crops
(d) Decrease in forest areas

Q.2 How can we conserve our health and environment? (Choose all the correct options)

(a) Grow organic crops
(b) Use natural fertilisers
(c) Manage waste water
(d) Use more air conditioning

Q.3 A steel factory burns firewood and charcoal for heating and melting the steel? What are the possible effects on the environment? (Choose all the correct options)

(a) Increase in global temperature
(b) Decrease in global temperature
(c) Increase in air pollution
(d) Decrease in air pollution

Q.4 What does conservation of energy mean? (Choose all options that apply)

(a) Saving energy
(b) Producing energy
(c) Using energy efficiently
(d) Creating energy sources

Q.5 Which of the following are non-renewable resources? (Choose all options that apply)

(a) Coal (b) Diesel
(c) Sun (d) Water

Q.6 Which of the following is an example of renewable resources?

(a) Coal (b) Solar energy
(c) CNG (d) Petroleum

Q.7 Which of the following options describe a green economy correctly? A green economy

(a) uses less resources
(b) uses more resources
(c) wastes less items
(d) wastes more items

Answers

1. (a,d) 2. (a,b,c) 3. (a,c) 4. (a,c) 5. (a,b)
6. (b) 7. (a,c)

B. Subjective Type Questions

Q.1 What are the five sources of energy available to us? Give two examples of each source?

Ans. Five sources of energy available to us are

(i) Nuclear fusion, e.g. Solar energy (Sun)
(ii) Gravitational energy, e.g. Gravity generated by Earth and Moon
(iii) Nuclear fission, e.g. Nuclear energy
(iv) Energy in the interior of the Earth, e.g. Geothermal energy
(v) Energy stored in chemical bonds, e.g. coal, petrol

Q.2 What are the sources of pollution?

Ans. Sources of pollution are as follows:

(i) Excessive use of chemicals in agriculture (like fertilisers, insecticides) affect the alkalinity of the soil causing land pollution.
(ii) Dangerous gases like chlorofluorocarbons or CFCs, methane, carbon dioxide from industrial processes causes air pollution.

Q.3 Classify the following under the three respective categories of natural resources : Air, iron, sand, petroleum, wind, clay, fish, forest, gold, pearls

Inexhaustible	Renewable	Non-renewable
...	...	...

Ans.

Inexhaustible	Renewable	Non-renewable
Wind	Fish	Iron
Air	Forest	Petroleum
Sand	Pearls	Gold
Clay		

Q.4 Write any three actions which you can take to conserve energy.

Ans. Three actions that can be taken to conserve energy are as follows:

(a) Switch off lights, fans when not in use.
(b) Use energy efficient bulbs that use less energy.
(c) Travel in a public transport or carpool instead of going alone in a car.

Q.5 Describe any three methods of water conservation.

Ans. Three methods of water conservation are as follows:

(a) Growing vegetation in catchment areas to hold in the soil.

(b) Rainwater harvesting to store rainwater.

(c) Prevention of throwing industrial wastes into sources of water.

Q.6 What is the purpose of soil conservation?

Ans. The purpose of soil conservation is to maintain soil fertility. Soil may loose its fertility due to soil erosion, heavy use of chemicals in agriculture and deforestation. Soil fertility can be maintained by adding manure, rotation of crops and planting trees.

Q.7 State any three ways by which we can save energy.

Ans. The ways to save energy are as follows:

(a) Use pressure cooker to save energy required for cooking.

(b) Using electric items like AC, geyser only when necessary as they use lot of electricity.

(c) Use renewable sources of energy wherever possible like using solar cooker, solar heater etc.

Q.8 What are green skills?

Ans. Refer to text on page no. 99 (Green skills).

Q.9 Give two examples of green skills that you can start learning from now.

Ans. Two examples of green skills that can be learnt:

(a) To reduce use of non-renewable sources of energy and use renewable sources wherever possible, e.g. to study in daytime use more of natural light instead of tubelight.

(b) To segregate household waste for proper waste management, e.g. keeping two separate dustbins for collection of dry and wet waste.

REVIEW EXERCISE

Including Competency Based Questions

Part I

Multiple Choice Questions

1. Which is an example of a natural resource?
(a) Natural gas (b) Copper
(c) Fertile land (d) All of these

2. Which type of resources can be replenished?
(a) Non-renewable resources
(b) Exhaustible resources
(c) Renewable resources
(d) Mineral resources

3. Which is an artificial resource?
(a) Plants (b) Plastics (c) Water (d) Air

4. Biomass and liquified petroleum gas are examples of
(a) Renewable resources (b) Non-renewable resources
(c) Energy resources (d) Inexhaustible resources

5. Which is not an effect of mining?
(a) Extinction of a species
(b) Formation of sinkholes
(c) Loss of biodiversity
(d) Contamination of groundwater

6. Which of the following is not an example of forest resource?
(a) Tannins (b) Horns and hides
(c) Wood (d) Gypsym

7. Fossil fuel emissions cause which of the following?
(a) Air pollution (b) Water pollution
(c) Land pollution (d) Noise pollution

8. Which of the following is a biodegradable pollutant?
(a) Lead (b) Plastic
(c) Cattle dung (d) Insecticide

9. Which is not a naturally occurring green house gas?
(a) Nitrous Oxide (b) Hydrofluorocarbons
(c) Ozone (d) Methane

10. Learning about the environment, mainly focuses on
(a) learning by doing
(b) direct contact with environment
(c) aesthetic appreciation
(d) acquiring knowledge about environment

11. If you are starting to use jute bags instead of plastic bags, then which 'R' you are doing?
(a) Reduce (b) Reuse
(c) Recycle (d) All 3R

12. To reduce wastage of any kind you should first
(a) avoid overuse of paper
(b) segregate waste before throwing
(c) prefer using recycled water
(d) All of the above

13. **Sustainable development goals are also known as**

(a) Green goals (b) Global goals
(c) Energy saving goals (d) Scientific goals

14. **Which of the following is not a component of green economy?**

(a) Organic farming
(b) Intensive agriculture
(c) Biomass and Biogas
(d) Waste management

15. **Which among the following job do not require any green skill?**

(a) Organic farmer
(b) Solar engineer
(c) Graphic designer
(d) Wind mill mechanic

16. **An area in which green skills contribute to sustainable development**

(a) rain water harvesting
(b) automotive manufacturing
(c) building factories
(d) None of the above

17. **Green project 'Swachh Cooperative' is about**

(a) teaching hygenic habits
(b) efficient sewage system
(c) disposal and management of waste
(d) providing energy efficient chulhas

18. **What are the main categories of natural resources?** Competency Based Ques.

I. Exhaustible Resources
II. Renewable Resources
III. Inexhaustible Resources
IV. Non-renewable Resources

(a) Both I and II (b) Both II and III
(c) Only III (d) All of these

19. **Which of the following activities is an example of overexploitation?** Competency Based Ques.

I. Excessive use of chemicals in agriculture
II. Mining for extracting valuable elements
III. Deforestation for non-forest purposes
IV. Separating waste before disposal

(a) Only I (b) Both II and III
(c) Only IV (d) All of these

20. **The government is running a compaign about the use of water and how to save more water by reducing its overuse and misuse and by encouraging the use of recycled water.**

Why is government putting so much importance on water and its conservation? Competency Based Ques.

(a) Water is important for life
(b) Water is an important natural resource
(c) Water is saved to avoid droughts
(d) Water is saved for producing energy

21. **A green economy is defined as low carbon producing, resource efficient and socially inclusive economy. In a green economy, growth in employment and income are driven by public and private investment into such economic activities, infrastructure and assets that allow reduced carbon emissions and pollution, enhanced energy and resource efficiency and prevention of the loss of biodiversity and ecosystem services.**

Which of the following are elements of green economy? Competency Based Ques.

(a) Generation and use of renewable energy
(b) Green jobs' generation
(c) Preservation and sustainable use of natural resources
(d) All of the above

22. **Which method is not mentioned for soil conservation in the given content?** Competency Based Ques.

I. Maintenance of soil fertility
II. Reforestation
III. Terracing
IV. Crop rotation

(a) Only II (b) Both I and IV
(c) Only IV (d) Both III and IV

23. **How can water conservation be achieved according to the given content?** Competency Based Ques.

I. Growing vegetation in catchment areas
II. Constructing dams and reservoirs
III. Treating sewage before releasing clear water into rivers
IV. Allowing unlimited water use in day-to-day life

(a) Both I, II and III (b) Only III
(c) Only IV (d) All of these

24. **What does "sustainable development" aim to achieve, according to the content?** Competency Based Ques.

I. Meeting the needs of the present without compromising the future
II. Maximizing economic growth at the expense of the environment
III. Ignoring the needs of future generations
IV. Exploiting natural resources without consequences

(a) Only I (b) Both I and II
(c) Only III (d) Only II

Answers

1. (d)	**2.** (c)	**3.** (b)	**4.** (c)	**5.** (a)
6. (d)	**7.** (a)	**8.** (c)	**9.** (b)	**10.** (d)
11. (a)	**12.** (d)	**13.** (b)	**14.** (b)	**15.** (c)
16. (a)	**17.** (c)	**18.** (d)	**19.** (b)	**20.** (a,b)
21. (d)	**22.** (c)	**23.** (a)	**24.** (a)	

Statement Based Questions

1. **Statement 1: Society interacts with the environment, and changes it at the same time.**

   Statement 2: Over the years, economic development has led to an increase in environmental pollution.
   (a) Both Statement 1 and Statement 2 are correct
   (b) Both Statement 1 and Statement 2 are incorrect
   (c) Statement 1 is correct but Statement 2 is incorrect
   (d) Statement 2 is correct but Statement 1 is incorrect

2. **Statement 1: Non-renewable resources are those that cannot easily be replaced once they are destroyed.**

   Statement 2: Fossil fuels are an example of non-renewable resources.
   (a) Both Statement 1 and Statement 2 are correct
   (b) Both Statement 1 and Statement 2 are incorrect
   (c) Statement 1 is correct but Statement 2 is incorrect
   (d) Statement 2 is correct but Statement 1 is incorrect

3. **Statement 1: Renewable resources are those that are constantly available or can be reasonably replaced or recovered.**

   Statement 2: Solar energy is an example of an inexhaustible resource.
   (a) Both Statement 1 and Statement 2 are correct
   (b) Both Statement 1 and Statement 2 are incorrect
   (c) Statement 1 is correct but Statement 2 is incorrect
   (d) Statement 2 is correct but Statement 1 is incorrect

4. **Statement 1: Deforestation results in loss of habitat for many plants and animals.**

   Statement 2: Pollution is caused by pollutants, which may be solid, liquid, or gaseous in nature.
   (a) Both Statement 1 and Statement 2 are correct
   (b) Both Statement 1 and Statement 2 are incorrect
   (c) Statement 1 is correct but Statement 2 is incorrect
   (d) Statement 2 is correct but Statement 1 is incorrect

5. **Statement 1: The three R's for saving the environment are Reduce, Reuse, and Recycle.**

   Statement 2: Recycling helps in conserving resources, reducing energy use during manufacture, and reducing pollution levels.
   (a) Both Statement 1 and Statement 2 are correct
   (b) Both Statement 1 and Statement 2 are incorrect
   (c) Statement 1 is correct but Statement 2 is incorrect
   (d) Statement 2 is correct but Statement 1 is incorrect

6. **Statement 1: Sustainable development is defined as development that meets the needs of the present without compromising the ability of future generations.**

   Statement 2: Sustainable agriculture involves using environmentally friendly methods of farming to avoid adverse effects on soil, water, and biodiversity.
   (a) Both Statement 1 and Statement 2 are correct
   (b) Both Statement 1 and Statement 2 are incorrect
   (c) Statement 1 is correct but Statement 2 is incorrect
   (d) Statement 2 is correct but Statement 1 is incorrect

7. **Statement 1: The Sustainable Development Goals (SDGs) were launched at the United Nations Sustainable Development Summit in New York in September 2015.**

   Statement 2: Green growth aims at achieving economic growth that is socially inclusive and environmentally sustainable.
   (a) Both Statement 1 and Statement 2 are correct
   (b) Both Statement 1 and Statement 2 are incorrect
   (c) Statement 1 is correct but Statement 2 is incorrect
   (d) Statement 2 is correct but Statement 1 is incorrect

8. **Statement 1: Conservation is the proper management of a natural resource to prevent its exploitation, destruction, or degradation.**

   Statement 2: Energy conservation refers to adopting various methods to check soil erosion.
   (a) Both Statement 1 and Statement 2 are correct
   (b) Both Statement 1 and Statement 2 are incorrect
   (c) Statement 1 is correct but Statement 2 is incorrect
   (d) Statement 2 is correct but Statement 1 is incorrect

9. **Statement 1: Reforestation involves planting trees and vegetation to reduce soil erosion.**

   Statement 2: Green consumer day is celebrated on 29 June of every year.
   (a) Both Statement 1 and Statement 2 are correct
   (b) Both Statement 1 and Statement 2 are incorrect
   (c) Statement 1 is correct but Statement 2 is incorrect
   (d) Statement 2 is correct but Statement 1 is incorrect

10. **Statement 1: Only economy is a part of society.**

    Statement 2: Constructing dams and reservoirs is essential for the survival of mankind, plants, and animals.
    (a) Both Statement 1 and Statement 2 are correct
    (b) Both Statement 1 and Statement 2 are incorrect
    (c) Statement 1 is correct but Statement 2 is incorrect
    (d) Statement 2 is correct but Statement 1 is incorrect

Answers

1. (a)	**2.** (a)	**3.** (a)	**4.** (a)	**5.** (a)
6. (a)	**7.** (a)	**8.** (c)	**9.** (c)	**10.** (d)

Assertion and Reason Based Questions

1. **Assertion : Conducting a resource audit is a crucial step in conserving natural resources.**

   Reason : A resource audit helps examine resource consumption and plan measures to prevent excessive use, promoting efficient and less wasteful utilization.
   (a) Both Assertion and Reason are true, and Reason is the correct explanation of Assertion.

(b) Both Assertion and Reason are true, but Reason is not the correct explanation of Assertion.
(c) Assertion is true, but Reason is false.
(d) Assertion is false, but Reason is true.

2. Assertion : Soil conservation involves practices such as reforestation and contour ploughing.

Reason : Reforestation and contour ploughing help reduce soil erosion and improve soil fertility.

(a) Both Assertion and Reason are true, and Reason is the correct explanation of Assertion.
(b) Both Assertion and Reason are true, but Reason is not the correct explanation of Assertion.
(c) Assertion is true, but Reason is false.
(d) Assertion is false, but Reason is true.

3. Assertion : Green skills are crucial for the transition from an unsustainable to a green economy.

Reason : Green skills contribute to jobs that protect ecosystems, reduce energy consumption, and minimize waste and pollution.

(a) Both Assertion and Reason are true, and Reason is the correct explanation of Assertion.
(b) Both Assertion and Reason are true, but Reason is not the correct explanation of Assertion.
(c) Assertion is true, but Reason is false.
(d) Assertion is false, but Reason is true.

4. Assertion : Overexploitation of natural resources can lead to the extinction of species and disrupt the ecological cycle.

Reason : When harvesting of resources exceeds their reproduction, it affects the natural populations' ability to recover.

(a) Both Assertion and Reason are true, and Reason is the correct explanation of Assertion.
(b) Both Assertion and Reason are true, but Reason is not the correct explanation of Assertion.
(c) Assertion is true, but Reason is false.
(d) Assertion is false, but Reason is true.

5. Assertion : Natural disasters such as floods and earthquakes are aggravated by human actions in exploiting natural resources.

Reason : Building structures like large dams and buildings can contribute to the impact of natural calamities.

(a) Both Assertion and Reason are true, and Reason is the correct explanation of Assertion.
(b) Both Assertion and Reason are true, but Reason is not the correct explanation of Assertion.
(c) Assertion is true, but Reason is false.
(d) Assertion is false, but Reason is true.

6. Assertion : The three Rs - Reduce, Reuse, and Recycle - are principles of modern waste management.

Reason : Implementing the three Rs helps in conserving resources, reducing energy consumption, and minimizing pollution.

(a) Both Assertion and Reason are true, and Reason is the correct explanation of Assertion.
(b) Both Assertion and Reason are true, but Reason is not the correct explanation of Assertion.
(c) Assertion is true, but Reason is false.
(d) Assertion is false, but Reason is true.

7. Assertion : Pollution caused by human activities, such as industrial emissions and plastic waste, has harmful effects on the environment.

Reason : Pollutants released into the air, water, and soil have detrimental effects on plants, animals, and human beings.

(a) Both Assertion and Reason are true, and Reason is the correct explanation of Assertion.
(b) Both Assertion and Reason are true, but Reason is not the correct explanation of Assertion.
(c) Assertion is true, but Reason is false.
(d) Assertion is false, but Reason is true.

Answers

1. (a)	2. (a)	3. (a)	4. (a)	5. (b)
6. (a)	7. (a)			

Part II

Very Short Answer Type Questions

1. What are the three Rs in waste management, and how do they contribute to environmental conservation?

Ans. Reduce, Reuse, Recycle—these practices minimize waste generation, conserve resources, and reduce environmental impact.

2. What is the greenhouse effect, and how does it contribute to global warming?

Ans. Greenhouse effect traps heat from burning fossil fuels, causing global warming by preventing Earth's heat escape.

3. How do pollutants from human activities contribute to environmental pollution?

Ans. Pollutants, solid, liquid, or gaseous, released by human activities contaminate air, water, and soil, harming the environment.

4. Why is education considered crucial for saving the environment?

Ans. Education empowers people with knowledge and skills to make informed choices, fostering responsible environmental stewardship.

5. What is the primary goal of soil conservation?

Ans. The primary goal of soil conservation is to prevent soil erosion and enhance soil fertility through various methods.

6. How can energy conservation contribute to saving fossil fuels?

Ans. Energy conservation involves efficient use, reducing waste, and can contribute to saving fossil fuels, leading to both environmental and economic benefits.

7. What does sustainable development aim to achieve?

Ans. Sustainable development aims to meet present needs without compromising the ability of future generations, balancing economic growth, environmental care, and social well-being.

8. Why is biodiversity essential for ecosystems?

Ans. Biodiversity is essential for ecological processes, including nutrient cycling, soil formation, air and water purification, and maintaining balance within ecosystems.

9. How is a 'green job' defined?

Ans. A 'green job' contributes to environmental preservation, sustainability, and includes roles in sectors like agriculture, manufacturing, research, and education focused on eco-friendly practices.

Short Answer Type Questions

1. Write three ill-effects of pollution.

Ans. Pollution of land, air and water is not good for the environment. The ill-effects of pollution are as follows:

1. **Land pollution** through contamination of soil may cause various diseases in human like dysentry, cholera, typhoid.
2. **Air pollution** through greenhouse effects causes many changes in climate leading to floods, famines, droughts etc.
3. **Water pollution** through dumping of industrial wastes makes the water unfit for drinking, kills aquatic life and affects tourism adversely.

2. How education can help in saving the environment?

Ans. Education is very important in saving the environment. It helps in three ways:

1. **Learning About the Environment** Education about the environment helps in acquiring knowledge and understanding of the surroundings and related issues.
2. **Learning Through the Environment** It helps in establishing direct contact with the environment through observation, learning by doing, exposure to the environment. This helps in developing the skills for efficient use of resources.
3. **Learning for the Environment** It aims at development of an informed response and responsibility towards the environment. This makes people more aware towards conservation of the environment.

3. What is sustainable development? Mention two strategies of sustainable development.

Ans. Sustainable development is defined as the development that meets the needs of the present without compromising the ability of future generation to meet their own needs. It aims to bring economic growth alongwith care for the environment and social well-being.

Strategies of sustainable development are as follows:

1. Scientific management of renewable resources especially bio-resources.
2. Reducing excessive use of non-renewable resources alongwith reusing and recycling of waste materials.

4. Define Green economy. Explain its two components.

Ans. Green economy is defined as the one that results in improved human well-being and social equity while significantly reducing environmental risks and ecological scarcities.

Two components of green economy are as follows:

1. Using the land resources to meet the requirement of people without causing damage to the environment.
2. Develop sustainable transport system that will cost less, help more people to move quickly and cause less or no damage to the environment.

5. How can green jobs be developed in construction and forestry?

Ans. Green jobs include jobs that help protect the ecosystem and diversity.

In construction the areas in which green jobs can be developed are in planning, design, manufacturing of buildings, lighting appliances etc. Green jobs in this sector are green builders, green design professionals, green workers.

In forestry the areas in which green jobs can be developed are in reforestation, afforestation projects, agroforestry and vertical farming. Green jobs in this sector are of natural scientists.

ASSESSMENT EXERCISE

Multiple Type Questions

1. Natural resource like forest are consumed directly when
   (a) they prevent soil erosion
   (b) they cause rainfall
   (c) they are used for eco-tourism
   (d) they regulate the climate
2. Which of the following is a finite resource?
   (a) Land
   (b) Gold
   (c) Kerosene
   (d) All of these
3. Ecological imbalances are created when there is
   (a) afforestation
   (b) recycling
   (c) green growth
   (d) heat radiation
4. Main source of water pollution is
   (a) rainwater pollutants
   (b) sewage water
   (c) atmospheric pollutants
   (d) melting of snow
5. Which of the following are essential for green economy?
   (a) Conservation of wildlife
   (b) Employment creation
   (c) Energy efficiency
   (d) Both (a) and (c)

Very Short Answer Type Questions

6. What is conservation?
7. How can we conserve soil?
8. Name methods for water conservation.
9. Define the term 'ecosystem'.
10. Explain the term sustainable development.

Short Answer Type Questions

11. Write two actions and two precautions that can be taken for saving the environment.
12. With the help of an example, explain how reduce, reuse and recycle can protect the environment from degradation.
13. Discuss how industrial affluents are the main cause of climate change.
14. Sustainable development and green growth are ways to conserve the environment along with development. Discuss.
15. Protection of the environment has become an important issue today. Suppose you start a new venture as an entrepreneur how will you contribute towards protecting the environment.
16. What are the benefits growth the chief aim to green economy? How does the increased carbon emissions impact the environment?
17. Explain any one example of Green Project.

Allinone®

COMPLETE STUDY | COMPLETE PRACTICE | COMPLETE ASSESSMENT

PART-B

Subject Specific Skills

CHAPTER 01

Introduction to Artificial Intelligence

Artificial Intelligence (AI) is a branch of computer science that's concerned with creating intelligent machines capable of tasks typically requiring human intelligence, like learning, problem-solving, and decision-making. These machines are powered by algorithms that process massive amounts of data to identify patterns and improve their performance over time. AI is already having a huge impact on our world, from self-driving cars to facial recognition software.

1.1 Intelligence

Intelligence in human beings is **the ability to learn from experiences, solve problems, think abstractly, and understand complex concepts.** It involves gathering information from the surrounding world, analyzing it, and using that knowledge to make decisions and adapt to new situations.

Intelligence involves being creative, learning from experiences, reasoning through problems, and being able to communicate effectively with others.

"The aggregate or global capacity of the individual to act purposefully, to think rationally and to deal effectively with his environment." *Psychologist David Wechsler*

1.2 Artificial Intelligence

"Artificial intelligence (AI) is about creating intelligent machines that can learn and perform tasks typically requiring human intelligence. It's not necessarily about replicating human thought, but rather about enabling machines to solve problems, adapt to new situations, and make data-driven decisions. Artificial intelligence (AI) is capable of many different tasks, including speech recognition, game play, and problem solving, frequently without direct human supervision."

Artificial (man made) + Intelligence (Ability to acquire and apply knowledge and skills) = Artificial Intelligence

For example, when you talk to **Siri, Alexa**, or **Google Assistant**, they use AI to grasp your voice commands and offer answers or do tasks. Services like Netflix and YouTube rely on AI to recommend movies or videos you might enjoy, taking into account your previous choices.

1.3 History of AI

Artificial Intelligence is not a new word and not a new technology for researchers. This technology is much older than you would imagine. Following are some milestones in the history of AI which defines the journey from the AI generation to till date development.

- **1943** American researchers Warren McCulloch and Walter Pitts present their model of **artificial neurons, considered the first artificial intelligence.**
- **1950** British mathematician Alan Turing proposes a **test for machine intelligence**. If a machine can fool humans into thinking it is human, then it has intelligence.
- **1956** American computer scientist John McCarthy **coins the term "artificial intelligence"** to describe "the science and engineering of making machines intelligent".

Info Wall

McCarthy presented his definition of artificial intelligence at a conference on the campus of Dartmouth College, USA in the summer of 1956. This conference led to the beginning of research in the field of artificial intelligence. McCarthy also created LISP ("List Processing"), programming language that still continues to be commonly used for several applications of artificial intelligence.

- **1961** General Motors installs the **first industrial robot**, Unimate, to replace humans in assembly tasks.
- **1964** Joseph Wizenbaum develops the **first natural language processing computer program**, ELIZA, which simulates human conversation.
- **1966** Shakey, the first general purpose mobile robot **capable of reasoning about its own actions**, is launched. It is considered the forerunner of autonomous cars.
- **1997** IBM's Deep Blue super computer **beats world chess champion** Garry Kasparov in one game.
- **2002** Roomba, **the first mass produced robotic hoover** sold by iRobot, is launched, capable of roaming and cleaning in the home.
- **2011** IBM's Watson system, capable of answering questions asked in natural language, **wins first prize** in the popular US TV quiz show Jeopardy!
- **2014** The Eugene computer program **passes the Turing Test** by convincing a third of the judges participating in the experiment that it was a human being.
- **2016** DeepMind's AlphaGo programme, based on a deep neural network, **beats Lee Sodol, the world Go champion** in five games.
- **2022** OpenAI launches ChatGPT, an **artificial intelligence chatbot** application trained to hold conversations and answer questions, to the public.

1.4 Types of Artificial Intelligence

Artificial Intelligence can be categorized in different ways. The two important bases on which AI can be categorized are:

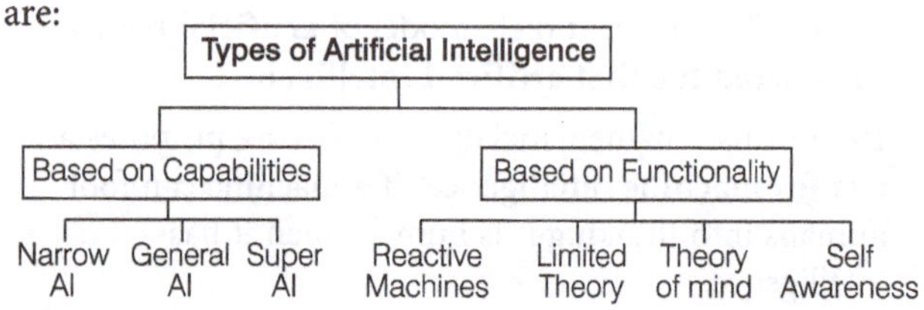

In this chapter, we will discuss about Narrow AI and Strong or General AI.

Based on Capabilities

Artificial intelligence that works with limited functionality and needs some prior information to be fed in order to accomplish a task is called **narrow AI**. One the order hand, any device or machine that is equipped with human-like intelligence is said to be showing **strong AI**.

1. Narrow or Weak AI

Artificial Narrow Intelligence (ANI) refers to AI systems that are designed and trained for a specific task or a narrow range of tasks. These systems excel at performing well-defined tasks within a limited domain but lack the ability to generalize their knowledge or skills beyond that domain.

Example Voice assistants like Siri or Alexa are examples of ANI. They can perform tasks like setting reminders, answering questions, or playing music within their specific domains but cannot perform tasks outside their programmed capabilities.

2. Strong or General AI (AGI - Artificial General Intelligence)

Artificial General Intelligence (AGI) refers to AI systems that possess the ability to understand, learn, and apply knowledge across a wide range of tasks and domains, similar to human intelligence. AGI would have the capacity for flexible adaptation and problem-solving in various contexts.

Example As of now, AGI only exists in theory and research, with no practical implementations. An AGI system would be able to excel in tasks ranging from language understanding and problem-solving to creativity and emotional intelligence, exhibiting human-like cognitive abilities across diverse domains.

Note *There is another form of AI called Artificial Superintelligence which is the highest form of AI using which machines will surpass human intelligence owing to their speed, capability to process astronomical amount of data and self-evolving smarter algorithms. What kind of world would that be with Super AI machines around is hard to predict.*

1.5 Advantages of Artificial Intelligence

Artificial Intelligence (AI) offers numerous advantages across various industries and sectors. Some key advantages include:

1. **Automation** AI can automate repetitive tasks, saving time and effort. For example, in factories, AI-powered robots can assemble products quickly and accurately, reducing human labour.
2. **Efficiency** AI algorithms can process vast amounts of data much faster than humans. This ability enhances efficiency in tasks like data analysis, where AI can quickly identify patterns or anomalies that might be challenging for humans to spot.
3. **Decision Making** AI can assist in decision-making processes by providing insights based on data analysis. For example, in healthcare, AI systems can analyze medical records to suggest potential

treatments or diagnosis, aiding doctors in making informed decisions.

4. **Personalization** AI enables personalized experiences by analyzing user preferences and behaviour. For example, streaming platforms use AI to recommend movies or music based on what users have previously watched or listened to.
5. **24/7 Availability** AI systems can work round the clock without fatigue. For example, chatbots provide customer service at any time, addressing queries and issues even outside of regular business hours.

1.6 Disadvantages of Artificial Intelligence

While Artificial Intelligence (AI) offers numerous benefits, there are several disadvantages and challenges associated with its development and deployment. Some of these disadvantages include:

1. **Job Loss** AI can do some tasks that people used to do. For example, in factories, robots powered by AI might replace some workers who used to assemble things.
2. **Unfair Decisions** Sometimes, AI systems can make decisions that are not fair because they learn from old data that might have biases. Like when a computer program used for hiring prefers one group of people over others without a good reason.
3. **Privacy Problems** AI needs a lot of information to work well, but sometimes, it collects too much personal data. Imagine if a shopping app collected more info about you than you wanted and shared it without your permission.
4. **Ethical Questions** AI might face situations where making the right choice is not easy. For example, imagine a self-driving car that has to decide between hitting one person or another in an accident.
5. **Hard to Understand** Some AI systems work like a mystery. They give answers, but it's tough for people to know how they reached those conclusions.

Try These 1.1

1 What do you understand by the term "AI"?

2 The main aim of artificial intelligence is to make the machine think and act like ______.

3 Distinguish between narrow intelligence and general intelligence.

4 Give three advantages and disadvantages of artificial intelligence.

1.7 Domains of AI

The major Domains of Artificial Intelligence are

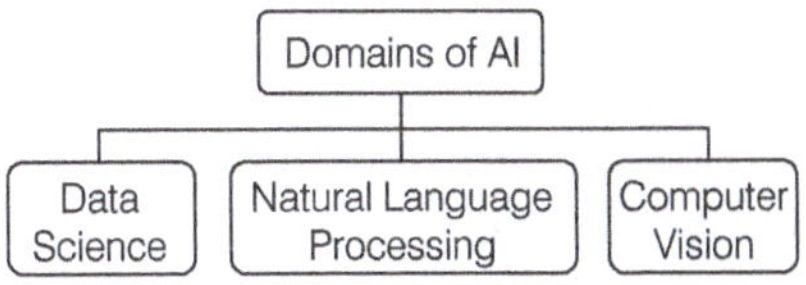

Data (Data Science)

Data is a collection of raw facts which can be processed to make information out of it. Data includes structured data (organized in databases) and unstructured data (like text, images, videos).

Data Science refers to the scientific study of data. It applying scientific methods, statistical techniques, computational tools, and domain expertise to explore, analyze, and extract insights from data.

Data science is related to

- **Data Mining** refers to the process of discovering patterns, trends, and insights from large datasets.
- **Machine Learning (ML)** is a discipline of artificial intelligence (AI) that provides machines with the ability to automatically learn from data and past experiences while identifying patterns to make predictions with minimal human intervention.
- **Big Data** refers to the massive volume of information that is too large and complex for traditional data processing techniques to handle efficiently. Big data is generated from various sources such as social media, sensors, mobile devices, and more.

Computer Vision (CV)

Computer vision is an artificial intelligence domain instructing computers to comprehend and interpret visual data. It involves tasks such as image recognition, object detection, video analysis, and image generation. CV helps AI systems to "see" and comprehends visual data, enabling applications in fields like autonomous vehicles, healthcare diagnostics, and augmented reality.

Natural Language Processing (NLP)

Natural Language Processing (NLP) is a domain of artificial intelligence that deals with the interaction between computers and humans in natural language. It involves the use of computational techniques to process and analyze natural language data, such as text and speech, with the goal of understanding the meaning behind the language.

It has two-sub categories:

- **Natural Language Understanding (NLU)** which involves the ability of computers to comprehend and interpret human language input. NLU also enables computers to communicate back to humans in their own languages (e.g., Siri and Google Assistant understand our speech).
- **Natural Language Generation (NLG)** simply means producing text from computer data. It acts as a translator and converts the computerized data into natural language. In this, a conclusion or text is generated based on collected data and input provided by the user. NLG is used in applications like chatbots, summarization tools, report generation, and content creation.

FacT BOT

The humanoid named Shalu which is developed by a kendriya vidyalya teacher Mr. Dinesh Patel can converse in 47 languages, it is possible through NLP. Modern day chatbots and virtual assistants (such as Siri, Alexa etc.) are based on NLP as their key technology.

1.8 Applications of Artificial Intelligence

1. Healthcare

AI algorithms can analyze medical images like X-rays and MRIs to detect abnormalities faster and more accurately than humans. Chatbots can provide round-the-clock assistance, answering patient queries and offering personalized health advice, thereby enhancing access to healthcare services.

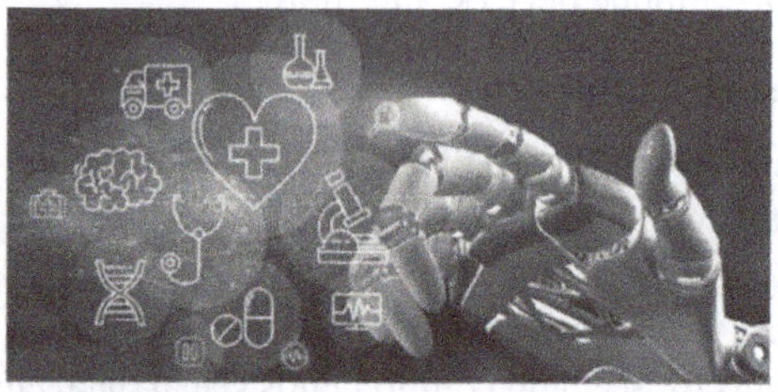

2. Automobiles

Artificial intelligence enhancing safety and efficiency in automobiles industries. AI interprets data in self-driving automobiles, such as Tesla's Autopilot, to ensure safe navigation. AI-powered systems also optimize fuel use and predict maintenance requirements, hence enhancing overall performance.

3. Education

Personalizing learning experiences is a key way artificial intelligence is transforming education. AI-powered tutoring systems like Khan Academy can adjust to students' learning styles and speed, improving comprehension. Language learning programs like Duolingo use AI to provide personalized exercises and targeted feedback, helping users identify and address weaknesses more effectively.

4. Digital Voice Assistants

AI is the brains behind smart assistants like Siri, Alexa, and Google Assistant. These virtual assistants understand our voice commands, allowing us to set reminders, play music, control smart home devices, and even get answers to our questions.

5. Facial Recognition

One of the most notable applications of AI in daily life is facial recognition. It replaces pin codes and fingerprints on cellphones to enable quick unlocking. Various algorithms that can identify a person's face with remarkable precision, social networking sites like Facebook use facial recognition to automatically recommend tagging friends in photos you submit. Airports are also using this technology to speed up boarding by using facial recognition to confirm identity, which makes travel easier.

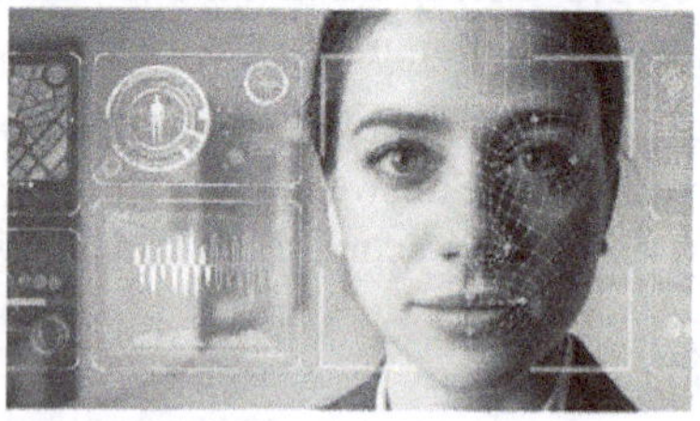

6. Humanoid Robots

Humanoid robots are finding uses in a surprising number of fields, from dangerous industrial tasks to providing companionship for people. Here are a few areas where you might encounter them:

- **Manufacturing** Humanoid robots can be used on assembly lines to perform delicate tasks or handle heavy materials. For instance, they can weld car parts or carefully assemble electronics with greater precision and tireless endurance than humans.
- **Space Exploration** Since they can mimic human movements, humanoid robots are being developed to assist astronauts in space. NASA's Robonaut 2 was one of the first humanoid robots to be sent to the International Space Station. These robots can help with routine tasks or even perform dangerous repairs outside the spacecraft.
- **Healthcare** Humanoid robots are being studied for use in physical therapy and rehabilitation. They can be used to guide patients through exercises or provide companionship and emotional support. For example, a robot named Pepper has been used to help reduce social isolation among elderly patients.
- **Research** Humanoid robots are valuable tools for researchers in a variety of fields. Studying how to build robots that move and interact like humans can lead to a better understanding of human biology and movement. This knowledge can then be used to create new prosthetics or improve surgical techniques.

Sophia is a humanoid robot developed by Hanson Robotics that is known for its realistic appearance and ability to simulate human conversation. She is the world's first robot citizen. While Sophia isn't currently being used in a commercial setting, it's a good example of the potential for humanoid robots to interact with people in a natural way. In the future, robots like Sophia could be used for education, entertainment, or even as companions for people who live alone.

1.9 Future Goals of Artificial Intelligence

The future of AI holds immense potential to reshape various aspects of human life and society. Here are some key points:

1. **Automation** AI will continue to automate routine tasks across industries, improving efficiency and productivity. This will lead to significant changes in the workforce, with a shift towards more skilled and creative roles.
2. **Personalization** AI algorithms will enable highly personalized experiences in areas such as marketing, healthcare, education, and entertainment. Products and services will be tailored to individual preferences and needs, enhancing user satisfaction.
3. **Healthcare** AI-powered tools will revolutionize healthcare by enabling early disease detection, personalized treatment plans, and improved patient outcomes. AI algorithms will analyze vast amounts of medical data to identify patterns and insights that can inform diagnosis and treatment decisions.
4. **Autonomous Systems** AI will drive the development of autonomous vehicles, drones, and robots that can perform tasks independently. These systems will revolutionize transportation, logistics, and manufacturing, leading to safer and more efficient operations.
5. **Ethical and Social Implications** As AI becomes more pervasive, ethical considerations surrounding data privacy, bias, transparency, and accountability will become increasingly important. Society will need to address these challenges to ensure that AI technologies benefit everyone equitably.
6. **Collaboration** Humans and AI will collaborate more closely in various domains, augmenting each other's capabilities. This human-AI partnership will lead to innovative solutions to complex problems and drive progress in science, engineering, and creative endeavors.

Try These 1.2

1. **Using computer vision, face recognition on phones is possible. (True/False)**
2. **What are some of the different fields where artificial intelligence is used?**
3. **What is the goal of AI in the future?**

Glossary

Artificial Intelligence (AI) It is the field of computer science concerned with creating intelligent machines that can perform tasks typically requiring human intelligence.

Artificial Narrow Intelligence (ANI) It refers to AI systems that are designed and trained for a specific task or a narrow range of tasks.

Artificial General Intelligence (AGI) It refers to AI systems that possess the ability to understand, learn, and apply knowledge across a wide range of tasks and domains, similar to human intelligence.

Data Science It refers to the scientific study of data.

Computer Vision It is an artificial intelligence domain instructing computers to comprehend and interpret visual data.

Natural Language Processing (NLP) It is a domain of artificial intelligence that deals with the interaction between computers and humans in natural language.

Let's Investigate

Game 1

It is a game of hand movements and it based on Data. Rules are:

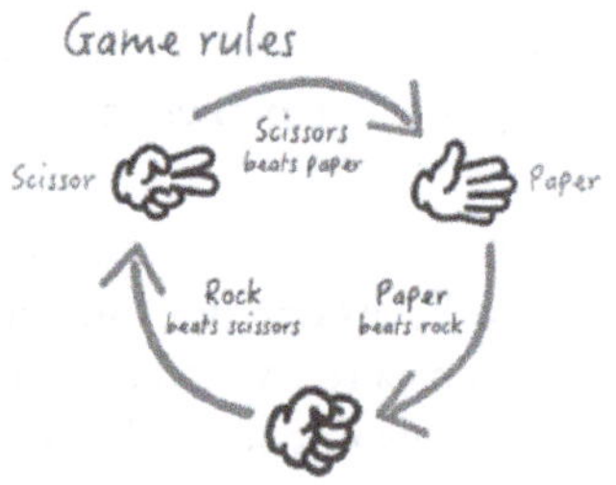

1. Requires two or more players.
2. Each player simultaneously forms one of the three shapes with an outstretched hand. These shapes have meanings as following:
   (a) Flat hand → Paper
   (b) Closed fist → Rock
   (c) A fist with index finger and middle finger like V → Scissors
3. This game has only two results: i. Draw or ii. Win
4. A player who decides to play a rock wins over the one who shows scissors (rock crushes scissors) but lose to one who plays a paper (Paper covers a rock). Scissors win over a paper (as Scissors cut paper). If both player shows same shape, the game is draw.
5. The players usually count 1,2,3 or speak Rock, Paper, Scissors and swing it in front of another.

Game 2

Semantris is a word association game created by Google AI that uses machine learning to understand how words relate to each other. This game is based on Natural Language Processing.

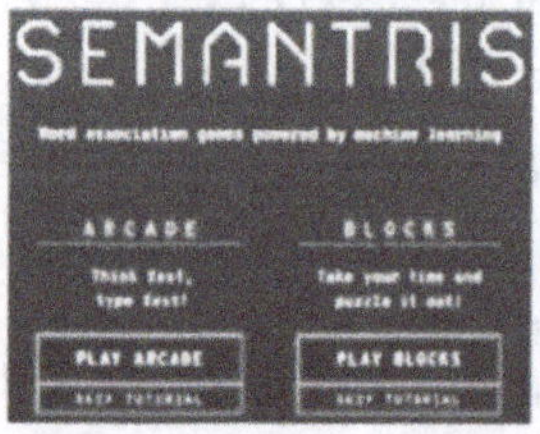

How to play:

1. Visit the website: https://experiments.withgoogle.com/semantris
2. Click on "Launch Experiment" to start the game.
3. Choose "Play Arcade" to begin.
4. The AI will give you a highlighted clue word.
5. Type in the word you think is most closely associated with the clue.

   The closer your word is to the AI's understanding, the higher your score.
6. See how well the machine understands your word choices!

This is a fun way to test your vocabulary and explore how machines learn about language. Enjoy the game!

Game 3

Quick, Draw! is a game developed by Google that utilizes Computer Vision and a neural network to engage players in a fun and interactive drawing challenge.

The objective of the game is for players to draw a given object or idea within a limited amount of time, usually 20 seconds.

To play game (Quick, Draw), follow these steps:

1. Open your web browser and go to https://quickdraw.withgoogle.com/.
2. Click on the "Let's Draw" button to start the game.
3. Click on the "Got it!" button to begin.
4. An item will be named on the screen for you to draw within 20 seconds.
5. Draw the named item on the white screen using your mouse or touchscreen.
6. The AI will guess what you are drawing as you draw.
7. Try to draw 6 objects correctly in a row to win the game!

NCERT FOLDER

Complete Explanations of all NCERT's Questions

A. Multiple Choice Questions

Q.1 Which one of the following is an application of AI?

(a) Remote controlled Drone
(b) Self-Driving Car
(c) Self-Service Kiosk
(d) Self-Watering Plant System

Q.2 This language is easy to learn and is one of the most popular languages for AI today

(a) C++ (b) Python
(c) Ruby (d) Java

Q.3 This field is enabling computers to identify and process images as humans do:

(a) Face Recognition (b) Model-view-controller
(c) Computer Vision (d) Eye-in-Hand System

Q.4 NLP stands for

(a) Neutral Learning Projection
(b) Neuro-Linguistic Programming
(c) Natural Language Processing
(d) Neural Logic Presentation

Q.5 Which of the following is not a domain of artificial intelligence?

(a) Data Management System
(b) Computer Vision
(c) Natural Language Processing
(d) Data Science

Q.6 How excited are you about this AI curriculum?

(a) Very Excited! (b) A bit excited
(c) Same as always (d) Not excited at all

Answers

1. (b) **2.** (b) **3.** (c) **4.** (c) **5.** (a) **6.** (a)

B. Subjective Type Questions

Q.1 How can AI be used as a tool to transform the world into a better place?

Ans. AI can be used as a tool to transform the world into a better place through:

- **Environment** AI can analyze data to predict weather patterns, optimize resource usage, and combat climate change.
- **Healthcare** AI can assist in medical diagnosis, personalize treatment plans, and accelerate drug discovery.
- **Education** AI tutors can provide personalized learning experiences and identify skill gaps for students.
- **Security** AI can analyze threats and patterns to improve cybersecurity and disaster prediction.
- **Efficiency** AI can automate tasks, optimize processes, and reduce waste across industries.

Q.2 Can you list down a few applications in your smartphone that widely make use of computer vision?

Ans. **Google Photos** For image recognition and search.

Face ID (iPhone) For facial recognition and security.

Snapchat For facial filters and augmented reality effects.

CamScanner For document scanning and text recognition.

Google Lens For identifying objects, text, and landmarks.

Q.3 Draw out the difference between the three domains of AI with respect to the types of data they use.

Ans. The three domains of AI differ in the types of data they use:

1. **Natural Language Processing (NLP)**
   - Uses text and speech data.
   - **Examples** documents, emails, conversations, and social media posts.
2. **Computer Vision (CV)**
   - Uses image and video data.
   - **Examples** photographs, video footage, and medical imaging.
3. **Data for AI**
   - Uses structured and unstructured data.
   - **Examples** databases, spreadsheets, sensor data, and logs.

Each domain processes different data types to derive insights and perform tasks specific to their applications.

Q.4 Identify the features and the domain of AI used in them:

(a)

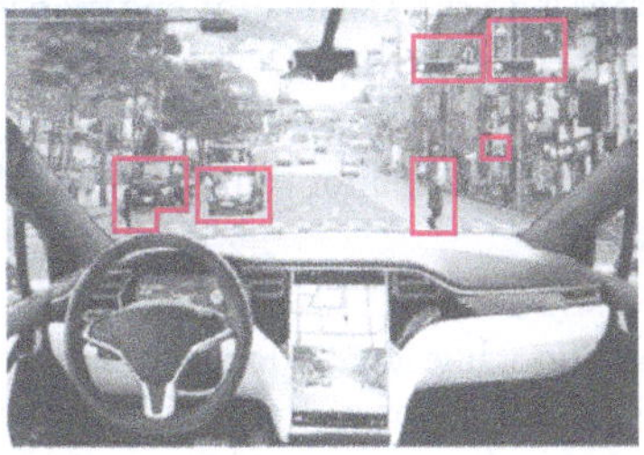

(b)

(c)

Ans. (a) **Domain** Computer Vision

Features This scenario uses computer vision techniques like object detection and image recognition. The AI identifies objects in the image (car, steering wheel, outside, line, person) and their positions.

(b) **Domain** Machine Learning, a subfield of Data Science.

Features This scenario might involve a machine learning model trained on a dataset of user interactions to predict which websites you'd likely want to open. A machine learning model, likely trained on user interaction data, would predict the websites you'd be interested in opening. This data could include browsing history, search queries, clicks, and time spent on specific websites.

(c) **Domain** Natural Language Processing (NLP)

Features This scenario employs speech recognition, a subfield of NLP. The AI converts the audio of the person speaking into text by identifying and understanding the spoken words

Q.5 Separate the following areas based on the kinds of domains widely used in them:

(a) Crop productivity
(b) Traffic regulation
(c) Maps and navigation
(d) Text editors and autocorrect
(e) Identifying and predicting disease

Ans. These areas based on the three domains of AI: Natural Language Processing (NLP), Computer Vision (CV), and Data for AI.

(a) **Crop Productivity** Data for AI (utilizing data such as weather patterns, soil quality, and crop yield data to optimize productivity)

(b) **Traffic Regulation** Computer Vision (using cameras and sensors to monitor traffic flow and detect violations)

(c) **Maps and Navigation** Computer Vision (for image recognition, like identifying landmarks or reading road signs) and Data for AI (for processing large amounts of geographic data and optimizing routes)

(d) **Text Editors and Autocorrect** Natural Language Processing (NLP) (for understanding and processing written text, suggesting corrections, and predicting next words)

(e) **Identifying and Predicting Disease** Data for AI (for analyzing medical data such as patient records, lab results, and imaging scans to identify patterns indicative of disease) and possibly NLP (for analyzing medical literature and reports).

Q.6 After the pandemic, it's been essential for everyone to wear a mask. However, you see many people not wearing masks when in public places. Which domain of AI can be used to build a system to detect people not wearing masks?

Ans. Computer Vision would be the domain of AI that can be used to build a system to detect people not wearing masks. Computer vision involves teaching computers to interpret and understand the visual world, including images and videos. By using techniques such as object detection and image classification, AI models can be trained to recognize whether individuals in public places are wearing masks or not. This can help enforce mask-wearing policies and promote public health during and after the pandemic.

Q.7 Search for an online game that recognizes the image drawn by you. Write down the observations including the AI domain used by it.

Ans. One popular online game that fits this description is "Quick, Draw!" by Google. In this game, players are given a prompt and have to quickly draw the object or concept described. The game then uses AI to guess what the player is drawing in real-time. Let's analyze it based on the three domains:

1. **Natural Language Processing (NLP)** The game uses NLP to interpret the prompts given to the players, as well as any text inputs provided by the players themselves.
2. **Computer Vision** Computer vision is at the core of the game's functionality. It analyzes the drawings made by players in real-time, recognizing patterns and shapes to guess what the player is attempting to draw.
3. **Data for AI** The game collects data on the drawings made by players, including both the images themselves and any associated metadata, such as the prompt given to the player. This data is used to train and improve the game's AI over time, enabling it to make more accurate guesses.

Overall, "Quick, Draw!" is an excellent example of an online game that utilizes AI across all three domains: NLP, computer vision, and data for AI.

REVIEW EXERCISE

Including Competency Based Questions

Part I

Multiple Choice Questions

1. Which of the following intelligence types have been implemented through Artificial Intelligence?
(a) Ability to use language for conversing
(b) Ability to recognise objects
(c) Ability to learn from experience
(d) All of the above

2. When was the term "Artificial Intelligence" first coined?
(a) 1956 (b) 1965 (c) 1970 (d) 1980

3. Who is considered the "Father of Artificial Intelligence"?
(a) John McCarthy (b) Alan Turing
(c) Marvin Minsky (d) Herbert Simon

4. Which domain of AI involves teaching computers to learn from data?
(a) Machine Learning (b) Natural Language Processing
(c) Robotics (d) Computer Vision

5. World's first robot citizen is
(a) Sophia (b) Lily (c) Eliza (d) Tay

6. Which AI domain focuses on enabling machines to comprehend, interpret, and generate human language?
(a) Machine Learning (b) Natural Language Processing
(c) Robotics (d) Expert System

7. What was the reality game show in which IBM Watson beat the existing champions?
(a) The Price of Right
(b) Jeopardy!
(c) Who Wants to Be a Millionaire?
(d) Wheel of Fortune

8. Which is an advantage of AI in healthcare?
(a) Reduced human errors in diagnostics
(b) High cost of implementation
(c) Limited access to healthcare facilities
(d) Increased doctor-patient interaction time

9. What is a potential disadvantage of AI in employment?
(a) Increased productivity
(b) Job displacement due to automation
(c) Enhanced workplace safety
(d) Equal job opportunities for all

10. Which AI application assists in optimizing logistics and supply chain operations?
(a) Healthcare (b) Agriculture
(c) Retail (d) Transportation

11. Mr. Dinesh Patel, a computer science teacher at kendriya vidyalya, has developed an educational humanoid namely Shalu, which can converse in 47 languages. Which AI technology helps Shalu, the robot, converse with us humans? **Competency Based Ques.**
(a) NLP (b) CV
(c) ML (d) Data Science

12. Which sector uses AI for weather forecasting and climate modeling?
(a) Environmental Sciences (b) Manufacturing
(c) Aerospace (d) Retail

13. Lavanaya is an environmental scientist developing an AI-powered system to predict weather patterns. At the initial stages, the system's forecasts were inconsistent and often inaccurate. As it processed more historical weather data and incorporated real-time information, its predictive accuracy significantly increased. Which technology primarily contributed to this improvement? **Competency Based Ques.**
(a) Natural Language Processing (NLP)
(b) Computer Vision
(c) Machine Learning (ML)
(d) All of the above

14. Which industry applies AI for enhancing customer service through automated responses?
(a) Hospitality (b) Construction
(c) Mining (d) Telecommunications

15. Heena is a passionate chef who recently started experimenting with a smart cooking assistant. Initially, her assistant struggled to suggest accurate ingredient substitutions when certain items were unavailable. However, after a few months of continuous usage and updates, the assistant began offering more precise and fitting alternatives for ingredients. What type of technology(ies) likely contributed to the improvement in the assistant's ability to suggest better ingredient substitutions over time? **Competency Based Ques.**

(a) Natural Language Processing (NLP)
(b) Machine Learning (ML)
(c) Data Analytics
(d) All of the above

16. **You're a customer service manager for a growing tech startup. With an influx of inquiries, your team struggles to handle the volume efficiently. Clients often face delays in receiving support, impacting customer satisfaction.**

To streamline customer support and enhance responsiveness, which AI tool should you integrate into your system? **Competency Based Ques.**

(a) Robotics
(b) Chatbots
(c) Natural Language Processing
(d) Computer Vision

17. **Which AI application focuses on understanding and generating human-like speech by machines?**

(a) Machine Translation
(b) Natural Language Processing
(c) Chatbots
(d) Speech Recognition

18. **Which industry uses AI for predictive maintenance of machinery and equipment?**

(a) Healthcare
(b) Agriculture
(c) Manufacturing
(d) Retail

19. **As a researcher, you're exploring innovative approaches to expedite the discovery of new medications for cancer treatment.**

To enhance drug discovery and development for cancer treatment, which field of AI algorithms would you use to analyze vast datasets and identify potential therapeutic compounds? **Competency Based Ques.**

(a) Healthcare
(b) Education
(c) Entertainment
(d) Aerospace

20. **Which AI application involves the simulation of intelligent behaviour in robots to perform tasks?**

(a) Natural Language Processing
(b) Robotics
(c) Computer Vision
(d) Machine Learning

21. **Which industry extensively uses AI for personalized recommendations and content curation?**

(a) Healthcare
(b) E-commerce
(c) Agriculture
(d) Manufacturing

22. **Which AI application focuses on training machines to understand and interpret visual data?**

(a) Machine Translation
(b) Natural Language Processing
(c) Computer Vision
(d) Speech Recognition

23. **Priya designed a sentiment analysis system for social media posts. Initially, the system had difficulty distinguishing between subtle emotions like sarcasm and irony. However, with continuous exposure to diverse text inputs, its accuracy in detecting nuanced sentiments notably improved.**

Which technology significantly contributed to this enhancement? **Competency Based Ques.**

(a) Natural Language Processing (NLP)
(b) Computer Vision
(c) Machine Learning (ML)
(d) All of the above

24. **Kriti created a facial recognition software that initially had difficulty recognizing faces in low-light conditions. As it processed more diverse images and lighting scenarios, its accuracy under challenging lighting environments notably increased. Which technology primarily contributed to this enhancement?** **Competency Based Ques.**

(a) Natural Language Processing (NLP)
(b) Computer Vision
(c) Machine Learning (ML)
(d) All of the above

Answers

1. (d)	2. (a)	3. (a)	4. (a)	5. (a)
6. (b)	7. (b)	8. (a)	9. (b)	10. (d)
11. (a)	12. (a)	13. (c)	14. (d)	15. (d)
16. (b)	17. (d)	18. (c)	19. (a)	20. (b)
21. (b)	22. (c)	23. (a)	24. (b)	

Statement Based Questions

1. **Statement 1 Narrow AI, also known as Weak AI, is designed to perform a specific task or solve a narrow problem.**

Statement 2 Narrow AI and General AI are terms used interchangeably to describe AI systems that can perform any intellectual task a human can.

(a) Both Statement 1 and Statement 2 are correct.
(b) Both Statement 1 and Statement 2 are incorrect.
(c) Statement 1 is correct but Statement 2 is incorrect.
(d) Statement 1 is incorrect but Statement 2 is correct.

2. **Statement 1 AI finds applications in domains like healthcare, finance, entertainment, and agriculture.**

Statement 2 AI is limited to only two domains - technology and robotics - and doesn't extend its applications beyond these areas.

(a) Both Statement 1 and Statement 2 are correct.
(b) Both Statement 1 and Statement 2 are incorrect.
(c) Statement 1 is correct but Statement 2 is incorrect.
(d) Statement 1 is incorrect but Statement 2 is correct.

3. Statement 1 Narrow AI focuses on performing specific tasks and is what we predominantly see in use today.

Statement 2 General AI possesses human-like intelligence and capabilities across various tasks.

(a) Both Statement 1 and Statement 2 are correct.
(b) Both Statement 1 and Statement 2 are incorrect.
(c) Statement 1 is correct but Statement 2 is incorrect.
(d) Statement 1 is incorrect but Statement 2 is correct.

4. Statement 1 Machine Learning is a subset of AI that focuses on algorithms and statistical models enabling systems to perform tasks without explicit instructions.

Statement 2 Natural Language Processing (NLP) is not considered a domain of Artificial Intelligence.

(a) Both Statement 1 and Statement 2 are correct.
(b) Both Statement 1 and Statement 2 are incorrect.
(c) Statement 1 is correct but Statement 2 is incorrect.
(d) Statement 1 is incorrect but Statement 2 is correct.

5. Statement 1 AI finds applications in autonomous vehicles, healthcare diagnostics, and personalized recommendations in various industries.

Statement 2 AI has limited real-world applications, mainly confined to the tech industry.

(a) Both Statement 1 and Statement 2 are correct.
(b) Both Statement 1 and Statement 2 are incorrect.
(c) Statement 1 is correct but Statement 2 is incorrect.
(d) Statement 1 is incorrect but Statement 2 is correct.

Answers

1. (c) **2.** (c) **3.** (a) **4.** (c) **5.** (c)

Assertion & Reason Based Questions

1. Assertion Computer Vision is not a domain of AI that enables machines to interpret visual information from the real world.

Reason It uses algorithms to process, analyze, and understand visual data from images or videos.

(a) Both Assertion and Reason are true and Reason is the correct explanation of Assertion.
(b) Both Assertion and Reason are true and Reason is not the correct explanation of Assertion.
(c) Assertion is true but Reason is false.
(d) Assertion is false but Reason is true.

2. Assertion AI has widespread applications across diverse fields.

Reason AI applications span industries like healthcare, finance, automotive, and entertainment, among others.

(a) Both Assertion and Reason are true and Reason is the correct explanation of Assertion.
(b) Both Assertion and Reason are true and Reason is not the correct explanation of Assertion.
(c) Assertion is true but Reason is false.
(d) Assertion is false but Reason is true.

3. Assertion AI helps in predicting future events based on past data.

Reason AI uses predictive analysis by analyzing historical information to forecast trends.

(a) Both Assertion and Reason are true and Reason is the correct explanation of Assertion.
(b) Both Assertion and Reason are true and Reason is the not correct explanation of Assertion.
(c) Assertion is true but Reason is false.
(d) Assertion is false but Reason is true.

4. Assertion AI is crucial in healthcare for early disease diagnosis.

Reason AI can process vast amounts of medical data and identify patterns that humans might miss.

(a) Both Assertion and Reason are true and Reason is the correct explanation of Assertion.
(b) Both Assertion and Reason are true and Reason is the not correct explanation of Assertion.
(c) Assertion is true but Reason is false.
(d) Assertion is false but Reason is true.

Answers

1. (d) **2.** (a) **3.** (a) **4.** (a)

Part II

Very Short Answer Type Questions

1. Who defined intelligence as "the global capacity to act purposefully, think rationally, and deal effectively with the environment"?

Ans. Psychologist David Wechsler.

2. What is Artificial Intelligence (AI)?

Ans. The field of computer science concerned with creating intelligent machines that can perform tasks requiring human intelligence.

3. Who coined the term Artificial Intelligence?

Ans. John McCarthy.

4. Which AI program beat the world chess champion Gary Kasparov in 1997?

Ans. Deep Blue developed by IBM.

5. What is Artificial Narrow Intelligence (ANI)?

Ans. AI systems designed for specific tasks, excelling within a limited domain but unable to generalize beyond it.

6. What is an example of Artificial General Intelligence (AGI)?

Ans. AGI currently exists only in theory and research, with no practical implementations.

7. What advantage does AI provide in healthcare?

Ans. AI can analyze medical images to detect abnormalities faster and more accurately than humans.

8. Which technology of AI used in FaceBook's DeepFace.

Ans. Computer Vision AI

Short Answer Type Questions

1. What is the difference between NLU and NLG?

Ans. NLU (Natural Language Understanding) involves comprehension of human language, while NLG (Natural Language Generation) focuses on creating human-like text or speech.

2. Define machine learning.

Ans. Machine learning is a branch of AI where algorithms learn from data, identifying patterns to make predictions or decisions without explicit programming.

3. What are the three domains of AI?

Ans. The three domains of AI are Narrow/Weak AI (focused on specific tasks), General AI (human-level intelligence), and Super intelligent AI (beyond human intelligence).

4. What do you understand by natural language processing?

Ans. Natural Language Processing (NLP) is an AI field enabling machines to understand, interpret, and generate human language, enabling communication between computers and humans.

5. Explain chatbots in brief.

Ans. Chatbots are AI-based programs designed to simulate human conversation, interacting with users *via* text or speech, offering information, support, or performing tasks autonomously.

6. Why training with information/data is important in Artificial Intelligent devices?

Ans. AI devices learn from information/data just like students learn from textbooks. This data teaches them how to perform tasks, recognize patterns, and make decisions. Without it, they wouldn't be intelligent - just like a student with a blank textbook! The quality of the data also matters - "garbage in, garbage out" applies to AI too.

Long Answer Type Questions

1. How does AI enhance and advance our homes?

Ans. AI has become a game-changer for our homes, making them smarter and more convenient. One way it helps is through smart assistants like Alexa or Google Home. These devices can control various things like lights, thermostats, and even appliances with just your voice commands, making tasks easier.

Another cool thing is AI-powered security systems. They use smart cameras and sensors to detect unusual activities and can alert you instantly through your phone, ensuring your home stays safe.

AI also boosts energy efficiency. Smart thermostats learn your preferences and adjust temperatures accordingly, saving energy and money. They can even anticipate when you're home or away.

Moreover, AI has entered our kitchen appliances, making cooking simpler. Smart ovens can suggest recipes, adjust cooking settings, and notify you when your meal is ready.

Lastly, AI enhances entertainment at home. Streaming platforms use AI to recommend shows and movies based on your preferences, giving you a personalized experience.

2. Explain how AI works in the following areas (any two):

(a) Google Search Engine

(b) Voice Assistants

(c) E-commerce websites

Ans. (a) **Google Search Engine** With the help of AI, Google Search Engine has been turned into intelligent search which is a new network of systems that produces direct answers. It uses voice and image searches and has incorporated deep learning to fasten the searches with more accuracy.

(b) **Voice assistant** AI is being used in voice assistants to recognize words spoken by the user. NLP has capabilities like "Speech-to-Text" convert the natural language of the user into text for further processing. As the digital assistant answers more and more queries, it "learns" using ML algorithms. The more tasks it performs, its ML algorithms help it "learn" from the tasks and the preferences of the user. As a result, the digital assistant improves its performance over time.

(c) **E-commerce website** With the use of big data, AI in E-Commerce is impacting customer choices by recording the data of previous purchases, searched products, and online browsing habits. Product recommendations provide multiple benefits for E-commerce retailers including: Higher number of returning customers.

3. How does Netflix recommend movies that match Rahul's interests? Explain the technology involved and provide some examples of other applications of this technology.

Ans. Netflix uses a recommendation system powered by artificial intelligence (AI) algorithms. When you watch a movie, the system analyzes various aspects such as genre, actors, directors, and your viewing history. Based on this data, it generates recommendations for similar content that you might enjoy. This process involves techniques like collaborative filtering, content-based filtering, and machine learning to personalize suggestions.

Similar technology is used by other platforms like Spotify for music recommendations, Amazon for product suggestions, and YouTube for video recommendations. These systems enhance user experience by providing relevant content tailored to individual preferences, increasing engagement and satisfaction.

4. Akash wants to understand why people think Artificial Intelligence is beneficial. Can you explain some of the advantages of AI, especially in areas like healthcare, transportation, and education? Competency Based Ques.

Ans. AI has many advantages, especially in fields like:

Healthcare AI can help doctors diagnose diseases more accurately and even assist in surgery with precision.

Transportation It can improve safety by helping in the development of self-driving cars and optimizing traffic flow.

Education AI can personalize learning experiences for students, providing tailored lessons and feedback to help them learn more effectively.

5. Raju is curious about the different domains of Artificial Intelligence and how they impact our daily lives. Could you explain the three main domains of AI and provide examples of how each domain is used in practical applications? Competency Based Ques.

Ans. Artificial Intelligence encompasses three main domains:

Data Science involves the analysis of large datasets to extract meaningful insights and make predictions. For example, recommendation systems like those used by streaming services such as Netflix or music platforms like Spotify rely on data science algorithms to suggest content based on users' preferences.

Computer Vision focuses on enabling machines to interpret and understand visual information from images and videos. Applications of computer vision include facial recognition technology used in smartphones for unlocking devices and image recognition systems employed in autonomous vehicles for identifying objects on the road.

Natural Language Processing (NLP) deals with enabling machines to understand and interpret human language. Virtual assistants like Siri and Alexa utilize NLP algorithms to understand voice commands and respond to user queries.

6. Arjun is curious about the disadvantages of Artificial Intelligence (AI). Can you explain to him in simple terms, considering his class 9th level of understanding? Competency Based Ques.

Ans. The disadvantages of Artificial Intelligence (AI) explained in simple terms:

1. **Job Losses** One big concern is that AI can take over jobs that humans do. For example, robots or computer programs can do some tasks faster and more accurately than people. This means some jobs, like driving trucks or answering customer service calls, might be done by AI, causing people to lose their jobs.
2. **Lack of Creativity** AI is good at processing data and following instructions, but it isn't creative like humans. AI can help design things or suggest ideas, but it can't come up with new and innovative concepts on its own.
3. **Ethical Issues** There are many ethical concerns with AI, like how it should be used and who controls it. For instance, using AI in surveillance might invade people's privacy. Also, if AI is used in making decisions like hiring for jobs, it needs to be fair and not biased.
4. **Security Risks** AI systems can be hacked or misused. If a malicious person takes control of an AI system, they could use it to cause harm, like spreading false information or even causing physical damage through robots.
5. **Lack of Understanding** Sometimes, AI systems can make decisions or take actions that humans don't understand because of the complex algorithms they use. This can be problematic if we can't explain why the AI did something, especially in critical areas like healthcare

ASSESSMENT EXERCISE

Multiple Choice Questions

1. Which AI program defeated the world chess champion, Gary Kasparov, in a highly-publicized match?
   (a) Deep Blue (b) Watson
   (c) Kismet (d) ELIZA
2. Which AI-driven technology aims to simulate human-like conversation?
   (a) Machine Learning (ML) (b) Robotics
   (c) Virtual Reality (VR) (d) Chatbots
3. Which of the following is an application of AI used to process and understand human languages?
   (a) Predictive Analytics (b) Autonomous Vehicles
   (c) Natural Language Processing (NLP) (d) Facial Recognition
4. What type of AI is designed to perform a specific task or solve a specific problem?
   (a) Artificial Narrow Intelligence (ANI)
   (b) Artificial General Intelligence (AGI)
   (c) Artificial Superintelligence (ASI)
   (d) Artificial Consciousness Intelligence (ACI)

Very Short Answer Type Questions

5. What do you understand by Humanoid Robots?
6. Write the Full form of NLU.
7. Name any two virtual voice assistants.

Short Answer Type Questions

8. What are three domain of AI?
9. Define Computer Vision (CV).
10. What potential risks are associated with our data being used for facial recognition purposes?

Long Answer Type Questions

11. How can Natural Language Processing be applied in evaluating subjective assessments in schools?
12. What are the major future goals of Artificial Intelligence?
13. What advantages come from using an AI system?

CHAPTER 02

AI Project Cycle

The AI project cycle is a step-by-step process for developing and deploying artificial intelligence solutions. It's like a roadmap that guides you through defining the problem you want to solve, collecting and analyzing data, building the AI model, and checking how well it works. By following this cycle, you can ensure your AI project is efficient, effective, and tackles the right problem from the start.

2.1 Project

A project is a series of tasks that need to be completed to reach a specific outcome. A project can also be defined as a set of inputs and outputs required to achieve a particular goal. Projects can range from simple to complex and can be managed by one person or a hundred.

Project Life Cycle

A project life cycle is a series of phases that a project goes through from initiation to completion. These phases typically include initiation, planning, execution, monitoring and controlling, and closure. Each phase has specific tasks, deliverables, and goals aimed at achieving project objectives.

2.2 AI Project Cycle

The AI project cycle is a step-by-step process that uses scientific methods to solve problems and draw conclusions. The AI project cycle is a structured roadmap for developing and deploying artificial intelligence projects to solve real-world problems. It guides organizations and individuals through a structured process that includes problem scoping, data acquisition, data exploration, modelling, and evaluation. This systematic approach helps define objectives, collect relevant data, uncover hidden insights, create models for AI systems, and assess their performance. By following the AI project cycle, stakeholders can enhance the efficiency and effectiveness of their AI initiatives.

The phases of the AI project cycle include

1. Problem Scoping
2. Data Acquisition
3. Data Exploration
4. Modelling
5. Evaluation
6. Deployment

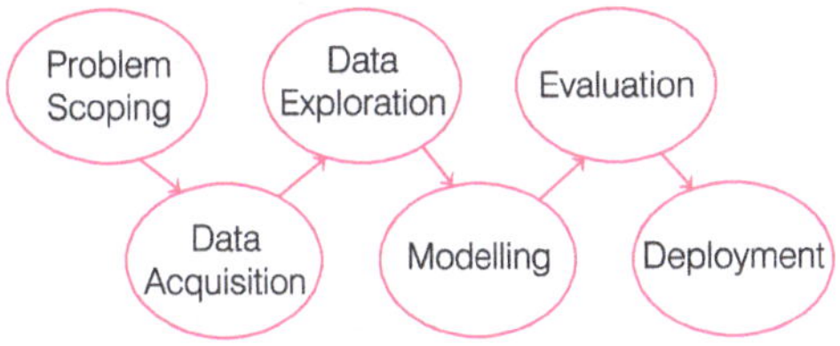

Fig. AI Project Cycle

Problem Scoping

Problem Scoping is the first phase of the AI project cycle. In this stage of project development, problems will be identified. It is then followed by designing, developing, or building, and finally testing the project.

Problem Scoping means selecting a problem which we might want to solve using our AI knowledge. The process of identifying the aim and scope of the problem that you wish to solve with the help of your project. This is "Problem Scoping".

The problem scoping refers to the identification of a problem and the vision to solve it. AI project cycle everything will be failed if problem scoping is failed or without appropriate problem scoping. Incorrect problem scoping also leads to failure of the project as well.

The 4Ws Problem Canvas

Problem scoping is the process of pinpointing a particular issue or opportunity that can be tackled using artificial intelligence. During this phase, we not only identify the problem but also set specific objectives, goals, and criteria for success. However, scoping a problem is no simple task. It requires a deep understanding of the issue so that we can work effectively and solve problem-solving.

To achieve this, we rely on an approach called the 4Ws problem canvas, which helps us gain a clearer and more defined understanding of the problem we're dealing with.

The 4Ws Problem canvas helps you in identifying the key elements related to the problem. Let us go through each of the blocks one by one.

Fig. 4Ws Canvas

Who This identifies all the stakeholders involved. Stakeholders are anyone impacted by the problem, directly or indirectly. This could be users, customers, employees, managers, or even external parties. Understanding who's affected helps tailor solutions.

What This focuses on the core problem itself. What exactly is the issue? Here, you gather evidence to confirm the problem exists and define its scope. Be specific! A vague "low sales" problem becomes more actionable when you pinpoint a drop in online sales or a decline in sales of a specific product line.

Where This considers the context and location of the problem. Does it occur everywhere, or in a specific department, region, or situation? Understanding the environment can help pinpoint root causes and guide potential solutions. For example, high product returns might be due to poor packaging during shipping, or unclear instructions included with the product.

Why This explores the importance of solving the problem. Why is it worth addressing? What are the negative consequences if left unaddressed? Highlighting the impact (e.g. lost revenue, customer dissatisfaction) strengthens the case for finding a solution.

These three canvases now become the base of why you want to solve this problem. Thus, in the "Why" canvas, think about the benefits which the stakeholders would get from the solution and how would it benefit them as well as the society.

The Problem Statement Template When the above 4Ws are filled, you need to prepare a summary of these 4Ws. This summary is known as the problem statement template. This template explains all the key points in a single template. So, if the same problem arises in the future this statement helps to resolve it easily. We can take a look at the Problem Statement Template and understand the key elements of it.

Our	[Stakeholder(s)] __________ __________ __________	Who
has/have a problem that	[issue, problem, need] __________ __________ __________	What
when/while	[Context, situation] __________ __________ __________	Where
An ideal solution would	[benefit of solution for them] __________ __________	Why

Fig. Problem Statement Template

Data Acquisition

As we move ahead in the AI project cycle, we come across the second stage which is data acquisition. As the term clearly mentions, this stage is about acquiring data for the project. While developing an AI system for predictive purposes, it's essential to begin by training it with relevant data.

Data acquisition consists of two words

Data Data refers to the raw facts, figures, information, or statistics. Data can be in the format of the text, video, images, audio, and so on and it can be collected from various source like interest, journals, newspapers and so on.

Acquisition Acquisition refers to acquiring data for the project.

So, Data acquisition means acquiring data needed to solve the problem.

Suppose you want to build a system that predicts how much an employee will earn in the future based on what they've earned in the past. To do this, you feed the system the historical salary information. We call this historical salary data "training data", while the dataset used for future salary predictions is called testing data.

Here, the specific kinds of information you want to collect are called data features. In our previous example, these data features could be things like the employee's salary amount, the percentage of salary increase they received, the time between salary raises, any bonuses they've earned, and more.

There are various methods to gather this data, such as follows

1. Surveys
2. Web scraping
3. Sensors
4. Cameras
5. Observations
6. API (Application Programming Interface)

One of the most dependable and trustworthy sources for data is government-hosted open-access websites. Examples of such government portals include data.gov.in and india.gov.in.

Data Features

Data features refer to the type of data you want to collect. In our previous example of future salary prediction, data features would be salary amount, increment percentage, increment period, bonus, etc.

In AI, data features are used to describe the input data that we feed into a machine learning model. These features help the model understand and make predictions.

Example Suppose you want to predict the price of a house. The features could include the number of bedrooms, the size of the house, the location, and the age of the house.

Type of data you want to collect. Here two terms are associated with this

1. **Training Data** Training data is a set of examples used to teach an AI model how to make predictions or perform a task. It's like giving practice problems to a student to help them learn. The model learns from the patterns in the training data and adjusts its internal parameters accordingly.

   Example Imagine you're teaching a robot to recognize different animals. You show it pictures of cats, dogs, and birds along with labels indicating what each animal is. The robot learns from these examples so that when you show it a new picture, it can correctly identify the animal.

2. **Testing Data** Testing data is another set of examples that we use to evaluate how well our AI model performs after it has been trained. It's like giving a student a test after they've studied to see how well they've learned the material.

   Testing data is separate from the training data to ensure that the model can generalize well to new, unseen examples.

   Example Going back to the animal recognition example, after training the robot with lots of pictures of animals, you give it a new set of pictures that it hasn't seen before. This testing set helps you assess if the robot can correctly identify animals it hasn't encountered during training.

   The testing data quality is essential for the machine learning model's performance, The data should represent the real world and be large enough to evaluate the model thoroughly.

Note *The training data and the test data are not different, they are usually divided from the main dataset in 80% - 20%.*

Info Wall

Andrew Ng said, "The training data is the food for the model, and the testing data is the dessert."

System Maps

A system map shows the components and boundaries of a system and the components of the environment at a specific point in time. With the help of System Maps, one can easily define a relationship amongst different elements which come under a system. Relating this concept to our module, the Goal of our project becomes a system whose elements are the data features mentioned above. Any change in these elements changes the system outcome too. For example, if a person received 200% increment in a month, then this change in his salary would affect the prediction of his future salary. The more the increment presently, the more salary in future is what the system would predict.

So how do we create a systems map? Here is a step-by-step guide to make a systems map.

The Steps

1. Developing a systems map relies on the thoroughness of knowledge about the problem. That is, when you have more information about the problem, your systems maps can be more detailed.
2. The best way to start once you enough information, is to write statements about how X leads to Y and under what conditions.
3. The next step is to separate information that belongs together and that does not.
4. Separate the contextual factors.
5. Establish connections between the major chunks that go together.
6. Gradually follow the chronological order to develop a narrative.
7. Create a systems diagram.
8. Refine the diagram till it accurately captures the story and provides information that is easier to understand.

9. Make sure you refine the diagram in such a manner that the connection between the main themes can be made explicit.

Try These 2.1

1 **What is the importante of AI project Cycle?**
2 **In the .... stage, broadly the aim and scope of the project undertaken are decided. (Problem Scoping/Data Acquisition)**
3 **What is 4 Ws canvas?**
4 **What is data features.**
5 **List some commonly used sources of data collection.**

Data Exploration

Data exploration is the third stage of AI project cycle. Data exploration is the process of arranging the gathered data uniformly for a better understanding. Data can be arranged in the form of a table, plotting a chart or making database. It is the first step of data analysis, after data acquisition, to explore and visualize data to uncover insights from the raw data. The extracted data then has to be studied using various techniques for understanding the structure of the data and identifying the trends, patterns, and inter-relationships within the data.

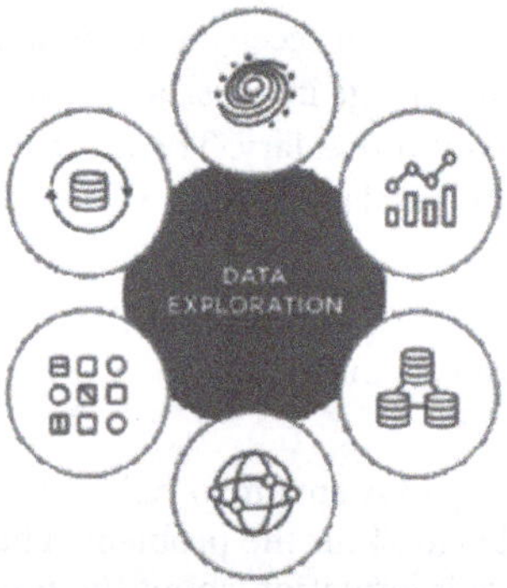

Data is a complicated, often just a bunch of numbers. But to make sense of it, we need to find the hidden patterns. That's where data visualization comes in. It's all about turning those numbers into pictures that are easy for people to understand. This allows you to include:

- **Spotting Trends and Patterns** When you look at a chart or graph, you can quickly see if something is going up, down, or staying the same. That helps you spot trends and patterns in the data.
- **Choosing the Right Tools** Data visualization helps you decide which method or model is best for further analysis. It's like picking the right tool for the job.
- **Sharing Insights** Once you've figured things out, you can show your findings to others. A picture is worth a thousand words, as they say. Visualizing data makes it easier to explain your insights to others.

To visualize data, you can use various types of visuals like bar graphs, histograms, line charts, and pie charts. These visuals make the data more approachable and understandable.

Data Visualization

Data visualization is the graphical representation of information and data in a pictorial or graphical format. Data visualization tools provide an accessible way to see and understand trends, patterns in data, and outliers. Data visualization tools and technologies are essential to analyzing massive amounts of information and making data-driven decisions.

The concept of using pictures is to understand data that has been used for centuries. General types of data visualization are Charts, Tables, Graphs, Maps, and Dashboards.

Advantages of Data Visualization

- A better understanding of data
- Provides insights into data
- Allows user interaction
- Provide real-time analysis
- Help to make decisions
- Reduces complexity of data
- Provides the relationships and patterns contained within data
- Define a strategy for your data model
- Provides an effective way of communication among users

Till now we learned about problem scoping and data acquisition. Now we have set your goal for your AI project and found ways to acquire data. When we acquired data the main problem with data is - the data is very complex. Because it's having numbers. To make use of these numbers user need a specific pattern to understand the data.

For example, if we are going to reading a book. We went to library and selected a book. The first thing you try to do is, just turning the pages and take a review and then select a book of your choice. Similarly, when we are working with data or going to analyze data we need to use data visualization.

Data Visualization Techniques

Here are some important data visualization **techniques** to know

1. **Pie Chart** Pie charts are one of the most common and basic data visualization techniques, used across a wide range of applications. Pie charts are ideal for illustrating proportions, or part-to-whole comparisons.

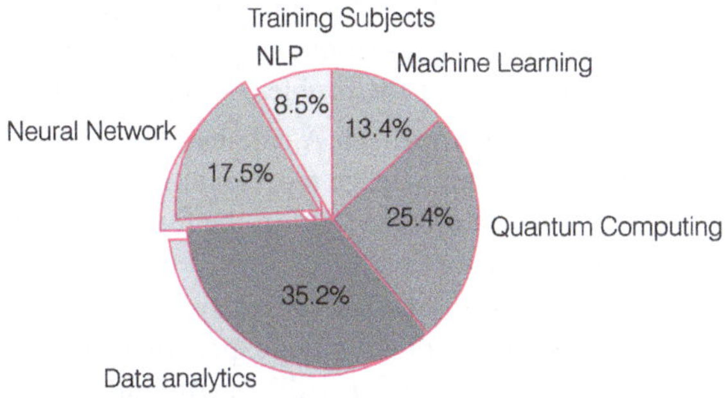

2. **Bar Chart** The classic bar chart, or bar graph, is another common and easy-to-use method of data visualization. In this type of visualization, one axis of the chart shows the categories being compared, and the other, a measured value. The length of the bar indicates how each group measures according to the value.

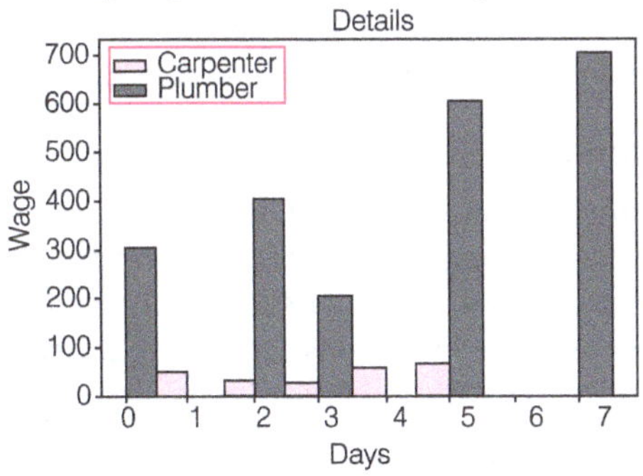

3. **Histogram** Histograms are especially useful for showing the frequency of a particular occurrence. For example, if you'd like to show how many clicks your website received each day over the last week, you can use a histogram. From this visualization, you can quickly determine which days your website saw the greatest and fewest number of clicks.

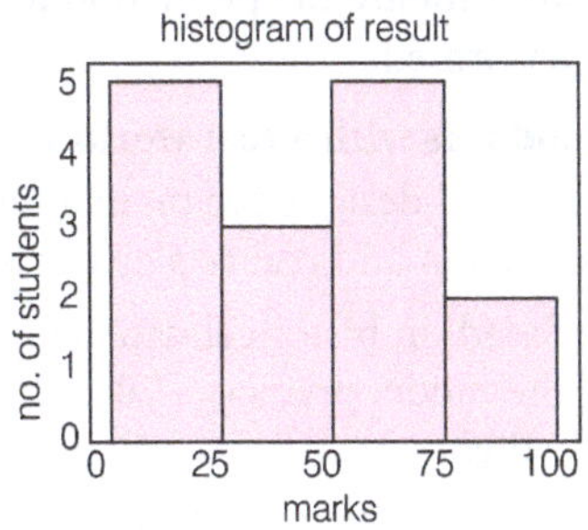

4. **Scatter Plot** An XY (Scatter) chart either shows the relationships among the numeric values in several data series or plots two groups of numbers as one series of XY coordinates.

   Additionally, the closer the data points are grouped together, the stronger the correlation or tends to be.

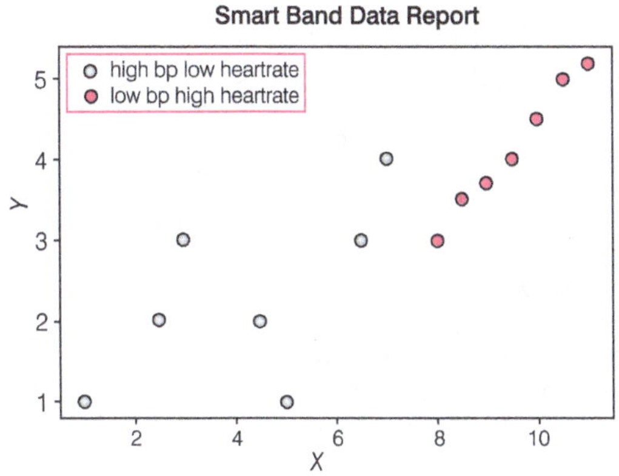

5. **Line Plot** Line plots are drawn by joining straight lines connecting data points where x-axis and y-axis values intersect. In Matplotlib, the plot() function represents this type of graph.

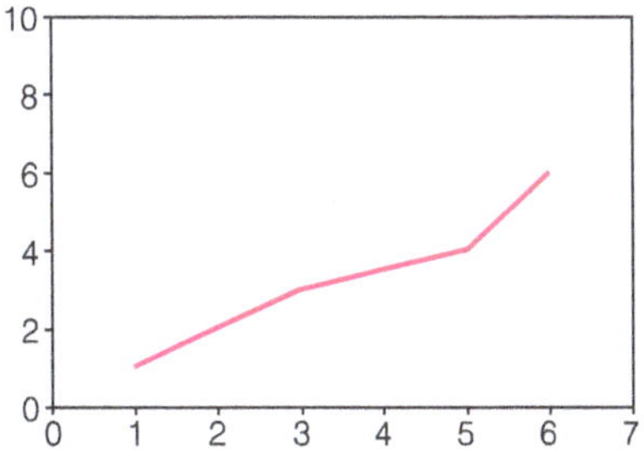

6. **Timeline** Timelines are the most effective way to visualize a sequence of events in chronological order. They're typically linear, with key events outlined along the axis. Timelines are used to communicate time-related information and display historical data.

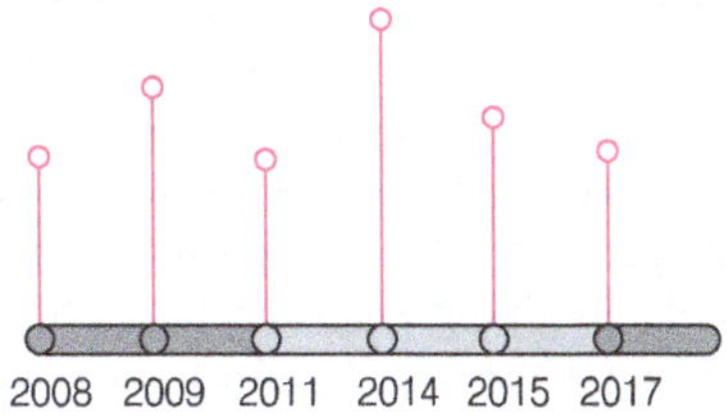

7. **Area Plot** The area plots spread across certain areas with bumps and drops (highs and lows) and are also known as stack plots.

In Matplotlib, the stackplot() function represents it.

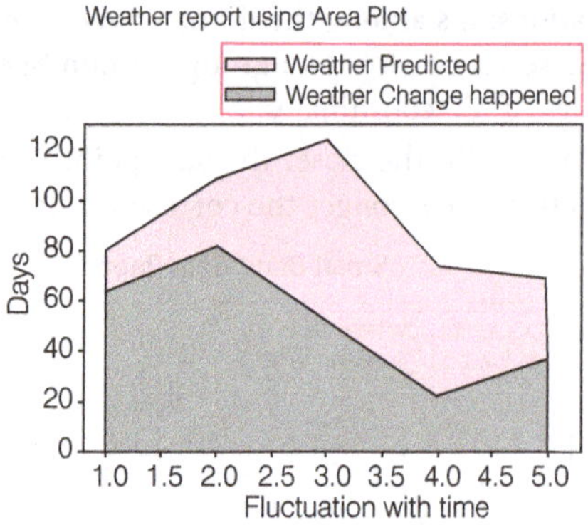

Try These 2.2

1. **Define data exploration.**
2. **What is the need of data visualization?**
3. **Mention some popular data visualization techniques.**
4. **Scatter chart also known as .... chart. (XY/Column)**

Modelling

Modelling is the process in which different models based on the visualized data can be created and even checked for the advantages and disadvantages of the model.

AI Model

An AI model is a program or algorithm that utilizes a set of data that enables it to recognize certain patterns. This allows it to reach a conclusion or make a prediction when provided with sufficient information. There are 2 Approaches to make a Machine Learning Model

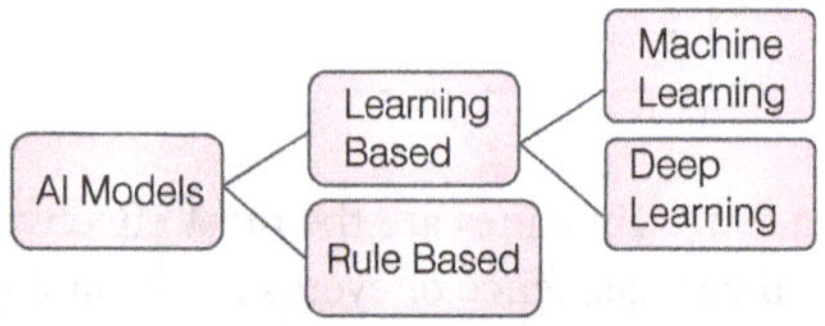

(i) **Learning Based Approach** Learning based approach is based on machine learning experience with the data fed.

The different types of learning based approaches are

- **Supervised Learning** The data that you have collected here is labelled and so you know what input needs to be mapped to what output. This helps you correct your algorithm if it makes a mistake in giving you the answer. Supervised Learning is used in classifying mail as spam.
- **Unsupervised Learning** The data collected here has no labels and you are unsure about the outputs. So, you model your algorithm such that it can understand patterns from the data and output the required answer. You do not interfere when the algorithm learns.
- **Reinforcement Learning** There is no data in this kind of learning, you model the algorithm such that it interacts with the environment and if the algorithm does a decent job, you reward it, else you punish the algorithm. (Reward or Penalty Policy). With continuous interactions and learning, it goes from being bad to being the best that it can for the problem assigned to it.

(ii) **Rule Based Approach** A rule-based system uses rules as the knowledge representation. These rules are coded into the system in the form of if-then-else statements.

The main idea of a rule-based system is to capture the knowledge of a human expert in a specialized domain and embed it within a computer system. A rule-based system is like a human being born with fixed knowledge. The knowledge of that human being doesn't change over time.

This implies that, when this human being encounters a problem for which no rules have been designed, then this human gets stuck and so won't be able to solve the problem. In a sense, the human being doesn't even understand the problem.

Evaluation

Evaluation is a process that critically examines a program. It involves collecting and analyzing information about a program's activities, characteristics, and outcomes. Its purpose is to make judgments about a program, to improve its effectiveness, and/or to inform programming decisions.

So, Evaluation is basically to check the performance of your AI Model. This is done by mainly two thing "Prediction" and "Reality".

- **Prediction** The output given by the machine after training and texting the data is known as a prediction.
- **Reality** This refers to the actual situation or event that the model is trying to predict. It's the ground truth, the data point we compare the prediction to see how well the model performed.

Let's understand this with a real-world scenario

Imagine an AI model designed to predict flight delays. Here's how prediction and reality play out in its evaluation:

- **Prediction** Based on historical data and current conditions, the model predicts a 20% chance of a delay for a specific flight.
- **Reality** The flight actually departs on time (no delay).

Here, we have two possible outcomes

- **True Negative** The model predicted no delay (negative), and reality confirms no delay (true). This is a successful prediction.
- **False Positive** The model predicted a delay (positive), but in reality, there was no delay (negative). This is an incorrect prediction.

Confusion Matrix

The comparison between the results of Prediction and reality is called the Confusion Matrix.

Confusion Matrix

	Reality Positive(1)	Reality Negative(0)
Predicted Positive(1)	True Positives (TPs)	False Positives (FPs)
Predicted Negative(0)	False Negatives (FNs)	True Negatives (TNs)

Prediction and Reality can be easily mapped together with the help of this Confusion Matrix.

Four Common AI Evaluation Methods

1. **Accuracy** This is a basic metric that measures the proportion of correct predictions made by the model. In the recommender system example, accuracy could be the percentage of users who bought recommended products.
2. **Precision** This metric focuses on the positive predictions and calculates the proportion of truly relevant items among those the model recommended. For the recommender system, precision would be the percentage of recommended products that User A actually bought.
3. **Recall** This metric considers all the relevant items and calculates the proportion of those that the model actually recommended. In the e-commerce scenario, recall would be the percentage of athletic socks User A was interested in (whether purchased or not) that the system recommended.
4. **F1-Score** This metric combines precision and recall into a single score, providing a balance between the two. It's useful when both precision and recall are important.

Deployment

Deployment is the method by which you integrate a machine learning model into an existing production environment to make practical business decisions based on data.

Deployment is the final stage where an AI model transitions from development to real-world use. It's like taking your creation out of the workshop and putting it to work.

Key steps in deployment involve

- Testing and validating the model to ensure it performs well in real-world situations, just like giving your creation a final test run.
- Integration with existing systems, which is like connecting your AI model to the tools and infrastructure it needs to function.
- Monitoring and maintenance, which means keeping an eye on your model's performance and making adjustments as needed, similar to how you might fine-tune a machine over time.

Examples of deployed AI showcase the power of AI in various fields, from self-driving cars navigating the roads to medical diagnosis systems assisting doctors to chatbots providing customer service on websites.

Deployment extends to mobile and web applications, making AI accessible and interactive for users.

Try These 2.3

1. **What is rule based and learning based AI model?**
2. **Explain confusion matrix.**
3. **Name four evaluation methods.**
4. **What do you understand by deployment?**

Glossary

Project A project is a series of tasks that need to be completed to reach a specific outcome. A project can also be defined as a set of inputs and outputs required to achieve a particular goal.

Problem Scoping The process of finalising the aim of a system or project means you scope the problem that you wish to solve with the help of your project.

Data visualisation It is the process of representing data visually or graphically, by using visual elements like charts, diagrams, graphs and maps etc.

Data Exploration The process of interpreting or exploring some useful information out of the large acquired data for a better understanding.

Modelling The process of selecting and implementing the model which match the requirements of a project.

Evaluation The evaluation of each and every model tried and choose the model which gives the most efficient and reliable results.

4W's canvas A framework to define a problem statement using Who, What, Where\When and Why.

Let's Investigate

Activity 1

Designing CottonAce App for Pest Management

Problem

Pest Infestation Damages Crops

Problem Scoping

The cotton industry in India comprises 6 million local farmers. Cotton crops frequently get infected with the Pink Bollworm, which is difficult to see with the naked eye. Small farmers struggle to eliminate these insects due to a lack of advanced tools and techniques.

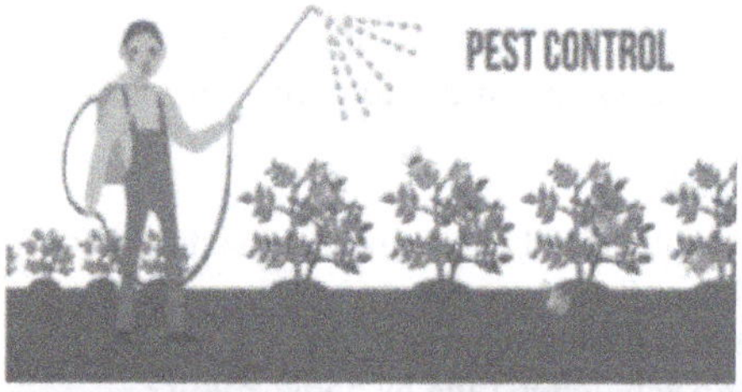

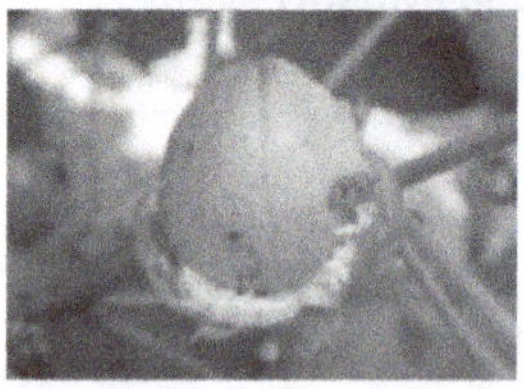

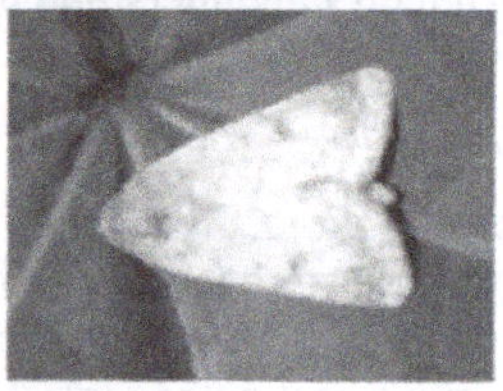

4W canvas for Pest Management

Our	Farmers	Who
Has a problem that	Cotton Crops got infected with pest -Pink Ballworm	What
When / while	On the crops in the field	Where
An ideal solution would	To create an AI-enabled app that aids farmers in – • Determining the correct amount of pesticides • Knowing the right time to spray pesticides • Increase in Production • Increase in the profit share of the farmers.	Why

Data Acquisition

In interaction with the farmers, different types of worms affecting the cotton crop are identified. The following data is collected:

- Images of the pests
- Farmer names
- Village names
- Farm size
- Pesticide usage

Data Exploration

Upon acquiring the data, it is noted that it is not uniform. Some images are small, others large. Some data is missing, while other data points have multiple copies. The data is cleaned, made uniform, and missing data is filled to enhance its comprehensibility.

Exploring the data helps researchers identify patterns and trends related to Pink Bollworm infestations, pesticide usage, crop yields, and other relevant factors.

Modelling

After exploring the data, an AI-enabled app is developed. Farmers use the app to click pictures of pests using their phone cameras. The AI app validates the images, recognizes the pests, and provides recommendations based on the number of pests identified and entomologists' guidelines.

Evaluation

The pest management system is tested by first emptying pest traps onto a blank sheet of paper and using the app to click pictures of pests. Initial results show a 70% accuracy rate. Further refinement of the model and exploration of other AI algorithms are undertaken to improve performance.

Deployment

After thorough testing, the pest management app, named CottonAce, is deployed and installed on farmers' mobile phones.

Note *CottonAce is a mobile application that helps farmers protect their crops from pests.*

Impact

- Small farms that used the app saw profit margins increase by up to 26.5%.
- Pesticide costs dropped by up to 38%.

Activity 2

A balloon debate is a fun and engaging activity where participants imagine they are in a hot air balloon that is losing altitude. The goal is to convince others why they should stay on the balloon, and each participant represents a different person, character, or concept. The debate continues until the participants have made their cases, and the group votes on who should stay on the balloon.

The impact of AI in our daily lives, you can organize the debate into two teams Team Pro (in favor of AI) and Team Con (against AI). Each team should have multiple students representing various aspects of the topic.

Team Pro (Pros of AI)

1. AI boosts efficiency and productivity by automating tasks, allowing humans to focus on more creative endeavors.
2. AI aids in medical advancements, leading to faster and more accurate diagnoses and personalized medicine.
3. AI enhances safety through autonomous vehicles and surveillance systems, reducing human errors and identifying security threats.
4. AI assists people with disabilities, providing them with independence and opportunities.
5. AI accelerates innovation and research, leading to breakthroughs in various fields.

Team Con (Cons of AI)

1. AI can lead to job displacement, particularly in sectors where routine tasks are easily automated.
2. Privacy concerns arise due to AI's reliance on data and the potential misuse of personal information.
3. AI systems may perpetuate societal biases present in training data, leading to discriminatory outcomes.
4. Security risks increase as AI systems become more sophisticated, making them vulnerable to cyber-attacks and misuse.
5. Overreliance on AI may result in a loss of human interaction and empathy, particularly in fields like healthcare and customer service.

Finally compile all the points of the team after a proper discussion on each point.

Pros of AI	Cons of AI

Activity 3

This activity will help you brainstorm a theme, identify a specific problem within that theme, and set a goal for your AI project.

Theme (Choose a theme relevant to your interests or current events)

Step 1 Brainstorming & Topic Selection

1. **Mind Map** Draw a mind map centered on your chosen theme. Write down any ideas, questions, or problems that come to mind related to the theme. This will help you explore different aspects of the theme.
2. **Discussion** Discuss the various topics you identified in your mind map. Consider these questions:
   - What problems or challenges exist within this theme?
   - How could AI potentially address these problems?
   - What are some potential benefits and drawbacks of using AI in this context?
3. **Topic Selection** Based on your discussion, select one specific topic within the theme that you find most interesting and has potential for an AI project.

Step 2 Problem Definition

Now, let's delve deeper into the chosen topic and define the specific problem you want your AI project to address.

1. **4Ws Problem Canvas** Fill out the following table to understand the problem better
   - **Who** Who is affected by this problem? (Individuals, organizations, society as a whole)
   - **What** What exactly is the problem? (Describe the specific issue)
   - **When** When and where does this problem occur? (Frequency, location)
   - **Why** Why is this a problem? (What are the negative consequences?)
2. **Problem Statement** Write a clear and concise problem statement using the following template People who [who are affected] struggle with [specific problem] because [reasons for the problem]. This has negative consequences such as [negative impacts].

Step 3 Goal Setting

Based on your problem definition, set a clear and achievable goal for your AI project.

Example

- **Theme** Education
- **Selected Topic** Personalized Learning for Students

4Ws Problem Canvas

- **Who** Students
- **What** Difficulty keeping up or being challenged in traditional one-size-fits-all learning environments
- **When** Throughout their educational journey
- **Why** Students may become disengaged or lose motivation if the learning pace is not tailored to their individual needs.

Problem Statement Students struggle to find a personalized learning experience that caters to their individual pace and needs because traditional classroom settings often follow a one-size-fits-all approach.

This can lead to disengagement, a lack of motivation, and hinder their academic potential.

Goal Develop an AI-powered educational assistant that personalizes learning materials and adapts to a student's individual needs and progress.

This activity provides a framework to brainstorm and define a problem you can address with your AI project. Remember, the goal should be specific, measurable, achievable, relevant, and time-bound (SMART).

Additional Tips

- Research existing solutions to your chosen problem. Can AI be used to improve upon them?
- Consider the feasibility of your project given your resources and timeline.
- Stay focused on a well-defined problem to ensure your AI project has a clear purpose.

This activity should give you a solid foundation for developing your AI project.

NCERT FOLDER

Complete Explanations of all NCERT's Questions

Problem Scoping

Q.1 What are the various stages of AI Project Cycle? Can you explain each with an example?

Ans. Various Stages of AI Project Cycle

(i) **Problem Identification** This stage involves identifying a problem or opportunity that can be addressed using AI techniques. For example, a company may identify a need to improve customer service response times.

(ii) **Data Acquisition** Once the problem is identified, relevant data needs to be collected and prepared for analysis. In our customer service example, this could involve gathering historical customer interactions and feedback data.

(iii) **Data Exploration** Explore the collected data to understand its characteristics, quality, and relationships between variables. This stage helps in identifying patterns and initial insights. Analyzing patient data to discover correlations between specific treatments and readmission rates, or identifying outliers and missing values that need to be addressed.

(iv) **Modelling** This stage involves selecting appropriate AI models and algorithms, training them on the prepared data, and tuning them for optimal performance. For instance, in our scenario, natural language processing (NLP) models might be used to analyze customer queries.

(v) **Evaluation** After building the model, it needs to be evaluated to ensure it meets the desired criteria and effectively addresses the problem. This evaluation could involve metrics like accuracy, precision, and recall in our customer service example.

(vi) **Deployment** Once the model is deemed satisfactory, it's deployed into the operational environment. In our case, the NLP model might be integrated into the company's customer service platform.

Q.2 How is an AI project different from an IT project?

Ans. Difference between an AI project and an IT project are as follows

Aspect	AI Project	IT Project
Focus	Developing intelligent models and systems	Developing and maintaining information systems
Data Usage	Heavily reliant on large datasets for training	Data management for processing and storage
Development	Iterative, experimental model training and tuning	Structured methodologies like Agile or Waterfall
Outcome	Systems that learn, predict, or automate tasks	Systems that meet business needs and improve efficiency
Skill Set	Algorithms, statistics, data science, programming	Software development, network management, cybersecurity

Q.3 Explain the 4Ws problem canvas in problem scoping.

Ans. The 4Ws problem canvas is a tool used in problem scoping to thoroughly understand the problem by addressing four key aspects: What, Who, Where, and When.

- **What** Describes the problem or opportunity in detail.
- **Who** Identifies the stakeholders involved or affected by the problem.
- **Where** Specifies the location or context in which the problem occurs.
- **When** Indicates the timeframe or frequency of the problem occurrence.

This canvas helps in clarifying the problem scope and understanding its various dimensions before proceeding with problem-solving activities.

Q.4 Why is there a need to use a Problem Statement Template during problem scoping?

Ans. Problem Statement Template provides a structured framework for defining the problem clearly and comprehensively. It ensures that all relevant information about the problem, its context, and its stakeholders are captured systematically. This template serves as a guide for the problem scoping process, helping stakeholders align their understanding of the problem and facilitating effective communication throughout the project lifecycle.

Q.5 What is Problem Scoping? What are the steps of Problem Scoping?

Ans. Problem scoping is the initial phase of a project where the problem or opportunity is defined, analyzed, and understood in detail. The steps involved in problem scoping typically include:

- **Problem Identification** Recognizing and articulating the problem or opportunity.
- **Problem Understanding** Gaining a deep understanding of the problem's context, causes, and implications.
- **Stakeholder Analysis** Identifying and engaging with stakeholders who are involved or affected by the problem.
- **Scope Definition** Clearly defining the boundaries and objectives of the problem-solving effort.
- **Data Collection** Gathering relevant data and information to inform the problem-solving process.
- **Problem Statement Formulation** Crafting a concise and precise statement that describes the problem and its key aspects.

Q. 6 Who are the stakeholders in the problem scoping stage?

Ans. Stakeholders in the problem scoping stage typically include

- **Project Sponsor** The individual or group funding the project and with a vested interest in its success.
- **Subject Matter Experts (SMEs)** Individuals with specialized knowledge or experience related to the problem domain.
- **End Users** Those who will ultimately use or be impacted by the solution.
- **Data Owners/Custodians** Individuals or departments responsible for providing access to relevant data.
- **Project Team Members** Those directly involved in scoping and solving the problem.
- **Regulatory Bodies** If applicable, regulatory agencies that govern the industry or domain related to the problem.

Data Acquisition

Q.1 How will you differentiate between Training Data and Testing Data? Elaborate with examples.

Ans.

	Training Data	Testing Data
Definition	A dataset of examples used during the learning process to fit the parameters.	A set of examples used solely to assess the performance of the fully specified classifier.
Usage	Used to train the model by adjusting its parameters.	Used to evaluate the performance of the trained model.
Dataset Proportion	Maximum portion of the dataset (usually around 80%).	A smaller portion of the dataset (usually around 20%).
Example	Training a model to recognize cats from images using a dataset of labeled images of cats and other objects.	After training, using a separate set of images containing cats and other objects to test the model's accuracy in correctly identifying cats.

Q.2 Name various methods for collecting data. For each method, can you name at least one project in which you may use that method of data collection?

Ans. The data acquisition stage is crucial in AI project cycles, as it lays the foundation for subsequent analysis and model development. Here are various methods for collecting data along with potential project examples:

(i) **Web Scraping**
- **Method** Automated extraction of data from websites.
- **Example Project** A project aiming to analyze customer reviews for sentiment analysis of a particular product or service.

(ii) **Surveys and Questionnaires**
- **Method** Gathering data through structured questions.
- **Example Project** Conducting a survey to gather feedback on user experience for improving a mobile application.

(iii) **Sensor Data Collection**
- **Method** Gathering data from physical sensors.
- **Example Project** Using IoT sensors to collect environmental data for predictive maintenance in manufacturing plants.

(iv) **Database Queries**
- **Method** Retrieving data from databases.
- **Example Project** Extracting historical sales data from a company's database for sales forecasting.

Q.3 What must you keep in mind while collecting data so it is useful?

Ans. When collecting data, ensure it's relevant to your objectives, accurate, collected ethically, and of sufficient quantity and quality for meaningful analysis.

Q.4 Imagine you are responsible to enable farmers from a village to take their produce to the market for sale. Can you draw a system map that encompasses all the steps and factors involved?

Ans. System Map for Connecting Farmers to Markets

Data Acquisition

Farmer Data
- Names, locations, types & quantities of produce
- Can be collected through surveys, village meetings, or mobile app

Market Data
- Location, types of produce accepted, current prices
- Data from local markets or government sources (agriculture departments)

Logistics Data
- Transportation options (trucks, bikes), costs, travel time
- Gathered from local transport providers or existing services

System Actors
- **Farmers** Provide data on their produce
- **Data Collector** Manages farmer data collection (surveys, app)
- **Market Aggregator** Gathers and maintains market data
- **Logistics Coordinator** Manages transportation options & costs
- **Matching Algorithm** (AI) Analyzes data to connect farmers with suitable markets

Data Flow
- Farmer data is collected (surveys, app)
- Market data is obtained (local markets, government sources)
- Logistics data is gathered (transport providers)
- All data is fed into the AI system

AI Model

The AI model analyzes data to
- Find the best market for each farmer's produce (considering price & distance)
- Recommend the most efficient transportation option

Outputs
- **Farmer Reports** Suggest markets, transport options, estimated earnings
- **Logistics Plan** Coordinates pick-up and delivery for produce

Benefits
- Increased income for farmers
- Reduced post-harvest losses
- Improved market access for villagers

Q.5 Name a few government websites from where you can get open-source data.

Ans. Here are a few government websites from where you can get open-source data:
- **Data.gov** is the federal government's open data site in the United States. It provides access to a wide variety of datasets from various government agencies.
- **Data.gov.in** is the Open Government Data Platform for India. It provides access to datasets from the Government of India and its various ministries and departments.

Data Exploration

Q.1 Which one of the following is the second stage of AI project cycle?

(a) Data Exploration (b) Data Acquisition
(c) Modelling (d) Problem Scoping

Ans. (b) Data Acquisition

Q.2 Which of the following comes under Problem Scoping?

(a) System Mapping (b) 4Ws Canvas
(c) Data Features (d) Web scraping

Ans. (b) 4Ws Canvas

Q.3 Which of the following is not valid for Data Acquisition?

(a) Web scraping (b) Surveys
(c) Sensors (d) Announcements

Ans. (d) Announcements

Q.4 If an arrow goes from X to Y with a - (minus) sign, it means that

(a) If X increases, Y decreases
(b) The direction of relation is opposite
(c) If X increases, Y increases
(d) It is a bi-directional relationship

Ans. (a) If X increases, Y decreases

Q.5 Which of the following is not a part of the 4Ws Problem Canvas?

(a) Who? (b) Why? (c) What? (d) Which?

Ans. (d) Which?

Q.6 What is the significance of Data Exploration after you have acquired the data for the problem scoped? Explain with examples.

Ans. Data exploration helps in understanding the characteristics and patterns in the data, identifying outliers, and refining hypotheses before analysis. For example, in healthcare, exploring patient data might reveal trends in disease prevalence or demographic patterns.

Q.7 What do you think is the relevance of Data Visualization in AI?

Ans. Data visualization in AI is crucial for interpreting complex datasets and communicating insights effectively. It helps analysts and stakeholders understand trends, patterns, and relationships in the data.

Q.8 List any five graphs used for data visualization.

Ans. Five common graphs for data visualization are

(i) Line graphs (ii) Bar charts
(iii) Scatter plots (iv) Histograms
(v) Pie charts

Q.9 How is Data Exploration different from Data Acquisition?

Ans. Data acquisition involves obtaining raw data, while data exploration involves analyzing and understanding the acquired data to derive insights and patterns.

Q.10 Use an example to explain at least one Data Visualization technique.

Ans. An example of data visualization technique is a scatter plot, which displays the relationship between two variables. For example, plotting the relationship between study hours and exam scores for a group of students can help visualize if there's a correlation between the two.

Modelling

Q.1 What are the various stages of the AI Project Cycle? Explain each with examples.

Ans. Refer to solution on page no. 136 Question no. 1.

Q.2 What is Artificial Intelligence? Give an example where AI is used in day-to-day life.

Ans. When a machine can mimic human intelligence, solve real-world problems, improve on its own from past experiences, and predict and make decisions on its own, it can be called Artificially Intelligent (AI).

One common example of AI in day-to-day life is virtual assistants like Siri, Google Assistant, or Amazon Alexa. These AI-powered assistants use natural language processing (NLP) to understand and respond to user commands or questions. They can perform various tasks such as setting reminders, answering queries, sending messages, playing music, and controlling smart home devices.

Q.3 How is Machine Learning related to Artificial Intelligence?

Ans. Machine learning is a subset of artificial intelligence that focuses on creating algorithms and models that enable computers to learn from and make predictions or decisions based on data. In essence, ML empowers AI systems to improve their performance over time without being explicitly programmed for every task.

Artificial intelligence, on the other hand, encompasses a broader spectrum of techniques and methodologies aimed at creating machines or systems that can mimic human intelligence, including reasoning, problem-solving, perception, and learning. While AI encompasses various disciplines like natural language processing, computer vision, robotics, and expert systems, machine learning stands out as a fundamental approach within AI for enabling systems to learn from data and improve their performance iteratively.

Q.4 Compare and contrast Rule-based and Learning-based approach in AI modelling indicating clearly when each of these may be used.

Ans. Rule-based approach relies on predefined rules and logic to make decisions or perform tasks. It's suitable when the problem domain is well-understood and the rules are clear and stable. It's often used in applications where transparency and interpretability are important, such as expert systems or legal reasoning. Learning-based approach, on the other hand, is training algorithms on data to recognize patterns and make decisions. It's ideal when the problem is complex and there's a lot of data available for training. Learning-based methods excel in tasks like image recognition, natural language processing, and recommendation systems, where the underlying patterns might be too intricate for rule-based systems to capture effectively.

Q.5 Identify which of the following are examples of classification/regression/clustering.

(i) Making a diagnosis for a patient on the basis of their symptoms
(ii) Price prediction for a house coming up on sale
(iii) HR shortlisting applications for interview based on information provided in candidates' resume

(iv) **Credit Card Fraud prevention**
(v) **SPAM filters**

Ans. (i) Classification (ii) Regression (iii) Classification (iv) Classification (v) Classification

Evaluation

Q.1 What is Evaluation?

Ans. Evaluation is the process of understanding the reliability of any AI model, based on outputs by feeding test dataset into the model and comparing with actual answers. There can be different Evaluation techniques, depending of the type and purpose of the model.

Q.2 What are various model evaluation techniques?

Ans. There are various techniques for model evaluation are:
- Accuracy
- Precision
- Recall
- F1-Score

Q.3 Why is model evaluation important in AI projects?

Ans. Model evaluation is essential for several reasons:
- Ensures model effectiveness
- Identifies biases and errors
- Improves model performance
- Provides insights for real-world deployment

Q.4 What do you understand by the terms True Positive and False Positive?

Ans. These terms are used in classification problems where the model predicts a binary outcome (positive or negative).
- **True Positive** (TP) A case where the model correctly predicts the positive. For example, a spam filter correctly identifying a spam email.
- **False Positive** (FP) A case where the model incorrectly predicts the positive. For example, a spam filter mistakenly marking a legitimate email as spam.

Deployment

Q.1 Does modelling mean creating an AI model?
(a) YES (b) NO

Ans. (b) NO

Q.2 Can we use AI on mobile phones?
(a) YES (b) NO

Ans. (a) YES

Q.3 What is deployment in the context of an AI project cycle?

Ans. Deployment as the final stage in the AI project cycle where the AI model or solution is implemented in a real-world scenario.

Q.4 Why is deployment an important phase in the AI project cycle?

Ans. Deployment is crucial because it's where the AI project delivers real value. After all the development and testing, deployment is where the rubber meets the road - the AI system starts impacting the business or solving the problem it was designed for.

Q.5 What are some common challenges in deploying AI models?

Ans. Deployment is crucial because it's where the AI project delivers real value. After all the development and testing, deployment is where the rubber meets the road - the AI system starts impacting the business or solving the problem it was designed for. Deploying AI models can be tricky. Here are a few common challenges
- **Integration** You need to seamlessly connect the AI model with existing systems and data flows.
- **Monitoring** Keeping an eye on the model's performance in the real world is essential. This way you can identify and address any issues that arise.
- **Maintaining Data Quality** AI models rely on good data. In deployment, you need to ensure a consistent flow of high-quality data to the model.

Revision Time

Q.1 Rearrange the steps of AI project cycle in correct order:
(a) **Data Acquisition** (b) **Problem Scoping**
(c) **Modelling** (d) **Data Exploration**
(e) **Deployment** (f) **Evaluation**

Ans. (b), (a), (d), (c), (f), (e)

Q.2 The process of breaking down the big problem into a series of simple steps is known as
(a) Efficiency (b) Modularity
(c) Both (a) and (b) (d) None of these

Ans. (b) Modularity

Q.3 The primary purpose of data exploration in AI project cycle is ....
(a) To make data more complicated
(b) To simplify complex data
(c) To discover patterns and insights in data
(d) To visualize data

Ans. (c) To discover patterns and insights in data

Q.4 Deployment is the final stage in the AI project cycle where the AI model or solution is implemented in a real-world scenario. (True/False)

Ans. True

Q.5 Identify A, B and C in the following diagram (Hint: How AI, ML &DL related to each other)

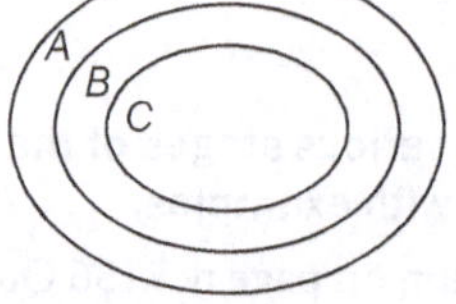

Ans. A → Artificial Intelligence (AI), B → Machine Learning (ML), C → Deep Learning (DL)

REVIEW EXERCISE

Including Competency Based Questions

Part I

Multiple Choice Questions

1 The AI Project Cycle is a .... that uses scientific methods to solve problems and draw conclusions.

(a) Step-by-step process (b) Random process
(c) Reverse process (d) None of these

2 The stages of the AI project cycle are

(a) Problem Scoping & Data Acquisition
(b) Data Exploration & Modelling
(c) Evaluation
(d) All of the above

3 In ...., we need to address the problem and what the advantages will be for the stakeholders once the problem is solved.

(a) Who (b) What
(c) Where (d) Why

4 Summarizes all of the important points in one place.

(a) Problem statement template
(b) Problem statement document
(c) Problem statement file
(d) None of the above

5 The method of collecting correct and dependable data to work with is known as ....

(a) Problem Scoping (b) Data Acquisition
(c) Data Exploration (d) Modelling

6 When you explore the data and try to put it uniformly for a better understanding. It is called ....

(a) Data acquisition (b) Problem scoping
(c) Data exploration (d) Modelling

7 Refers to developing algorithms, also called models which can be trained to get intelligent.

(a) Data acquisition (b) Problem scoping
(c) Data exploration (d) Modelling

8 .... element helps us to understand and categorize who is directly and indirectly affected by the problem.

(a) Who (b) What
(c) Where (d) Why

9 .... section aids us in analyzing and recognizing the nature of the problem.

(a) Who (b) What
(c) Where (d) Why

10 What does data acquisition involve in the AI Project Cycle?

(a) Analyzing data patterns
(b) Collecting relevant data for the project
(c) Implementing machine learning algorithms
(d) Generating predictions without data

11. What is the primary purpose of extracting data features in the context of an AI project?

(a) To confuse the machine learning algorithm
(b) To visualize factors affecting the problem statement
(c) To make the project conflict with other AI projects
(d) To acquire irrelevant data

12 Which of the following is mentioned as a reliable source for authentic information in data acquisition?

(a) Random internet websites
(b) Private databases without proper sources
(c) Government-hosted open-access websites
(d) Social media platforms

13 Data Acquisition involves acquiring .... for the project.

(a) Computers (b) Data
(c) Software (d) Servers

14 In an AI project, historical salary information used for training is termed as ....

(a) Testing data
(b) Prediction data
(c) Training data
(d) Acquired data

15 Which of the following is a method to collect data?

(a) Observations (b) Web scraping
(c) Sensors (d) All of these

16 What does API stand for?

(a) Advanced Programming Interface
(b) Application Programming Interface
(c) Algorithmic Protocol Integration
(d) Automated Processing Interface

17 System map in AI is primarily used to:

(a) Visualize the timeline of an AI project
(b) Identify and illustrate the components and relationships within an AI system
(c) Display statistical data
(d) Track the financial expenses of an AI project

18 **What is the primary objective of data exploration?**
(a) Analyzing data
(b) Visualizing data
(c) Understanding data
(d) Extracting insights

19 **What is the purpose of data visualization in data analysis?**
(a) To complicate data interpretation
(b) To obscure trends and patterns
(c) To simplify data understanding
(d) To hinder communication of insights

20 **Which data visualization technique is best suited for illustrating proportions or part-to-whole comparisons?**
(a) Bar Chart
(b) Scatter Plot
(c) Pie Chart
(d) Histogram

21 **What is the drawback of using a pie chart for complex data sets?**
(a) Inability to display trends
(b) Lack of clarity
(c) Difficulty in interpretation
(d) Limited use of color

22 **What is the main advantage of using a scatter plot?**
(a) Illustrating proportions
(b) Displaying part-to-whole comparisons
(c) Identifying trends or correlations
(d) Showing time-related information

23 **Which of the following is a key benefit of using a system map in AI?**
(a) Simplifies complex processes and helps in understanding relationships
(b) Provides detailed project timelines
(c) Highlights individual performance metrics
(d) Outlines the financial budget of an AI project

24 **Which stage of the AI project cycle involves gathering and filtering data from various sources?**
(a) Data Exploration (b) Data Visualization
(c) Data Acquisition (d) Data Analysis

25 **Which visualization technique is best suited for illustrating the frequency of a particular occurrence?**
(a) Scatter Plot (b) Choropleth Map
(c) Word Cloud (d) Histogram

Answers

1. (a)	2. (d)	3. (d)	4. (a)	5. (b)
6. (c)	7. (d)	8. (a)	9. (b)	10. (b)
11. (b)	12. (c)	13. (b)	14. (c)	15. (d)
16. (b)	17. (b)	18. (c)	19. (c)	20. (c)
21. (b)	22. (c)	23. (a)	24. (c)	25. (d)

Statement Based Questions

1 **Statement 1 The "Who" block helps analyze people directly or indirectly affected by the problem.**

Statement 2 The "What" block focuses on identifying the context or situation of the problem.
(a) Both Statement 1 and Statement 2 are correct
(b) Both Statement 2 and Statement 2 are incorrect
(c) Statement 1 is correct but Statement 2 is incorrect
(d) Statement 2 is correct but Statement 1 is incorrect

2 **Statement 1 The phases of the AI project cycle include Data Exploration.**

Statement 2 The initial steps of requirement gathering, planning, and designing in a project cycle may vary in order depending on the project.
(a) Both Statement 1 and Statement 2 are correct
(b) Both Statement 1 and Statement 2 are incorrect
(c) Statement 1 is correct but Statement 2 is incorrect
(d) Statement 2 is correct but Statement 1 is incorrect

3 **Statement 1 Evaluation is the first stage of the AI project cycle.**

Statement 2 Precision in the evaluation phase measures how well the model avoids false alarms.
(a) Both Statement 1 and Statement 2 are correct
(b) Both Statement 1 and Statement 2 are incorrect
(c) Statement 1 is correct but Statement 2 is incorrect
(d) Statement 2 is correct but Statement 1 is incorrect

4. **Statement 1 Good quality training data is crucial for the performance of a machine learning model.**

Statement 2 Testing data should have the same distribution of features as the actual dataset.
(a) Both Statement 1 and Statement 2 are correct
(b) Both Statement 1 and Statement 2 are incorrect
(c) Statement 1 is correct but Statement 2 is incorrect
(d) Statement 2 is correct but Statement 1 is incorrect

5 **Statement 1 Observations can be a time-consuming data source.**

Statement 2 Sensors are part of IoT and collect physical data.
(a) Both Statement 1 and Statement 2 are correct
(b) Both Statement 1 and Statement 2 are incorrect
(c) Statement 1 is correct but Statement 2 is incorrect
(d) Statement 2 is correct but Statement 1 is incorrect

6. **Statement 1 The data with which the machine can be trained is the testing data.**

Statement 2 The data with which the model is evaluated is the training data.
(a) Both Statement 1 and Statement 2 are correct
(b) Both Statement 1 and Statement 2 are incorrect
(c) Statement 1 is correct but Statement 2 is incorrect
(d) Statement 2 is correct but Statement 1 is incorrect

7 Statement 1 Data visualization helps in spotting trends and patterns in the data.

Statement 2 Data visualization reduces the complexity of data.

(a) Both Statement 1 and Statement 1 are correct

(b) Both Statement 1 and Statement 1 are incorrect

(c) Statement 1 is correct but Statement 2 is incorrect

(d) Statement 2 is correct but Statement 1 is incorrect

Answers

1. (a) 2. (a) 3. (d) 4. (a) 5. (a)
6. (b) 7. (a)

Assertion and Reason Based Questions

1 Assertion Problem Identification is the first step in the AI project cycle.

Reason A well-defined problem statement helps in focusing on the root cause of the problem and avoids unnecessary details or assumptions.

(a) Both Assertion and Reason are true, and Reason is the correct explanation of Assertion.

(b) Both Assertion and Reason are true, but Reason is not the correct explanation of Assertion.

(c) Assertion is true, but Reason is false.

(d) Both Assertion and Reason are false.

2. Assertion Data Acquisition is a crucial stage in the AI project cycle as it involves gathering relevant information for the project.

Reason Data Acquisition involves acquiring raw facts, figures, or statistics necessary for training AI systems.

(a) Both assertion and reason are true, and the reason is the correct explanation of the assertion.

(b) Both assertion and reason are true, but the reason is not the correct explanation of the assertion.

(c) Assertion is true, but the reason is false.

(d) Assertion is false, but the reason is true.

3 Assertion Testing data should be new and unseen to ensure the model's ability to generalize to different scenarios.

Reason The testing data quality is essential for the machine learning model's performance.

(a) Both Assertion and Reason are true, and the Reason is the correct explanation for the Assertion.

(b) Both Assertion and Reason are true, but the Reason is not the correct explanation for the Assertion.

(c) Assertion is true, but the Reason is false.

(d) Assertion is false, but the Reason is true.

4 Assertion Data visualization in data exploration leverages familiar visual cues such as shapes, dimensions, colors, lines, points, and angles.

Reason Humans process visual data better than numerical data, making it challenging for data scientists to communicate meaning without visual components.

(a) Both Assertion and Reason are true, and Reason is the correct explanation of Assertion.

(b) Both Assertion and Reason are true, but Reason is not the correct explanation of Assertion.

(c) Assertion is true, but Reason is false.

(d) Assertion is false, but Reason is true.

5 Assertion Bar charts are an effective method for data visualization when comparing categories and measured values.

Reason Bar charts can become problematic when there are too many categories included and may oversimplify complex data sets.

(a) Both Assertion and Reason are true, and Reason is the correct explanation of Assertion.

(b) Both Assertion and Reason are true, but Reason is not the correct explanation of Assertion.

(c) Assertion is true, but Reason is false.

(d) Assertion is false, but Reason is true.

Answers

1. (a) 2. (a) 3. (a) 4. (a) 5. (b)

Part II

Very Short Answer Type Questions

1 What is the AI Project Cycle?

Ans. The AI Project Cycle is a step-by-step process that a company must follow in order to derive value from an AI project and to solve the problem.

2 What are the different AI Project stages?

Ans. The different AI Project stages are:

(i) Problem Scoping (ii) Data Acquisition
(iii) Data Exploration (iv) Modelling
(v) Evaluation (vi) Deployment

3 What is Problem Scoping?

Ans. Problem scoping is the process of understanding a problem, determining the various factors that affect the problem, and defining the project's purpose.

4 In the AI project cycle, what is the first phase, and what does it involve?

Ans. The first phase of the AI project cycle is "Problem Scoping," which involves identifying and finalizing the problem that the AI project aims to solve.

5 What are some methods of data acquisition in the context of AI projects?

Ans. Methods of data acquisition include surveys, web scraping, sensors, cameras, observations, and API (Application Programming Interface).

6 In the AI project cycle, what is the purpose of the "Evaluation" stage?

Ans. The "Evaluation" stage assesses the efficiency of the AI model by testing it with a separate dataset, considering factors such as precision, accuracy, F1 score, and recall.

7 What role does training data play in machine learning?

Ans. Training data is essential for teaching algorithms and ensuring accuracy.

8 How does testing data differ from training data in AI?

Ans. Training data is used to teach the AI model, helping it learn patterns. Testing data evaluates the model's performance on unseen data, ensuring it generalizes well.

Short Answer Type Questions

1 What is a project, and why is it important to break it down into individual tasks?

Ans. A project is a series of tasks aimed at achieving a specific goal. Breaking down a project into individual tasks is essential for better management, accountability, and utilizing team strengths. It helps in clear delegation, understanding expectations, and meeting deadlines effectively.

2 Explain the significance of problem scoping in the AI project cycle and provide an example scenario where problem scoping is essential.

Ans. Problem scoping is vital in the AI project cycle as it involves defining the scope and aim of the problem to be solved. For example, in developing a facial recognition system for enhanced security, problem scoping includes identifying authorized personnel, obtaining their data, and creating a system to prevent unauthorized access.

3 What is the role of data exploration in the AI project cycle, and how does data visualization contribute to understanding complex data?

Ans. Data exploration in the AI project cycle involves finding hidden patterns in complex data. Data visualization, through methods like charts and graphs, helps in spotting trends, choosing the right tools for analysis, and sharing insights. It makes data more understandable and aids in decision-making.

4 What is the first step in scoping a problem for an AI project?

Ans. The first step in scoping a problem for an AI project is Problem Identification. This involves creating a concise and specific description of the current situation, the desired situation, and the gap between them. It includes clear identification of the problem, finding the root cause, and framing the problem correctly.

5 What is Data Acquisition, and why is it important in the AI Project Cycle?

Ans. Data Acquisition is the process of obtaining relevant data for a project. In the AI Project Cycle, it's essential for training AI systems with adequate information to make accurate predictions or decisions. This stage ensures that the system learns from real-world data, enabling it to understand patterns and relationships. Without proper data acquisition, AI systems may produce unreliable outcomes or fail to perform effectively.

6 How does data exploration differ from data acquisition?

Ans. Data exploration involves analyzing and visualizing the collected data to uncover patterns and insights, while data acquisition is the process of gathering and filtering data from various sources.

7 Can you name some popular data visualization techniques?

Ans. Some techniques include pie charts, bar charts, histograms, Gantt charts, heat maps, and various types of diagrams and maps used to represent data visually.

Long Answer Type Questions

1 What are the phases involved in the development of an artificial intelligence project?

Ans. The AI project development involves crucial phases:

(i) **Problem Scoping** Identify and define the issue to solve, setting clear objectives and boundaries.

(ii) **Data Acquisition** Gather relevant data from various sources using methods like surveys, web scraping, and sensors.

(iii) **Data Exploration** Analyze and understand collected data, visualizing patterns and anomalies to guide modelling techniques.

(iv) **Modelling** Develop mathematical models representing data relationships, tailored to the problem's complexity and available data.

(v) **Evaluation** Assess model performance against predefined metrics using validation datasets to ensure reliability and meet objectives.

(vi) **Deployment** Deployment is the method by which you integrate a machine learning model into an existing production environment to make practical business decisions based on data.

2 Write the problem approach in AI Problem Scoping.

Ans. Problem scoping in AI involves identifying issues through the 4Ws Problem Canvas:

- **Who?** Identifying stakeholders affected, like financial experts and regulatory bodies in a fraud detection project.
- **What?** Detailing the problem with evidence from sources like historical data in fraud detection.
- **Where?** Understanding where the problem is prominent, like specific industries prone to fraud.
- **Why?** Addressing reasons for solving the problem, such as safeguarding financial assets and societal benefits.

3 Wildlife India, an autonomous organization dedicated to the rehabilitation of injured wild animals, is keen on monitoring the treated animals by tracking details like their location and thermal information. Which method are most suitable for collecting this specific set of data? **Competency Based Ques.**

Ans. Sensors would be the most suitable method for collecting location and thermal information of treated wild animals. Wildlife India can use GPS trackers or radio telemetry tags to monitor the animals' locations accurately. These devices can provide real-time data on the animals' movements, allowing for effective tracking and management.

Additionally, thermal sensors can be deployed to monitor the animals' body temperatures, helping to assess their health and recovery progress. Using sensors ensures continuous and reliable data collection without relying on human observations, which can be limited in accuracy and consistency. Overall, sensors offer a robust and comprehensive approach to monitoring the treated animals, enabling Wildlife India to make informed decisions for their rehabilitation and conservation efforts.

4 What are some common techniques used in data exploration?

Ans. Data exploration techniques encompass a range of methods, including statistical analysis, visualization, and data clustering. Analysts utilize tools like histograms, scatter plots, and box plots to visualize data distributions and identify outliers. Statistical measures such as mean, median, and mode help understand data variance and central tendencies. Moreover, data clustering enables analysts to group similar data points for deeper analysis. By combining these techniques, analysts can gain insights into data structures, relationshipspatterns, facilitating informed decision-making and further analysis.

5 A wildlife conservation organization has gathered data on the population of endangered species in various national parks. The released statistics include 800 elephants, 600 rhinos, 400 tigers, and 300 pandas. What is the best visualization to represent this type of data in data visualization tools? **Competency Based Ques.**

Ans. The best visualization for representing the population of endangered species in various national parks would be a bar chart. A bar chart allows for clear comparison between different categories, making it easy to see the differences in population sizes of elephants, rhinos, tigers, and pandas across the national parks. Each species can be represented by a different colored bar, and the length of each bar corresponds to the population size. This visualization effectively communicates the relative sizes of the populations and allows for easy interpretation of the data.

ASSESSMENT EXERCISE

Multiple Type Questions

1. Which of the following is not a stage in the AI Project Cycle
   (a) Problem Scoping (b) Data Acquisition
   (c) Data Exploration (d) Prototyping
2. While finalising the aim of this system, you scope the problem which you wish to solve with the help of your project. This is called ....
   (a) Data acquisition (b) Problem Scoping
   (c) Data exploration (d) Modelling
3. Which of the following would you study in the problems scoping stage of an AI project.
   (a) Domain and parameters specific to the problem
   (b) Data specific to the problem
   (c) Data required for testing
   (d) Algorithm and solution specific to the problem
4. What is the role of API (Application Programming Interface) in data acquisition for AI projects?
   (a) API is a source of raw visual data
   (b) API collects physical data through sensors
   (c) API is a messenger that takes requests and provides responses
   (d) API is a method of gathering data through surveys
5. It refers to human or mechanical watching, noticing or perceiving of what people actually do or what events take place in a specific working environment.
   (a) Survey (b) Interview
   (c) Observation (d) API

Very Short Answer Type Questions

6. Why is analyzing the current state important in scoping a problem for an AI project?
7. In the 4Ws Canvas, what does the "Why" block focus on?
8. What is the first step in scoping a problem in the AI project cycle?
9. What are some techniques used in data exploration?

Short Answer Type Questions

10. List different sources from where you can collect data.
11. Explain the significance of training data in predictive AI systems.
12. Describe the Role of AI in data exploration.
13. Why is data visualization important in data exploration?

Long Answer Type Questions

14. What is a problem scoping stages in AI project cycle?
15. What is data exploration, and why is it an essential step in data analysis?

CHAPTER 03

Ethics

AI ethics is a field concerned with the responsible development and use of artificial intelligence. It focuses on minimizing risks and maximizing benefits by addressing issues like bias in AI systems, data privacy, and the fairness of automated decisions.

3.1 Introduction to Ethics

Ethics is basically a set of principles or standards that guide people's behaviour and decisions about what is right and wrong. It helps individuals determine how they should act in different situations, considering what is fair, just, and morally acceptable.

Ethics influences how we interact with others, make choices, and live our lives in a way that aligns with our values and the principles society considers good or acceptable. Essentially, it's about doing the right thing based on moral beliefs and values.

Morals

Morals are the principles that guide our behavior and our understanding of what is right or wrong. They are influenced by our upbringing, culture, and personal beliefs. Moral principles help us to make choices that are fair, just, and kind.

For example, honesty is a moral value. So, if you find someone's wallet, your morals would tell you to return it, even though there's no legal consequence for keeping it.

3.2 AI Related to Ethics

AI and ethics are closely connected because AI systems are designed to make decisions, just like humans do. But since AI learns from data and patterns, it can sometimes make choices that might not be fair or right. Ethics in AI means figuring out rules and guidelines to make sure AI behaves in ways that align with our values and doesn't harm anyone. It involves considering things like privacy, fairness, transparency, and the impact AI might have on people's lives.

Artificial Intelligence (AI) ethics refers to the moral principles and guidelines that govern the development, deployment, and use of AI technologies. It's like a set of rules or values that help make sure AI systems are fair, safe, and respectful to people.

Imagine AI as a really smart tool that can learn, make decisions, and do things on its own, like recommending movies, driving cars, or helping doctors diagnose diseases. But sometimes, these AI systems can make mistakes or do things that might not be fair or right.

AI ethics demands that AI systems be:

- **Fair** Treating everyone equally without favoring any group.
- **Private** Respecting people's personal information and not sharing it without permission.
- **Transparent** Allowing people to understand how decisions are made.
- **Accountable** Having clear responsibility for when things go wrong.
- **Safe** Designed to avoid causing harm to people and society.
- **Unbiased** Free from discrimination against any particular group.

Note Biased Data will create Bias Decisions.

3.3 Bias

AI bias means favoring someone or something. When Biased Data is fed to an AI machine while creating the model then the machine will also be biased. AI Bias is an anomaly in the result produced through AI based programs and algorithms because of prejudiced assumptions made during the algorithm development process or prejudices in the training data. For example,

1. Most of virtual assistants have a female voice and not a male voice.
2. Security systems are trained, based on an individual's race of gender rather than their actions, movements to commit the crime ,etc.
3. In US, a healthcare algorithm was used to decide extra medical facilities for people, AI produced faulty results and favoured white patients over black patients.

Note *In 2018, Amazon abandoned its AI recruitment tool because it was discovered to be biased against female candidates.*

The scenario shows us how important it is to make sure AI systems don't learn from biased data. If they do, they might end up making unfair decisions without even realizing it. So, it's crucial to check and fix these biases to make AI systems are fair to everyone.

Training Data in AI

Data plays an important role in an AI model's functioning. AI models uses training data to learn and perform its task with high accuracy. Training data may be biased during collection process that will produced biased results. Training Data is a huge collection of labelled information that is used to build an AI model.

For example,

Let us consider that a person Mr. X likes a color 'Red' very much. Now, if another dataset stores that 'Red' colour is preferred for aggressive nature, then without much representation, this dataset may link that person with aggressive nature. So this is an example of AI bias.

Reason of AI Bias

The reasons you listed are all important factors that contribute to AI bias in various ways:

- **Human bias in decisions** Our own biases can creep into AI systems at different stages. For instance, programmers might unknowingly weight certain factors in an algorithm that reflect their own biases.
- **Flawed and unbalanced data collection** If the data used to train an AI is flawed or gathered in a biased way, the AI will learn those biases and perpetuate them.
- **Under- or over-representation of specific features** When certain features (like race or gender) are under-represented in the training data, the AI might not be able to handle those variations well, leading to biased outcomes.
- **Wrong assumptions** If the developers make incorrect assumptions about the data or the real world, the AI might inherit those assumptions and produce biased results.
- **No proper bias testing** If AI systems aren't rigorously tested for bias, these biases might go undetected and cause problems later.
- **No bias mitigation** Even after identifying bias, if there aren't steps taken to reduce its effects, the AI will remain biased.

Note *Bias in data collection refers to flawed or unbalanced data with over- or under- representation of data related to specific features or groups or ethnicity etc. in the final data- collection.*

3.4 AI Access

AI Access explain the gap in society, where only upper-class people who can afford AI-enabled devices have the opportunity to access it and people below the poverty line don't have access to it.

Because of this, a gap has emerged between these two classes of people and it gets widened with the rapid advancement of technology.

The Government has to bring balance in the society by providing infrastructure to common students/people so that everyone will get a chance to access emerging technologies like AI. AI access means making AI more accessible or available to all.

Principles of AI Ethics

The following principles in AI Ethics affect the quality of AI solutions

- **Human Rights** AI systems should be developed and used in a way that respects human rights and fundamental freedoms. This means avoiding applications that discriminate against individuals or groups, or that could be used for surveillance or other intrusive purposes.
- **Bias** AI algorithms can inherit biases from the data they are trained on. This can lead to unfair or discriminatory outcomes.

  For example, if an AI used for loan approvals is biased against certain demographics. Mitigating bias is essential for creating fair and trustworthy AI.

- **Privacy** AI systems often collect and use large amounts of personal data. It's important to ensure that this data is collected, used, and stored ethically, with proper user consent and strong data security measures.
- **Inclusion** AI development should involve diverse teams and consider the needs of all potential users. This helps to avoid building solutions that exclude or disadvantage certain groups of people. By ensuring inclusion, AI can be a powerful tool for promoting equality and accessibility.

Try These 3.1

1 **List some ethical issues related to AI.**

2 **Give some examples of AI bias.**

3 **How is training data useful for AI? Why should it be fair?**

4 **The data used by AI algorithms to build AI models is known as .... data. (Testing/Training)**

Glossary

AI Ethics refers to the moral principles and guidelines that govern the development, deployment, and use of AI technologies.

AI bias refers to unfair or prejudiced outcomes that can occur when artificial intelligence systems are trained on data that contains biases.

Training Data A collection of labelled, annotated information that's used to build an AI model.

Let's Investigate

Activity

In this activity, students will explore the Moral Machine website, a platform that gathers a human perspective on moral decisions made by machine intelligence, such as self-driving cars.

Students will play the role of major stakeholders, and they have to decide what is ethical and what is not for a given scenario.

Materials

- Computers with internet access
- Projector (optional)
- Whiteboard or chart paper (optional)

Procedure

1. Begin by introducing the concept of self-driving cars and the ethical dilemmas that they present.
2. Divide the students into small groups.
3. Instruct the students to visit the Moral Machine website (https://www.moralmachine.net/).
4. Explain to the students that they will be presented with a series of moral dilemmas in which a self-driving car must choose the lesser of two evils.
5. For each dilemma, the students should discuss the following questions:
   - What is the situation?
   - What are the possible outcomes?
   - What is the most ethical decision for the self-driving car to make?
   - Why?
6. After the students have had time to discuss each dilemma, have each group share their thoughts with the class.
7. As a class, discuss the different perspectives that were raised.
8. Debrief the activity by asking the students the following questions:
   - What are some of the challenges of programming self-driving cars to make ethical decisions?
   - Who should be responsible for making decisions about the ethics of self-driving cars?
   - How can we ensure that self-driving cars are programmed in a way that is fair and unbiased?
   - Extension Activities
   - Have the students design their own moral dilemmas for self-driving cars.
   - Have the students research the ethical guidelines that are being developed for self-driving cars.
   - Have the students debate the pros and cons of self-driving cars.

This activity can be adapted to fit the needs of your students and the time constraints of your class. It is a great way to get students thinking about the ethical implications of artificial intelligence.

NCERT FOLDER

Complete Explanations of all NCERT's Questions

A. Objective Type Questions

Q.1 The guiding principles to decide what is good or bad is known as ....

Ans. ethics

Q.2 When building AI solutions, we need to ensure that they follow ....

Ans. ethical principle

Q.3 Praneet has taken extra packets of mouth freshener after dinner from a restaurant. Is it considered as theft? Is it -Moral or Ethical concern?

Ans. Both Moral and Ethical

Q.4 Rakshit and Aman are talking about purchasing a new mobile. They discuss various features which they want in their mobile. Aman finds that, he started getting notification of various models of Mobiles that meets his requirement? Write which ethical concern the above example depicts.

Ans. Rakshit and Aman's situation depicts the ethical concern of privacy. Their online discussions influencing targeted advertising is a potential privacy intrusion.

Q.5 "Preference for one over the other" is known as ....

Ans. Bias

Q.6 Artificial Intelligence and machine learning systems can display unfair behaviour if not trained properly. (True/False)

Ans. True

Q.7 Search for images of personal secretary on Google, displaying predominantly the images of Women is an example of ....

Ans. gender bias

Q.8 An Ethical AI framework makes sure that transparency, fairness and accountability is develop into the systems to provide unbiased results. (True/False)

Ans. True

B. Subjective Type Questions

Q.1 Differentiate between Ethics and Moral with suitable examples.

Ans. Difference between Ethics and Morals

Ethics	Morals
The guiding principles to decide what is good or bad.	The beliefs dictated by our society.
These are values that a person themselves chooses for their life. **Examples** • Is it good to speak the truth in all situations? • Is it good to be loyal under all circumstances? • Is it necessary to always be generous?	Morals are not fixed and can be different for different societies. **Examples** • Always speak the truth • Always be loyal • Always be generous

Q.2 Define principles of AI ethics.

Ans. Refer to text on page no. 148 (Principles of AI Ethics).

Q.3 Explain Data privacy.

Ans. Data privacy is a major concern in AI ethics because AI systems rely on vast amounts of data, which can contain personal information.

This raises issues of:

- **Collection** Is data collected fairly and with user knowledge?
- **Use** Is data used only for its intended purpose?
- **Bias** Can biased data lead to biased AI decisions?
- **Security** Is personal data secure from breaches?

Ethical AI requires data privacy measures to protect individuals and ensure responsible AI development.

Q.4 Craft a description of how considerations for inclusivity are addressed during the development of AI models.

Ans. Inclusivity is considered in AI development:

- **Diverse Teams** People from various backgrounds bring different perspectives to identify and mitigate biases in data and algorithms.
- **Inclusive Data** Data collection considers diverse populations to avoid bias towards certain groups.
- **Fairness in Design** AI systems are designed to be accessible and avoid discrimination based on factors like age, race, or disability.

Q.5 Write major issues around AI ethics.

Ans. Some major issues around AI ethics are:

- **Bias** AI systems can inherit and amplify biases from the data they're trained on, leading to discriminatory outcomes.
- **Privacy** AI development often relies on vast amounts of personal data, raising concerns about collection, storage, and misuse.
- **Transparency** Many AI systems are complex and opaque, making it difficult to understand how they reach decisions.
- **Security** AI systems can be vulnerable to hacking or manipulation, potentially causing harm.

Q.6 A company had been working on a secret AI recruiting tool. The machine-learning specialists uncovered a big problem: their new recruiting engine did not like women chefs. The system taught itself that male candidates are preferable. It penalised resumes that included the word "women chef". This led to the failure of the tool.

a. What aspect of AI ethics is illustrated in the given scenario?

b. What could be the possible reasons for the ethical concern identified?

Ans. a. Bias in AI is illustrated in this scenario.

b. Possible reasons for the bias:

- **Training Data** The AI might have been trained on a dataset with a historical underrepresentation of women chefs. This can lead the model to associate "women chef" with qualities not typically desired in chefs.
- **Word Association** The algorithm might have misinterpreted "women chef" as a negative term due to subconscious societal biases reflected in how the training data is written.

Q.7 As Artificially Intelligent machines become more and more powerful, their ability to accomplish tedious tasks is becoming better. Hence, it is now that AI machines have started replacing humans in factories. While people see it in a negative way and say AI has the power to bring mass unemployment and one day, machines would enslave humans, on the other hand, other people say that machines are meant to ease our lives. If machines over take monotonous and tedious tasks, humans should upgrade their skills to remain their masters always.

What according to you is a better approach towards this ethical concern? Justify your answer.

Ans. A balanced approach is best towards the ethical concern of AI replacing humans in factories. Embracing AI for its efficiency and potential to take over monotonous tasks can lead to greater productivity and innovation.

However, it is crucial to simultaneously invest in education and training programs to help workers develop new skills and adapt to evolving job markets. This way, humans can remain in control and benefit from technological advancements, ensuring that AI serves to enhance human life rather than detract from it.

REVIEW EXERCISE

Including Competency Based Questions

Part I

Multiple Choice Questions

1 What is ethics?

(a) A set of rules for programming AI
(b) A set of principles guiding behaviour and decisions
(c) The study of robotics
(d) A programming language

2 Why is ethics important in the context of AI?

(a) It ensures AI systems are always correct
(b) It prevents the development of AI technologies
(c) It addresses concerns about fairness, safety, and privacy
(d) It only focuses on maximizing profit

3 What does AI bias refer to?

(a) A positive trait of AI systems
(b) Unfairly favoring or discriminating against certain groups of people
(c) A programming error in AI algorithms
(d) The speed at which AI makes decisions

4 How can AI bias be mitigated according to the provided information?

(a) By reducing the diversity of training data.
(b) By designing algorithms without considering fairness.
(c) By regularly auditing AI systems.
(d) By excluding diverse perspectives from development teams.

5 What does Ethical AI prioritize in terms of social well-being?

(a) Serving the interests of corporations.
(b) Working for the benefit of mankind.
(c) Maximizing individual profits.
(d) Focusing solely on technological advancement.

6 Which principle of Ethical AI ensures transparency and accountability?

(a) Social Well-being
(b) Avoiding Unfair Bias
(c) Transparency and Explainability
(d) Value Alignment

7 In the context of AI ethics, what are the key aspects covered under the term "Fairness"? **Competency Based Ques.**

I. Treating everyone equally
II. Favoring specific groups
III. Considering historical biases
IV. Ensuring equal distribution of resources

(a) Both I and III (b) Only II
(c) Both I and IV (d) Only III

8. Which of the following is a major factor contributing to bias in AI systems?

(a) Overfitting to the training data
(b) The use of neural networks
(c) Human biases embedded in the training data
(d) High computational power

9 How does ethical AI contribute to a better future for AI? **Competency Based Ques.**

I. By setting regulations to reduce risks such as mass surveillance
II. By promoting exclusive profit generation
III. By prioritizing human rights violations
IV. By ensuring systems are transparent and explainable

(a) Both I and IV
(b) I, III, and IV
(c) Both II and IV
(d) All of the above

10 How can the negative impact of job displacement due to AI automation be mitigated?

(a) Ignoring the impact on jobs
(b) Focusing on reskilling and upskilling workers
(c) Increasing automation without considering consequences
(d) Limiting the development of AI technologies

11 A tech company developed an AI system for processing job applications. However, it was found that the system consistently rejected applications from candidates with certain ethnic backgrounds. Which AI ethics principle is violated in this scenario? **Competency Based Ques.**

(a) Trust, Privacy and Control
(b) Bias and Fairness
(c) Accountability
(d) Transparency

12 A new AI-driven medical diagnosis system was introduced in a hospital. After a few months, it was discovered that the system occasionally provided incorrect diagnoses without any clear explanation. What AI ethical issue is highlighted in this situation? **Competency Based Ques.**

(a) Human rights and AI
(b) Accountability
(c) Unbiased
(d) Human-AI interaction

13 What is the primary concern regarding the use of AI in autonomous weapons systems?

(a) They can be easily hacked and controlled by adversaries
(b) They lack the ability to make ethical decisions in warfare situations
(c) They have the potential to cause unintended harm and escalate conflicts
(d) They are prohibitively expensive to develop and maintain

14 What is the main ethical concern related to the use of AI in employment and workforce management?

(a) The potential loss of jobs due to automation and displacement of human workers
(b) The unequal distribution of wealth and resources resulting from AI-driven economic changes
(c) The invasion of privacy through constant monitoring and surveillance of employees
(d) The risk of AI systems making biased or discriminatory hiring decisions

15 Which of the following is not a potential consequence of widespread job automation by AI?

(a) Increased unemployment and economic inequality
(b) Greater job satisfaction and work-life balance for workers
(c) Displacement of certain industries and professions
(d) Shift in the nature of work towards more creative and human-centric tasks

16 Which ethical principle emphasizes the importance of ensuring that AI systems treat all individuals fairly and without bias?

(a) Autonomy (b) Beneficence
(c) Justice (d) Non-maleficence

17 How can AI be used to promote social good?

(a) By developing AI systems that prioritize profit over ethical considerations

(b) By creating AI algorithms that perpetuate bias and discrimination
(c) By using AI to address societal challenges such as healthcare and poverty
(d) By limiting access to AI technology to only certain groups of people

18 **What is the purpose of AI transparency?**
(a) To ensure AI systems are kept secret from the public
(b) To provide explanations for how AI systems make decisions
(c) To increase the complexity of AI algorithms
(d) To eliminate bias from AI systems

19 **What role does public policy play in AI ethics?**
(a) Public policy has no impact on AI ethics
(b) Public policy can help regulate the development and use of AI systems
(c) Public policy is solely concerned with maximizing profits for AI companies
(d) Public policy focuses on eliminating all AI technologies

20 **Which of the following is not a potential ethical concern related to AI?**
(a) Bias in algorithms leading to discriminatory outcomes
(b) Loss of human jobs due to automation
(c) Privacy violations through mass surveillance
(d) Advancements in medical research and treatment options

Answers

1. (b)	2. (c)	3. (b)	4. (c)	5. (b)
6. (c)	7. (c)	8. (c)	9. (a)	10. (b)
11. (b)	12. (b)	13. (c)	14. (d)	15. (b)
16. (c)	17. (c)	18. (b)	19. (b)	20. (d)

Statement Based Questions

1 **Statement 1 AI ethics involves considering principles like fairness, transparency, and accountability.**

Statement 2 Privacy is one of the ethical issues related to AI, ensuring personal information is handled carefully.
(a) Both Statement 1 and Statement 2 are correct
(b) Both Statement 1 and Statement 2 are incorrect
(c) Statement 1 is correct but Statement 2 is incorrect
(d) Statement 2 is correct but Statement 1 is incorrect

2 **Statement 1 Bias in AI can occur when AI systems inherit biases present in the data they are trained on.**

Statement 2 In 2018, Amazon abandoned an AI recruitment tool found to be biased against male candidates.
(a) Both Statement 1 and Statement 2 are correct
(b) Both Statement 1 and Statement 2 are incorrect
(c) Statement 1 is correct but Statement 2 is incorrect
(d) Statement 2 is correct but Statement 1 is incorrect

3 **Statement 1 Transparency in AI refers to the challenge of understanding how AI algorithms arrive at their decisions.**

Statement 2 The lack of transparency in AI algorithms can hinder accountability and raise concerns about potential misuse.
(a) Both Statement 1 and Statement 2 are correct
(b) Both Statement 1 and Statement 2 are incorrect
(c) Statement 1 is correct but Statement 2 is incorrect
(d) Statement 2 is correct but Statement 1 is incorrect

4 **Statement 1 Ethics is a set of principles guiding people's behaviour and decisions about what is right and wrong.**

Statement 2 AI and ethics are closely connected because AI systems are designed to make decisions just like humans do.
(a) Both Statement 1 and Statement 2 are correct
(b) Both Statement 1 and Statement 2 are incorrect
(c) Statement 1 is correct but Statement 2 is incorrect
(d) Statement 2 is correct but Statement 1 is incorrect

Answers

1. (a) 2. (c) 3. (a) 4. (a)

Assertion & Reason Based Questions

1 **Assertion Ethics plays a crucial role in guiding individuals' behaviour and decision-making, considering principles of fairness, justice, and moral acceptability.**

Reason Ethics provides a set of principles or standards that help individuals determine what is right or wrong in various situations, influencing how people interact with others, make choices, and align their actions with societal values.
(a) Both Assertion and Reason are true, and Reason is the correct explanation of the Assertion.
(b) Both Assertion and Reason are true, but Reason is not the correct explanation of the Assertion.
(c) Assertion is true, but Reason is false.
(d) Assertion is false, but Reason is true.

2 **Assertion The lack of transparency in AI algorithms can hinder accountability and lead to concerns about potential misuse.**

Reason Many AI algorithms operate as black boxes, making it challenging to understand how they arrive at their decisions, which can impact trust in their outcomes.
(a) Both Assertion and Reason are true, and Reason is the correct explanation of the Assertion.
(b) Both Assertion and Reason are true, but Reason is not the correct explanation of the Assertion.
(c) Assertion is true, but Reason is false.
(d) Assertion is false, but Reason is true.

3 **Assertion Inclusive development teams contribute to reducing unintentional biases in AI systems.**

Reason Diverse backgrounds and perspectives within development teams help ensure a more comprehensive and fair approach.

(a) Both Assertion and Reason are true, and Reason is the correct explanation of the Assertion.
(b) Both Assertion and Reason are true, but Reason is not the correct explanation of the Assertion.
(c) Assertion is true, but Reason is false.
(d) Assertion is false, but Reason is true.

4 **Assertion AI bias can occur due to biases present in training data, algorithmic development, and feedback loops.**

Reason Training data bias influences how AI systems learn, algorithmic bias results from design choices, and feedback loops reinforce biases through continuous learning.

(a) Both Assertion and Reason are true, and Reason is the correct explanation of the Assertion.
(b) Both Assertion and Reason are true, but Reason is not the correct explanation of the Assertion.
(c) Assertion is true, but Reason is false.
(d) Assertion is false, but Reason is true.

5 **Assertion Diverse training data is crucial in mitigating AI bias.**

Reason A robot trained on limited data may develop biased perceptions, leading to unfair decisions.

(a) Both Assertion and Reason are true, and Reason is the correct explanation of the Assertion.
(b) Both Assertion and Reason are true, but Reason is not the correct explanation of the Assertion.
(c) Assertion is true, but Reason is false.
(d) Assertion is false, but Reason is true.

Answers

1. (a) **2.** (b) **3.** (a) **4.** (a) **5.** (a)

Part II

Very Short Answer Type Questions

1 **What is AI bias, and how does it occur?**

Ans. AI bias is unfair outcomes in AI systems due to human bias in decisions, flawed and unbalanced data collection and no proper bias testing.

2 **How can diverse training data mitigate AI bias?**

Ans. Diverse training data ensures fair AI by exposing systems to varied examples, preventing skewed outcomes or discrimination.

3 **Why is ethical AI design crucial in AI development?**

Ans. Ethical design ensures fairness, transparency, and accountability in AI algorithms, preventing unintentional biases and promoting equitable outcomes.

4 **How does regular auditing help mitigate AI bias?**

Ans. Regular audits identify and correct biases in AI systems over time, ensuring continuous fairness and addressing emerging issues promptly.

5 **Why is inclusive development essential for reducing AI bias?**

Ans. Inclusive development teams bring diverse perspectives, minimizing unintentional biases and creating AI systems that cater to a broader range of users.

6 **Why is transparency important in AI?**

Ans. Transparency helps understand AI decisions, fostering trust and accountability, crucial for ensuring fairness and ethical behaviour.

7 **How can regulations contribute to a better future for AI ethics?**

Ans. Regulations can reduce AI risks, addressing issues like mass surveillance and human rights violations for a balanced and ethical AI.

8 **Name one feature of Ethical AI that promotes social well-being.**

Ans. Ethical AI prioritizes social well-being, working for the benefit of individuals, society, and the environment.

Short Answer Type Questions

1 **Describe reason of AI bias.**

Ans. Refer to text on page no. 148 (Reason of AI bias).

2 **What are Morals?**

Ans. Refer to text on page no. 147 (Morals).

3 **Give some examples of AI bias.**

Ans. Refer to text on page no. 148 (Bias).

Long Answer Type Questions

1 **Write about the AI ethical issues.**

Ans. AI presents several ethical issues, including:

1. **Bias and Discrimination** AI systems can perpetuate or even amplify biases present in training data, leading to unfair treatment based on race, gender, or other attributes.
2. **Privacy Concerns** AI technologies often require vast amounts of data, raising concerns about surveillance, data security, and user consent.

3. **Autonomous Decision-Making** The use of AI in critical areas like healthcare and criminal justice raises questions about accountability and the appropriateness of machine-made decisions.
4. **Job Displacement** Automation and AI can lead to significant job losses, particularly in industries reliant on repetitive tasks, necessitating discussions on retraining and economic support.
5. **Transparency** Many AI systems operate as "black boxes," making it difficult to understand their decision-making processes, which can hinder accountability.
6. **Weaponization** The development of autonomous weapons systems poses significant risks, including the potential for unintended escalations in conflict.
7. **Misinformation** AI can be used to create deepfakes and other misleading content, contributing to the spread of false information and impacting public trust.

2 In 2014, Amazon developed an AI recruiting system to streamline their hiring process. It was found to be discriminatory against women as the data used to train the model was from the past 10 years, where most selected applicants were men due to the male dominance in the tech industry. Amazon scraped this system in 2018.This is an example of which AI ethical issue and also name the other ethical issues.

Competency Based Ques.

Ans. This situation demonstrates the problem of bias and fairness in AI. Amazon's recruiting system unfairly favored men over women because it was trained on data from a time when men were more likely to be hired in the tech industry. This resulted in discrimination against female applicants. To address this issue, Amazon discontinued the system in 2018.

This scenario shows how Amazon's AI recruiting system unfairly favored men over women, which is an example of the ethical issue of bias and fairness in AI. The system's training data from the past 10 years reflected a male-dominated tech industry, leading to discrimination against female applicants.

Other ethical issues involved include privacy concerns regarding the data used in the system and the potential for misuse of personal information. Additionally, there may have been issues related to transparency and accountability in how the AI system was developed and implemented. Overall, this situation highlights the importance of addressing multiple ethical considerations in AI applications.

ASSESSMENT EXERCISE

Multiple Choice Questions

1. Why is transparency important in AI ethics?
   (a) It makes AI systems smarter
   (b) It ensures that AI algorithms are kept secret
   (c) It helps users understand how AI systems make decisions
   (d) It slows down the decision-making process
2. In the context of AI ethics, what is the problem of inclusion?
   (a) Ensuring AI algorithms are exclusive
   (b) Making AI systems treat everyone fairly and inclusively
   (c) Excluding certain groups intentionally
   (d) Ignoring ethical considerations in AI development
3. What is one ethical issue related to AI and privacy?
   (a) Using AI to enhance personal privacy
   (b) AI systems sharing personal information without permission
   (c) Privacy has no relevance to AI
   (d) AI is not capable of handling personal data
4. What is the Cambridge Analytica scandal related to?
   (a) AI bias in hiring
   (b) Privacy concerns with AI
   (c) Job displacement due to automation
   (d) Ethical issues in self-driving cars
5. What does AI bias refer to?
   (a) The tendency of artificial intelligence to favor certain individuals or groups over others.
   (b) Unfair or prejudiced outcomes resulting from biased data or algorithms.
   (c) The accuracy of AI systems in recognizing diverse patterns.
   (d) The speed at which AI systems process information.
6. Which of the following is not a way in which AI bias can occur?
   (a) Training Data Bias
   (b) Algorithmic Bias
   (c) Feedback Loop Bias
   (d) Real-time Decision Bias

Very Short Answer Type Questions

7. How do ethical AI frameworks address unfair bias?
8. How does ethical AI contribute to human-centered principles?
9. Name some ethical issues of AI.

Short Answer Type Questions

10. What is AI bias? Give example.
11. Discuss the bias in data collections.

Long Answer Type Question

12. What are the possible reasons of AI bias?

Data Literacy

CHAPTER 04

Data literacy is foundational for understanding AI. It's the ability to read, work with, and analyze data. This is crucial for AI because AI systems are trained on data, and any biases or errors in that data can be reflected in the AI's outputs. So, data literacy empowers people to understand how AI works, assess its limitations, and ensure it's used fairly and effectively.

4.1 Introduction to Data Literacy

Data literacy is the ability to read, understand, create, and communicate data as information. It involves a combination of skills, knowledge, and attitudes that enable individuals to effectively work with data.

Data refers to raw, unprocessed facts and figures that are collected through observation, measurement, or research. Data can take various forms, including numbers, text, images, and more. It is the fundamental building block of information.

Literacy generally refers to the ability to read and write. However, in broader terms, it encompasses the skills needed to effectively communicate, interpret, and understand information.

4.2 Data Pyramid

The data pyramid, also known as the **DIKW pyramid**, represents the different stages of working with data and transforming it into something more meaningful.

The pyramid consists of four levels

- **Data** This is the foundation of the pyramid and refers to raw, unprocessed facts and figures. It can be structured or unstructured and come in various forms like text, numbers, images, audio, and video.
- **Information** Data is processed and organized to become information. This stage involves adding context and meaning to the raw data, making it understandable.
- **Knowledge** Information is analyzed and interpreted to uncover patterns, trends, and relationships. This level provides insights into "how" things happen.
- **Wisdom** At the top of the pyramid lies wisdom, which is the ability to make sound decisions and take effective actions based on the knowledge gained from data and information.

Let's understand the data pyramid with an example

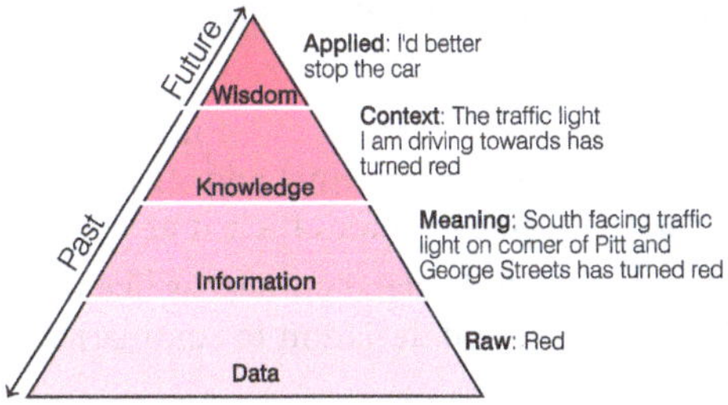

4.3 Impact of Data Literacy

Data literacy is becoming increasingly important as our world gets bombarded with information. It's essentially the ability to understand, work with, and communicate data effectively. This skill empowers people to make informed decisions, identify trends, and unlock the value of data.

Here's how data literacy can make a big impact:

For Individuals

- **Empowerment** Data literacy allows people to analyze information for themselves and draw their own conclusions. This fosters critical thinking and independence.

- **Better Decision Making** By understanding data, people can make more informed choices in all aspects of life, from personal finances to healthcare.

For Businesses

- **Increased Efficiency** Data-driven decisions can streamline operations, reduce waste, and improve overall business efficiency.
- **Improved Innovation** Data can reveal hidden patterns and trends that can inform new product development and marketing strategies.
- **Competitive Advantage** Businesses that leverage data literacy can gain a significant edge over competitors who rely on intuition or outdated methods.

For Society

- **Informed Citizens** Data literacy equips people to critically evaluate information and avoid misinformation, which is especially important in today's digital age.
- **Better Policy Making** Data can guide policymakers in creating evidence-based solutions for social and economic challenges.

How to Become Data Literate

Becoming data literate involves understanding how to gather, analyze, and interpret data effectively. Data literacy empowers you to understand, work with, and interpret data to inform your decisions.

Here's how you can develop this skillset, along with an example

- **Data Collection and Organization** Learn how data is gathered (surveys, experiments) and structured (spreadsheets, databases) for efficient analysis.
- **Basic Statistics** Understand core ideas like mean, median, and standard deviation to summarize data sets.
- **Data Visualization** Grasp how charts and graphs (bar charts, pie charts) present data insights in an easily digestible way.

Imagine you're analyzing fitness tracker data for a group. You can

- **Collect** Compile data on steps walked, calories burned, and sleep patterns.
- **Organize** Put this data into a spreadsheet with columns for each metric and rows for each participant.
- **Analyze** Calculate average steps walked and identify trends (e.g., weekends have lower activity levels).
- **Visualize** Create a bar chart to see which participant walked the most steps on average.

Importance of Data Literacy

Data literacy is important for several reasons

1. **Informed decision-making** Data literacy enables individuals and organizations to make informed decisions based on evidence rather than relying on intuition or guesswork. Data-driven decision-making leads to better outcomes, more efficient processes, and increased competitiveness.
2. **Increased efficiency and productivity** Data literacy helps employees identify patterns, trends, and anomalies in data, which can lead to process improvements, cost reductions, and increased operational efficiency.
3. **Innovation and growth** By harnessing the power of data, organizations can identify new opportunities, develop innovative products and services, and drive business growth. Data literacy is essential to effectively leverage data for innovation.
4. **Competitive advantage** As data becomes increasingly important in virtually every industry, businesses with a data-literate workforce are better positioned to compete and succeed in the market. Data literacy can provide a significant competitive advantage by enabling organizations to capitalize on the wealth of data available.
5. **Risk management** Data literacy helps organizations identify potential risks and vulnerabilities, allowing them to proactively address issues and implement effective risk management strategies.
6. **Compliance and regulation** Many industries are subject to strict data regulations, and organizations must be able to manage and understand their data to maintain compliance. Data literacy plays a critical role in ensuring that businesses can meet these requirements.
7. **Employee empowerment and job satisfaction** Employees who are data literate feel more confident in their roles and are better equipped to contribute to their organization's success. This can lead to increased job satisfaction, engagement, and retention.
8. **Enhanced collaboration** Data literacy fosters a culture of data-driven decision-making across the organization, promoting cross-functional collaboration and a shared understanding of business objectives and challenges.

Data Literacy Process Framework: A Well-Structured Approach

This framework offers a methodical way to develop data literacy abilities at different awareness levels. For successful implementation, it places a strong emphasis on an iterative approach and audience focus.

Planning

You've identified key aspects of planning - defining goals, understanding participants, and setting a timeframe. Consider including success metrics in the planning phase. How will you define a "successful" data literacy program for your audience?

Communication

Tailor communication strategies for different participant groups. Use clear and concise language for those less familiar with data concepts.

Assessment

Consider using a variety of assessment tools beyond just one. This could include surveys, skills tests, or group discussions to gain a more comprehensive understanding of participant needs.

Develop Culture

Develop strategies to reinforce data-driven decision making beyond the program itself. This could involve recognizing data-driven successes or creating data visualization dashboards that promote a data-centric culture.

Prescriptive Learning

Select educational materials based on participant requirements and program objectives. This guarantees that people find worthwhile and relevant content. To help learners retain information, think about incorporating interactive learning elements and chances for real-world application.

Evaluation

Define clear evaluation metrics aligned with your success criteria. This allows for focused measurement of program effectiveness.

Use a mix of quantitative and qualitative data collection methods for a well-rounded assessment. This could include surveys, skills tests, and interviews.

Try These 4.1

1. **Define the term "Data Literacy".**
2. **Write the impact of data literacy for soceity.**
3. **Explain data pyramid.**

4.4 Data Privacy

Data privacy, also known as information privacy, is all about control over your personal information. It refers to the right of individuals to determine how their data is collected, used, shared, and protected by organizations.

Example When you sign up for a social media account, the platform collects information like your name, email address, and maybe even your birthday.

Data privacy means you have the right to know what data is being collected, why it's being collected, and how it will be used. You should also be able to control who sees your information on the platform and have the ability to delete your account if you want.

Importance of Data Privacy

Data privacy is important for a number of reasons, both for individuals and for society as a whole. Here are some key points

- **Protection of personal information** Data privacy safeguards your personal information from unauthorized access. This includes sensitive data like social security numbers, financial records, and health information. By controlling your data, you reduce the risk of identity theft, fraud, and other crimes.
- **Trust and confidence** Data privacy is essential for building trust between individuals and organizations. When you share data with a company, you expect them to handle it responsibly. Good data privacy practices show that a company can be trusted with your information.
- **Security** Data breaches can be devastating. Hackers can steal personal information and use it for malicious purposes. Strong data privacy measures help to prevent these breaches from happening.
- **Autonomy** Data privacy gives you control over your personal information. You should decide who has access to your data and how it is used.

4.5 Data Security

Data security is all about protecting digital information. This includes guarding against unauthorized access, corruption, or theft of that information. Data security measures are designed to protect throughout its entire lifecycle, from creation to storage to use and disposal.

Some key aspects of data security are

- **Confidentiality** This ensures that only authorized people can access the data.
- **Integrity** This ensures that the data is accurate and hasn't been tampered with.
- **Availability** This ensures that the data is accessible to those who need it when they need it.

Importance of Data Security

Data security is vital in today's world for a number of reasons

- **Protection of Valuable Assets** Data is the lifeblood of many organizations, containing sensitive information like financial records, trade secrets, and customer data. Strong data security safeguards this information from unauthorized access, corruption, or theft.
- **Maintaining Trust** Data breaches can severely damage an organization's reputation. By implementing robust security measures, organizations can build trust with their customers and partners, assuring them that their information is well-protected.
- **Compliance with Regulations** Many industries have regulations mandating specific data security practices. Organizations must comply with these regulations to avoid hefty fines and legal repercussions.
- **Mitigating Financial Losses** Data breaches can be incredibly expensive, leading to financial losses from litigation, regulatory fines, and the cost of recovery. Strong data security helps prevent these financial burdens.
- **Safeguarding Privacy** Data security protects individual privacy by preventing unauthorized access to personal information. This is especially important in the age of identity theft and online scams.

Note *Data security and Privacy in AI systems is not just about safeguarding information it's about maintaining trust, preserving privacy and ensuring the integrity of AI decision-making processes.*

4.6 Cyber Security

Cybersecurity, also called **information technology security**, is the practice of protecting computers, servers, mobile devices, electronic systems, networks, and data from malicious attacks.

These attacks can aim to

- Access sensitive information
- Change or destroy information
- Extort money from users with ransomware
- Disrupt normal business processes

Steps for Improving Cyber Security

Here are some key steps you can follow to improve your cyber security posture

Protect Your Data

- **Strong Passwords** Create complex and unique passwords for all your accounts and enable two-factor authentication (2FA) whenever possible. 2FA adds an extra layer of security by requiring a second verification step beyond your password.
- **Account Security** Be cautious about the information you share online and be wary of unsolicited messages or requests for personal details.

Prevent Malware

Security Software Use reputable antivirus and anti-malware software to detect and remove malicious programs. Keep them up-to-date with the latest scans and definitions.

Avoid Phishing Attacks

- **Be Wary of Links** Don't click on suspicious links or attachments in emails, even if they appear to be from legitimate sources.
- **Verify Senders** Be cautious of emails requesting urgent action or personal information. Verify the sender's email address and be wary of generic greetings.

Backup Your Data

- **Regular Backups** Regularly back up your important data to a secure external drive or cloud storage service. This ensures you have a copy of your data in case of a cyber attack or device failure.

Keep Your Devices Safe

- **Software Updates** Install software updates for your operating system, applications, and firmware whenever they become available. These updates often include security patches to fix vulnerabilities.
- **Secure Connections** Avoid using public Wi-Fi for sensitive activities and consider using a virtual private network (VPN) for added security.
- **Mobile Device Security** Use a strong PIN or password to lock your mobile device and enable features like remote wipe in case it's lost or stolen.

Advantages of Data Literacy

- **Smarter Decisions** Data literacy helps you ditch guesswork and make choices based on facts. By understanding data, you can analyze information, identify trends, and use evidence to make better decisions in all aspects of life, from school projects to personal choices.

- **Problem-Solving Powerhouse** Imagine being a detective with data as your clues! Data literacy equips you with critical thinking skills to tackle challenges. You can analyze data to understand problems, find root causes, and develop effective solutions.
- **Innovation Station** Data can spark amazing ideas! With data literacy, you can uncover hidden patterns and relationships in information. This can lead to new inventions, creative solutions, and advancements in all fields.
- **Standing Out from the Crowd** In today's data-driven world, data literacy is a valuable skill. Being able to understand and work with data can give you an edge in school, future careers, and even citizen participation.

Disadvantages of Data Literacy

- **Information Overload** There's data everywhere! Data literacy can help you navigate this information flood, but it can also be overwhelming at first. Learning to prioritize reliable sources and filter out irrelevant data is an important skill to develop.
- **Misleading Data** Not all data is created equal. Data can be biased, incomplete, or even manipulated. Data literacy equips you with the tools to critically evaluate data sources and avoid being misled.
- **Tech Savvy Needed** Working with data often involves some technology. While the basics can be learned by anyone, data literacy may require some familiarity with tools like spreadsheets or data visualization software.

Applications of Data Literacy

The applications of data literacy are

- **Business** In the business world, data literacy is essential for making sound decisions about everything from marketing and sales to product development and operations. By understanding data, businesses can identify trends, target customers more effectively, and improve their overall performance. For example, a company might use data to identify trends in customer behaviour, understand what products are selling well, and target their advertising more effectively.
- **Science** Scientists use data to test hypothesis, conduct research, and make new discoveries. Data literacy is essential for scientists to be able to interpret and communicate their findings effectively.
- **Healthcare** Data literacy is becoming increasingly important in healthcare. By understanding data, healthcare providers can make more informed decisions about patient care, track the spread of diseases, and develop new treatments.
- **Education** Educators can use data to track student progress, identify areas where students are struggling, and personalize instruction accordingly. Data can also be used to develop more effective curriculum and teaching methods.

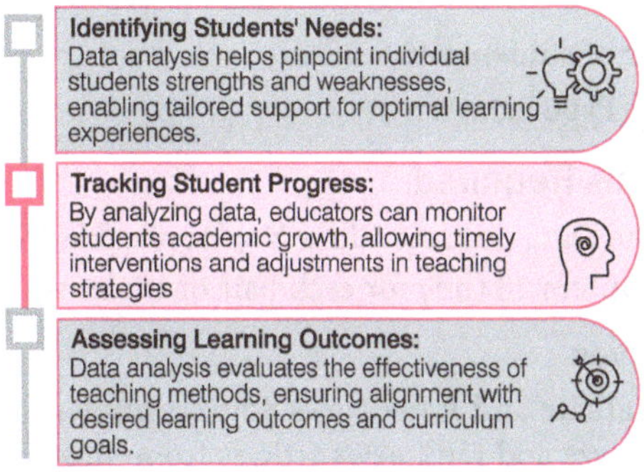

- **Government** Governments use data to develop policies, allocate resources, and track the effectiveness of programs. Data literacy is essential for government officials to be able to make sound decisions based on evidence.
- **Personal Life** Data literacy can also be beneficial in our personal lives. For example, we can use data to track our finances, monitor our health, and make informed decisions about our careers.

Try These 4.2

1. **Write the Importance of Data Privacy.**
2. **What do you understand by Data Security.**
3. **Write the few steps for improving Cyber Security.**
4. **Write any two advantages of Data Literacy.**
5. **What are the applications of data literacy in Business and Healthcare.**

Glossary

Data It refers to raw, unprocessed facts and figures that are collected through observation, measurement, or research.

Literacy It generally refers to the ability to read and write.

Data literacy It is the ability to read, understand, create, and communicate data as information.

Data pyramid It also known as the DIKW pyramid, is a model that shows the hierarchy of information processing.

Data privacy It also known as information privacy, is all about control over your personal information. It refers to the right of individuals to determine how their data is collected, used, shared, and protected by organizations.

Data security It is all about protecting digital information.

Cybersecurity It also called information technology security, is the practice of protecting computers, servers, mobile devices, electronic systems, networks, and data from malicious attacks.

Let's Investigate

Number of students 40 Students

Activity Type Pair Activity

Materials Required

- **Online Data Sources Clues** Not Applicable (NA)
- **Computers** 20 (one for each pair of students)

Objectives

1. **Evaluate and Rank News Sources** Students will analyze and rank news articles from most accurate to least accurate.
2. **Critical Thinking** Develop critical thinking skills by assessing the credibility and accuracy of different news sources.
3. **Data Literacy** Understand the importance of data literacy in making informed decisions.

Procedure

1. **Introduction** (10 minutes)
   - Explain the importance of data literacy and how it impacts decision-making.
   - Discuss the role of news articles in shaping public perception and opinion.
2. **Pairing and Setup** (5 minutes)
   - Pair up the students.
   - Assign each pair a computer.
3. **Activity Instructions** (10 minutes)
   - Each pair will choose a trending news topic.
   - They will search for and select five news articles covering the chosen topic from different sources.
4. **Analysis and Ranking** (40 minutes)
   - Each pair will read and analyze the articles.
   - They will rank the sources from most accurate to least accurate based on
     - **Author credentials** Evaluate the background and expertise of the author.
     - **Source reputation** Consider the credibility and reputation of the news outlet.
     - **Evidence and References** Check for the presence of verifiable facts, data, and references.
     - **Bias and Objectivity** Assess the objectivity and potential bias in the reporting.
     - **Consistency** Compare the information with other sources for consistency.
   - Fill in the table provided.
5. **Presentation** (20 minutes)
   - Each pair will present their findings, explaining their ranking and the reasons behind their choices.
6. **Discussion and Conclusion** (15 minutes):
   - Discuss as a class the different rankings and the reasoning behind them.
   - Highlight the importance of being critical of the information sources and making informed decisions.

Example Table Entry

Trending News Topic Climate Change Initiatives

Rank	Data Source	Author of the Source	Weblink to the Source	How was the situation described by the Source	Key figures in the source
1	The New York Times	Jane Doe	Link	Detailed with evidence and expert quotes	Dr. John Smith (Climate Scientist), EPA report
2	BBC News	John Roe	Link	Balanced, multiple viewpoints	UK Environment Minister, Greenpeace report
3	CNN	Alex Johnson	Link	General overview, some expert opinions	UN Climate Panel, local activists
4	BuzzFeed News	Emily Davis	Link	Casual tone, limited expert input	Social media influencers, NGO representatives
5	A Random Blog	Anonymous Blogger	Link	Personal opinion, no verifiable sources	None

NCERT FOLDER

Complete Explanations of all NCERT's Questions

Multiple Choice Questions

Q. 1 Cultivating Data Literacy means

(a) Utilize vocabulary and analytical skills
(b) Acquire, develop, and improve data literacy skills
(c) Develop skills in statistical methodologies
(d) Develop skills in Math

Q. 2 Data Privacy and Data Security are often used interchangeably but they are different from each other

(a) True (b) False

Q. 3 The .... provides guidance on using data efficiently and with all levels of awareness.

(a) data security framework
(b) data literacy framework
(c) data privacy framework
(d) data acquisition framework

Q. 4 .... allows us to understand why things are happening in a particular way

(a) Data
(b) Information
(c) Knowledge
(d) Wisdom

Q. 5 .... is the practice of protecting digital information from unauthorized access, corruption, or theft throughout its entire lifecycle.

(a) Data security
(b) Data literacy
(c) Data privacy
(d) Data acquisition

Answers

1. (b) **2.** (a) **3.** (b) **4.** (c) **5.** (a)

REVIEW EXERCISE

Including Competency Based Questions

Part I

Multiple Choice Questions

1 What is data literacy?

(a) The ability to sing and dance with data
(b) The ability to read, understand, create, and communicate data as information
(c) The ability to count numbers accurately
(d) The ability to speak multiple languages fluently

2 What is the fundamental building block of information?

(a) Wisdom (b) Knowledge
(c) Data (d) Information

3 What does the Data Pyramid represent?

(a) The hierarchy of ancient civilizations
(b) Different stages of working with data and transforming it into something meaningful
(c) A mathematical problem-solving technique
(d) A new model of storytelling

4 What is the top level of the Data Pyramid?

(a) Information
(b) Data
(c) Wisdom
(d) Knowledge

5 How can data literacy impact individuals?

(a) By making them forgetful
(b) By empowering them to analyze information and make informed decisions
(c) By limiting their creativity
(d) By reducing their critical thinking abilities

6 What advantage do businesses gain from data literacy?

(a) Increased confusion
(b) Decreased efficiency
(c) Improved innovation and competitive advantage
(d) Reduced customer satisfaction

7 **Which skill is not involved in becoming data literate?**
(a) Data collection and organization
(b) Basic statistics
(c) Data encryption
(d) Data visualization

8 **What does data privacy refer to?**
(a) The sharing of personal secrets
(b) The handling of personal information, including who can access it and how it's used
(c) The government's control over data
(d) The deletion of personal data

9 **What does data security aim to protect against?**
(a) Unwanted data collection
(b) Unauthorized access, corruption, or theft of digital information
(c) Data deletion
(d) Data miscommunication

10 **What is a key aspect of data security?**
(a) Transparency (b) Integrity
(c) Accessibility (d) Redundancy

11 **What is cyber security primarily concerned with protecting?**
(a) Physical assets
(b) Digital information and systems
(c) Financial investments
(d) Environmental resources

12 **How can individuals prevent malware attacks?**
(a) By sharing passwords openly
(b) By clicking on all links in emails
(c) By using reputable antivirus software and being cautious of suspicious links
(d) By ignoring security updates

13 **What is one advantage of data literacy mentioned in the content?**
(a) Information overload (b) Misleading data
(c) Smarter decisions (d) Lack of tech savvy

14 **In which field is data literacy not important?**
(a) Business
(b) Education
(c) Fashion design
(d) Healthcare

15 **What can data literacy empower individuals to do in their personal lives?**
(a) Track finances and monitor health
(b) Become less responsible
(c) Rely solely on evidence for decision-making
(d) Ignore data completely

Answers

1. (b)	**2.** (c)	**3.** (b)	**4.** (c)	**5.** (b)
6. (c)	**7.** (c)	**8.** (b)	**9.** (b)	**10.** (b)
11. (b)	**12.** (c)	**13.** (c)	**14.** (c)	**15.** (c)

Statement Based Questions

1 **Statement 1 Data literacy involves the ability to read, understand, create, and communicate data as information.**

Statement 2 Data literacy only refers to the skills needed to interpret numerical data.
(a) Both Statement 1 and Statement 2 are correct
(b) Both Statement 1 and Statement 2 are incorrect
(c) Statement 1 is correct but Statement 2 is incorrect
(d) Statement 2 is correct but Statement 1 is incorrect

2 **Statement 1 The DIKW pyramid represents the stages of transforming data into information, knowledge, and wisdom.**

Statement 2 In the data pyramid, knowledge is the second stage.
(a) Both Statement 1 and Statement 2 are correct
(b) Both Statement 1 and Statement 2 are incorrect
(c) Statement 1 is correct but Statement 2 is incorrect
(d) Statement 2 is correct but Statement 1 is incorrect

3 **Statement 1 Data literacy helps individuals make more informed decisions in personal and professional life.**

Statement 2 Data literacy only benefits businesses and has no impact on society.
(a) Both Statement 1 and Statement 2 are correct
(b) Both Statement 1 and Statement 2 are incorrect
(c) Statement 1 is correct but Statement 2 is incorrect
(d) Statement 2 is correct but Statement 1 is incorrect

4 **Statement 1 Data privacy refers to your right to control your personal information, including who can access it and how it's used.**

Statement 2 Data privacy is important for individuals, businesses and organizations.
(a) Both Statement 1 and Statement 2 are correct
(b) Both Statement 1 and Statement 2 are incorrect
(c) Statement 1 is correct but Statement 2 is incorrect
(d) Statement 2 is correct but Statement 1 is incorrect

Answers

1. (c) **2.** (a) **3.** (d) **4.** (a)

Assertion & Reason Based Questions

1 **Assertion Data literacy is crucial for individuals to make informed decisions.**

Reason Data literacy involves only the ability to read and write numerical data.
(a) Both Assertion and Reason are true, and Reason is the correct explanation of Assertion.
(b) Both Assertion and Reason are true, but Reason is not the correct explanation of Assertion.
(c) Assertion is true, but Reason is false.
(d) Assertion is false, but Reason is true.

2 Assertion The top level of the DIKW pyramid is wisdom.

Reason Wisdom in the DIKW pyramid is achieved by organizing and processing raw data into information.

(a) Both Assertion and Reason are true, and Reason is the correct explanation of Assertion.
(b) Both Assertion and Reason are true, but Reason is not the correct explanation of Assertion.
(c) Assertion is true, but Reason is false.
(d) Assertion is false, but Reason is true.

3 Assertion Data privacy helps to protect individuals' personal information from unauthorized access.

Reason Data privacy ensures that only authorized people can access, modify, and use personal data.

(a) Both Assertion and Reason are true, and Reason is the correct explanation of Assertion.
(b) Both Assertion and Reason are true, but Reason is not the correct explanation of Assertion.
(c) Assertion is true, but Reason is false.
(d) Assertion is false, but Reason is true.

Answers

1. (c) **2.** (c) **3.** (a)

Part II

Very Short Answer Type Questions

1 What is data literacy?

Ans. Data literacy is the ability to read, understand, create, and communicate data as information.

2 What does the data pyramid represent?

Ans. The data pyramid represents the different stages of working with data and transforming it into something more meaningful.

3 What is the importance of data literacy for businesses?

Ans. Data literacy can lead to increased efficiency, improved innovation, and a competitive advantage for businesses.

4 What are some key aspects of data security?

Ans. Confidentiality, integrity, and availability are key aspects of data security.

5 Write about education in applications of data literacy.

Ans. Educators can use data to track student progress, identify areas where students are struggling, and personalize instruction accordingly.

Short Answer Type Questions

1 What is data literacy, and why is it important?

Ans. Data literacy is the ability to understand, work with, and communicate data effectively. It's crucial because it empowers individuals and organizations to make better decisions by analyzing information accurately.

2 Explain the stages of the data pyramid.

Ans. The data pyramid consists of four levels: data, information, knowledge, and wisdom. Data is the raw facts, information adds context, knowledge involves analysis, and wisdom leads to informed decision-making.

3 Why is data privacy important?

Ans. Data privacy safeguards personal information, builds trust, ensures security, and grants autonomy over data usage and access.

4 What are some key steps for improving cybersecurity?

Ans. Steps include using strong passwords, avoiding phishing attacks, regularly backing up data, keeping devices updated, and protecting data with security software like antivirus programs.

5 What are the advantages of data literacy?

Ans. Data literacy empowers individuals to make smarter decisions, solve complex problems, innovate, and stand out in a data-driven world.

It enables critical thinking, evidence-based decision-making, and leveraging data for personal and professional growth.

6 Explain the Data Pyramid and its significance in data processing.

Ans. The Data Pyramid represents the stages of working with data, from raw facts to actionable wisdom. It starts with data, progresses to information, then knowledge, and finally wisdom.

This framework is essential for transforming data into meaningful insights and informed decision-making.

7 What are the key aspects and importance of data security?

Ans. Data security involves ensuring confidentiality, integrity, and availability of digital information.

It's vital for protecting valuable assets, maintaining trust with stakeholders, complying with regulations, mitigating financial losses, and safeguarding individual privacy in today's digital landscape.

Long Answer Type Questions

1 How might understanding the data pyramid help someone make more informed decisions, and what are the practical steps involved in this process?

Ans. Since the data pyramid illustrates the process of converting raw data into actionable wisdom, comprehension of it is essential for making well-informed decisions. Organizing and contextualizing data into relevant information is the first step in the process. Data is made up of unprocessed facts in various forms. By adding context and clarity, this step prepares the ground for a more in-depth examination.

Information is then subjected to analysis in order to find connections, patterns, and trends, which turns it into knowledge. Because it sheds light on the underlying causes and connections among the data, this knowledge phase is crucial. Ultimately, using this information to guide decisions and carry out wise acts is how wisdom is attained.

In practice, this method involves careful data gathering, organized chaos, careful trend analysis, and application of results to actual situations. Every stage builds on the one before it, ultimately leading to the capacity to make educated, calculated decisions that drive innovation and success.

2 Why is data literacy becoming crucial in today's society, and what are some examples of its impact on various fields?

Ans. Data literacy has grown more and more important in today's world in a variety of industries. For example, in the business world, having strong data literacy skills enables professionals to spot market possibilities, streamline processes, and improve client experiences. Educators can improve learning results by customizing teaching tactics to each student's requirements through the use of data literacy.

Data literacy in healthcare helps doctors diagnose patients, monitor health trends, and create individualized treatment programs. By applying insights to create policies that effectively address social issues and distribute resources, governments may reap the benefits of data literacy.

In general, data literacy fosters critical thinking and well-informed decision-making across a wide range of sectors, enabling people and organizations to navigate an increasingly data-driven world.

ASSESSMENT EXERCISE

Multiple Choice Questions

1. Which level of the data pyramid involves the ability to make sound decisions and take effective actions based on the knowledge gained from data and information?
   (a) Data (b) Information (c) Knowledge (d) Wisdom
2. What is one key impact of data literacy on society?
   (a) Increased efficiency in business operations
   (b) Improved innovation in product development
   (c) Empowerment to analyze information independently
   (d) Informed citizens capable of evaluating information critically
3. In the context of data privacy, what does the principle of autonomy refer to?
   (a) Ensuring data is accurate and hasn't been tampered with
   (b) The right to control personal information and decide who can access it
   (c) Protection against unauthorized access and data breaches
   (d) Building trust between individuals and organizations
4. Which of the following is a step to improve cybersecurity by preventing malware?
   (a) Use strong and unique passwords
   (c) Regularly back up important data
   (c) Be cautious about unsolicited messages
   (d) Use reputable antivirus and anti-malware software
5. What is a primary application of data literacy in the field of education?
   (a) Developing effective marketing strategies
   (b) Tracking the spread of diseases
   (c) Identifying areas where students are struggling
   (d) Allocating resources and tracking program effectiveness

Very Short Answer Type Questions

6. What is the foundation of the data pyramid?
7. What does information represent in the data pyramid?
8. How can data literacy benefit individuals in their personal lives?

Short Answer Type Questions

9. What is the Data Pyramid?
10. Why is data security important?
11. Describe key steps to improve cybersecurity.

Long Asnwer Type Questions

12. Write the Application of Data Literacy.
13. Explain Data Pyramid with example.

CHAPTER 05

Acquiring, Processing and Interpreting Data

Data is the fuel for AI. Just like a car needs gas to run, AI systems require vast amounts of data to learn and improve. This data is used for training, where the AI model is exposed to examples and refines its ability to recognize patterns, make predictions, or perform tasks. Acquiring this data can involve collecting sensor information, user interactions, or pre-existing datasets. Once collected, the data needs processing to clean and organize it for the AI.

5.1 Introduction

Extracting knowledge from data involves a three-step journey: acquiring, processing, and interpreting. First, you need to acquire the data. This could involve collecting new information through surveys or experiments, or finding existing data from databases or online sources. Once you have the data, it likely needs processing. This might involve cleaning the data to remove errors, organizing it into a usable format, and transforming it into a structure suitable for analysis. Finally, with clean and processed data, comes interpretation. This is where you make sense of the data by looking for patterns, trends, or relationships. By interpreting the data, you can draw conclusions and gain insights that inform decisions or answer your initial questions.

Data

Data is fundamental to AI in much the same way food is to a human. AI systems, especially those that learn through machine learning, require massive amounts of data to function. This data acts as a training tool, allowing the AI to learn and improve its abilities.

Let's learn about the various types of data.

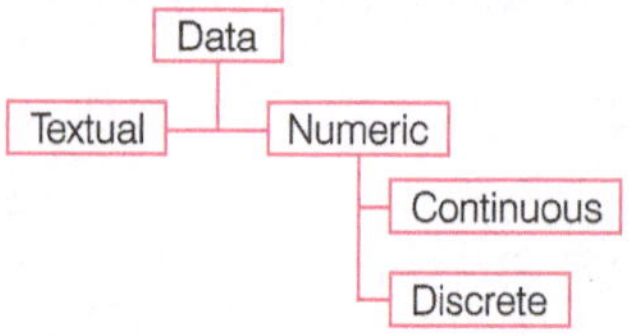

Textual Data

Textual data refers to information that can be categorized based on attributes or qualities. It is also known as categorical or qualitative data. Textual data is characterized by its linguistic structure and can be unstructured (Free-Form text) or semi-structured (text with some organizational elements, like tags or metadata).

Numerical Data

This refers to data that consists of numbers. It is quantitative and can be measured and ordered.

Numerical data can generally be classified into two main types

1. **Discrete Data** This type of data consists of distinct, separate values with no intermediate values possible. Discrete data usually arise from counting and can only take certain numerical values. The number of students in a class, the number of cars in a parking lot, or the number of books on a shelf are all examples of discrete data.
2. **Continuous Data** Continuous data, on the other hand, can take on any value within a given range. It often arises from measurement and can be broken down into smaller parts, with infinite possibilities between any two values. Examples include measurements like height, weight, temperature, or time.

Difference between Textual Data and Numerical Data

Aspect	Textual Data (Qualitative)	Numerical Data (Quantitative)
Type	Consists of strings of characters.	Consists of numbers.
Representation	Represents words, sentences, or paragraphs.	Represents quantities, measurements, or counts.
Example	"apple", "blue sky", "The quick brown fox."	5,10.25,1000
Analysis	Often requires natural language processing (NLP) techniques.	Analyzed using statistical methods.
Operations	May involve text processing like tokenization, stemming, or lemmatization.	Arithmetic operations like addition, subtraction, etc.
Data Types	Includes text, categorical variables.	Includes integers, floats, and decimals.
Context	Contextual understanding is important.	Contextual understanding might be necessary but not as critical.
Examples	Text documents, social media posts, emails.	Measurements, financial data, sensor readings.

The list of items categorized by whether they represent quantitative or qualitative data:

Quantitative Data (Numerical and Measurable)

- Temperature (in degrees Celsius, Fahrenheit, etc.)
- Shoe size (numerical value)
- Weight of a person (in kilograms, pounds, etc.)
- Age (in years)
- Height (in centimeters, inches, etc.)
- Distance (in kilometers, miles, etc.)
- Number of customers served (numerical count)
- Sales figures (numerical amount)
- Response time on a survey (in seconds)

Qualitative Data (Descriptive and Non-numerical)

- Gender (male, female, non-binary, etc.) - While there can be numerical codes assigned to genders, it's not inherently numerical data.
- Favourite color (descriptive term, not a number)
- Customer satisfaction (descriptive feedback, not a number)
- Movie genre (descriptive category)
- Customer feedback (written text, not a number)
- Reason for purchase (descriptive explanation)
- Brand preference (descriptive term)
- Emotional response (descriptive terms like happy, sad, angry)

Types of Data used in Three Domains of AI

The three domains of Artificial Intelligence (AI) you mentioned all rely on different types of data for their tasks:

- **Computer Vision (CV)** This field deals with enabling machines to interpret and understand the visual world. The data used in CV is primarily images and videos. These **images and videos** can be of various formats, including digital photographs, satellite imagery, and medical scans. The goal of CV algorithms is to extract meaningful information from these images, such as identifying objects, recognizing faces, and understanding scenes.
- **Natural Language Processing (NLP)** This domain focuses on how computers can understand and process human language. The data used in NLP is primarily **text**. This text can come from various sources, such as books, articles, social media posts, and conversations. NLP algorithms aim to extract meaning from this text, such as identifying the sentiment of a piece of writing, translating languages, and generating text that is similar to human-written text.
- **Statistical Data** This is a broader category that encompasses all types of data that can be used to identify patterns and trends. Statistical data can be used in all three domains of AI, but it is particularly important for tasks such as machine learning. Examples of statistical data include numerical data (e.g., sales figures, sensor readings), categorical data (e.g., customer demographics, product categories), and time series data (e.g., stock prices, weather data). Statistical techniques are used to analyze this data and extract insights that can be used to improve the performance of AI systems.

5.2 Data Acquisition

Data acquisition refers to the process of collecting, measuring, and analyzing data from various sources to obtain useful information. This process is essential in many fields, including scientific research, industrial applications, and business analytics. It involves collecting data that will be used to train, validate, and test models, ensuring they perform effectively and accurately. It also known as **acquiring data.**

Let's understand the three key steps involved in data acquisition for AI models :

1. Data Discovery

Data discovery is the process of identifying and obtaining relevant datasets that can be used for training AI models. This step is crucial because the quality and relevance of the data significantly impact the performance of the model. Here's how data discovery typically works :

- **Online Repositories** There are numerous online platforms where datasets are shared, such as Kaggle, UCI Machine Learning Repository, and government data portals like data.gov.
- **APIs and Web Scraping** Sometimes, relevant data can be collected from various websites using APIs or web scraping techniques. For instance, social media platforms, financial websites, and e-commerce sites often provide APIs that can be used to collect data.
- **Collaborations and Partnerships** Collaborating with other organizations or institutions can provide access to proprietary datasets that are not publicly available.
- **Internal Databases** For organizations, internal databases can be a rich source of data, including customer records, sales data, and operational metrics.

2. Data Augmentation

Data augmentation is a technique used to increase the diversity and quantity of training data without actually collecting new data. This is especially useful in situations where the existing dataset is limited or imbalanced. Common data augmentation techniques include:

- **Image Data Augmentation** Techniques like rotation, flipping, cropping, scaling, and adding noise can create variations of existing images to improve model robustness.
- **Text Data Augmentation** Techniques such as synonym replacement, random insertion, random deletion, and back-translation can be used to generate variations in text data.
- **Synthetic Data Generation** Using algorithms to generate data that mimics the properties of the original dataset. For example, Generative Adversarial Networks (GANs) can create realistic images or text.

3. Data Generation

When existing data is insufficient, data generation becomes necessary. This involves creating new data points that simulate real-world data. Some approaches include:

- **Simulated Environments** Creating virtual environments where data can be generated. For example, self-driving car companies use simulators to generate driving scenarios that are hard to capture in the real world.
- **Procedural Content Generation** Techniques that use algorithms to generate large amounts of data programmatically. This is often used in video game development and virtual worlds.
- **Synthetic Data** Using tools and frameworks to generate synthetic data that statistically mirrors the real data. This can be done using various statistical methods or machine learning models like GANs.

Try to understand **the three steps with and example of speech recognition model.**

Acquiring Data-Sample Data Discovery

Let's say we want to collect data for making a speech recognition model.

- We will require audio recordings of various people speaking different phrases in different accents.
- We can search and download these audio recordings from the internet or use open-source datasets like LibriSpeech.
- This process is called data discovery.

Acquiring Data-Sample Data Augmentation

- Data augmentation in speech recognition means increasing the amount of audio data by adding copies of existing recordings with small changes.
- The original audio recording remains the same, but we create new versions by modifying parameters such as pitch, speed, or adding background noise.
- This helps to create a more robust model by slightly changing the existing data.

Acquiring Data-Sample Data Generation

- Data generation refers to creating or recording new audio data using microphones or other recording devices.
- For example, recording various speakers in different environments (like quiet rooms, noisy streets, etc.) to capture a diverse set of audio samples.
- The recorded audio data is then stored on a computer in a suitable format, such as WAV or MP3, for further processing and model training.

Sources of Data

Data can be acquired from two main categories: primary and secondary sources.

1. **Primary data** is collected firsth and by the researcher for the specific purpose of their study. This data is

original and has not been previously collected by anyone else. There are several ways to collect primary data, including:

- **Surveys** Surveys are a popular way to collect data from a large group of people. They can be conducted online, in person, or by mail.
- **Interviews** Interviews are a good way to collect in-depth data from a smaller group of people. They can be conducted in person, by phone, or online.
- **Experiments** Experiments are used to test a hypothesis by manipulating variables and observing the results.
- **Observations** Observations can be used to collect data about people's behaviour or about the natural world.

2. **Secondary data** is data that has already been collected by someone else for a different purpose. This data can be a good way to save time and money, but it is important to be aware of the limitations of secondary data. Some of the common sources of secondary data include:

    - **Government publications** Government agencies collect a lot of data on a variety of topics. This data is often available for free online or in libraries. You can find government data on a variety of topics on government websites (.gov). Non-governmental organizations (NGOs) also collect and publish data on a variety of topics.
    - **Research reports** Research reports can be a good source of data on a specific topic. They can be found online, in libraries, or by purchasing them from the researcher.
    - **Books and articles** Books and articles can also be a good source of secondary data. They can be found online, in libraries, or by purchasing them from a bookstore.
    - **Websites** Many websites collect and publish data. It is important to be critical of the data you find on websites and to make sure it is from a reputable source.

Difference between Good data and Bad data

Feature	Good Data	Bad Data
Accuracy	Reflects reality	Errors/Inconsistencies
Completeness	All relevant info	Missing values
Consistency	Consistent format	Inconsistent format
Relevance	Addresses the question	Irrelevant data
Timeliness	Up-to-date	Outdated data
Accessibility	Easy to access	Difficult to access

Web Scraping

Data acquisition from websites, often called web scraping, is a technique for collecting specific information from websites. It allows you to automate the process of gathering data that would be tedious or impossible to collect manually. This data can be anything from product prices on an e-commerce site to news articles or social media posts. Here's a breakdown of web data acquisition:

The Process

1. Define what data you want to collect. Is it product details, text content, or specific elements like prices or titles?
2. Websites are built with code. Familiarize yourself with the underlying HTML structure of the target website. This will help you identify patterns in how the data you need is organized.
3. There are several tools and methods for web scraping. Here are a few options:
    - **Coding** You can write scripts using languages like Python with libraries like Beautiful Soup to parse the website's HTML and extract data.
    - **Web scraping tools** Visual tools like scrapy or web scraping APIs can simplify the process, especially for beginners.
4. Once you understand the website's structure and have your tool ready, you can extract the data. This typically involves navigating the website's code and isolating the specific elements containing your target data.
5. The extracted data needs a home. You can save it in various formats like CSV, Excel, or even databases depending on your needs.

Ethical Concern in Data Acquisition

While gathering data and choosing datasets, certain ethical issues can be addressed before they occur

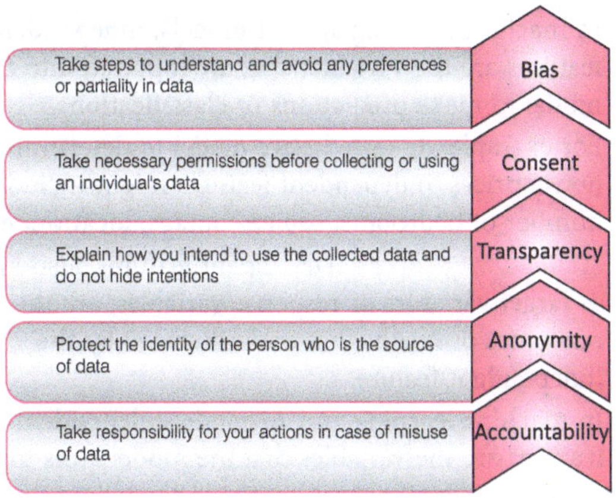

Features of Data and Data Preprocessing

Usability of data

Usability of data is crucial in ensuring that the data serves its intended purpose effectively and efficiently. The three primary factors determining the usability of data-structure, cleanliness, and accuracy-play significant roles in this process.

There are three primary factors determining the usability of data:

1. **Structure** Defines how data is organized and stored. A well-structured dataset is easier to understand, manipulate, and analyze. Structured data allows for more efficient storage and processing, optimizing performance in data handling and analysis.
2. **Cleanliness** Clean data is free from duplicates, missing values, outliers, and other anomalies that may affect its reliability and usefulness for analysis. Data cleaning is the process of identifying and correcting these issues.
3. **Accuracy** Accuracy indicates how well the data reflects real-world values, ensuring reliability. Accurate data closely reflects actual values without errors, enhancing the quality and trustworthiness of the dataset.

Features of Data

Data features, also known as attributes or variables, are the individual pieces of information that make up a dataset. They act like building blocks, providing the details used to describe and analyze the data.

Here's a breakdown of the two types of features you mentioned:

1. **Independent Features** Independent features, also known as input variables or predictors, are the attributes or characteristics that are manipulated or controlled in a study or analysis.

   In machine learning and AI models, independent features are the variables that are inputted into the model to make predictions or classifications.

   For example, in a predictive model to determine house prices, independent features might include the number of bedrooms, square footage, location, etc.
2. **Dependent Features** Dependent features, also known as target variables or response variables, are the outcomes or results that are influenced by the independent features.

   In machine learning and AI models, dependent features are the variables that the model aims to predict or classify based on the independent features.

   Using the previous example, the dependent feature in a house price prediction model would be the actual sale price of the house.

Try These 5.1

1. **Write the difference between quantitative and qualitative data.**
2. **Explain primary data.**
3. **What do you understand by data generation.**

5.3 Data Processing and Data Interpretation

Data Processing

Data in its raw form is not useful to any organization. Data processing is the method of collecting raw data and translating it into usable information. It is usually performed in a step-by-step process by a team of data scientists and data engineers in an organization. The raw data is collected, filtered, sorted, processed, analyzed, stored, and then presented in a readable format.

Data processing is essential for organizations to create better business strategies and increase their competitive edge. By converting the data into readable formats like graphs, charts, and documents, employees throughout the organization can understand and use the data.

Now that we've established what we mean by data processing, let's examine the data processing cycle.

All About the Data Processing Cycle

The data processing cycle consists of a series of steps where raw data (input) is fed into a system to produce actionable insights (output). Each step is taken in a specific order, but the entire process is repeated in a cyclic manner. The first data processing cycle's output can be stored and fed as the input for the next cycle, as the illustration below shows us.

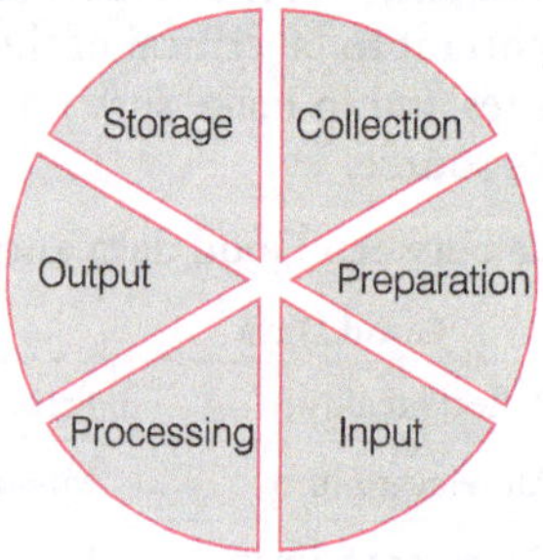

Generally, there are six main steps in the data processing cycle :

Step 1 **Collection** The collection of raw data is the first step of the data processing cycle. The type of raw data collected has a huge impact on the output produced. Hence, raw data should be gathered from defined and accurate sources so that the subsequent findings are valid and usable. Raw data can include monetary figures, website cookies, profit/loss statements of a company, user behavior, etc.

Step 2 **Preparation** Data preparation or data cleaning is the process of sorting and filtering the raw data to remove unnecessary and inaccurate data. Raw data is checked for errors, duplication, miscalculations or missing data, and transformed into a suitable form for further analysis and processing. This is done to ensure that only the highest quality data is fed into the processing unit.
The purpose of this step to remove bad data (redundant, incomplete, or incorrect data) so as to begin assembling high-quality information so that it can be used in the best possible way for business intelligence.

Step 3 **Input** In this step, the raw data is converted into machine readable form and fed into the processing unit. This can be in the form of data entry through a keyboard, scanner or any other input source.

Step 4 **Data Processing** In this step, the raw data is subjected to various data processing methods using machine learning and artificial intelligence algorithms to generate a desirable output. This step may vary slightly from process to process depending on the source of data being processed (data lakes, online databases, connected devices, etc.) and the intended use of the output.

Step 5 **Output** In this step, the processed data is delivered in a comprehensible format, such as graphs, charts, tables, or reports, which are easy to interpret. The output is crucial for making informed decisions, gaining insights, or further analyzing the data.

Step 6 **Storage** The final step is storing the processed data securely for future use. Proper storage ensures that data can be retrieved and reused efficiently. This step often involves organizing data into databases or data warehouses, where it can be accessed for ongoing analysis or reference.

Data Interpretation

Data interpretation is a data review process that utilizes analysis, evaluation, and visualization to provide in-depth findings to enhance data-driven decision-making. Further, there are many steps involved in data interpretation, as well as different types of data and data analysis processes that influence the larger data interpretation process. This article will explain the different data interpretation methods, the data interpretation process, and its benefits. Firstly, let's start with an overview of data interpretation and its importance.

Understanding Some Keywords Related to Data

- **Data Acquisition** This stage focuses on collecting data from various sources. This may involve internal databases, external APIs, web scraping, surveys, or sensor networks.
- **Data Processing** After raw data is collected, it often needs cleaning and preparation. This includes handling missing values, correcting inconsistencies, and transforming the data into a suitable format for analysis.
- **Data Analysis** This is where the exploration and manipulation of data happens. Data analysts use various techniques like statistical analysis, machine learning, and data visualization to uncover patterns, trends, and relationships within the data.
- **Data Interpretation** It's crucial to interpret the results of the analysis accurately. This involves explaining what the findings mean in the context of the original problem or question.
- **Data Presentation** The final step involves communicating the insights effectively to stakeholders. This may involve creating reports, dashboards, or visualizations that clearly present the findings and their implications.

Methods of Data Interpretation

There are two methods for Data Interpretation based on two type of data:

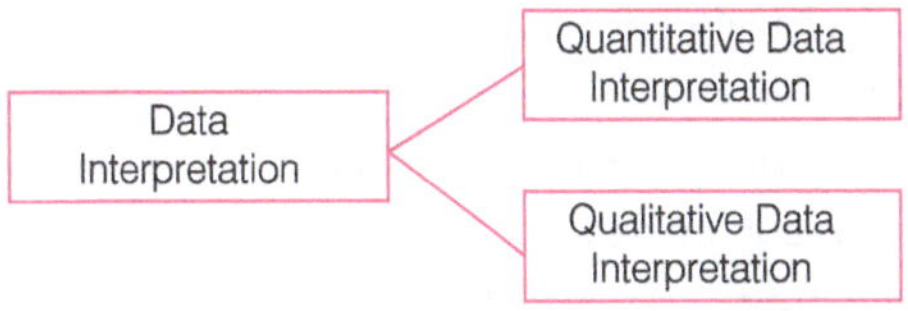

1. Qualitative Data Interpretation

Used for non-numerical data, data that involves words, images, or descriptions. This method focuses on understanding the meaning behind the data, through techniques like interviews, focus groups, and thematic analysis.

Interpretation methods for qualitative data involve techniques like:

- **Thematic analysis** Here, you identify recurring themes or patterns within the data. For instance, analyzing interview transcripts about customer experiences might reveal a common theme of frustration with a particular product feature.
- **Grounded theory** This method involves developing a theory based on the data itself, rather than starting with a pre-existing hypothesis. Imagine studying customer reviews of a new restaurant. Grounded theory might help you identify unexpected categories, like the importance of comfortable furniture or the prevalence of family dining.

Qualitative Data Collection Methods

Data collection methods for qualitative data are distinct from those used for quantitative data. Qualitativc data is non-numerical and focuses on understanding experiences, feelings, and motivations. Here are some common methods for collecting qualitative data:

- **Interviews** One-on-one interviews allow researchers to delve deep into individual perspectives and experiences.
- **Focus Groups** Group discussions moderated by a researcher can reveal group dynamics and shared experiences.
- **Observations** Researchers can observe people in their natural environment to understand behaviors and interactions.
- **Open-Ended Surveys** While surveys can provide some quantitative data, open ended questions allow for rich qualitative responses.
- **Document Analysis** Textual materials like diaries, letters, or social media posts can offer insights into people's thoughts and feelings.

5 Steps to Qualitative Data Analysis

1. Collect Data
2. Organize
3. Set a code to the Data Collected
4. Analyze your data
5. Reporting

2. Quantitative Data Interpretation

Used for numerical data, data that can be counted or measured. This method involves statistical analysis, modeling, and tools to uncover patterns and trends in numbers.

Interpretation methods for quantitative data involve techniques like:

- **Statistical analysis** This uses statistical tools to summarize and understand the data. You might calculate average sales figures across different regions, or use correlation analysis to see if there's a relationship between customer age and product preference.
- **Data visualization** Here, you create charts and graphs to represent the data visually. A bar chart could show how sales vary by product category, or a line graph might track changes in customer satisfaction over time.

Quantitative Data Collection Methods

- **Surveys** This is a widespread method for gathering numerical data through questionnaires. Surveys can be delivered via phone, online, or in person, and use closed-ended questions like multiple choice or rating scales. This allows for easy quantification of responses.
- **Experiments** Researchers control and manipulate variables in an experiment to measure their cause-and-effect relationships. Dala is collccted through observations or measurements during the experiment.
- **Observations** Here, researchers systematically observe and record data about a phenomenon without manipulating anything. This can be done in a natural setting (naturalistic observation) or a controlled environment.
- **Longitudinal Studies** These studies involve collecting data from the same group of participants over an extended period, allowing researchers to track changes and trends.
- **Polls** Similar to surveys, polls collect data through quick questions, often with a focus on opinions or preferences.

Feature	Qualitative Interpretation	Quantitative Interpretation
Data Type	Words, Text, Descriptions	Numbers, Values
Focus	"Why" and "How"	"How Much" and "How Many"
Analysis Method	Thematic Analysis, Identifying Patterns	Statistical Analysis (e.g., averages, correlations)
Outcome	Understanding Experiences, Opinions, Reasons	Measuring Trends, Relationships
Objectivity	Subjective, Open to Interpretation	Objective, Fixed Values
Example	"Customers found the product to be confusing."	"70% of customers completed the purchase."

4 Steps to Quantitative Data Analysis

1. Relate measurement scales with variables

2. Connect descriptive statistics with data
3. Decide a measurement scale
4. Represent data in an appropriate format

Types of Data Interpretation

Data can be presented in three main ways:

1. **Textual** This involves presenting data in written form, such as sentences, paragraphs, or reports. Textual data is good for explaining complex concepts or providing detailed descriptions.
2. **Tabular** In the tabular method, data is arranged in vertical and horizontal rows. It is the easiest way of representing data but not the easiest of interpreting data. Generally, questions based on tabular method comproses of data regarding Production/Profit/sales of different companies in a year, List of students in a class, list of defective items, Income of different persons, etc.

   In tabular form method, either rows and columns are used to represent the discrete non-connected data while other represents connected continuous variable.

	A	B	C	D	E	F	G
1	id	first_name	last_name	email	gender	ip_address	
2	1	Anstice	Sincock	asincock0@v	Female	124.76.249.59	
3	2	Lethia	Timmens	ltimmens1@	Female	14.193.225.111	
4	3	Carolin	Hallybone	challybone2(	Female	17.45.122.149	
5	4	Ad	Brewitt	abrewitt3@v	Male	117.68.14.35	
6	5	Mariele	Mount	mmount4@v	Female	215.176.15.211	
7	6	Dave	Rowney	drowney5@g	Male	217.248.75.59	
8	7	Base	Birkin	bbirkin6@tar	Male	4.253.91.17	
9	8	Ansell	Trow	atrow7@prir	Male	77.188.159.187	
10	9	Joyann	Gripton	jgripton8@q	Female	42.221.170.135	
11	10	Felipa	Kerwen	fkerwen9@p	Female	26.181.115.43	
12							
13							

3. **Graphic** This involves presenting data in visual formats, such as charts, graphs, and maps. Graphic data is good for showing trends, patterns, and relationships between data points.

   In Unit 1, we already learned about various kinds of graphs.

Importance of Data Interpretation

Data interpretation is vital because it unlocks the hidden meaning of raw data. Imagine a giant warehouse full of boxes - that's data. Interpretation is the key that lets you open the boxes, see what's inside (information), and understand its significance.

Here's why data interpretation is so important:

- **Informed Decisions** Data by itself doesn't tell you what to do. Interpretation allows you to analyze trends, identify patterns, and uncover insights that inform better choices. This is crucial in anything from business strategy to scientific research.
- **Problem Solving** Data can reveal problems you might not have noticed. Interpretation helps you pinpoint the root causes and develop effective solutions.
- **Improved Performance** By interpreting data on things like customer behavior or employee productivity, you can identify areas for improvement and make adjustments to optimize performance.
- **Predictive Power** Data trends can shed light on future possibilities. Through interpretation, you can anticipate upcoming issues or opportunities.

Try These 5.2

1. **Explain data processing.**
2. **What are the two methods of data interpretation?**
3. **Write the importance of data interpretation.**

5.4 Project Interactive Data Dashboard and Presentation

Data Visualization (Using Tableau)

Data visualization is the graphical representation of information and data. By using visual elements like charts, graphs, and maps, data visualization tools provide an accessible way to see and understand trends, outliers, and patterns in data.

Advantages

Our eyes are drawn to colors and patterns. We can quickly identify red from blue, and squares from circles. Our culture is visual, including everything from art and advertisements to TV and movies. Data visualization is another form of visual art that grabs our interest and keeps our eyes on the message. When we see a chart, we quickly see trends and outliers. If we can see something, we internalize it quickly. It's storytelling with a purpose. If you've ever stared at a massive spreadsheet of data and couldn't see a trend, you know how much more effective a visualization can be.

Some other advantages of data visualization include:

- Easily sharing information.
- Interactively explore opportunities.
- Visualize patterns and relationships.

Disadvantages

While there are many advantages, some of the disadvantages may seem less obvious. For example, when viewing a visualization with many different datapoints, it's easy to make an inaccurate assumption or sometimes the visualization is just designed wrong so that it's biased or confusing.

Some other disadvantages include :

- Biased or inaccurate information.
- Correlation doesn't always mean causation.
- Core messages can get lost in translation.

Importance of Data Visualisation

Data visualization is crucial because it helps us understand information in a much clearer way. Here's a breakdown of its importance:

- **Makes complex data understandable** Raw data, especially in large amounts, can be overwhelming and difficult to grasp. Visualizations like charts, graphs, and maps present this data in a way that's easier to interpret, allowing you to see patterns, trends, and outliers that might otherwise be missed.
- **Identifies trends and patterns** By visualizing data, you can easily spot connections and relationships between different pieces of information. This can help you identify trends over time, patterns within subgroups, and potential areas for further investigation.
- **Communicates information effectively** Data visualizations are a powerful tool for communication. They can be used to present complex findings to a wider audience, even those without a strong data background. A well-designed visualization can capture attention, simplify explanations, and leave a lasting impression.
- **Supports decision-making** By providing clear insights from data, visualizations can inform better decision-making. They allow you to weigh different options, assess risks and potential outcomes, and ultimately make more data-driven choices.

Data Visualization Tools

The following are the 10 best Data Visualization Tools

1. Tableau	2. Looker
3. Zoho Analytics	4. Sisense
5. IBM Cognos Analytics	6. Qlik Sense
7. Domo	8. Microsoft Power BI
9. Klipfolio	10. SAP Analytics Cloud

Tableau

Tableau is a powerful tool used for data visualization and business intelligence. It allows users to create interactive charts, graphs, maps, and dashboards to explore and understand data easily. Here's a breakdown of what Tableau can do:

- **Data Visualization** Tableau makes it easy to create different charts and graphs from your data, even if you don't have any coding experience. You can use drag-and-drop functionality to create visualizations that best suit your needs.
- **Data Analysis** Tableau goes beyond just creating visuals; it helps you analyze the data and uncover hidden insights. You can drill down into specific data points, filter data sets, and create calculations to get a deeper understanding of your information.
- **Communication and Sharing** With Tableau, you can create dashboards and stories to share your data insights with others. These dashboards can be interactive, allowing viewers to explore the data themselves.

Download and install Tableau

To download and install Tableau, follow these steps:

Step 1 Download Tableau

1. **Visit the Tableau Website**
   - Go to the Tableau website.
2. **Choose Your Version**
   - Depending on your needs, you can choose Tableau Desktop, Tableau Public, or Tableau Server. For most individual users, Tableau Desktop or Tableau Public will be suitable.
3. **Start Free Trial or Download Tableau Public**
   - For Tableau Desktop, click on "Try Tableau for Free" or "Free Trial" to get a trial version.
   - For Tableau Public, click on "Download Tableau Public" which is free to use but has some limitations.
4. **Fill in the Required Information**
   - If you're downloading the free trial of Tableau Desktop, you may need to provide some personal information such as your name, business email, and company name.
5. **Download the Installer**
   - Once you've filled in the information, the download should start automatically. If not, there should be a link to manually start the download.

Step 2 Install Tableau

1. **Run the Installer**
   - Locate the downloaded installer file (usually in your Downloads folder) and double-click on it to start the installation process.

2. **Follow the Installation Wizard**
    - Follow the on-screen instructions in the installation wizard. You'll need to agree to the license agreement and choose an installation directory (the default is usually fine for most users).
3. **Complete the Installation**
    - Once the installation process is complete, you can choose to launch Tableau immediately.

Step 3 Activate Tableau (for Tableau Desktop)

1. **Launch Tableau Desktop**
    - If you choose to launch Tableau immediately after installation, it will open. Otherwise, you can open it from your start menu or desktop shortcut.
2. **Sign In or Activate**
    - You will be prompted to sign in with your Tableau account. Use the same email and password you used to start the free trial.
    - If you have a product key, you can enter it during this step to activate Tableau Desktop.

Step 4 Start Using Tableau

- Once you've signed in or activated your copy, you can start creating visualizations and exploring your data.

To pull in the data, click on Microsoft Excel in the top left corner.

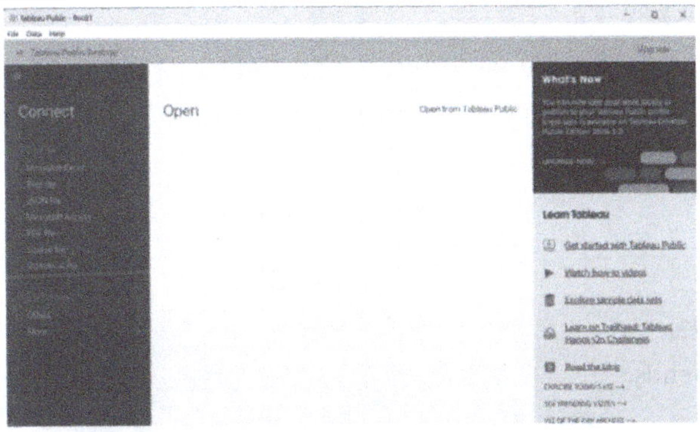

- Click Sheet1 in the bottom left corner of the screen

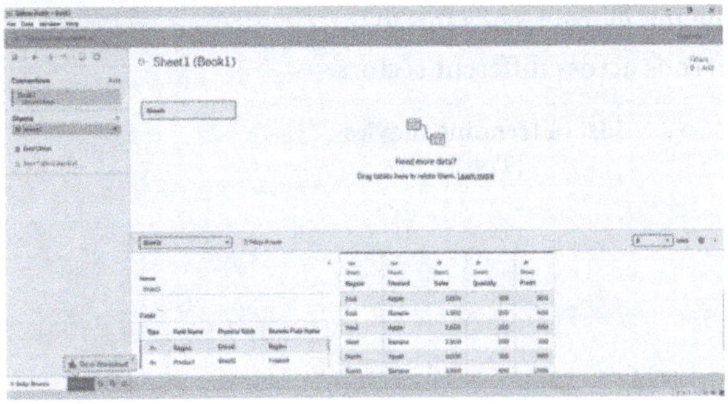

- First, let's recreate the bar chart we made to visualize the product and region as per profit!
- Hover over the word "Product". You will notice a blue oval appear behind it.
- Click and drag "Product" up and to the right, releasing it next to the word Columns when a little orange arrow appears.

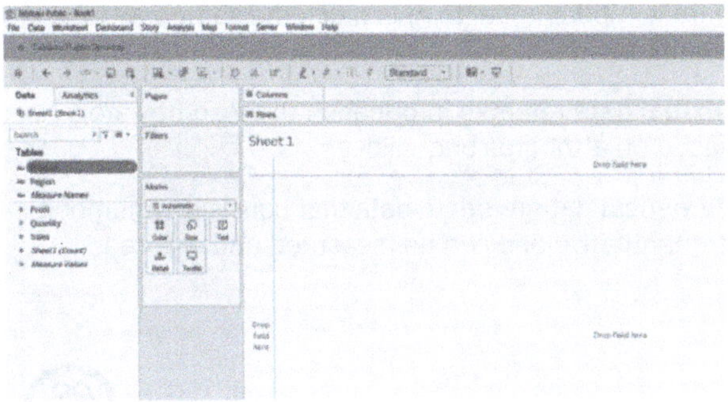

Now drag "Profit" to Rows, following the same steps as above.

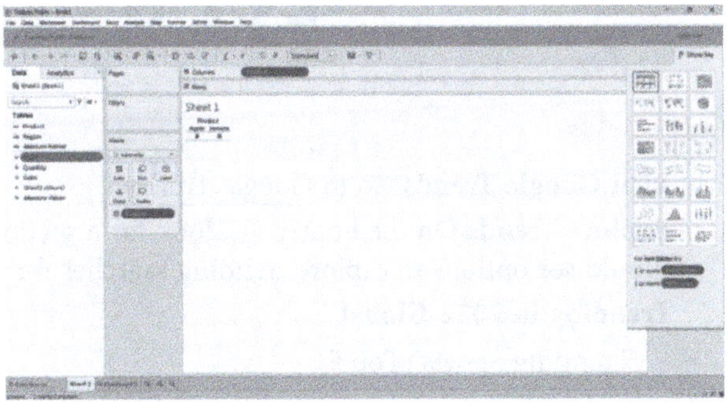

Tableau made us a bar graph

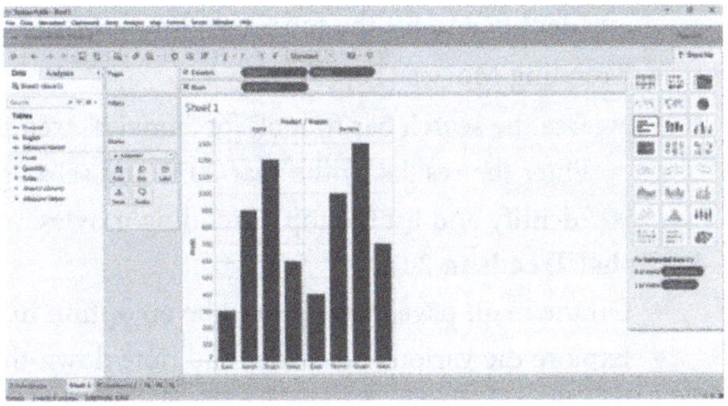

In the upper right corner, click "Show Me" will see all of the different types of visualizations that Tableau can create using Genre and Sheet Count 1.

Note *You may also use Ms Excel or Datawrapper (https://www.datawrapper.de/) for the data visualization instead of Tableau.*

Try These 5.3

1 What are the advantages of data visualization?
2 Name any four data visualization tools.
3 Write the importance of data visualization.

Glossary

Data is fundamental to AI in much the same way food is to a human.

Textual data refers to information that can be categorized based on attributes or qualities.

Numerical data refers to data that consists of numbers. It is quantitative and can be measured and ordered.

Data acquisition refers to the process of collecting, measuring, and analyzing data from various sources to obtain useful information.

Data acquisition from websites, often called **web scraping**, is a technique for collecting specific information from websites.

Data processing is the method of collecting raw data and translating it into usable information.

Data interpretation is a data review process that utilizes analysis, evaluation, and visualization to provide in-depth findings to enhance data-driven decision-making.

Data visualization is the graphical representation of information and data.

Let's Investigate

Activity

1. **Visit Google Trends** Go to Google Trends.
2. **Explore Trends** On the homepage, look for a section that allows you to explore trends from previous years. You should see options to explore trending searches for different years.
3. **Trending in 2022-Global**
   - Trending Sports (Top 5)
     - Use the search bar to look for "sports" trends in 2022.
     - Filter the results by the year 2022 and select global trends.
     - Identify and list the top 5 trending sports.
   - Trending Movies (Top 5)
     - Use the search bar to look for "movies" trends in 2022.
     - Filter the results by the year 2022 and select global trends.
     - Identify and list the top 5 trending movies.
4. **Global Trends in 2022**
   - On the main page, there should be an option to view the top global trends for 2022.
   - Explore the various categories and note down the top trends across different sectors.

List of trending athletes (Top 5)	List of trending movies (Top 5)

NCERT FOLDER

Complete Explanations of all NCERT's Questions

Multiple Choice Questions

Q.1 What are the basic building blocks of qualitative data?

(a) Individuals (b) Units
(c) Categories (d) Measurements

Q.2 Which among these is not a type of data interpretation?

(a) Textual (b) Tabular
(c) Graphical (d) Raw data

Q.3 Quantitative data is numerical in nature.

(a) True (b) False

Q.4 A Bar Graph is an example of?

(a) Textual (b) Tabular
(c) Graphical (d) None of the above

Q.5 .... relates to the manipulation of data to produce meaningful insights.

(a) Data Processing (b) Data Interpretation
(c) Data Analysis (d) Data Presentation

Answers

1. (c) 2. (d) 3. (a) 4. (c) 5. (b)

Subjective Questions

Q.1 At which stage of the AI project cycle does Tableau software prove useful?

Ans. Tableau software proves useful in the data exploration and visualization stage of the AI project cycle.

Q.2 Name any five graphs that can be made using Tableau software.

Ans. Here are five graphs you can create using Tableau software:

- **Bar charts** Great for comparing categories or showing trends over time.
- **Line charts** Ideal for visualizing trends and continuous data.
- **Scatter plots** Useful for exploring relationships between two variables.
- **Pie charts** Effective for showing proportions of a whole.
- **Heatmaps** Excellent for visualizing data with multiple dimensions, like sentiment analysis across different products and regions.

Q.3 In the below excel sheet-

C26 fx

	A	B	C	D	E	F
1	Song Name	Album	Artist	Genre	Year	Song Length
2	Blinding Lights	Blinding Lights	The Weeknd	R&B	2019	3:20
3	Savage Love	Savage Love	Jason Derulo	Hip-Hop	2020	2:49
4	Watermelon Sugar	Fine Line	Harry Styles	Pop	2019	3:54
5	Happy	Happy	Pharrell Williams	Pop	2013	3:53
6	Panini	EP 7	Lil Nas X	Hip-Hop	2019	1:55
7	Cake by the Ocean	DNCE	DNCE	Pop	2016	3:39
8	7 Rings	thank u, next	Ariana Grande	Pop	2019	2:59
9	24K Magic	24K Magic	Bruno Mars	Funk	2016	3:46

(i) Is the Year qualitative or quantitative?

Ans. Year is quantitative

(ii) Is Song Length discrete or continuous?

Ans. Song Length is continuous.

(iii) Is the Genre discrete or continuous?

Ans. Genre is discrete.

Q.4 What is the importance of data visualization?

Ans. Data visualization is important because it helps us understand complex data by turning it into visual representations like charts and graphs. This makes it easier to see patterns, trends, and outliers that might be missed in raw data. In short, it helps us see the bigger picture.

REVIEW EXERCISE

Including Competency Based Questions

Part I

Multiple Choice Questions

1 What type of data is represented by words, sentences, or paragraphs?

(a) Discrete Data (b) Continuous Data
(c) Textual Data (d) Numerical Data

2 Which of the following is an example of discrete data?

(a) Temperature
(b) Height
(c) Number of books on a shelf
(d) Weight

3 Which domain of AI primarily uses text data for its tasks?

(a) Computer Vision (CV)
(b) Natural Language Processing (NLP)
(c) Statistical Data
(d) Reinforcement Learning

4 What is the purpose of data augmentation in AI?

(a) To delete unnecessary data
(b) To increase the diversity and quantity of training data
(c) To measure the accuracy of data
(d) To store data in a database

5 Which method involves collecting data by observing people's behaviour or the natural world?

(a) Surveys (b) Interviews
(c) Experiments (d) Observations

6 What type of data includes information like gender, favourite colour, and movie genre?

(a) Quantitative Data
(b) Numerical Data
(c) Discrete Data
(d) Qualitative Data

7 Which of the following is a primary source of data?

(a) Government publications
(b) Research reports
(c) Surveys
(d) Books and articles

8 What is web scraping used for in data acquisition?

(a) To clean data
(b) To automate the process of gathering data from websites
(c) To structure data
(d) To generate synthetic data

9 Which factor determines how well data reflects real-world values?

(a) Structure (b) Cleanliness
(c) Accuracy (d) Format

10 In a machine learning model to predict house prices, what would be considered an independent feature?

(a) Sale price of the house (b) Number of bedrooms
(c) Location (d) Both (b) and (c)

11 What does data discovery involve in the context of data acquisition for AI models?

(a) Generating new data points
(b) Identifying and obtaining relevant datasets
(c) Augmenting existing data
(d) Cleaning and structuring data

12 Which of the following is NOT an example of quantitative data?

(a) Temperature (b) Customer satisfaction
(c) Sales figures (d) Shoe size

13 What technique can create new versions of existing audio recordings by modifying parameters like pitch or speed?

(a) Data discovery (b) Data cleaning
(c) Data generation (d) Data augmentation

14 Which type of data can take on any value within a given range and often arises from measurement?

(a) Discrete Data
(b) Continuous Data
(c) Textual Data
(d) Qualitative Data

15 What is the primary goal of data used in the field of Computer Vision (CV)?

(a) To interpret and understand text data
(b) To extract meaningful information from images and videos
(c) To analyze numerical and categorical data
(d) To generate synthetic data

16 What is the primary objective of data processing?

(a) Converting raw data into usable information
(b) Collecting as much raw data as possible
(c) Storing raw data for future reference
(d) Filtering out irrelevant information

17 **Which step of the data processing cycle involves checking for errors, duplication, and missing data?**

(a) Collection (b) Preparation

(c) Input (d) Data Processing

18 **What is the purpose of the "Input" step in the data processing cycle?**

(a) To analyze the data using statistical methods

(b) To convert raw data into machine-readable form

(c) To filter out unnecessary data

(d) To present data in a readable format

19 **Which type of data interpretation focuses on understanding experiences, opinions, and reasons?**

(a) Quantitative Interpretation

(b) Statistical Interpretation

(c) Qualitative Interpretation

(d) Correlation Interpretation

20 **What is the main advantage of data visualization?**

(a) Making complex data more difficult to understand

(b) Concealing trends and outliers in data

(c) Identifying biased or inaccurate information

(d) Presenting information in a clearer and more understandable way

21 **Which tool is commonly used for data visualization and business intelligence?**

(a) Microsoft Word (b) Adobe Photoshop

(c) Tableau (d) Google Sheets

22 **What is the primary function of Tableau?**

(a) Creating interactive charts and dashboards

(b) Editing videos

(c) Writing code

(d) Sending emails

23 **How can Tableau be obtained for use?**

(a) By purchasing it from a retail store

(b) By downloading it from the official website

(c) By subscribing to a streaming service

(d) By borrowing it from a friend

Answers

1. (c)	2. (c)	3. (b)	4. (b)	5. (d)
6. (d)	7. (c)	8. (b)	9. (c)	10. (d)
11. (b)	12. (b)	13. (d)	14. (b)	15. (b)
16. (a)	17. (b)	18. (b)	19. (c)	20. (d)
21. (c)	22. (a)	23. (b)		

Statement Based Type Questions

1 **Statement 1: Textual data consists of numbers.**

Statement 2: Textual data can be categorized based on attributes or qualities.

(a) Both Statement 1 and Statement 2 are correct

(b) Both Statement 1 and Statement 2 are incorrect

(c) Statement 1 is correct but Statement 2 is incorrect

(d) Statement 2 is correct but Statement 1 is incorrect

2 **Statement 1: Data discovery involves creating new data points to simulate real-world data.**

Statement 2: Data augmentation increases the diversity and quantity of training data without collecting new data.

(a) Both Statement 1 and Statement 2 are correct

(b) Both Statement 1 and Statement 2 are incorrect

(c) Statement 1 is correct but Statement 2 is incorrect

(d) Statement 2 is correct but Statement 1 is incorrect

3 **Statement 1: Web scraping involves defining the data to be collected and understanding the HTML structure of the target website.**

Statement 2: The extracted data from web scraping cannot be saved in formats other than CSV.

(a) Both Statement 1 and Statement 2 are correct

(b) Both Statement 1 and Statement 2 are incorrect

(c) Statement 1 is correct but Statement 2 is incorrect

(d) Statement 2 is correct but Statement 1 is incorrect

4 **Statement 1: Primary data is collected firsthand by the researcher for the specific purpose of their study.**

Statement 2: Surveys, interviews, experiments, and observations are common methods of collecting primary data.

(a) Both Statement 1 and Statement 2 are correct

(b) Both Statement 1 and Statement 2 are incorrect

(c) Statement 1 is correct but Statement 2 is incorrect

(d) Statement 2 is correct but Statement 1 is incorrect

5 **Statement 1: Structure refers to how data is organized and stored, impacting its efficiency in storage and processing.**

Statement 2: Clean data is free from duplicates, missing values, and outliers, ensuring its reliability and usefulness for analysis.

(a) Both Statement 1 and Statement 2 are correct

(b) Both Statement 1 and Statement 2 are incorrect

(c) Statement 1 is correct but Statement 2 is incorrect

(d) Statement 2 is correct but Statement 1 is incorrect

Answers

1. (d)	2. (d)	3. (c)	4. (a)	5. (a)

Assertion Reason Based Type Questions

1 **Assertion: Data processing is essential for organizations to create better business strategies and increase their competitive edge.**

Reason: Data processing involves converting raw data into usable information through various steps like collection, preparation, input, and processing.

(a) Both assertion and reason are true, and the reason is the correct explanation of the assertion.

(b) Both assertion and reason are true, but the reason is not the correct explanation of the assertion.

(c) Assertion is true, but the reason is false.
(d) Assertion is false, but the reason is true.

2 Assertion: Data interpretation methods include qualitative and quantitative approaches.

Reason: Qualitative data interpretation focuses on non-numerical data, while quantitative data interpretation deals with numerical data.

(a) Both assertion and reason are true, and the reason is the correct explanation of the assertion.
(b) Both assertion and reason are true, but the reason is not the correct explanation of the assertion.
(c) Assertion is true, but the reason is false.
(d) Assertion is false, but the reason is true.

3 Assertion: Data visualization helps in making complex data understandable by presenting it in visual formats like charts and graphs.

Reason: Visualizations like charts, graphs, and maps present data in a way that's easier to interpret, allowing for the identification of patterns and trends.

(a) Both assertion and reason are true, and the reason is the correct explanation of the assertion.
(b) Both assertion and reason are true, but the reason is not the correct explanation of the assertion.
(c) Assertion is true, but the reason is false.
(d) Assertion is false, but the reason is true.

4 Assertion: Tableau is a powerful tool for data visualization and business intelligence.

Reason: Tableau allows users to create interactive charts, graphs, maps, and dashboards to explore and understand data easily.

(a) Both assertion and reason are true, and the reason is the correct explanation of the assertion.
(b) Both assertion and reason are true, but the reason is not the correct explanation of the assertion.
(c) Assertion is true, but the reason is false.
(d) Assertion is false, but the reason is true.

Answers

1. (a) **2.** (a) **3.** (a) **4.** (a)

Part II

Very Short Answer Type Questions

1 What type of data is represented by words and sentences?

Ans. Textual data.

2 What is the primary data type used in Natural Language Processing (NLP)?

Ans. Text.

3 How is data augmentation beneficial in speech recognition?

Ans. It increases data diversity by modifying existing recordings.

4 What is the process of collecting, measuring, and analyzing data called?

Ans. Data acquisition.

5 What is data processing?

Ans. The method of collecting raw data and translating it into usable information.

6 Why is data processing essential for organizations?

Ans. To create better business strategies and increase competitive edge.

7 What is the purpose of the preparation step in data processing?

Ans. To remove unnecessary and inaccurate data.

8 What is done in the input step of data processing?

Ans. Converting raw data into machine-readable form and feeding it into the processing unit.

9 What is data interpretation?

Ans. A data review process utilizing analysis, evaluation, and visualization to provide in-depth findings.

10 What is the focus of qualitative data interpretation?

Ans. Understanding the meaning behind non-numerical data.

11 What is the primary outcome of quantitative data interpretation?

Ans. Measuring trends and relationships in numerical data.

12 What are the two main types of numerical data?

Ans. Discrete and continuous data.

13 What is the primary purpose of acquiring data in AI systems?

Ans. Data acts as a training tool, enabling AI to learn and enhance its capabilities, much like food for humans.

14 How does continuous data differ from discrete data?

Ans. Continuous data can take any value within a range, while discrete data consists of distinct, separate values with no intermediate values possible.

15 Describe the difference between textual data and numerical data representation.

Ans. Textual data represents words or sentences, while numerical data represents quantities or measurements.

16 What are the main types of data used in Natural Language Processing (NLP)?

Ans. The primary type of data used in NLP is text data, sourced from various mediums like books, articles, and social media posts.

17 How does data augmentation contribute to improving model robustness?

Ans. Data augmentation increases the diversity and quantity of training data by creating variations of existing data, enhancing the model's ability to generalize to unseen data.

18 How can Tableau help in data visualization?

Ans. By allowing users to create interactive charts, graphs, maps, and dashboards to explore and understand data easily.

Short Answer Type Questions

1 What are the two main types of data and their defining characteristics?

Ans. **Textual Data** Qualitative, non-numeric information categorized based on attributes or qualities, such as names or labels.

Numerical Data Quantitative, consisting of numbers that can be measured or ordered, categorized into discrete and continuous types.

2 Explain the process of data acquisition in AI models with three key steps and examples relevant to speech recognition.

Ans. **Data Discovery** Identifying and obtaining relevant datasets, such as audio recordings from sources like LibriSpeech.

Data Augmentation Increasing data diversity by modifying existing recordings, like adjusting pitch or adding background noise.

Data Generation Creating new audio data, such as recording speakers in various environments, to capture a diverse set of samples.

3 Enumerate three primary factors crucial for determining the usability of data, and briefly explain their significance.

Ans. **Structure** Organizes data for easier manipulation and analysis, optimizing storage and processing efficiency.

Cleanliness Ensures data reliability by removing duplicates, outliers, and other anomalies, enhancing its usefulness.

Accuracy Reflects real-world values without errors, enhancing the quality and trustworthiness of the dataset for analysis.

4 What is data processing, and why is it essential for organizations?

Ans. Data processing involves translating raw data into usable information through collection, filtering, sorting, analysis, and presentation. It's vital for organizations to create better strategies and gain a competitive edge by converting data into readable formats like graphs and charts.

5 What are the main steps in the data processing cycle, and why is data preparation crucial?

Ans. The data processing cycle includes steps like collection, preparation, input, processing, output, and storage. Data preparation, specifically, involves sorting and filtering raw data to remove errors and ensure high-quality input for analysis, which is essential for accurate results.

6 Explain the methods of data interpretation and give an example of each.

Ans. Data interpretation includes qualitative and quantitative methods. Qualitative methods, like thematic analysis, focus on understanding non-numerical data through identifying recurring themes. Quantitative methods, such as statistical analysis, involve interpreting numerical data to uncover patterns or relationships, like calculating average sales figures or using correlation analysis.

Long Answer Type Questions

1 Discuss the significance of data interpretation and its methods in enhancing decision-making processes.

Ans. Data interpretation plays a crucial role in extracting actionable insights from raw data. By employing qualitative and quantitative interpretation methods, organizations can delve into the meaning behind their data, uncover hidden correlations, and forecast trends effectively. Qualitative methods like thematic analysis and grounded theory provide depth to understanding non-numerical data, while quantitative techniques such as statistical analysis and data visualization enable the exploration of numerical data. These methods facilitate informed decision-making by offering comprehensive insights into experiences, opinions, trends, and relationships within datasets.

2 Explain the process of installing and activating Tableau Desktop for data visualization purposes.

Ans. Installing Tableau Desktop involves several straightforward steps. First, users download the installer from the Tableau website and choose the appropriate version (Desktop or Public). After filling in required information for a trial version or downloading Tableau Public, the installation process begins by running the installer and following on-screen instructions. Once installed, Tableau Desktop is activated by signing in with a Tableau account or entering a product key. Users can then start utilizing Tableau for data visualization by accessing various features like creating charts, graphs, and dashboards through intuitive drag-and-drop functionality.

3 What is Data Interpretation? Write its importance.

Ans. Refer to text on page no. 173 and 175 (Data Interpretation, Types of Data Interpretation).

ASSESSMENT EXERCISE

Multiple Choice Questions

1. Which type of data involves information that follows a specific pattern or set of rules and is stored in a tabular form?
   (a) Unstructured Data (b) Semi-Structured Data
   (c) Structured Data (d) Big Data
2. Which of the following is a method to collect primary data?
   (a) Government publications (b) Research reports
   (c) Surveys (d) Books and articles
3. What is a common limitation of secondary data?
   (a) It is always free
   (b) It is collected firsthand by the researcher
   (c) It may not be specific to the researcher's needs
   (d) It includes conducting experiments
4. Which of the following is NOT a factor determining the usability of data?
   (a) Structure (b) Cleanliness
   (c) Accuracy (d) Cost
5. What type of data interpretation involves statistical analysis and data visualization?
   (a) Qualitative Data Interpretation (b) Quantitative Data Interpretation
   (c) Grounded Theory (d) Thematic Analysis
6. In the data processing cycle, which step involves transforming raw data into a machine-readable form?
   (a) Collection (b) Preparation
   (c) Input (d) Data Processing
7. It refers to human or mechanical watching, noticing or perceiving of what people actually do or what events take place in a specific working environment.
   (a) Survey (b) Interview
   (c) Observation (d) API

Very Short Answer Type Questions

8. What is primary data?
9. What is web scraping?
10. Name the three primary factors determining the usability of data.

Short Answer Type Questions

11. Explain the types of Data Interpretation.
12. Write the advantages of using Tableau.
13. Give the examples of qualitative data.

Long Answer Type Questions

14. Explain the different sources of data used in data collection. Provide examples for each source.
15. What is the importance of data visualisation?

CHAPTER 06

Math for AI (Statistics and Probability)

Math is the backbone of Artificial Intelligence (AI). Linear algebra helps manipulate data and forms the foundation for machine learning algorithms. Statistics and probability come into play to deal with uncertainty in data. AI systems use probability to reason about incomplete information and make predictions, while statistics helps analyze data, identify patterns, and improve the accuracy of those predictions.

6.1 Math Related to AI

In the world of artificial intelligence (AI), mathematics plays a crucial role. Imagine AI as a brain, and mathematics as its language. Just like how we use words to communicate, AI uses numbers and equations to understand and process information. One important concept in AI is called algorithms, which are step-by-step instructions that tell the computer what to do. These algorithms often rely on mathematical formulas to make decisions or solve problems.

Mathematics and AI intersect significantly in machine learning, where AI systems learn from experience without explicit programming. Mathematics is crucial for creating models and algorithms that recognize data patterns and make predictions. A strong foundation in algebra, calculus, and statistics is essential for students interested in AI, enabling them to understand and innovate in the field.

AI algorithms use mathematical models to learn from data, relying on concepts such as linear algebra, calculus, and probability theory. These techniques help AI identify patterns in complex datasets and make predictions.

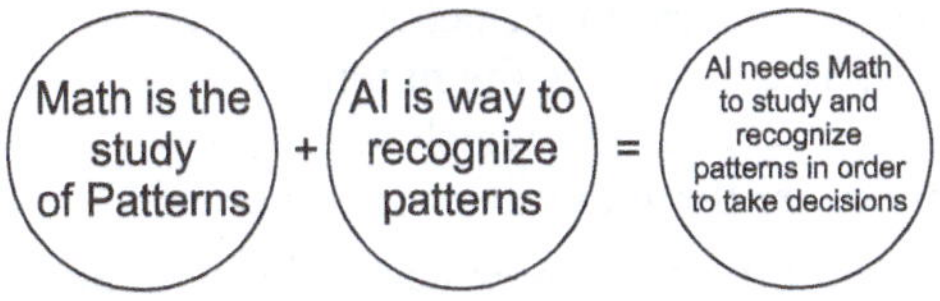

Math provides the tools to analyze and manipulate data. This is crucial for AI because AI systems need to be able to process massive amounts of data in order to learn effectively. Techniques from statistics and linear algebra are particularly important in this area.

The primary purpose of AI is to create an acceptable model for human understanding. And these models can be prepared with the ideas and strategies from various branches of mathematics.

Consider self-driving cars. Their goal is to recognize objects and people in video images. Math powers these cars in the form of minimization procedures and backpropagation. Math helps AI scientists solve challenging, deep abstract problems using traditional methods and techniques that have been known for hundreds of years.

Uses of Math

Math is the foundation that allows AI to learn and perform many kinds of tasks. Here's a breakdown of how each branch of mathematics contributes to AI:

- **Statistics (Exploring data)** This is crucial for understanding the data that AI models are trained on. Statistical methods are used to summarize and analyze data, identify patterns and trends, and assess the validity of machine learning models. For instance, calculating the mean, median, and standard deviation of a dataset helps AI understand the central tendency and spread of the data.
- **Calculus (training and improving AI model)** Calculus provides the tools to optimize the inner workings of AI models. Techniques like gradient descent use calculus to adjust the parameters of a model in tiny steps, minimizing errors and improving the model's performance over time.
- **Linear Algebra (finding out unknown or missing values)** This branch of math deals with vectors,

matrices, and linear transformations. Linear algebra is essential for representing data in a way that AI models can understand and manipulate. It's also used in techniques like matrix factorization to fill in missing data points or reduce the dimensionality of data for faster processing.

- **Probability (predicting different events)** Probability is key for AI systems that make predictions about the future. By calculating the likelihood of different outcomes, AI models can make informed decisions and handle uncertainty in real-world situations. For example, spam filters use probability to classify emails as spam or not spam based on the presence of certain keywords.

Advantages of Learning Math for AI

Math is the foundation for much of the magic behind AI: Here are few advantages of Learning Math for AI

- **Stronger Analytical Thinking** Math trains you to break down problems logically, identify patterns, and find solutions through a step-by-step process. This analytical approach is crucial for designing and troubleshooting AI systems.
- **Understanding the Magic Behind AI** AI algorithms rely heavily on mathematical concepts. Linear algebra helps with tasks like image recognition, calculus is used to optimize machine learning models, and probability and statistics are essential for analyzing data and evaluating AI performance.
- **Making Informed Decisions** Math equips you to assess the strengths and weaknesses of different AI models. You can use mathematical reasoning to choose the right approach for a specific problem and interpret the results accurately.

6.2 Statistics

Statistics is the field of study concerned with the collection, organization, analysis, interpretation, and presentation of data.

Statistical techniques helps to prepare the data for learning. Statistics use to clean the data, identify outliers, and choose the right features for training the models. This leads to more accurate and efficient learning. The real world is messy, and data is rarely perfect. Statistics helps us quantify this uncertainty and build models that are robust to errors and variations in the data.Statistics provides a common ground for AI and humans. We can use statistical concepts to explain our decisions and conclusions in a way that humans can understand.

There are many different activities that can be done in statistics, such as:

- **Collecting data** This could involve conducting a survey, experiment, or observation.
- **Organizing data** This could involve creating a table, chart, or graph.
- **Analyzing data** This could involve calculating measures of central tendency, variance, and standard deviation, as well as other statistical tests.
- **Interpreting data** This could involve drawing conclusions from the data and making recommendations based on those conclusions.

Statistics is a branch of mathematics that deals with the collection, organization, analysis, and interpretation of data. It is used in many fields, including business, economics, social science, and natural science.

Here are the different parts of statistics:

Measure of Central Tendency

A measure of central tendency is a single value that attempts to describe a whole set of data by identifying the central position within that set of data. There are three main measures of central tendency:

- **Mean** The mean, often referred to as the average, is the sum of all the values in a data set divided by the number of values. It is the most common measure of central tendency.
- **Median** The median is the middle value in a data set when the data is ordered from least to greatest. If there are two middle values, the median is the mean of those two value.

  Example of a Median

  - To find the median value in a list with an odd amount of numbers, one would find the number that is in the middle with an equal amount of numbers on either side of the median. To find the median, first arrange the numbers in order, usually from lowest to highest.

    For example, in a data set of {3, 13, 2, 34, 11, 26, 47}, the sorted order becomes {2, 3, 11, 13, 26, 34, 47}. The median is the number in the middle {2, 3, 11, 13, 26, 34, 47}, which in this instance is 13 since there are three numbers on either side.
  - To find the median value in a list with an even amount of numbers, one must determine the middle pair, add them, and divide by two. Again, arrange the numbers in order from lowest to highest.

For example, in a data set of {3, 13, 2, 34, 11, 17, 27, 47}, the sorted order becomes {2, 3, 11, 13, 17, 27, 34, 47}. The median is the average of the two numbers in the middle {2, 3, 11, 13, 17, 26 34, 47}, which in this case is 15 or (13 + 17) ÷ 2 = 15.

- **Mode** The mode is the most frequent value in a data set. A data set can have one mode, two modes (bimodal), or even more modes (multimodal).

  Examples of the Mode

  In the following list of numbers, 16 is the mode since it appears more times in the set than any other number:

  3, 3, 6, 9, 16, 16, 16, 27, 27, 37, 48

  A set of numbers can have more than one mode (this is known as bimodal if there are two modes) if there are multiple numbers that occur with equal frequency and more times than the others in the set.

  3, 3, 3, 9, 16, 16, 16, 27, 37, 48

  In the above example, both the number 3 and the number 16 are modes as they each occur three times and no other number occurs more often.

Variance and Standard Deviation

Variance and standard deviation are measures of how spread out the data is from the mean.

Variance

The variance is the average squared deviation from the mean. In other words, it is a measure of how much the data points vary from the average value.

Understanding Variance In statistics, variance measures variability from the average or mean. It is calculated by taking the differences between each number in the data set and the mean, then squaring the differences to make them positive, and finally dividing the sum of the squares by the number of values in the data set. Software like Excel can make this calculation easier.

Variance is calculated by using the following formula:

$$\sigma^2 = \frac{\sum_{i=1}^{n}(x_i - \bar{x})^2}{N}$$

where, x_i = Each value in the dataset

$\bar{x}$ = Mean of all values in the dataset

N = Number of values in the dataset

Standard deviation

The standard deviation is the square root of the variance. It is another measure of how spread out the data is from the mean, but it is expressed in the same units as the original data.

Standard Deviation Formula Standard deviation is calculated by taking the square root of a value derived from comparing data points to a collective mean of a population. The formula is:

$$\text{Standard Deviation} = \sqrt{\frac{\sum_{i=1}^{n}(x_i - \bar{x})^2}{n-1}}$$

where, x_i = Value of the ith point in the data set

$\bar{x}$ = The mean value of the data set

n = The number of data points in the data set

6.3 Applications of Statistics

Statistics is a powerful tool that has many applications across various fields. Here are some of the areas you mentioned :

Sports

Statistics are heavily used in sports to analyze player performance, team strategies, and even predict game outcomes. This field is known as sports analytics and it uses complex mathematical models to crunch vast amounts of data.

Info Wall

The Tokyo 2020 Olympics, originally scheduled for summer 2020, were postponed due to the global Covid-19 pandemic.
Statistics revealed that COVID cases sharply increased in Japan during the planned period of Olympics.

Disaster Management

Statistics play a vital role in disaster management by helping to assess risks, predict the spread of disasters, and allocate resources effectively. For instance, by analyzing historical data on floods, statisticians can create flood maps that identify areas at high risk.

Disease Prediction

Statistical analysis is crucial in disease prediction and control. By studying historical data on disease outbreaks, statisticians can identify trends and patterns that can help predict future outbreaks. This information is then used to develop preventive measures and allocate resources for healthcare.

Fact BOT

By analyzing COVID statistics, the government can see areas with rising cases and target those areas for additional testing, resources, and vaccination efforts.

Weather Forecast

Weather forecasting relies heavily on statistics. Meteorologists collect vast amounts of data on atmospheric conditions, such as temperature, pressure, humidity, and wind speed. They then use statistical models to analyze this data and predict future weather patterns.

Few More Facts

- Kids watch around 1.5-3 hours of TV per day while being in childcare.
- 72% of teens often (or sometimes) check for messages or notifications as soon as they wake up, while roughly four-in-ten feel anxious when they do not have their cellphone with them.
- 77% of children don't get enough physical exercise.
- Almost a quarter (23%) of children aged five to 16 believe that playing a computer game with friends is a form of exercise.
- 69% of all children experience one or more sleep-related problems at least a few nights a week.
- Only 54% of US children aged 3 to 5 years attend full-day preschool programs.

6.4 Probability

One fundamental concept in AI is probability, which helps AI systems make decisions under uncertainty. For instance, in machine learning, probability theory is used to model uncertainty in data and make predictions.

Probability is basically a way of measuring how likely something is to happen. It's a branch of mathematics that deals with chance and uncertainty, and it uses numbers between 0 and 1 to express how probable an event is.

This is any event where there's more than one possible outcome, and you can't be sure what will happen beforehand. Flipping a coin, rolling a die, or picking a card from a deck are all chance events.

Formula for Probability

The probability formula is defined as the possibility of an event to happen is equal to the ratio of the number of favourable outcomes and the total number of outcomes.

$$P(A) = \frac{\text{Number of favorable outcomes to A}}{\text{Total number of possible outcomes}}$$

Example : Imagine a fair coin. There are two possible outcomes: heads or tails. Since the coin is fair, both outcomes are equally likely. So, the probability of getting heads is 1/2 (or 0.5), and the probability of getting tails is also 1/2 (0.5).

There are 6 pillows in a bed, 3 are red, 2 are yellow and 1 is blue. What is the probability of picking a yellow pillow?

The probability is equal to the number of yellow pillows in the bed divided by the total number of pillows, i.e. 2/6 = 1/3.

The probability of an event is a number between 0 and 1. The closer the number is to 1, the more likely the event is to happen. Conversely, the closer it is to 0, the less likely it is.

Probalility Related to AI

Probability is fundamental to many aspects of Artificial Intelligence (AI). AI systems are constantly dealing with uncertainty, and probability theory provides a mathematical framework for reasoning about these uncertainties.

Here are a few ways probability is used in AI

- Machine learning algorithms learn from data, and much of that data is inherently noisy or incomplete. Probability theory allows us to represent the uncertainty in the data and make predictions about future data points.

  For example, a spam filter might use a probabilistic model to represent the likelihood that an email is spam, given the words it contains.
- Robots operate in the real world, which is a complex and unpredictable environment. Probability theory allows robots to reason about the uncertainty in their sensor readings and make decisions about how to move and interact with their surroundings.
- Computer vision systems are tasked with understanding the visual world, which is often ambiguous or cluttered. Probability theory allows computer vision systems to represent the uncertainty in their interpretations of images and videos.

  For example, a facial recognition system might use a probabilistic model to represent the likelihood that a particular face is in an image.

The concept of probability is a fundamental aspect of mathematics and statistics, and it can be expressed in various ways to describe different levels of certainty about events. Here's a summary of these expressions with explanations and examples:

1. Certain Events

An event that will happen without any doubt.

Probability : 1 (or 100%).

Example : The probability that the sun will rise tomorrow is 1. This event is certain because it is based on astronomical phenomena that have been consistent over time.

2. Likely Events

An event that has a higher probability of occurring than another event.

Probability : Greater than 0.5 but less than 1.

Example : The probability of drawing a heart from a standard deck of cards (52 cards) is 13/52 or 1/4 (0.25). If you know the deck is stacked in a way that favors hearts, this probability increases, making drawing a heart more likely than drawing another suit.

3. Unlikely Events

An event that has a lower probability of occurring than another event.

Probability : Greater than 0 but less than 0.5.

Example : The probability of flipping a coin and getting heads 10 times in a row is quite low, making this an unlikely event. The probability for this is (1/2)^10, which is approximately 0.00098 or 0.098%.

4. Impossible Events

An event that has no chance of occurring.

Probability : 0.

Example : The probability of drawing a red ball from a bag that contains only blue balls is 0. Since there are no red balls in the bag, it is impossible to draw one.

5. Equal Probability Events

Events that have the same probability of occurring.

Probability : The same value for each event.

Example : When rolling a fair six-sided die, the probability of landing on any given number (1, 2, 3, 4, 5, or 6) is 1/6. Each outcome is equally likely, with a probability of 1/6.

Let's consider a bag containing 7 yellow stars and 3 blue stars. We can use this example to illustrate different types of probabilities:

Certain Events

Drawing a star from the bag is a certain event. No matter what, you will always draw a star because the bag only contains stars.

Likely Events

Drawing a yellow star is more likely than drawing a blue star. Since there are more yellow stars (7) than blue stars (3), the probability of drawing a yellow star is higher.

Unlikely Events

Drawing a blue star is less likely than drawing a yellow star. The probability of drawing a blue star is lower because there are fewer blue stars (3) compared to yellow stars (7).

Impossible Events

Drawing a green star is an impossible event. Since there are no green stars in the bag, the probability of drawing a green star is zero.

Equal Probability Events

If we consider a scenario where we draw two stars from the bag one after another without replacement, the probability of drawing a yellow star first and then a blue star is the same as drawing a blue star first and then a yellow star. Both sequences have the same chance because they depend on the same counts of stars. Let's try to understand the concept of probability using a relatable example. Consider a relatable scenario. You want to go to the amusement park next Sunday. Your parents decide to make a deal with you.

Scenario 1

Scenario 2

Scenario 3

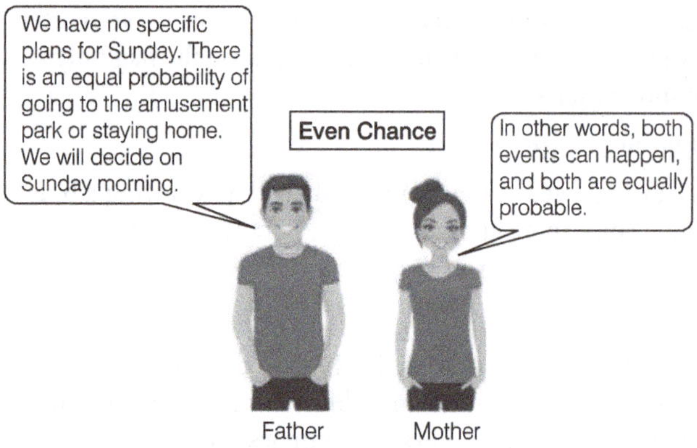

Scenario 4

Applications of Probability

1. **Sports-Cricket Batting Average** Understanding the probability of scoring runs, particularly boundaries, helps in estimating a player's batting average. This insight can inform strategies and predictions in cricket matches.
2. **Weather Forecasting** Weather forecasters rely heavily on probability to predict weather conditions accurately. By analyzing historical data and current atmospheric conditions, they assign probabilities to different weather outcomes, such as rain, snow, or clear skies, enabling people to plan their activities accordingly.
3. **Traffic Estimation** Probability plays a crucial role in estimating traffic conditions. By considering factors like time of day, location and weather, individuals can make informed decisions about when to travel to avoid heavy traffic. This application of probability helps in optimizing travel routes and reducing commute times.
4. **Finance and Investment** Probability is extensively used in finance and investment to assess risks and returns. For instance, investors might calculate the probability of a stock reaching a certain price level within a given time frame using historical data and market indicators to make informed investment decisions.
5. **Healthcare** In healthcare, probability is used in various ways such as predicting the likelihood of a patient developing certain diseases based on their medical history, genetic predispositions, and environmental factors. It's also used in clinical trials to determine the effectiveness of new treatments or medications.
6. **Gaming and Gambling** Probability plays a crucial role in gaming and gambling industries. Casinos use probability to determine the odds of winning for different games such as roulette, blackjack, or slot machines. Similarly, game developers use probability to design game mechanics and balance gameplay, ensuring a fair and enjoyable experience for players.
7. **Insurance** Insurance companies rely on probability to assess risks and set premiums for various types of insurance policies. They use statistical models to calculate the probability of certain events such as accidents, natural disasters, or illnesses occurring within a given population, allowing them to price their policies accordingly and manage their financial exposure.

Try These 6.1

1. **Write the use of Math in AI.**
2. **Write some example of mean, median, mode.**
3. **What are the formula of probability?**
4. **What are the applications of probability?**

Glossary

Statistics It is the field of study concerned with the collection, organization, analysis, interpretation, and presentation of data.

Mean The mean, often referred to as the average, is the sum of all the values in a data set divided by the number of values.

Median The median is the middle value in a data set when the data is ordered from least to greatest.

Mode The mode is the most frequent value in a data set.

Probability The probability formula is defined as the possibility of an event to happen is equal to the ratio of the number of favourable outcomes and the total number of outcomes.

Let's Investigate

Activity 1

Purpose Observing and analyzing the numbers and Find the pattern.

Problem 1 : Missing Number Series

In each of the series, the missing number can be found by looking at the difference between consecutive terms. Here's how to find the missing number in each case:

- Series 1: 2, 4, 6, 8, 10, 12, ? The difference between consecutive terms is always 2 (4 - 2 = 2, 6 - 4 = 2, and so on). Therefore, the missing number is the last term (12) plus the difference (2): 12 + 2 = 14.
- Series 2: 4, 10, 16, 22, 28, ? The difference between consecutive terms is always 6 (10 - 4 = 6, 16 - 10 = 6, and so on). The missing number is the last term (28) plus the difference (6): 28 + 6 = 34.
- Series 3: 34, 31, 28, 25, 22, ? The difference between consecutive terms is always 3 (31 - 34 = -3, 28 - 31 = -3, and so on). Here, we have a subtraction instead of addition. So, the missing number is the last term (22) minus the difference (3): 22 - 3 = 19.

Problem 2 : Predicting Profit

Following the pattern of increasing profits by INR 500 each year, the predicted profit for year 5 would be:

- Last year's profit (Year 4) + Increase in profit per year
- 2500 (INR) + 500 (INR) = 3000 (INR)

Therefore, the predicted profit for year 5 is INR 3000.

Activity 2

Purpose To find connections between sets of images and using that to solve problems, think smartly, and grasp tricky ideas. Complete the sequence in the left column by identifying the correct missing piece in the right column out of A or B.

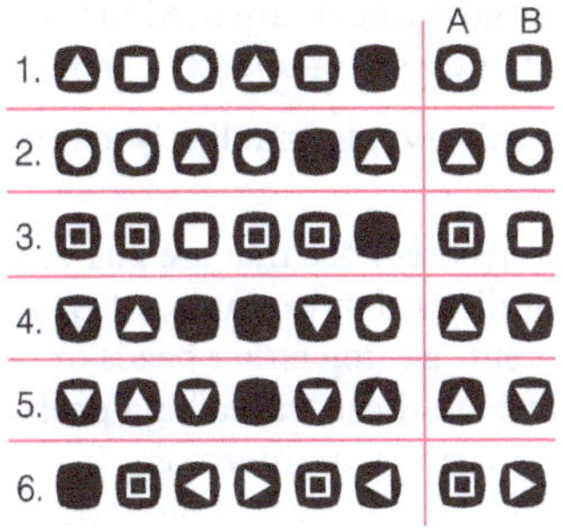

Activity 3 :

Purpose To implement the concept of data collection, analysis, and interpretation.

Activity Introduction

- In this activity, students will engage in data collection and tabulation.
- Data collection plays a key role in Artificial Intelligence as it forms the basis of statistics and interpretation by AI.
- This activity will also require students to answer a set of questions based on the recorded data.

Data Collection

1. Preparation

- Before starting the video, prepare a table with the following columns: Colour of Car, Tally, and Total Count.
- The colours to include are: Red, Blue, Black, White, Silver, and Other.

2. Watch the Video

- Visit the following link: Car Spotting Video
- As you watch the video, use tally marks to record each car you see based on its colour.

Example Table

Colour of Car	Tally	Total Count
Red		
Blue		
Black		
White		
Silver		
Other		

Data Analysis

1. How many cars are spotted in total?
2. Which colour has been spotted the maximum amount of times?

Data Interpretation

1. What is the most common colour choice for the residents of this area?
   (Hint The colour observed the maximum number of times.)

NCERT FOLDER

Complete Explanations of all NCERT's Questions

A. Multiple Choice Questions

Q.1 If you are to throw an arrow to this pie chart, in which color is the arrow more likely to fall?

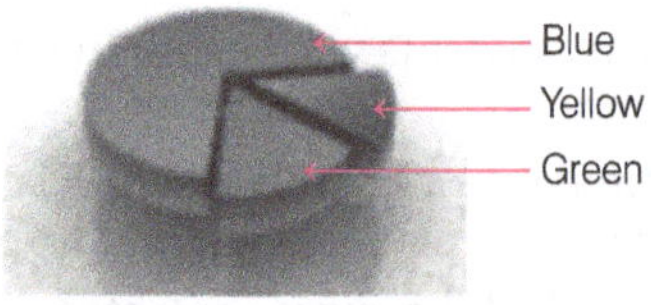

(a) Red (b) Blue (c) Yellow (d) Green

Q.2 If you select a balloon without looking, how likely is it that you will pick a blue one?

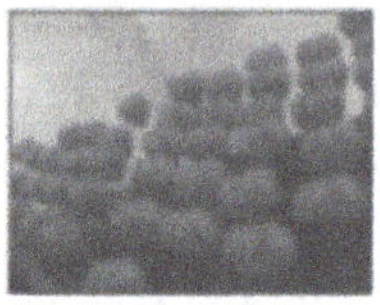

(a) Probable (b) Certain (c) Unlikely (d) Impossible

Q.3 With one throw of a 6-sided die, what's the probability of getting an even number?

(a) 1/5 (b) 2/5 (c) 5/6 (d) 1/2

Q.4 Which of the following is an equation?

(a) $2x + 5$ (b) $x + 2 = 4x$

(c) $x^2 + 2x$ (d) $5 + 5x + 5x^2$

Q.5 What is the value of x? $10x - 8 = 6x$

(a) 8 (b) 4 (c) 2 (d) 6

Q.6 Which two are examples of descriptive statistics?

(a) Median and correlation.

(b) Mean and standard deviation.

(c) Mode and regression analysis.

(d) Variance and Hypothesis testing.

Q.7 What is the probability of getting head when you toss a coin once?

(a) 0.75 (b) 1 (c) 0 (d) 0.5

Q.8 Getting seven in die throwing is a possible event. (True/False).

Q.9 The median of the data: 155, 160, 145, 149, 150, 147, 152, 144, 148 is

(a) 149 (b)150 (c)147 (d)144

Answers

1. (b) 2. (d) 3. (d) 4. (b) 5. (c)
6. (b) 7. (d) 8. (F) 9. (a)

B. Match the column

Q.1 Match the following:

	A		B
(i)	Probability	(a)	exploring data
(ii)	Calculus	(b)	finding out unknown or missing values
(iii)	Statistics	(c)	predicting different events
(iv)	Linear Algebra	(d)	training and improving AI model.

Ans. (i) (c), (ii) (d), (iii) (a), (iv) (b)

C. Subjective Type Questions

Q.1 Explain the relationship between Mathematics and Artificial Intelligence, providing justification for their interconnection.

Ans. Mathematics serves as the backbone of Artificial Intelligence (AI), providing the theoretical framework and tools necessary for understanding and developing AI algorithms. Concepts from various branches of mathematics such as calculus, linear algebra, probability theory, and statistics are used extensively in AI for modeling, optimization, decision-making, and machine learning.

Q.2 Aman is confused, how probability theory is utilized in artificial intelligence, help Aman by providing two examples to illustrate its importance.

Ans. Probability theory plays a crucial role in AI by providing a mathematical framework for dealing with uncertainty. For example, in machine learning, probabilistic models like Bayesian networks are used to represent and reason about uncertainty in data. Another example is in natural language processing, where probabilistic models such as Hidden Markov Models are used for tasks like speech recognition and part-of-speech tagging.

Q.3 Define Certain events and likely events with examples.

Ans. Certain events are those that are guaranteed to happen, with probability 1. For example, when you flip a fair coin, the event "getting either heads or tails" is certain. Likely events are those with a high probability of occurring, but not guaranteed. For instance, in rolling a fair six-sided die, the event "rolling a 3 or a 4" is likely.

Q.4 Write any two examples of impossible and equal probability events.

Ans. Impossible events are those with zero probability of occurring. For example, rolling for a seven with a fair six-sided die is an impossible event. Equal probability events are those with the same likelihood of occurring. For instance, when you roll a fair six-sided die, each face has an equal probability of 1/6 of appearing.

Q.5 Radhika collected the data of the age distribution of cases admitted during a day in a hospital.

Age (in years)	10	12	14	15	16
Cases admitted (in a day)	5	7	9	22	11

Find the average number of cases admitted in hospital. Also, draw a line graph to represent the data graphically.

Ans. To find the average number of cases admitted in the hospital, we can use the formula :

Average = (Sum of all cases admitted) / (Number of data points)

Let's calculate the sum of all cases admitted:

Sum = 5 + 7 + 9 + 22 + 11 = 54

Now, there are 5 data points, so the average is:

Average = 54 / 5 = 10.8

So, the average number of cases admitted in the hospital is 10.8 per day.

Now, let's create a line graph to represent the data:

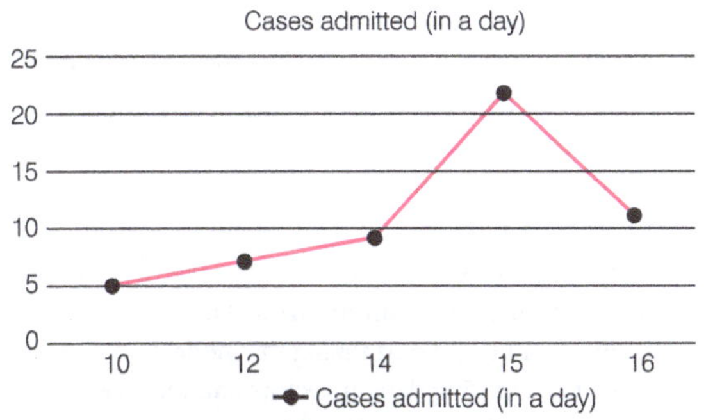

Q.6 Identify the likely, unlikely, impossible and equal probability events from the following

(a) Tossing a coin

(b) Rolling an 8 on a standard die

(c) Throwing ten 5's in a row

(d) Drawing a card of any suite

Ans. (a) **Tossing a coin** This is an equal probability event. There are two possible outcomes (heads or tails), and each outcome has an equal chance of happening.

(b) **Rolling an 8 on a standard die** This is an unlikely event. A standard die has six sides, and only one side has an 8. So, the probability of rolling an 8 is 1 out of 6, which is a low chance.

(c) **Throwing ten 5's in a row** This is an impossible event. While unlikely things can happen, throwing ten 5s in a row is extremely improbable. There are 6 possible outcomes when rolling a die (1-6), and getting a 5 ten times in a row is statistically very unlikely.

(d) **Drawing a card of any suite** This is a likely event. There are four suits in a standard deck (hearts, diamonds, clubs, spades), and you only need to draw a card from any of those suits. There are 52 cards total, and 4 of them satisfy the condition (one from each suit), so the chance of drawing a card of any suit is quite high.

Q.7 Why is math necessary for designing an AI project?

Ans. Math is the language of AI for a few reasons:

- **Foundations of AI algorithms** Many AI algorithms rely on complex mathematical formulas to analyze data, recognize patterns, and make predictions. This could involve anything from linear algebra for image recognition to calculus for optimizing machine learning models.
- **Data representation and manipulation** Real-world data is often messy and needs to be processed and transformed before feeding it into an AI system. Math provides the tools to represent this data in a way that computers can understand and manipulate.
- **Evaluation and performance** You need to be able to measure how well your AI system is performing. Math provides the framework to define metrics and assess the effectiveness of your design.

REVIEW EXERCISE

Including Competency Based Questions

Part I

Multiple Choice Questions

1 What is the primary role of statistics in artificial intelligence?
(a) To write code for AI algorithms
(b) To clean and prepare data for AI models
(c) To design user interfaces for AI applications
(d) To optimize hardware for AI processing

2 Which branch of mathematics is essential for optimizing the parameters of AI models?
(a) Algebra (b) Geometry
(c) Calculus (d) Trigonometry

3 What mathematical technique is commonly used to adjust the parameters of AI models to minimize errors?
(a) Regression analysis (b) Gradient descent
(c) Matrix factorization (d) Monte Carlo simulation

4 Which measure of central tendency is the most common and is calculated as the sum of all values divided by the number of values?
(a) Mode (b) Median
(c) Mean (d) Range

5 In a data set {2, 3, 11, 13, 26, 34, 47}, what is the median value?
(a) 11 (b) 13
(c) 26 (d) 34

6 What is the mode in the data set {3, 3, 6, 9, 16, 16, 16, 27, 27, 37, 48}?
(a) 3 (b) 16
(c) 27 (d) 48

7 How is variance calculated in a data set?
(a) By taking the sum of the data points
(b) By calculating the average of the data points
(c) By finding the average squared deviation from the mean
(d) By dividing the sum of the squares by the number of values

8 Which field uses statistical analysis to evaluate player performance and predict game outcomes?
(a) Finance
(b) Marketing
(c) Sports
(d) Education

9 Which statistical measure is the square root of the variance?
(a) Mean (b) Mode
(c) Standard deviation (d) Median

10 In machine learning, what role does probability theory play?
(a) It helps design user interfaces for AI applications
(b) It models uncertainty in data and makes predictions
(c) It optimizes hardware for AI processing
(d) It writes code for AI algorithms

11 What is the function of linear algebra in AI?
(a) Training AI models
(b) Summarizing data
(c) Representing and manipulating data
(d) Predicting future events

12 What is one of the activities involved in the field of statistics?
(a) Conducting a survey
(b) Writing AI algorithms
(c) Designing hardware for AI
(d) Developing user interfaces

13 Which application of statistics helps in predicting disease outbreaks and allocating healthcare resources?
(a) Disaster management (b) Disease prediction
(c) Weather forecast (d) Business analysis

14 How does AI use calculus to improve its models?
(a) By analyzing and summarizing data
(b) By training and optimizing the models
(c) By representing data in vectors and matrices
(d) By predicting different outcomes

15 What does the term "bimodal" mean in statistics?
(a) A dataset with no modes
(b) A dataset with one mode
(c) A dataset with two modes
(d) A dataset with multiple modes

Answers

1. (b)	2. (c)	3. (b)	4. (c)	5. (b)
6. (b)	7. (c)	8. (c)	9. (c)	10. (b)
11. (c)	12. (a)	13. (b)	14. (b)	15. (c)

Statement Based Questions

1 Statement 1: Probability helps AI systems to reason under uncertainty and make optimal choices.

Statement 2: Statistics is used to extract meaningful insights and identify patterns in data for AI.

(a) Both Statement 1 and Statement 2 are correct
(b) Both Statement 1 and Statement 2 are incorrect
(c) Statement 1 is correct but Statement 2 is incorrect
(d) Statement 2 is correct but Statement 1 is incorrect

2 Statement 1: Linear algebra is used to represent data in a way that AI models can understand and manipulate.

Statement 2: Calculus is used in AI for predicting different events.

(a) Both Statement 1 and Statement 2 are correct
(b) Both Statement 1 and Statement 2 are incorrect
(c) Statement 1 is correct but Statement 2 is incorrect
(d) Statement 2 is correct but Statement 1 is incorrect

3 Statement 1: Standard deviation measures the average squared deviation from the mean.

Statement 2: Median is the middle value in a data set when the data is ordered from least to greatest.

(a) Both Statement 1 and Statement 2 are correct
(b) Both Statement 1 and Statement 2 are incorrect
(c) Statement 1 is correct but Statement 2 is incorrect
(d) Statement 2 is correct but Statement 1 is incorrect

4 Statement 1: Probability is a measure of how likely an event is to happen, expressed as a number between 0 and 1.

Statement 2: The sum of probabilities of all possible outcomes of a chance event is always equal to 1.

(a) Both Statement 1 and Statement 2 are correct
(b) Both Statement 1 and Statement 2 are incorrect
(c) Statement 1 is correct but Statement 2 is incorrect
(d) Statement 2 is correct but Statement 1 is incorrect

5 Statement 1: Weather forecasting relies on probability to predict future weather conditions based on historical data and current atmospheric conditions.

Statement 2: In sports, probability is used to calculate the likelihood of a specific outcome, such as a player hitting a home run in baseball.

(a) Both Statement 1 and Statement 2 are correct
(b) Both Statement 1 and Statement 2 are incorrect
(c) Statement 1 is correct but Statement 2 is incorrect
(d) Statement 2 is correct but Statement 1 is incorrect

Answers

1. (a) **2.** (c) **3.** (d) **4.** (a) **5.** (a)

Assertion & Reason Based Questions

1 Assertion: Statistics is a crucial tool for AI because it helps in preparing data for learning by identifying outliers and choosing relevant features.

Reason: Statistical techniques enable the cleaning of data, which leads to more accurate and efficient learning in AI systems.

(a) Both Assertion and Reason are true, and Reason is the correct explanation of Assertion.
(b) Both Assertion and Reason are true, but Reason is not the correct explanation of Assertion.
(c) Assertion is true, but Reason is false.
(d) Assertion is false, but Reason is true.

2 Assertion: Calculus is essential in AI for optimizing the performance of models by adjusting parameters using techniques like gradient descent.

Reason: Calculus provides tools to represent and manipulate data in AI systems effectively.

(a) Both Assertion and Reason are true, and Reason is the correct explanation of Assertion.
(b) Both Assertion and Reason are true, but Reason is not the correct explanation of Assertion.
(c) Assertion is true, but Reason is false.
(d) Assertion is false, but Reason is true.

3 Assertion: Standard deviation is a measure of how spread out data points are from the mean and is expressed in the same units as the original data.

Reason: Variance is the square root of the standard deviation.

(a) Both Assertion and Reason are true, and Reason is the correct explanation of Assertion.
(b) Both Assertion and Reason are true, but Reason is not the correct explanation of Assertion.
(c) Assertion is true, but Reason is false.
(d) Assertion is false, but Reason is true.

4 Assertion : Probability theory is crucial in AI for modeling uncertainty in data and making informed decisions under certain conditions.

Reason: In facial recognition technology, AI uses probability theory to precisely identify features like the shape of a nose or the distance between eyes.

(a) Both Assertion and Reason are true, and Reason is the correct explanation of Assertion.
(b) Both Assertion and Reason are true, but Reason is not the correct explanation of Assertion.
(c) Assertion is true, but Reason is false.
(d) Assertion is false, but Reason is true.

Answers

1. (a) **2.** (a) **3.** (c) **4.** (a)

Part II

Very Short Answer Type Questions

1 What branch of math helps AI understand data patterns?

Ans. Statistics

2 Which mathematical technique is used to optimize AI model parameters?

Ans. Gradient descent

3 How does probability benefit AI systems?

Ans. It helps AI make decisions under uncertainty.

4 What is the role of linear algebra in AI?

Ans. It helps represent and manipulate data.

5 Why is calculus important for training AI models?

Ans. It optimizes the model's performance by minimizing errors.

6 What foundational concepts empower machines to make intelligent decisions?

Ans. Statistics and probability, particularly in analyzing data and handling uncertainty.

7 How does mathematics contribute to AI algorithms?

Ans. Mathematics, including linear algebra, calculus, and probability theory, forms the basis for AI models and predictions.

8 Why is statistics crucial for AI?

Ans. Statistics enables understanding and analyzing data, identifying patterns, and making informed predictions in AI systems.

9 How does calculus improve AI models?

Ans. Calculus optimizes AI models by adjusting parameters through techniques like gradient descent for enhanced performance.

10 Why is linear algebra important in AI?

Ans. Linear algebra helps represent and manipulate data for AI models, essential for understanding and processing information efficiently.

11 What role does probability play in AI systems?

Ans. Probability helps AI systems make decisions under uncertainty and model data variability for accurate predictions.

12 What are the primary measures of central tendency?

Ans. Mean, median, and mode are the main measures of central tendency in statistics.

13 Define variance and its importance in statistics.

Ans. Variance measures data variability from the mean, crucial for understanding the spread of data points in a dataset.

14 How does mathematics support various fields beyond AI?

Ans. Mathematics, particularly statistics, is applied in diverse fields such as sports analytics, disaster management, finance, and education.

Short Answer Type Questions

1 How does mathematics contribute to the foundation of AI?

Ans. Mathematics serves as the language of AI, enabling machines to process information through numbers and equations, essential for creating algorithms and machine learning models that recognize patterns and make predictions.

2 What role does statistics play in preparing data for AI learning?

Ans. Statistics aids in cleaning data, identifying outliers, and selecting relevant features for training AI models. This ensures more accurate and efficient learning by quantifying uncertainty and building robust models.

3 Can you explain the significance of measures of central tendency in statistics?

Ans. Measures like mean, median, and mode provide insights into the central position within a dataset. They help in understanding data distribution, essential for analyzing trends and making informed decisions in AI.

4 How do variance and standard deviation measure data spread?

Ans. Variance quantifies the average squared deviation from the mean, indicating data variability. Standard deviation, the square root of variance, expresses data spread in the same units as the original data, aiding in assessing data consistency.

5 In what ways does probability theory benefit AI systems?

Ans. Probability theory enables AI systems to make decisions under uncertainty by modeling probabilistic outcomes.

This is crucial in machine learning for handling data uncertainty and making informed predictions, enhancing the reliability of AI algorithms.

Long Answer Type Questions

1. How does statistics contribute to the robustness of AI models?

Ans. Statistics plays a crucial role in ensuring the robustness of AI models by addressing the uncertainties and imperfections in data.

It helps in identifying outliers, cleaning data, and selecting relevant features for training models. By quantifying uncertainty, statistics enables the creation of models that are resilient to errors and variations in data, enhancing their accuracy and efficiency in making predictions.

Additionally, statistical techniques such as hypothesis testing and confidence intervals allow for the validation and generalization of AI models, ensuring they perform reliably on new, unseen data. This comprehensive approach helps in building robust AI systems that can withstand the challenges of real-world applications.

2. Explain the significance of calculus in optimizing AI models.

Ans. Calculus provides the mathematical framework for optimizing the performance of AI models. Techniques like gradient descent utilize calculus to adjust the parameters of models iteratively, minimizing errors and improving performance over time.

By enabling precise adjustments based on the rate of change of variables, calculus ensures that AI models converge towards optimal solutions, enhancing their effectiveness in tasks such as pattern recognition and decision-making.

Moreover, advanced calculus methods such as partial derivatives and multivariable functions allow for the optimization of complex models with numerous parameters, facilitating the fine-tuning necessary for achieving high accuracy and efficiency in diverse AI applications.

3. How does probability theory aid AI systems in handling uncertainty?

Ans. Probability theory is essential for AI systems to make decisions under uncertainty. By modeling uncertainty in data, probability theory enables AI systems to quantify the likelihood of different outcomes and make informed decisions. This is crucial in various applications, such as natural language processing and autonomous vehicles, where AI systems must navigate complex and uncertain environments.

Probability theory provides a solid foundation for reasoning about uncertainty, allowing AI systems to make optimal choices and adapt to changing circumstances effectively.

Additionally, techniques such as Bayesian inference and probabilistic graphical models offer powerful tools for updating beliefs based on new information, further enhancing the decision-making capabilities of AI systems in dynamic settings.

ASSESSMENT EXERCISE

Multiple Choice Questions

1. In a self-driving car simulation, there is a 70% chance of encountering a pedestrian crossing the street and a 40% chance of encountering a red light. These events are considered independent. What is the probability of encountering both a pedestrian and a red light?
   (a) 110% (This probability is not possible)
   (b) 28%
   (c) 56%
   (d) There is not enough information to determine the probability.

2. Which of the following is the most appropriate measure of central tendency for a dataset with a large number of outliers?
   (a) Mean (b) Median
   (c) Mode (d) All of the above

3. An AI for spam filtering is trained on a dataset where 80% of emails are spam. If a new email is classified as spam, what is the probability that it actually is spam (assuming the AI is not perfect)?
   (a) 100% (We cannot be certain without more information)
   (b) 80%
   (c) This depends on the accuracy of the AI.
   (d) None of the above

4. Which mathematical concept is used to represent the uncertainty of an event in probabilistic reasoning for AI?
   (a) Calculus (b) Probability Theory
   (c) Linear Algebra (d) Set Theory

Very Short Answer Type Questions

5. What is the role of statistics in AI?
6. What is median?
7. Write the formula of Probability.
8. Why is linear algebra important in AI?

Short Answer Type Questions

9. How Probability plays an important role in AI?
10. Write the application of statistics.

Long Answer Type Questions

11. Explain how math related to AI.
12. What are the application of Probability?

CHAPTER 07

Generative AI

Generative AI is a type of artificial intelligence that can create entirely new content, like text, images, music, and even videos. It works by analyzing existing data to learn patterns and relationships. Then, it uses this knowledge to generate fresh content that follows those patterns. This has the potential to revolutionize many fields, from art and design to software development.

7.1 Introduction

Generative AI, short for generative artificial intelligence, is a type of AI that can create new content, like text, images, music, and even videos. It's essentially like a creative machine that learns by analyzing existing data and then uses that knowledge to generate entirely new things.

Generative AI Models

Generative AI models are trained and learn the datasets and design within the data based on large datasets and patterns. They can generate new examples that are similar to the training data. These models are capable of generating new content without any human instructions.

In simple words, it generally involves training AI models to understand different patterns and structures within existing data and using that to generate new original data.

Although the topic of generative AI has bloomed recently, the technology itself is not new. The idea of computers mimicking human thinking abilities has entertained science-fiction writers since the dawn of computerization. Artificial intelligence began to be treated more like reality than fantasy when English mathematician and computer scientist **Alan Turing** published his paper "Computing Machinery and Intelligence" in 1950, introducing the concept of machines capable of reasoning similarly to humans.

Since then, artificial intelligence and its generative branch have rapidly progressed. However, let's focus on the current decade. While AI and machine learning are nothing new, in 2022 discussion about them ramped up. That's when names like ChatGPT, DALL-E, and Midjourney began to appear. These are among the first generative AI models available to the general public due to their easy-to-use interfaces and ability to understand queries written in natural language used by humans in conversations, unlike earlier models operated in programming languages.

7.2 Generative AI Timeline

- 1956 Introduction of Artificial Intelligence as a science;
- 1958 Frank Rosenblatt proposed the scheme of a device that simulates the process in the human brain - perceptron, the world's first neural network;
- 1964 Creation of one of the first functioning generative AI-ELIZA chatbot;
- 1982 RNN is created, which takes prior information into account and generates sentences;
- 1997 A type of RNN with a more complex architecture called LSTM is developed, which allows efficient processing of long sequences of data and identifies patterns;
- 2013 Creation of a generative model called variational autoencoders (VAE);
- 2014 Creation of GANs, which were a breakthrough in generative AI as they were among the first to generate high-quality images. GAN has received more attention, also due to the higher degree of complexity of the theoretical basis of VAE compared to the more straightforward concept underlying GAN;

- **2015** Introduction of diffusion models that function by incorporating noise into the existing training data and then reversing the process to restore the data;
- **2017** Deep learning architecture referred to as transformer was proposed;
- **2018** Groundbreaking Generative pre-trained transformers (GPT), a type of large language model, was introduced by OpenAI;
- **2021** AI platform DALL-E intended for generating and editing unique artworks and photorealistic images was launched;
- **2022** Open source Stable Diffusion and proprietary Midjourney AI image-generating tools were introduced;
- **2023** GPT-4 was released in March 2023, capable of generating longer texts up to 25000 words.

Continued Milestones in GenAI

The evolution of Generative AI has been marked by a number of important breakthroughs that have each added a new chapter to its history.

Here are some pivotal moments that have reshaped the landscape of GenAI:

- **WaveNet (2016)** DeepMind's WaveNet marked a significant advancement in generative models for audio. WaveNet could generate realistic-sounding human speech, which opened doors for more human-like AI assistants and highly accurate text-to-speech synthesis.
- **Progressive GANs (2017)** Progressive GANs, developed by NVIDIA, were a milestone in producing high-resolution, photo-realistic images. These GANs were able to generate images with unprecedented detail and clarity by progressively adding layers during the training process.
- **GPT-2 and GPT-3 (2019, 2020)** OpenAI's generative pre-trained transformer (GPT) models marked a significant leap in the field of GenAI for text. They demonstrated the ability to generate coherent and contextually relevant sentences, making them useful for a wide range of applications, from writing assistance to the chatbot population.
- **DALL-E (2022)** OpenAI launched DALL-E to the public. DALL-E is a deep learning model that can generate digital images from natural language prompts.
- **ChatGPT (2022)** Open AI released ChatGPT, a conversational chatbot based on GPT, and the platform reached one million users within five days.
- **GPT-4 (2023)** The latest GPT model is reportedly more accurate and has advanced reasoning capabilities. Premium ChatGPT users now have optional access to GPT-4 within the chatbot.

Each of these milestones brought Generative AI closer to its current capabilities, overcoming challenges related to computational power, data quality, and training stability.

7.3 Working of Generative AI

Generative AI operates using machine learning, particularly a specialized branch known as deep learning. Deep learning employs artificial neural networks, which are virtual models inspired by the neural networks in animal brains.

What sets deep learning apart from other machine learning methods is its capability to learn in a semi-supervised or unsupervised manner. This means deep learning models can process vast amounts of unlabeled data with minimal human intervention. In unsupervised learning, the model receives data without specific instructions and autonomously analyzes it to discover patterns. The foundational models developed through this approach serve as the basis for various generative AI applications.

Generative AI technology can identify patterns in human-generated information, learn from them, and reproduce them by utilizing deep learning. It creates original content in response to user inputs known as "prompts," thereby generating creative results inspired by these requests.

7.4 Impact and Future of Generative AI

Generative AI shows potential for wide use in diverse industries. Educators and healthcare professionals could use it to develop learning plans or patient rehabilitation training. Graphic and fashion designers could generate new ideas for visual assets, logos, styles and patterns. Personalized digital assistants can develop individual diet and exercise plans, make travel reservations and pay bills. Developers can accelerate coding. Users will more easily engage in chat-like conversations with their devices. Generative AI also shows near-limitless potential for scientific research and analysis.

The potential benefits of generative AI for on-device applications alone can further improve the user experience through enhanced data privacy and security, reduced latency, increased performance and contextual personalization while lowering the required costs and energy consumption of cloud-based AI.

Generative AI will continue to play a crucial role in shaping the future of technology by pushing the boundaries of what machines can achieve. New advancements in generative AI may spur laptop replacements and a general move from the cloud to on-device processing. Personal AI assistants will make smartphones even more indispensable. Creatives and marketers will see an increase in productivity levels, time-to-market and efficiency. Consumers will increasingly demand that their devices work together across open ecosystems, and extended reality experiences will redefine our world.

Try These 7.1

1 **What is Generative AI?**
2 **In which year was GPT-4 released?**
3 **What is the impact of Generative AI on the future?**

Types of Generative AI

Generative AI comes in a variety of forms, each with unique advantages and uses. Some of the most typical varieties are given below

GAN (Generative Adversarial Network)

GAN stands for Generative Adversarial Network. It's a type of artificial intelligence (AI) that uses two neural networks to create new data, like images, music, or even text.

Working

GANs consist of two main components - a Generator Network and a Discriminator Network.

These networks don't collaborate in the traditional sense. Instead, they have an "adversarial" relationship, where they compete with each other.

The Generator tries to create new data (images, text, etc.) that are indistinguishable from real data.

The Discriminator acts like a critic, trying to identify whether the data it sees is real or generated by the Generator.

This competition is a continuous loop. The Generator receives feedback from the Discriminator's analysis and uses it to improve its creations. Over time, the Generator gets better at producing realistic data, while the Discriminator gets better at spotting fakes.

Applications

Examples of what GANs can be used for:

- Generating realistic portraits of people who don't exist.
- Transforming images from day to night or *vice versa* (applying artistic styles).
- Creating images based on a textual description.
- Even generating realistic videos!

Beyond these, GANs have a wide range of applications in various fields:

- **Drug discovery** Simulating molecules for medical research.
- **Game development** Creating realistic game environments.
- **Fashion design** Generating new clothing designs.
- **Music composition** Composing new music pieces in a specific style.

VAE (Variational Autoencoders)

VAEs, which stands for Variational Autoencoders, are a type of artificial neural network used for generating new data. They work by learning the underlying structure of a dataset and then using that knowledge to create new data points that resemble the originals.

Working

Encoder-decoder architecture Like autoencoders, VAEs have two main parts: an encoder and a decoder. The encoder compresses the input data into a latent space representation, which captures the essential features. The decoder then uses this latent representation to reconstruct the original data as accurately as possible.

Unlike regular autoencoders, VAEs introduce a probabilistic element to the latent space. The encoder doesn't just output a single point, but rather a probability distribution over possible latent codes. This allows for more diverse and interesting data generation.

Applications

- **Image generation** VAEs are great for generating new images that resemble the training data. You can train a VAE on a dataset of faces and use it to create new, realistic-looking faces.
- **Image reconstruction** VAEs can also be used for image reconstruction tasks. For example, if you have a corrupted image, a VAE can be trained to remove the noise and reconstruct a clean version.
- **Creative text formats** Similar to generating new faces, VAEs can be used to generate different creative text formats. Imagine training a VAE on a collection of poems and using it to create new drafts for a writer, keeping the same style and flow.
- **Music composition** By learning the patterns in musical pieces, VAEs can generate new sounds and even compose entirely new pieces of music that adhere to a specific genre or style.

RNN (Recurrent Neural Network)

Recurrent neural networks (RNNs) are powerful tools for dealing with sequential data thanks to their unique ability to consider past information.

Working

Unlike traditional neural networks that treat each input independently, RNNs excel at understanding the relationships between elements in a sequence. This makes them ideal for tasks like language processing, where the meaning of a word depends on the words before it.

RNNs have an internal state, often called a hidden layer, that acts like a memory. This hidden layer stores information about past inputs, allowing the network to use that knowledge to predict what might come next.

Applications

RNNs are used in various applications that involve sequential data. Here are some examples:

- **Text Generation** RNNs can be trained on a large corpus of text to learn the writing style of a particular author or genre. Then, they can be used to generate new text that mimics that style.
- **Next Word Prediction** This is a common application in language processing. RNNs can analyze a sequence of words and predict the most likely word to come next. This is used in features like autocorrect and text suggestions on your phone.

Transformal Model

Transformer models are a specific kind of neural network architecture designed to handle sequential data, like text or speech.

Working

Unlike older models, they rely on a mechanism called self-attention. This allows them to analyze the relationships between different parts of the sequence, understanding how words depend on each other across long distances in a sentence. Additionally, they can process the sequence in parallel, making them faster.

Applications

Transformer models have become the go-to choice for many Natural Language Processing (NLP) tasks. They excel in tasks like:

- **Machine translation** Accurately translating text from one language to another.
- **Text-to-speech** Converting written text into natural-sounding speech.
- **Text generation** Creating new text content, like poems or code.
- **Sentiment analysis** Determining the emotional tone of a piece of text.

7.5 Conventional vs Generative AI

Conventional AI and Generative AI are two distinct approaches to artificial intelligence, each with its own strengths and applications:

Conventional AI *vs* Generative AI

Conventional AI (Traditional AI)

- **Rule-based** Relies on explicit programming and predefined rules.
- **Strengths**
  - **Transparent** Easy to understand how it arrives at a decision.
  - **Reliable** Performs consistently within its programmed parameters.
  - **Well-suited** for tasks with clear rules and defined goals (e.g., playing chess, spam filtering).
- **Limitations**
  - **Inflexible** Struggles with adapting to new situations outside its programming.
  - **Lacks creativity** Limited to generating outputs based on the data it is trained on.

Generative AI

- **Data-Driven** Learns from vast amounts of data to identify patterns and generate new content.
- **Strengths**
  - **Creative** Can produce novel and unexpected outputs like text, images, or music.
  - **Adaptable** Can learn and improve over time as it encounters new data.
  - **Potential for generalization** Can apply learnings to solve problems beyond the specific data it was trained on.

- **Limitations**
  - **Black Box** Can be difficult to understand the reasoning behind its outputs.
  - **Requires a lot of data for training** May not perform well with limited datasets.
  - **Potential for Bias** Can inherit biases present in the data it is trained on.

Try These 7.2

1. Explain GAN.
2. Write the applications of VAE.
3. What are the limitations of Generative AI?

Advantages of Generative AI

Generative AI, a subset of artificial intelligence that involves creating new content or data that resembles a given set of input data, offers a wide range of benefits across various fields. Here are some key advantages:

1. Creativity and Content Generation

Art and Design Generative AI can create unique artworks, design patterns, and graphics, enabling artists and designers to explore new creative possibilities.

Info Wall

The Next Rembrandt project used data analysis and 3D printing to create a new painting in the style of Rembrandt
(Watch video: Video source: The Next Rembrandt. (2016, April 5). The Next Rembrandt [Video]. YouTube. https://www.youtube.com/watch?v=IuygOYZ1Ngo)

Writing and Music It can assist in generating text for stories, articles, and even scripts, as well as composing original music pieces.

Note *AIVA is an AI composer that can create original pieces of music in various genres.*
(Watch video: Video source: TED. (2018, October 1). How AI could compose a personalized soundtrack to your lif |Pierre Barreau [Video]. YouTube. https://www.youtube.com/watch?v=wYb3Wimn01s)

2. Efficiency and Automation

Customer Service AI-powered chatbots and virtual assistants can handle customer inquiries and provide support, improving response times and reducing the need for human intervention.

Data Synthesis Generative models can create synthetic data for training other AI models, especially when real data is scarce or sensitive.

3. Enhanced Personalization

Marketing Generative AI can create personalized marketing content, such as emails, advertisements, and social media posts, tailored to individual preferences and behaviors.

Entertainment It can generate personalized recommendations for movies, music, and other media based on user preferences.

4. Innovation in Science and Medicine

Drug Discovery Generative models can assist in designing new drugs by predicting molecular structures that might be effective against specific diseases.

Medical Imaging AI can generate synthetic medical images to augment datasets, aiding in the training of diagnostic models.

5. Improving Accessibility

Language Translation AI can generate translations and captions in multiple languages, making content accessible to a broader audience.

Assistive Technologies Generative AI can create assistive tools for individuals with disabilities, such as generating descriptive text for images to aid the visually impaired.

6. Problem Solving and Decision Making

Simulation and Modeling Generative AI can create simulations of complex systems (e.g., weather patterns, financial markets) to help in decision-making and planning.

Optimization It can generate various scenarios and solutions for optimization problems in logistics, manufacturing, and resource management.

7. Enhanced User Experience

Gaming AI can create dynamic and immersive game environments, including procedurally generated levels, characters, and narratives.

Virtual Reality (VR) and Augmented Reality (AR) Generative models can create realistic virtual environments and augment real-world experiences.

8. Economic and Business Impact

Cost Reduction Automation of content creation and customer service can significantly reduce operational costs.

Innovation Generative AI drives innovation by enabling the creation of new products, services, and business models.

Disadvantages of Generative AI

Generative AI has transformative potential across many fields, but it also comes with significant limitations. Here are some key limitations including the ones you've mentioned :

1. Data Bias

Generative AI models learn from the data they are trained on. If the training data is biased or lacks diversity, the model will reflect those biases, leading to skewed or unfair outcomes. This can be particularly problematic in applications like facial recognition, where biased training data can result in higher error rates for certain demographic groups.

In natural language processing (NLP), biased data can perpetuate stereotypes or reinforce existing prejudices in generated text, leading to ethical and social issues.

2. Uncertainty

Generative AI models, especially those based on neural networks, can produce unexpected and unpredictable results. This unpredictability can be an asset in creative applications, such as art and music generation, but a liability in applications requiring high reliability and precision, like medical diagnosis or autonomous driving.

The decision-making process of generative models is often opaque, making it difficult to understand or predict how they will behave in new or unseen situations.

3. Computational Demands

Training and running generative AI models, particularly large ones like GPT-4, require substantial computational resources. This includes powerful hardware (e.g., GPUs or TPUs) and significant energy consumption, which can be both costly and environmentally impactful.

The need for high computational power can limit the scalability of deploying generative AI models, especially in resource-constrained environments or applications requiring real-time processing.

4. Ethical Concerns

Generative AI can be used to create realistic fake content, including deepfakes and misleading information, which can be weaponized to deceive and manipulate people.

Generating content that mimics the style or substance of existing works raises questions about intellectual property rights and the potential for plagiarism.

5. Quality Control

The quality of output from generative models can vary widely. Ensuring consistently high-quality results can be challenging, especially when the model is applied to diverse or complex tasks.

Small errors in the generated content can propagate and amplify, leading to significant flaws in the final output, which can be particularly detrimental in applications requiring high accuracy.

7.6 Generative AI Tools

Generative AI tools have found their way into various real-world scenarios, revolutionizing industries and enhancing productivity in numerous ways.

1. **Text Generation with GPT-3** Employ GPT-3 for content creation, chatbots, and summarization tasks. Its ability to understand context and generate human-like text makes it valuable for automating various writing tasks.
2. **Image Generation with DALL-E** DALL-E can create images from textual descriptions, making it useful for generating visual content for design projects, prototyping, and artistic endeavors. It can also be used in e-commerce for generating product images based on descriptions.
3. **Music Generation with MuseNet** MuseNet can compose music in various styles and genres, enabling musicians, filmmakers, and content creators to generate original soundtracks, background music, and jingles quickly.
4. **Video Generation with Deep Video Portraits** Deep Video Portraits can synthesize realistic videos of people speaking based on audio input, which can be applied in dubbing, video editing, and virtual avatars for online communication.
5. **Code Generation with GPT (Code Completion)** Generative AI models like GPT can assist developers by providing code completion suggestions, generating code snippets based on requirements, and even helping in code refactoring tasks.
6. **Design Generation with Generative Adversarial Networks (GANs)** GANs can be utilized in design tasks such as generating graphic designs, architectural layouts, fashion designs, and interior decor concepts based on input parameters and constraints.
7. **Language Translation with Transformer Models** Transformer models like BERT and T5 excel at language translation tasks, enabling businesses to

localize content efficiently and accurately across multiple languages.

8. **Data Augmentation with StyleGAN** StyleGAN can generate synthetic data resembling real data, which is useful in augmenting datasets for machine learning models, improving their robustness and generalization.
9. **Story Generation with StoryAI** StoryAI can create narrative text based on prompts, making it valuable for generating plot ideas, interactive storytelling, and content generation in gaming and entertainment industries.
10. **Personalization with Recommendation Systems** Generative models can enhance recommendation systems by generating personalized recommendations for products, content, and services based on user preferences, behavior, and historical data.

Ethical Issues of using Generative AI

Generative AI brings a wave of exciting possibilities but also raises ethical concerns that need careful consideration. Here's a breakdown of the points you mentioned:

Ownership As generative AI creates increasingly original content, the question of who owns it becomes murky. In creative fields, it's unclear whether the AI or the human who provided the prompt or training data should be credited as the author. Copyright laws might need revisions to address this.

Human Agency As the line between human and machine-generated content blurs, concerns arise about human agency. If AI takes over significant content creation, it could lead to a decline in human creativity and a sense of powerlessness over the information we consume.

Bias Generative AI models are only as good as the data they're trained on. Biases in the training data can be amplified by the AI, leading to discriminatory outputs. This is especially risky in areas like loan approvals or criminal justice where AI-generated recommendations can have life-altering consequences.

Misinformation The ability to create realistic-looking fake content with generative AI is a major concern. Deepfakes and fabricated news articles can be used to manipulate public opinion and sow discord. This undermines trust in institutions and can have serious implications for democracy.

Privacy Generative AI tools often require user data for training. There's a risk of privacy breaches if this data isn't anonymized or secured properly. Additionally, AI-generated content might inadvertently reveal sensitive information present in the training data.

Potential Negative Impacts and Considerations Surrounding Generative AI

Negative Impacts

- **Misinformation** Generative AI can create convincing fakes (like deepfakes) that spread misinformation and manipulate public opinion.
- **Job displacement** As AI gets better at tasks like content creation, some jobs currently done by humans might be automated.
- **Privacy risks** AI could be used to generate personal information for malicious purposes.
- **Bias** AI models trained on biased data can perpetuate those biases in their outputs.

The Path Forward : Responsible Use

Solutions to mitigate these risks

- **Training data** Using diverse and representative data sets helps reduce bias in AI outputs.
- **Scrutiny** Checking AI-generated content for misinformation and bias is crucial.
- **Privacy** User privacy and consent should be prioritized.
- **Ownership** Clear guidelines around who owns generative content are needed.
- **Public discussion** Open discussions about the ethical and social implications of generative AI are essential.

By focusing on responsible development and use, generative AI has the potential to greatly benefit society.

Try These 7.3

1. **What are the advantages of Generative AI?**
2. **Write about any five Generative Tools.**
3. **What are the ethical issues of using Generative AI?**

Glossary

Generative AI (Generative Artificial Intelligence) It is a type of AI that can create new content, like text, images, music, and even videos.

GPT It is OpenAI's generative pre-trained transformer (GPT) models.

GAN stands for Generative Adversarial Network.

VAEs stands for Variational Autoencoders.

RNN stands for Recurrent Neural Networks.

Let's Investigate

Activity 1

Purpose

- To understand the difference between real and AI-Generated Images.
- Examine the images and determine whether either of the images is a real image or an AI- generated image. Also, give reasons for your answer.

		Reason

Activity 2

The video title, "Intel is unlocking the potential of generative AI", suggests that the video is about generative AI, a type of artificial intelligence that can create new content, like text, images, or code.

Watch the video

https://www.youtube.com/watch?v=26fJ_ADteHo and Share your views

Your View

Activity 3

GAN Paint Overview

- GAN Paint allows users to interactively modify images by activating and deactivating neurons in a generative adversarial network (GAN).
- Each left button (e.g., "door", "brick") represents a set of 20 neurons, which can influence the image by drawing relevant elements like trees, doorways, and roofs.
- Direct manipulation of neurons provides insight into how the network understands and constructs visual elements.

Steps to Use GAN Paint

1. Select a Base Image :
   - Visit Link: https://ganpaint-v2.vizhub.ai/.
   - Choose a base image from the available library.
2. Modify the Image:
   - Use the brush tool to add or modify objects and textures on the image.
   - Select different features from the left button menu (e.g., add a "door" or "brick").
   - Observe how the GAN network generates and adjusts the image to create realistic alterations.
3. Experiment and Create :
   - Try different combinations of features and observe the changes.
   - Experiment with various textures and objects to see the range of the GAN's capabilities.
   - Enjoy the creative process and explore the boundaries of what the GAN can generate.

Before painting

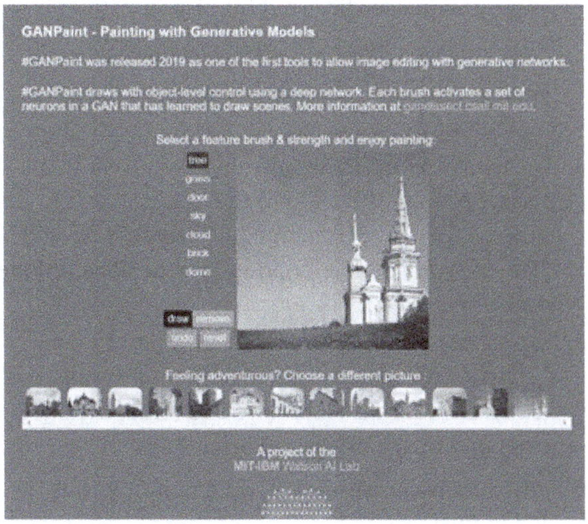

After draw a tree and clouds in the picture :

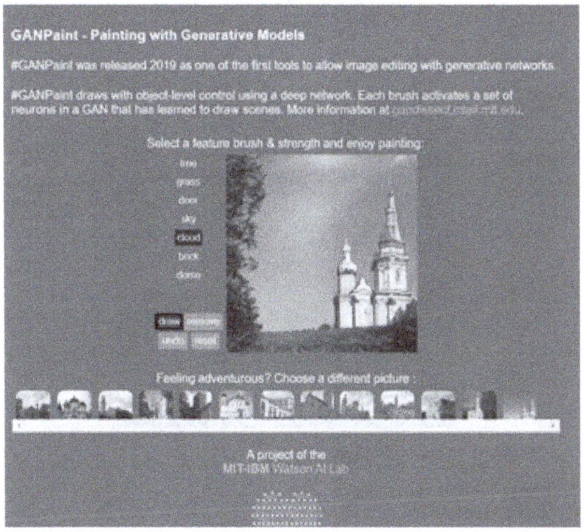

Activity 4

Part 1 Artbreeder

This activity will guide you through generating images using text prompts on Artbreeder.

1. Head to Artbreeder: Open your web browser and visit https://artbreeder.com/.
2. Create a New Image: Click on the "Create" menu in the top bar. From the dropdown menu, select "New Image" under the "Prompter" category.
3. ** Unleash your Creativity:** Now comes the fun part! Think of a cool and descriptive text prompt that sparks your imagination. This prompt will be the inspiration for the AI to generate an image. Here are some examples to get you started :

- A majestic waterfall cascading down a mountainside shrouded in mist.
- A futuristic city built on the clouds.
- A playful pod of dolphins leaping through a bioluminescent ocean.

4. **Let the AI Work its Magic** Once you have your perfect prompt, type it into the designated field and click on the "Create" button. Artbreeder's AI will then use your text description to generate a unique image.
5. **Experiment and Refine** Don't be afraid to try different prompts and see what kind of results you get. Artbreeder also allows you to refine the generated image using its editing tools.

A majestic waterfall cascading down a mountainside shrouded in mist.

Part 2 Runway ML

Now, let's explore the creative potential of Runway ML's AI Magic Tools.

1. **Runway's Playground** Head over to Runway's website at https://runwayml.com/.
2. **Discover the Magic** Explore the various AI Magic Tools available on the Runway platform. Each tool offers unique functionalities powered by artificial intelligence.
3. **Get Hands-on** Choose a tool that piques your interest. Runway provides a user-friendly interface, so follow the tool's instructions to generate new and exciting content.

Here is the example :

Part 3: ChatGPT

Link: https://chat.openai.com/

I asked ChatGPT to introduce itself. And here is the response

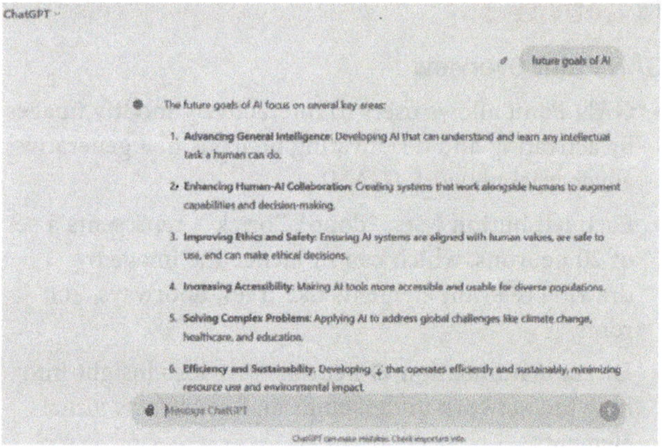

Part 4: Gemini

Link: https://gemini.google.com/

I asked Gemini to introduce itself. And here is the response!

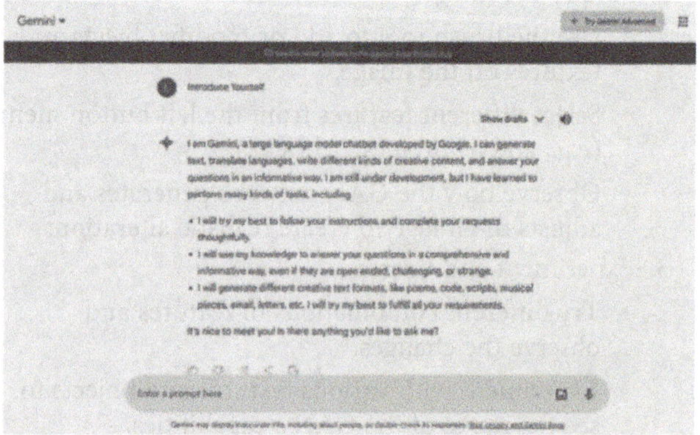

NCERT FOLDER

Complete Explanations of all NCERT's Questions

Subjective Type Questions

Q.1 What do you understand about Generative Artificial Intelligence? Give any two examples.

Ans. Generative Artificial Intelligence refers to AI systems that can create new content, such as text, images, audio, and more, by learning patterns from existing data. Examples include:

1. **GPT-4** A language model developed by OpenAI that can generate coherent and contextually relevant text based on a given prompt.
2. **DALL-E** Another AI by OpenAI that generates images from textual descriptions, creating unique visuals based on the input provided.

Q.2 Write any two AI tools each for the following-

Generative AI image generation tools

Generative AI text generation tools

Generative AI audio generation tools

Ans. Generative AI Image Generation Tools

1. **DALL-E** Created by OpenAI, it generates images from textual descriptions using deep learning techniques.
2. **Midjourney** A research lab and service known for its powerful AI capable of creating art and images based on text prompts.

Generative AI Text Generation Tools

1. **GPT-4** Developed by OpenAI, it generates coherent and contextually relevant text based on user prompts.
2. **Jasper** An AI content platform designed to help with copywriting, blog posts, and other text generation tasks.

Generative AI Audio Generation Tools

1. **OpenAI's Jukedeck** An AI tool for creating custom music tracks for various uses, like videos and presentations.
2. **AIVA (Artificial Intelligence Virtual Artist)** Composes original music across various genres, often used for soundtracks and media projects.

Q.3 Give full forms of the following-

1. GANs
2. VAEs
3. RNNs

Ans. The full forms of the given acronyms are :

1. **GANs** Generative Adversarial Networks
2. **VAEs** Variational Autoencoders
3. **RNNs** Recurrent Neural Networks

Q.4 How Generative AI can be helpful in following fields-

1. Architecture
2. Coding
3. Music
4. Content Creation

Ans. Generative AI can be highly beneficial in the following fields

1. **Architecture** Generative AI can assist in creating innovative design concepts, optimizing structural layouts, and generating complex, sustainable architectural forms that consider environmental factors.
2. **Coding** It can automate code generation, offer intelligent code suggestions, and debug programs, enhancing developer productivity and reducing the time required for software development.
3. **Music** AI can compose original music, create accompaniments, and assist in sound design, helping musicians and producers generate new melodies and harmonies or explore novel musical styles.
4. **Content Creation** Generative AI can produce written content, create graphics, and generate videos, aiding content creators by providing ideas, drafting initial versions, and enhancing creativity and efficiency.

Q.5 Sakshi has been assigned a homework essay on the topic, "The Impact of Climate Change on Coral Reefs." The essay requires Sakshi to research and explain various aspects of climate change, such as ocean acidification and rising sea temperatures, and their effects on coral reef ecosystems. His friend suggested using some text generation tool. List some guidelines for Sakshi to prevent misuse of Generative AI and use it constructively.

Ans. Some guidelines for Sakshi to use generative AI constructively and avoid misuse are:

1. **Use as a Supplement** Use AI-generated content as a starting point or for inspiration, not as the final submission.
2. **Verify Information** Cross-check AI-generated facts with credible sources to ensure accuracy.

3. **Add Personal Analysis** Incorporate personal insights and analysis to make the essay original and reflective of her understanding.
4. **Cite Sources** Properly cite any information or ideas derived from AI tools to maintain academic integrity.
5. **Learn from the Content** Use the AI output to learn and expand knowledge on the topic, not to bypass the research process.
6. **Edit Thoroughly** Review and edit the AI-generated content for coherence, relevance, and alignment with the essay requirements.
7. **Avoid Plagiarism** Ensure that the essay is her own work and does not simply replicate AI-generated text.

Q.6 How do you think generative AI can revolutionize the creative industry, such as art and fashion, by enabling the generation of unique and innovative designs?

Ans. Generative AI can be a game-changer for creative industries by:

- **Automating repetitive tasks** AI can handle things like generating variations on a theme, freeing up artists to focus on conceptual ideas.
- **Creating unique designs** AI can produce entirely new design elements, pushing creative boundaries.
- **Democratizing creativity** AI tools can allow anyone to create professional-looking content, fostering a wider creative pool.

Q.7 Considering the ethical challenges associated with generative AI, what are your thoughts on establishing guidelines or regulations to ensure responsible use of these technologies? How can we balance the potential benefits and risks?

Ans. Generative AI presents exciting possibilities but also ethical landmines. Here's why guidelines and regulations might be necessary:

- **Curbing Misinformation** Generative AI can create incredibly realistic deepfakes or text that can be misused to spread misinformation. Guidelines could stress transparency about AI-generated content and fact-checking mechanisms.
- **Taming Bias** AI reflects the biases in its training data. Regulations could mandate diverse training datasets and bias detection tools to mitigate unfair or discriminatory outputs.
- **Protecting Privacy and IP** Generative AI might raise privacy concerns if trained on personal data. Regulations could require user consent and data anonymization. Copyright laws might also need revising to address AI-generated content.
- **Ensuring Accountability** Who's responsible if AI-generated content causes harm? Guidelines could establish accountability for developers and users based on the intended use of the AI.

Balancing benefits and risks requires a nuanced approach :

- **Transparency** Clear labeling of AI-generated content helps users discern real from artificial.
- **Human Oversight** AI should be a tool, not an autonomous decision-maker. Human oversight can ensure ethical application.
- **Impact Assessments** Before deploying generative AI, assess its potential societal impacts to identify and mitigate risks.
- **Public Education** Increasing awareness of generative AI's capabilities and limitations can help people navigate the information landscape more critically.
- Generative AI is a powerful tool, and responsible use is key. By establishing guidelines and fostering open discussions, we can harness its potential for good while minimizing the risks.

REVIEW EXERCISE

Including Competency Based Questions

Part I

Multiple Choice Questions

1 What is Generative AI primarily focused on?

(a) Completing tasks
(b) Analyzing data
(c) Creating new content
(d) Understanding human instructions

2 When was the concept of machines capable of reasoning similarly to humans introduced?

(a) 1956 (b) 1958
(c) 1964 (d) 1950

3 What was the first functioning generative AI created in 1964?

(a) GAN (b) LSTM
(c) ELIZA chatbot (d) Transformer

4 Which milestone in 2014 was a breakthrough in generative AI for generating high-quality images?

(a) RNN creation (b) LSTM development
(c) GAN creation (d) VAE creation

5 Which type of AI is most commonly used for tasks such as image and speech synthesis?

(a) Conventional AI (b) Generative AI
(c) Symbolic AI (d) Expert systems

6 Which model is specifically designed to handle sequential data like text or speech?

(a) VAE (b) GAN
(c) RNN (d) Transformer

7 What is the primary application of GANs?

(a) Drug discovery (b) Music composition
(c) Fashion design (d) All of these

8 Which advantage of Generative AI is highlighted by its use in personalized marketing content?

(a) Creativity and Content Generation
(b) Efficiency and Automation
(c) Enhanced Personalization
(d) Innovation in Science and Medicine

9 Which disadvantage of Generative AI is exemplified by the potential for biased outcomes in facial recognition?

(a) Data Bias
(b) Uncertainty
(c) Computational Demands
(d) Ethical Concerns

10 What is one application of Generative AI mentioned in the context of gaming?

(a) Language Translation
(b) Drug Discovery
(c) Simulation and Modeling
(d) Creating dynamic game environments

11 Which Generative AI tool is specifically designed for code generation and completion?

(a) DALL-E (b) GPT
(c) MuseNet (d) StoryAI

12 What ethical concern arises from the potential use of Generative AI to create fake content?

(a) Data Bias (b) Job displacement
(c) Misinformation (d) Privacy risks

13 Which solution is suggested to mitigate bias in AI outputs?

(a) Scrutiny (b) Training data diversity
(c) User privacy (d) Ownership guidelines

14 In which year was GPT-4 released?

(a) 2019 (b) 2020
(c) 2021 (d) 2023

15 Which type of AI relies on explicit programming and predefined rules?

(a) Generative AI (b) Conventional AI
(c) Deep learning (d) Supervised learning

16 Which model is specifically designed for image generation based on textual descriptions?

(a) GPT (b) RNN
(c) DALL-E (d) VAE

17 What advantage of Generative AI is highlighted by its application in drug discovery?

(a) Creativity and Content Generation
(b) Enhanced Personalization
(c) Innovation in Science and Medicine
(d) Efficiency and Automation

18 Which disadvantage of Generative AI is exemplified by the need for substantial computational resources?

(a) Data Bias
(b) Uncertainty
(c) Computational Demands
(d) Ethical Concerns

Answers

1. (c) 2. (d) 3. (c) 4. (c) 5. (b)
6. (c) 7. (d) 8. (c) 9. (a) 10. (d)
11. (b) 12. (c) 13. (b) 14. (d) 15. (b)
16. (c) 17. (c) 18. (c)

Statement Based Questions

1 Statement 1: Generative AI can create new content such as text, images, music, and videos.

Statement 2: Generative AI models operate using machine learning, particularly deep learning.

(a) Both Statement 1 and Statement 2 are correct
(b) Both Statement 1 and Statement 2 are incorrect
(c) Statement 1 is correct but Statement 2 is incorrect
(d) Statement 2 is correct but Statement 1 is incorrect

2 Statement 1: VAEs (Variational Autoencoders) are used for generating new data by learning the underlying structure of a dataset.

Statement 2: GANs (Generative Adversarial Networks) use two neural networks, Generator and Discriminator, in an adversarial relationship to create new data.

(a) Both Statement 1 and Statement 2 are correct
(b) Both Statement 1 and Statement 2 are incorrect
(c) Statement 1 is correct but Statement 2 is incorrect
(d) Statement 2 is correct but Statement 1 is incorrect

3 Statement 1: RNNs (Recurrent Neural Networks) are ideal for sequential data processing due to their ability to consider past information.

Statement 2: Transformer models rely on self-attention mechanisms to understand relationships between different parts of a sequence.

(a) Both Statement 1 and Statement 2 are correct
(b) Both Statement 1 and Statement 2 are incorrect
(c) Statement 1 is correct but Statement 2 is incorrect
(d) Statement 2 is correct but Statement 1 is incorrect

4 Statement 1: Generative AI is a subset of conventional AI that relies on predefined rules for generating new content.

Statement 2: Generative AI can lead to job displacement as it automates tasks like content creation.

(a) Both Statement 1 and Statement 2 are correct
(b) Both Statement 1 and Statement 2 are incorrect
(c) Statement 1 is correct but Statement 2 is incorrect
(d) Statement 2 is correct but Statement 1 is incorrect

Answers

1. (a) 2. (a) 3. (a) 4. (d)

Assertion & Reason Based Questions

1 Assertion: Generative AI models can create new content, such as text, images, music, and videos, without any human instructions.

Reason: These models are trained to understand patterns and structures within existing data and use that knowledge to generate new original data.

(a) Both the assertion and reason are true, and the reason is the correct explanation of the assertion.
(b) Both the assertion and reason are true, but the reason is not the correct explanation of the assertion.
(c) The assertion is true, but the reason is false.
(d) Both the assertion and reason are false.

2 Assertion: Generative Adversarial Networks (GANs) consist of two main components - a Generator Network and a Discriminator Network.

Reason: The Generator network creates new data, while the Discriminator network tries to identify whether the data it sees is real or generated by the Generator.

(a) Both the assertion and reason are true, and the reason is the correct explanation of the assertion.
(b) Both the assertion and reason are true, but the reason is not the correct explanation of the assertion.
(c) The assertion is true, but the reason is false.
(d) Both the assertion and reason are false.

3 Assertion: Recurrent Neural Networks (RNNs) are particularly suitable for tasks like language processing, where the meaning of a word depends on the words before it.

Reason: RNNs have an internal state, often called a hidden layer, that acts like a memory and stores information about past inputs.

(a) Both the assertion and reason are true, and the reason is the correct explanation of the assertion.
(b) Both the assertion and reason are true, but the reason is not the correct explanation of the assertion.
(c) The assertion is true, but the reason is false.
(d) Both the assertion and reason are false.

4 Assertion: Transformer models have become the go-to choice for many Natural Language Processing (NLP) tasks due to their ability to analyze the relationships between different parts of a sequence.

Reason: Unlike older models, transformer models rely on self-attention mechanisms, allowing them to understand how words depend on each other across long distances in a sentence.

(a) Both the assertion and reason are true, and the reason is the correct explanation of the assertion.
(b) Both the assertion and reason are true, but the reason is not the correct explanation of the assertion.
(c) The assertion is true, but the reason is false.
(d) Both the assertion and reason are false.

Answers

1. (a) 2. (a) 3. (a) 4. (a)

Part II

Very Short Answer Type Questions

1 What is the main function of Generative AI?

Ans. To create new things based on learned data.

2 When was the concept of machines reasoning like humans introduced?

Ans. 1950, by Alan Turing.

3 What was the breakthrough in generative AI in 2014?

Ans. Creation of GANs for high-quality image generation.

4 What is the key characteristic of deep learning?

Ans. Learning from vast amounts of unlabeled data.

5 What is GAN and its function?

Ans. Generative Adversarial Network, creates new data like images.

6 What was the milestone in audio generation in 2016?

Ans. Introduction of WaveNet by DeepMind.

Short Answer Type Questions

1 What are some examples of Generative AI models and their applications?

Ans. Generative AI models like GPT-3, DALL-E, and GANs have various applications. GPT-3 can generate human-like text, DALL-E creates images from textual descriptions, and GANs produce realistic images. These models find applications in art, design, writing, music composition, and more.

2 How has Generative AI evolved over the years, and what are some significant milestones in its development?

Ans. Generative AI has evolved significantly since its inception. Milestones include the creation of ELIZA chatbot in 1964, GANs in 2014 for high-quality image generation, and GPT-3 in 2020 for generating coherent text. These milestones have pushed the boundaries of what AI can achieve creatively.

3 What are the advantages of using Generative AI in various industries?

Ans. Generative AI offers benefits like enhanced creativity, automation of tasks, personalized experiences for users, and innovation in fields like healthcare and gaming. It can also lead to cost reduction and improved efficiency in businesses.

4 What are some popular Generative AI tools available for users, and how can they be utilized?

Ans. Popular Generative AI tools include GPT-3 for text generation, DALL-E for image generation, and MuseNet for music composition. These tools can be utilized for tasks like content creation, design, code generation, and storytelling, among others.

5 How do Generative AI models contribute to innovation and problem-solving in various domains?

Ans. Generative AI models contribute to innovation by generating new ideas, automating tasks, aiding in decision-making through simulations, and optimizing processes. They find applications in drug discovery, game development, language translation, and more.

Long Answer Type Questions

1 How has Generative AI evolved over time, and what significant milestones mark its progression?

Ans. Generative AI has evolved significantly since its inception. Key milestones include the creation of ELIZA in 1964, marking one of the first functioning generative AIs, and the development of GANs in 2014, which revolutionized image generation. Additionally, the introduction of GPT models by OpenAI in 2018 and subsequent iterations like GPT-3 and GPT-4 have propelled text generation capabilities to new heights. These milestones have reshaped the landscape of Generative AI, pushing boundaries and unlocking new creative potentials.

2 What distinguishes Generative AI from conventional AI, and what advantages does it offer across various industries?

Ans. Generative AI, unlike conventional AI, relies on data-driven learning to create new content rather than following predefined rules. Its strengths lie in creativity, adaptability, and potential for generalization. Across industries, Generative AI offers benefits such as enhanced creativity in art and design, efficiency and automation in customer service, personalized marketing, innovation in science and medicine, improved accessibility, problem-solving, and decision-making, enhanced user experience, and economic impact through cost reduction and innovation.

3 What ethical concerns accompany the use of Generative AI, and what measures can be taken to address them?

Ans. Generative AI raises ethical concerns such as ownership of generated content, human agency in content creation, bias amplification, misinformation, and privacy risks. To address these concerns, measures like using diverse and representative training data to reduce bias, scrutinizing AI-generated content for misinformation and bias, prioritizing user privacy and consent, establishing clear guidelines on ownership of generative content, and fostering public discussion on the ethical and social implications of Generative AI are essential. These steps can help ensure responsible development and use of Generative AI for the benefit of society.

ASSESSMENT EXERCISE

Multiple Choice Questions

1. Generative AI is a field of artificial intelligence focused on:
   (a) Solving complex mathematical problems.
   (b) Optimizing existing data for better analysis.
   (c) Creating entirely new content, like images or text.
   (d) Simulating real-world physics for games.
2. The history of generative AI can be traced back to which concept?
   (a) Expert systems for decision making.
   (b) Artificial neural networks inspired by the human brain.
   (c) Symbolic logic and reasoning.
   (d) Evolutionary algorithms for optimization.
3. Which of these is NOT a common type of Generative AI model?
   (a) Generative Adversarial Networks (GANs)
   (b) Variational Autoencoders (VAEs)
   (c) Support Vector Machines (SVMs)
   (d) Transformers
4. Generative AI can be used in
   (a) Drug discovery by creating new molecule simulations.
   (b) Stock market prediction by analyzing past trends.
   (c) Basic web search functionalities.
   (d) Installing software updates on your computer.
5. A potential challenge of using Generative AI for creative tasks like music generation could be:
   (a) The AI can generate music in any style perfectly.
   (b) The AI may struggle to capture the originality or emotional depth of human creations.
   (c) The AI requires too much computational power to run.
   (d) It's impossible to teach AI about music theory.

Very Short Answer Types Questions

6. Name the commonly used Generative AI.
7. Write the full form of RNN and VAE.
8. Write the two Applications of Transformer model.

Short Answer Type Questions

9. Explain the term Generative AI
10. What are the advantages of generative AI
11. Write the working of GANs.
12. What do you understand by RNN.

Long Answer Type Questions

13. What are the applications of Generative AI.
14. Distinguish between Conventional and Generative AI.
15. Write a short note on the Future of Generative AI.

CHAPTER 08

Python Overview

Python is a versatile, high-level programming language known for its readability and simplicity. It supports multiple programming paradigms, including procedural, object-oriented, and functional programming. With a comprehensive standard library and a large ecosystem of third-party packages, Python is widely used in web development, data analysis, artificial intelligence, and more.

8.1 Program

A computer program is a set of instructions written in a programming language that a computer can understand and execute. These instructions enable the computer to perform specific tasks, like calculations, data manipulation, and controlling hardware.

Programs are the building blocks of software applications and the operating system, which is the core software that manages the computer's resources.

8.2 Introduction to Python

Python is a general purpose interpreted, interactive, object oriented and high-level programming language. It was initially designed by **Guido Van Rossum** in 1991 and developed by Python Software Foundation.

This programming language lets you work quickly across integrated systems more efficiently. Python is dynamically typed and garbage collected. Because of its simplicity in coding and powerful features, it works brilliantly for both beginners to experts.

Python is based on two programming languages which are as follows:

- ABC language, is an interactive programming and teaching language, originally intended as a good replacement of BASIC.
- Modula-3 supports interfaces, objects and generics.

Python interpreters are available for many operating systems such as Windows, MacOS etc.

Python uses English keywords frequently where as other languages use punctuations. Python uses whitespace indentation rather than curly brackets to delimit blocks.

Python for AI

Python is a widely used programming language for artificial intelligence due to its readability, extensive libraries, and strong community support. Data scientists and engineers heavily rely on Python to build and prototype AI systems, making it a popular choice for developing next-generation AI solutions.

Lisp, Prolog, C++, Java, and Python are some of the programming languages that can be used to create AI applications. Python is the most popular of these because of the following reasons:

1. **Easy to use and Readable** Python's syntax is clear and concise, resembling natural language, making it easier to learn and understand for beginners and those maintaining code.
2. **Object-Oriented and Procedural Programming** Python supports both Procedural and Object-Oriented programming. Functions promote code reusability, while classes and objects allow modeling real-world entities.
3. **Portability** Python code is portable across different operating systems (Windows, Mac, Linux) without major modifications due to the use of a bytecode interpreter.
4. **Free and Open-Source** Python is free to use and distribute for any purpose, including commercial

projects, under an OSI-approved open-source license.

5. **Extensive Standard Library** Python boasts a rich standard library containing modules for various tasks like string manipulation, networking, and file handling. This reduces the need to write code from scratch.

Applications of Python

Python is a high-level, general-purpose programming language. It is different from other languages such as C and Java that are designed to be compiled to machine code. Python is easy to learn and can be used to write virtually anything that can be described in code.

There are different types of Python applications

- Web and Internet Development
- Desktop GUI Application
- Software Development
- Business Application
- Database Access
- Games and 3D Graphics

Try These 8.1

1. **What is a program?**
2. **Who developed the Python Language?**
3. **Why is Python used for Artificial Intelligence?**
4. **What are the applications of Python?**

8.3 Getting Started with Python

Python is a cross-platform programming language, which means it runs on a variety of platforms including Windows, MacOS or Linux operating system.

A Python interpreter must be installed on our computer in order to write and run Python programs.

Python works on a number of popular operating systems, including windows server operating system.

Installation of Python on the windows server operating system is a simple.

You must download the Python setup from Python.org and running it on your server.

Downloading Python

To download a Python setup, follow the steps given below

(i) Enter Python.org in URL. A window will be appear. Select Downloads tab, after this a pop-up will appear.

(ii) Click on Python 3.7.3 button to download.

The file named 3.7.3.exe should start downloading into your standard download folder.

(iii) Move this file to more permanent location, so that you can install Python.

Installing Python

To install Python, follow the steps given below

(i) Open Downloads folder where Python setup was saved. Double click on the file python-3.7.3.exe.

(ii) An Open File-Security Warning dialog box will appear as shown below.

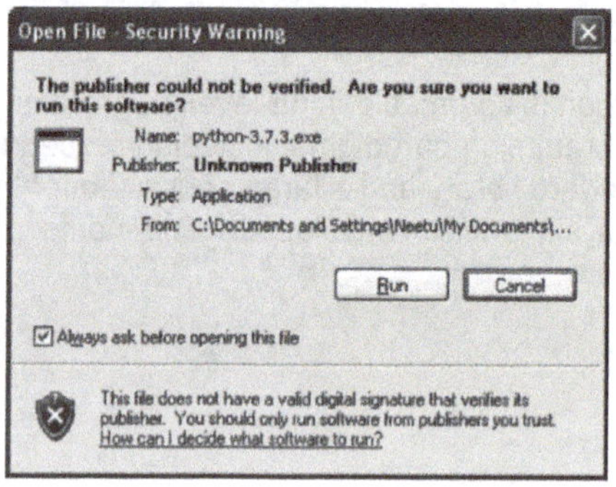

(iii) Click on Run button.

A Python 3.7.3 (32-bit) Setup pop-up window will appear.

(iv) Highlight the install now (or upgrade now) message and then click it. A user account control pop-up window will appear, that asked the question. Do you want to allow the following program to make changes to this computer?

(v) Click on Yes button.

A new Python 3.7.3 (32-bit) Setup pop-up window will appear, with a Setup Progress message and a progress bar.

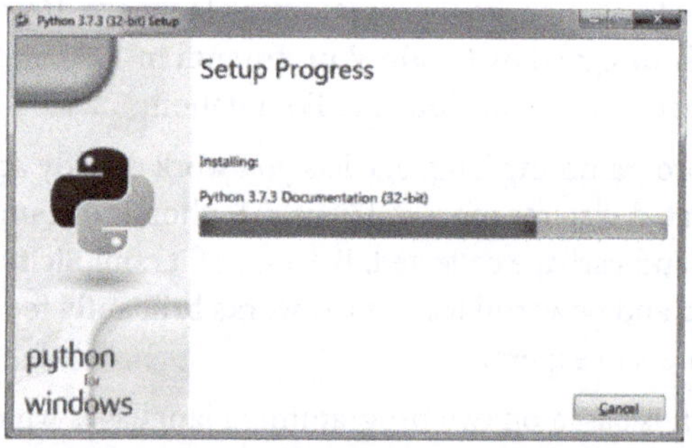

During installation, it will show the various components that are installing and move the progress bar towards completion. Soon, a new Python 3.7.3 (32 bit) Setup pop-up window will appear, with a "Setup was successful" message.

(vi) Click the Close button.

8.4 Working in Python

Generally programmers write stand alone scripts, that are independent to live environments. Then, they save it with a .py extension, which indicates to the operating system and programmer that the file is actually a Python program. After the interpreter is invoked, it reads and interprets the file.

User can run a program with three ways in Python

(i) Python (Command line)

Python is an interpreted language which can directly run on command prompt with no argument.

To start Python with command line, follow given step

Start → All Programs → Python 3.7 → Python 3.7 (32-bit).

Python 3.7 (32-bit) window will appear in your computer, where you can write code and execute it.

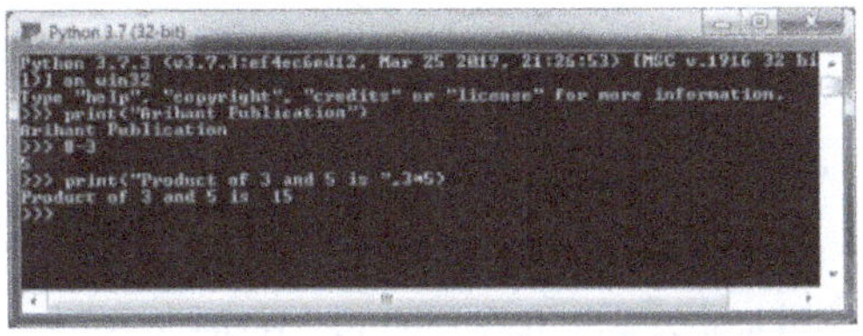

Python gives the output after you entered statement and press enter key. In command line mode, you type

```
>>> print ("Arihant Publication")
Arihant Publication
>>> print (8-3)
5
>>> print ("Product of 3 and 5 is", 3 * 5)
Product of 3 and 5 is 15
```

Indentation plays a very crucial role in Python programming.

For example, if you give extra space between >>> print, it will give syntax error.

(ii) Interactive Mode IDLE (Python GUI)

IDLE stands for Integrated Development Environment. You can run Python from a Graphical User Interface (GUI) environment as well, if you have a GUI application on your system that supports Python.

If you are not able to set-up the environment properly, then you can take help from your system admin.

Make sure the Python environment is properly set-up and working perfectly fine.

To start Python with IDLE, follow the given step

Start → All Programs → Python 3.7 → IDLE (Python 3.7 (32-bit)).

Python 3.7.3 Shell window will appear.

In that window, >>> sign will appear, here you can write your code and press Enter.

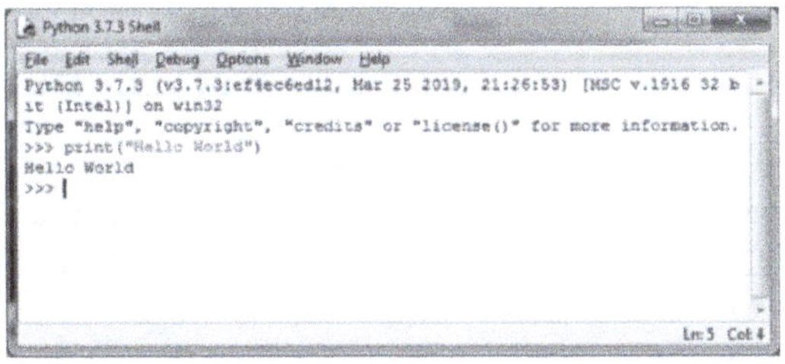

If you want to exit from the IDLE window, there are various options

Press Ctrl+D from keyboard.

or Click File → Exit.

or Click on cross ☒ button on title bar.

(iii) Python Script Mode

Python gives the output immediately as you entered code and press Enter button. But if you want to see all output after completion of code, then you can use Python script mode. To work with Python script mode, you will have to follow given steps:

Step 1 Create Script/Program File

To create script/program file, follow the given instructions:

- Start button → All Programs → Python 3.7 → IDLE (Python 3.7 (32-bit)).
- Python 3.7.3 shell window will appear on your screen. From here select File → New File window.

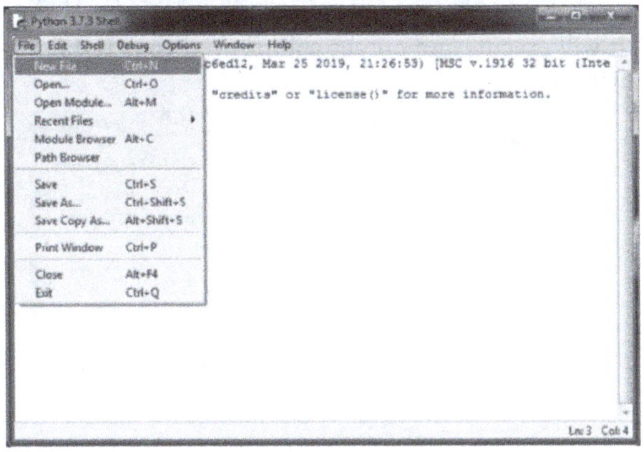

- Named untitled window will appear where you can write your code.

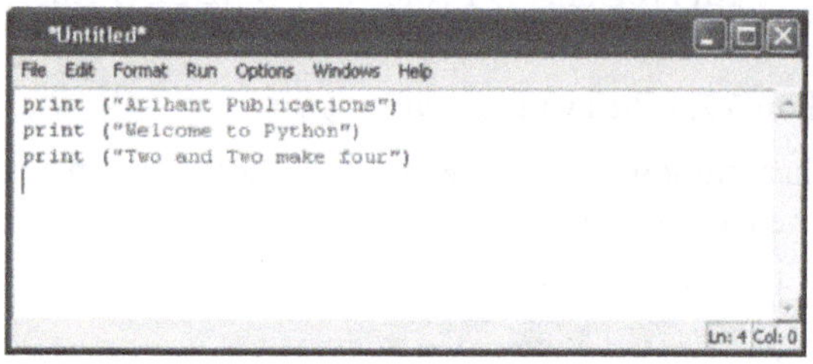

- After finish your code, select File → Save As.
- Save As dialog box will appear. Enter program name in File name text field with .py extension and click on Save button.

Step 2 Run Script/ Program File

To run script/program file after creation of script, follow the given instructions:

- Now, open the IDLE file, which was opened in Step1.
- Select File → Open and type file name in File name: box which file you want to open for executing.
- Click on Open button. Filename.py file will appear on your screen.
- Select Run → Run Module

  or press F5 key from keyboard.

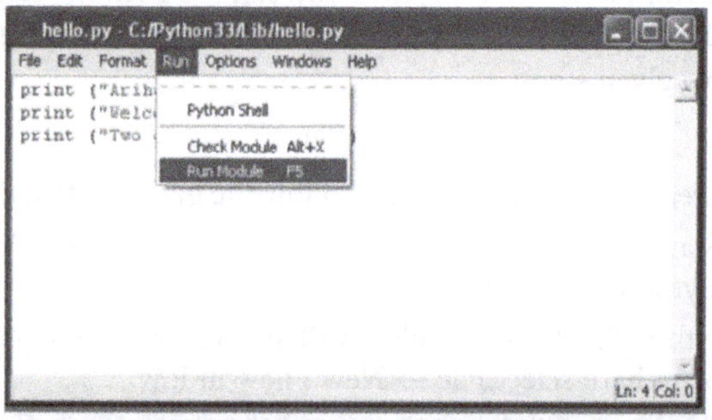

- It will execute and output will print in your IDLE window.

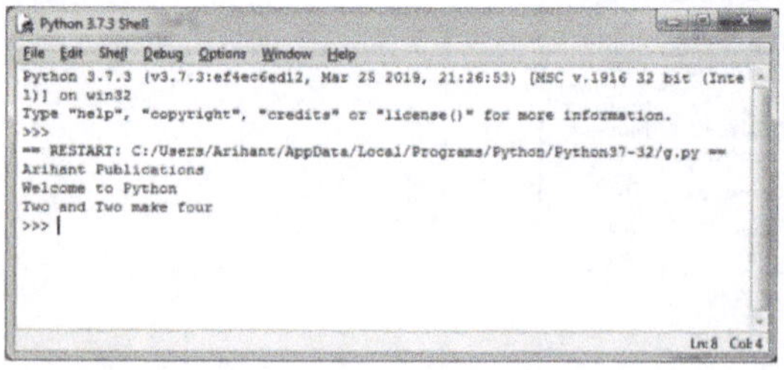

8.5 Structure of Python Program

```
#Python Program 1
print("Hello")
Name = "Sam"
print("Learner", end =" ")
print (Name)
A = 50
B = 300
print (A, "Times", B, "is", A*B)
```

Code Explanation

Line 1 in the above code starting with # is a comment line, which means the line is non- executable and it is only for the programmer's reference.

Line 2 will simply display

Hello

Line 3 will assign a string value "Sam" to a variable Name

Line 4 will display Learner and will allow the next output to get displayed in the same line

Line 5 will display Sam in the same line as Learner

Line 6 will assign an integer 50 to a variable A

Line 7 will assign an integer 300 to a variable B

Line 8 will display 50 Times 300 is 15000

So, the complete output of the Python Code will be

Hello
Learner Sam
50 times 300 is 15000

Try These 8.2

1. What steps are used in downloding Python?
2. How many ways can a user able to use to start programming in Python.
3. Describe Python Script Mode.

Glossary

Program A computer program is a set of instructions written in a programming language that a computer can understand and execute.

Python It is a general purpose interpreted, interactive, object oriented and high-level programming language.

IDLE Integrated Development Environment.

Let's Investigate

Activity

CodeCombat is essentially an adventure/dungeon-delving -type game that teaches the basics of coding for kids. Players can only control their characters by writing actual code using actual programming language, like JavaScript or Python. The steps to play CodeCombat are :

Getting Started

1. **Head to the Website** Open a web browser and go to https://codecombat.com/.
2. **Create an Account (Optional)** For free play, creating an account is not mandatory. However, creating a free account allows students to track their progress, earn rewards, and access additional features. To create an account, click on "Sign Up" in the top right corner.

Choosing a Learning Path

1. **Explore Levels** CodeCombat offers various learning paths depending on the student's coding experience and desired focus. For Class 9 students, the following paths are good options :
   - **Kithgard Dungeon** This introductory path teaches basic programming concepts like variables, loops, and functions using Python.
   - **Backwoods Forest** This path builds on the basics and introduces conditional statements (if/else), arrays, and object properties using JavaScript.
2. **Select a Level** Within each path, there are multiple levels with increasing difficulty. Students can choose a level based on their comfort level.

Coding and Playing

1. **Read the Level Introduction** Each level provides instructions and explains the objective.
2. **Write Code** The game interface displays a code editor where students will write their code using Python or JavaScript (depending on the chosen path).
3. **Run the Code** Once the code is written, students can click the "Run" button to see how their code affects the game world. The game provides visual feedback on the success or errors in the code.
4. **Experiment and Learn** If the code doesn't work as expected, students can analyze the feedback, make adjustments to their code, and try again. This experimentation process is key to learning and improving coding skills.

REVIEW EXERCISE

Including Competency Based Questions

Part I

Multiple Choice Questions

1 Python is based on

(a) ABC language (b) Modula 3
(c) Both (a) and (b) (d) None of these

2 Python was initially designed by

(a) Guido Van Rossum (b) Charles Babbage
(c) Grace Hopper (d) Dennis Ritchie

3 Which of the following is/are advantage(s) of Python?

(a) Easy to use (b) Object oriented
(c) Portability (d) All of these

4 The extension of Python files is

(a) .pyth (b) .python
(c) .py (d) .p

5 Python interpreters are available for operating system(s)

(a) Windows (b) MacOS
(c) Both (a) and (b) (d) None of these

6 In Python programming, which is considered as keyword?

(a) var (b) data (c) time (d) and

7 **When writing a program, which elements belong to the character set used in coding?**
(a) Alphabets (A-Z, a-z)
(b) Digits (0-9)
(c) Special characters (!, @, #, etc.)
(d) All of the above

8 **In programming languages, which of the following are examples of data types?**
i. Integer
ii. Float
iii. Character
iv. Loop
(a) Only i and ii (b) i, ii, and iii
(c) ii, iii, and iv (d) Only iii

9 **When writing a computer program, which of the following are used to store information?**
i. Variables
ii. Datatypes
iii. Type conversion
iv. Comments
(a) Only i (b) i and ii
(c) ii and iii (d) i, ii, and iii

Answers

1. (c) 2. (a) 3. (d) 4. (c) 5. (c)
6. (d) 7. (d) 8. (a) 9. (b)

Statement Based Questions

1 **Statement 1 : Python is a high-level programming language.**
Statement 2 : Python was created by Guido van Rossum.
(a) Both Statement 1 and Statement 2 are correct
(b) Both Statement 1 and Statement 2 are incorrect
(c) Statement 1 is correct but Statement 2 is incorrect
(d) Statement 2 is correct but Statement 1 is incorrect

2 **Statement 1 : Python code is compiled before it is executed.**
Statement 2 : Python uses an interpreter to execute code line by line.
(a) Both Statement 1 and Statement 2 are correct
(b) Both Statement 1 and Statement 2 are incorrect
(c) Statement 1 is correct but Statement 2 is incorrect
(d) Statement 2 is correct but Statement 1 is incorrect

3 **Statement 1 : Python is used for web development.**
Statement 2 : Python cannot be used for scientific computing.
(a) Both Statement 1 and Statement 2 are correct
(b) Both Statement 1 and Statement 2 are incorrect
(c) Statement 1 is correct but Statement 2 is incorrect
(d) Statement 2 is correct but Statement 1 is incorrect

4 **Statement 1 : Python has a simple syntax that is easy to learn.**
Statement 2 : Python is platform-independent, meaning it can run on different operating systems.
(a) Both Statement 1 and Statement 2 are correct
(b) Both Statement 1 and Statement 2 are incorrect
(c) Statement 1 is correct but Statement 2 is incorrect
(d) Statement 2 is correct but Statement 1 is incorrect

5 **Statement 1 : Python is widely used in AI and machine learning applications.**
Statement 2 : Python does not have libraries for AI development.
(a) Both Statement 1 and Statement 2 are correct
(b) Both Statement 1 and Statement 2 are incorrect
(c) Statement 1 is correct but Statement 2 is incorrect
(d) Statement 2 is correct but Statement 1 is incorrect

Answers

1. (a) 2. (d) 3. (c) 4. (a) 5. (c)

Assertion & Reason Based Questions

1 **Assertion (A): Python is an interpreted language.**
Reason (R): Python code is executed line by line at runtime by the Python interpreter.
(a) Both A and R are correct and R is the correct explanation of A.
(b) Both A and R are correct but R is not the correct explanation of A.
(c) A is correct but R is incorrect.
(d) A is incorrect but R is correct.

2 **Assertion (A) : Python is an object oriented language.**
Reason (R) : In Python, everything is an object.
(a) Both A and R are correct and R is the correct explanation of A.
(b) Both A and R are correct but R is not the correct explanation of A.
(c) A is correct but R is incorrect.
(d) A is incorrect but R is correct.

3 **Assertion (A) : Python is not a highly readable programming language.**
Reason (R) : Python uses indentation to define the structure of the code, making it easy to read and understand.
(a) Both A and R are correct and R is the correct explanation of A.
(b) Both A and R are correct but R is not the correct explanation of A.
(c) A is correct but R is incorrect.
(d) A is incorrect but R is correct.

4 Assertion (A): Python is a high level language.

Reason (R): Python code can be easily understand by humans.

(a) Both A and R are correct and R is the correct explanation of A.

(b) Both A and R are correct but R is not the correct explanation of A.

(c) A is correct but R is incorrect.

(d) A is incorrect but R is correct.

Answers

1. (a) **2.** (a) **3.** (d) **4.** (a)

Part II

Very Short Answer Type Questions

1 Who developed the Python?

Ans. Python was initially designed by Guido Van Rossum in 1991 and developed by Python Software Foundation.

2 Python is which type of programming language?

Ans. Python is an Object Oriented Programming language.

3 What is the extension of Python files?

Ans. Python files have extension .py.

4 Python is based on which type of programming language?

Ans. Python is based on two types of programming languages as

(i) ABC language (ii) Modula-3

5 Python is portable language. Give reason.

Ans. Python is portable language because it can run on any machine or platform without any changes.

6 Give an advantage of Python language.

Ans. Python is an easy to use and easy readability language.

7 How can you start Python with command line?

Ans. Start → All Programs → Python version → Python (32-bit).

8 What will be the output of following code at command line?

```
>>>print (''Sum of 10 and 20 is'', 10+20)
```

Ans. Sum of 10 and 20 is 30.

9 What is the full form of IDLE?

Ans. Integrated Development Environment.

10 Abhay is working on IDLE (Python GUI). He has finished his coding and now wants to exit from IDLE. How can he exit from IDLE?

Ans. Press Ctrl+D or File → Exit or Click on cross ☒ title bar.

Short Answer Type Questions

1 What is Python? Explain.

Ans. Python is a general purpose interpreted, interactive, object oriented and high level programming language.

It was initially designed by Guido Van Rossum in 1991 and developed by Python Software Foundation.

2 Python is free and open source, what is it mean?

Ans. Python language is developed under an OSI-approved open source license,which makes it free to use and distribute, including for commercial purposes.

3 What is the difference between interactive mode and script mode in Python?

Ans. Interactive mode is used when an user wants to run one single line or one block of code. While script mode is used when the user is working with more than one single code or a block of code.

4 What is the output of the following code?

```
print (''Welcome to Python.'')
print (''Practice makes a man perfect.'')
print (''Difference between 10 and 5 is'', 10 - 5)
```

Ans. Welcome to Python.

Practice makes a man perfect.

Difference between 10 and 5 is 5

5 What do you mean by IDLE in Python?

Ans. IDLE is Integrated Development Environment for editing and running Python 2.X or Python 3 programs. The IDLE GUI (Graphical User Interface) is automatically installed with the Python interpreter. IDLE was designed specifically for using with Python.

IDLE has a number of features to help you develop your Python programs including powerful syntax highlighting.

Long Answer Type Questions

1 Write the applications of Python?

Ans. Python is a versatile programming language with a wide range of applications, including:

- **Web Development** Python is popular for building web applications due to its simplicity and frameworks like Django and Flask that make development faster. These frameworks handle many of the complexities of web development, so you can focus on the core functionality of your application.
- **Data Science and Machine Learning** Python is a leader in data science and machine learning because of its extensive libraries like Pandas, NumPy, and Scikit-learn.

These libraries provide tools for data manipulation, analysis, and creation of machine learning models.

- **Scientific Computing** Python is a great choice for scientific computing because of its ease of use and powerful libraries like SciPy and Matplotlib. These libraries allow for numerical computations, data analysis, and visualization.
- **Automation** Python can be used to automate tasks on your computer, such as file manipulation, data processing, and web scraping. Libraries like Selenium and Beautiful Soup can automate interactions with web pages.
- **Game Development** Python can be used to create games, both simple and complex. Libraries like Pygame provide a foundation for building games.
- **Desktop Applications** Python can be used to create desktop applications with graphical user interfaces (GUIs) using libraries like Tkinter or PyQt.
- **Other Applications** Python is also used in many other domains, including image processing, audio processing, network programming, and system administration.

2 Write down the steps for downloading and installing Python.

Ans. To download a Python setup, follow the steps given below

(i) Enter Python.org in URL. A window will be appear. Select Downloads tab, after this a pop-up will appear.

(ii) Click on Python 3.7.3 button to download.

The file named 3.7.3.exe should start downloading into your standard download folder.

(iii) Move this file to more permanent location, so that you can install Python.

To install Python, follow the steps given below

(i) Open Downloads folder where Python setup was saved. Double click on the file python-3.7.3.exe.

(ii) An Open File-Security Warning dialog box will appear as shown below.

(iii) Click on Run button.

A Python 3.7.3 (32-bit) Setup pop-up window will appear.

(iv) Highlight the install now (or upgrade now) message and then click it. A user account control pop-up window will appear, that asked the question. Do you want to allow the following program to make changes to this computer?

(v) Click on Yes button.

A new Python 3.7.3 (32-bit) Setup pop-up window will appear, with a Setup Progress message and a progress bar.

During installation, it will show the various components that are installing and move the progress bar towards completion. Soon, a new Python 3.7.3 (32 bit) Setup pop-up window will appear, with a "Setup was successful" message.

(vi) Click the Close button.

3 What are the different ways to run programs in Python?

Ans. Refer to text on page no. 217 and 218 (Working in Python).

ASSESSMENT EXERCISE

Multiple Choice Questions

1. Which of the following is not an advantage of Python?
   (a) Interpreted (b) Integration
   (c) Memory consumption (d) Extensive Support Libraries
2. User can run a program with .... ways in Python.
   (a) two (b) three
   (c) four (d) five
3. Python uses rather than curly brackets to delimit blocks.
   (a) whitespace indentation (b) square brackets
   (c) parentheses (d) None of these

Very Short Answer Type Questions

4. In which year, Python was developed?
5. Python is an interpreted language. Explain.
6. Where can you install Python in your computer?

Short Answer Type Questions

7. How can you start Python with IDLE?
8. What is the output of the following statement?

```
>>> a=25;
>>> print (a)
```

9. Give any two advantages of Python Programming language.
10. Python is weak in mobile computing. Give reason.
11. How many ways can user run a program in Python?
12. Give output of the following code.

```
>>>print(''Hello world!!!'')
>>>print(''Python Program'')
>>>print(''Honesty is the best policy'')
```

Long Answer Type Questions

13. What do you mean by script mode in Python?
14. Write the uses of Python in AI.

CHAPTER 09

Python Fundamental

Python fundamentals are the building blocks of Python programming. They encompass things like data types (numbers, text, etc.), variables (storing data), operators (performing calculations). By grasping these basics, you'll be able to write simple Python programs and progress to more complex tasks.

The term IPO stands for Input, Process, and Output. This cycle is a fundamental concept in computer science and system analysis. It describes the flow of information, where data is entered (input), manipulated (process), and presented as a result (output).Sometimes, we need to transfer some input to useful output. For this, program is used to process this input and produce an appropriate output.

In many languages, some elements are used to write programs. So, for working in any language you must to know all elements, which are used to write code. In Python, various elements are used as character set, token, expressions, statements, input, output etc.

9.1 Python Character Set

Character set is a set of valid characters that a language can recognise. A character represents any digit, alphabet and special symbol. The character used in a Python source program belongs to unicode standard.

Python supports the following character set.

Alphabets A to Z (uppercase), a to z (lowercase)

Digits 0 to 9

Special Characters Space ( ) + - * /\ ^ & % # $ { } [ ] ! _ (underscore) >< ? @ . ; : ' " etc.

White Space Blank space, Horizontal tab ('), Carriage return, Newline, formfeed

Other Characters Python can process any of the ASCII and unicode characters as data or as literals

9.2 Python Tokens

A progarm consists of various statements and statement comprises a sequence of atomic units called tokens.

Python tokens are:

- Identifiers
- Keywords
- Constants
- Operators
- Puntuators

In this chapter, we will discuss about -identifiers,keywords and operators.

Identifiers

Identifiers are the fundamental building blocks program which are used to give the name to data items included by the programmer. It is required in all programming languages, where the programmer has to include items like variables, objects, classes, functions, arrays, etc., to specify their names. The identifier is a sequence of characters taken from Python character set.

The rules in Python for identifiers are

(i) Only alphabets, digits and underscores are permitted.

(ii) Identifier name cannot start with a digit.

(iii) Keywords cannot be used as identifier.

(iv) Uppercase and lowercase letters are distinct because Python is case sensitive language.
(v) Special characters are not allowed.

For example, Some valid identifiers : Name, name, name_1, _sum, FirstName etc.

Some invalid identifiers: global, name 1, 2num etc.

Keywords

Keywords are predefined reserved words by the programming language that have some special or predefined meanings. These are reserved for special purpose and must not be used as identifier names. Some commonly used keywords in Python, which are listed below

False	assert	del	for	in	or	while
None	break	elif	from	is	pass	with
True	class	else	global	lambda	raise	yield
and	continue	except	if	nonlocal	return	
as	def	finally	import	not	try	

Operators

Operators are those tokens that perform a specific task/computation when applied on variable or some other objects in an expression (known as operands). Operators are used in programs to operate on data and variables. Python carries a wide range of operators. Operators in Python are mostly made of signs or little bit letters. Since, it mainly relies on symbols and less on English words so it makes Python code shorter. There are two types of operators as follows:

(i) **Unary Operators** Those operators that work on single operand to form an expression are known as unary operators. Following are some unary operators:

+	unary plus
–	unary minus
~	Bitwise complement
not	logical negation

(ii) **Binary Operators** The operators that work upon two operands are known as binary operators. There are various types of binary operators in Python as follows.

(a) **Arithmetic operator** These operators are used to do arithmetic operations. These operators are

+	Addition
–	Subtraction
*	Multiplication
/	Division
%	Remainder / Modulus
**	Exponent (raise to power)
//	Floor division

(b) **Logical operators** These operators are used to make a decision on two conditions. Logical operators are typically used with boolean values and what they return is also a boolean value. These operators are

and	Logical AND
or	Logical OR

(c) **Relational operators** Relational operators compare two operands to one another. These operators are

<	less than
>	greater than
< =	less than or equal to
> =	greater than or equal to
==	equal to
! =	Not equal to

(d) **Assignment operators** Assignments operators are used to assign the value of an expression to a variable. These operators are

=	assignment
/=	assign quotient
+=	assign sum
* =	assign product
% =	assign remainder
– =	assign difference
* * =	assign exponent
// =	assign floor division

(e) **Bitwise operators** Bitwise operators work on bits and perform bit by bit operation. These operators are

&	Bitwise AND
^	Bitwise XOR
|	Bitwise OR

(f) **Shift operators** These operators are used to shift value left or right. These operators are

<<	shift left
>>	shift right

(g) **Identity operators** These operators are

is	is the identity same ?
is not	is the identity not same?

(h) **Membership operators** These operators are

in	whether variable in sequence
not in	whether variable not in sequence

9.3 Expressions

An expression is a combination of operators, constants and variables as per rule of the language. Any part in a program which can have a value, is an expression. It will have operands and operators together to produce a value.

e.g. `4 * i, x + y/10, (a < b) etc.`

From the above program, we have 5 expressions

50, 35, x – y + 10, (z – 5), z < 30

9.4 Variable

Variable is a container object that stores a meaningful value that can be used throughout the program.

In a Python program, to store different types of values such as, name of a shop and quantities of items (goods) available in the shop during the run time. We require some sort of storage area called **variables**. Each variable has a specific type, which determines the size and layout of the variable's memory, the range of values that can be stored within that memory and the set of operations that can be applied to the variable. A variable is an identifier that is used to represent specific data item. The data item may be a whole number, a fractional number, a sequence of characters, a single character, etc.

Creating a Variable

Creating of variables means providing an initial value when it is declared. A variable can be created anywhere in Python program.

e.g. Name = 'Neha'
Subject = 'Computer'
Marks = 80

Above is an assignment statements which used to assign values to a variables. The equal (=) sign causes the value on the right hand side of the variables to be assigned to the variable on the left.

Rules for Variables

- A variable name must start with a letter or the underscore character
- A variable name cannot start with a number
- A variable name can only contain alphanumeric characters and underscores (Az, 09, and _)
- Variable names are casesensitive (age, Age and AGE are three different variables)
- A variable name cannot be any of the Python keywords.

Try These 9.1

1. **Write the name of character set which are supported by Python.**
2. **How many types of comments used in Python?**
3. **Name any five keywords used in a program.**
4. **Write the rules or naming convention for the variables.**

9.5 Data Types

The data that needs to be processed by a computer can be in various form. It can be numbers with or without decimal places or it can be just a single character or a sequence of characters. The data to be handled by the computer can also be in group. All computer programming languages support wide variety of data that can be stored, processed and manipulated in a computer system. 'Data type is a term that is used to show the kind of data values or the type of data that is expected to be handled.' Data types are used to identify the type of data and associated operations to handle it. Python has five standard data types which shown in figure below

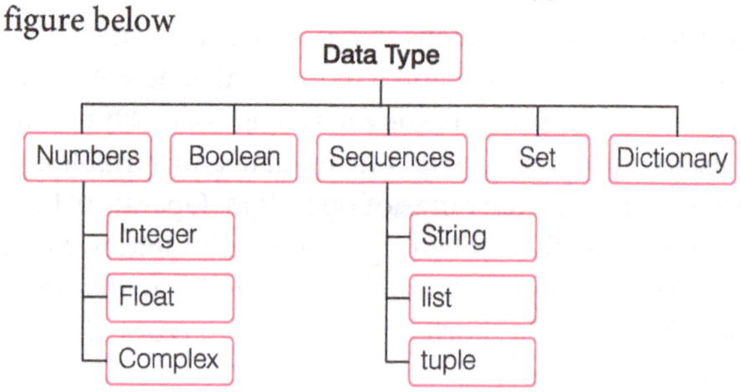

1. Numbers

Numbers data type contains only numeric value in Python. The types of numbers data type are as follows :

(i) Integers

Integers are the whole numbers having different storage range supported by particular machine. Integers have no fractional parts. They can be positive or negative.

There are two types of integers in Python as follows:

(I) **Integers (signed)** It is a simple whole numbers integers. In Python 3.X, integers are represented by of any length and its length is limited that depends on memory availability. It is signed representation.

(II) **Booleans** These represent the values either True or False. True value is represent as 1 and False value is represent as 0.
e.g. 8, 17, -195 etc.

(ii) Floating Point Numbers

The float type in Python designates a floating point number. Float values are specified with a decimal point. The decimal point signals that it is a floating point number not an integer. e.g. 159.12, 734.30 etc. Integer and floating points are separated by decimal points. 1 is integer and 1.0 is floating point number. Floating point numbers can also be written in exponent notation.

e.g. 786.456 would be written as 7.86456E02.

Floating point numbers are used for measurable quantities like distance, area, temperature etc, and typically have fractional parts. Floating point identifier represents real numbers.

(iii) Complex Numbers

A complex number is a number expressed in the form a+bi, where, a (real part) and b (imaginary part) are real numbers and i is the imaginary part. So, we can say that complex number is made up of both real numbers and imaginary numbers. e.g. 2 + 3i, 1 + 4i, 2 – 5i etc. Here, you will learn about how to declare complex numbers in Python and extract their real and imaginary parts.

```
>>> a=complex(2.3)
>>>print(a)
(2+3i)
>>>a.real
2.0
>>>a.imag
3.0
```

where , a.real will give the real part of complex number and a.imag will give the imaginary part of complex number.

2. Boolean

Data type with one of the two builtin values, True or False. Boolean objects that are equal to True are truthy (true), and those equal to False are falsy (false). However non-Boolean objects can be evaluated in a Boolean context as well and determined to be true or false. It is denoted by the class bool.

```
print(type(True))
print(type(False))
print(false)
```

Output

<class 'bool'>
<class 'bool'>

NameError : name 'false' is not defined

Note *True and False with capital 'T' and 'F' are valid Booleans otherwise python will throw an error.*

3. Sequence

The sequence Data Type in Python is the ordered collection of similar or different Python data types. Sequences allow storing of multiple values in an organized and efficient fashion. There are several sequence data types of Python:

(i) Strings

Strings are sequence of character data. The string type in Python is called str. String literals may be delimited using either single quotes or double quotes.

e.g. "Rahul", 'ABC', "??\+", '$ABC' etc.

```
>>>print("Arihant Publications")
Arihant Publications
>>>type("Arihant Publications")
<class 'str'>
```

A string in Python can contain as many characters as you want. The string limit is depend on your machine's memory resources. A string can also be empty.

```
>>>'  '
'  '
```

(ii) Lists

Lists are a very useful variable type in Python. A list can contain a series of values. List variables are declared by using brackets [ ] following the variable name and separated by comma(,). Lists are mutable that means they can be change after creation. e.g.

x = [ ]
y = [1, 2, 3, 'Neha']
z = [23, 34, 56, 67]

All lists in Python are zero based indexed. When referencing a member or the length of a list the number of list elements is always the number shown plus one.
In IDLE Python,

```
>>>value = [34, 45, 'Neha', 56, 'Kabir']
>>>value1 = ['Riya', 23, 43.3]
print(value)
print(value[0])
print(value[1:3])
print(value1[1])
print(value*2)
print(value+value1)
```

Output

[34, 45, 'Neha', 56, 'Kabir']
34
[45, 'Neha']
23

[34, 45, 'Neha', 56, 'Kabir', 34, 45, 'Neha', 56, 'Kabir']

[34, 45, 'Neha', 56, 'Kabir', 'Riya', 23, 43.3]

If you want to change any element in list then follow this,

```
>>>value[1] = 'Riya'
>>>value
[34, 'Riya', 'Neha', 56, 'Kabir']
```

(iii) Tuples

Tuple is an ordered sequence of items same as list. The only difference is that tuples are immutable and lists are mutable. Tuples once created cannot be modified. Tuples are used to writeprotect data and are usually faster than list as it cannot change dynamically. Tuples are defined by parentheses ( ).

e.g.
```
sub = ('Maths' , 'English', 'Hindi',
'Computer')
add_sub = ('Games', 'Dancing')
print (sub)
print (sub [1])
print (sub [2:])
print (add_sub * 1)
print (sub + add_sub)
```

Output

('Maths', 'English', 'Hindi', 'Computer')

English

('Hindi', 'Computer')

('Games', 'Dancing')

('Maths', 'English', 'Hindi', 'Computer', 'Games', 'Dancing')

4. Set

In Python, a set is an unordered collection of unique elements. Sets are defined using curly braces {} or the set() function and are commonly used to eliminate duplicate items from a list or to perform mathematical set operations like union, intersection, and difference. Elements in a set must be immutable, which means you can include strings, numbers, and tuples, but not lists or other sets. Sets are highly efficient for membership tests and support various methods to manage the collection of elements.

Example of creating and using a set:

```
# Creating a set
fruits = {"apple", "banana", "cherry", "apple", "cherry"}
print(fruits)  # Output will be {'apple', 'banana',
                                        'cherry'}
# Adding an element to the set
fruits.add("orange")
print(fruits)  # Output will be {'apple', 'banana',
                               'cherry', 'orange'}
# Removing an element from the set
fruits.remove("banana")
print(fruits)  # Output will be {'apple', 'cherry',
                                        'orange'}
# Checking membership
print("apple" in fruits)  # Output will be True
print("banana" in fruits)  # Output will be False
```

5. Dictionary

Dictionaries in Python are lists of key: value pairs. This is a very powerful data type to hold a lot of related information that can be associated through keys. The main operation of a dictionary is to extract a value based on the key name. Dictionaries can also be used to sort, iterate and compare data. Dictionaries are created by using braces { } with pairs separated by a comma (,) and the key values associated with a colon (:). In dictionaries, the key must be unique.

e.g.
```
dict = {'Name': 'Neha' , 'Salary' : 25000,
'Post': 'Coordinator'}
print (dict. keys ( ))
print (dict. values ( ))
print (dict ['Salary'])
print (dict ['Post'])
```

Output

dict_keys(['Name', 'Salary', 'Post'])

dict_values(['Neha', 25000, 'Coordinator'])

25000

Coordinator

Mutable and Immutable Types

Every variable in Python holds an instance of an object. There are two types of objects in Python as follows:

1. **Mutable Types** The values of mutable types can be changed after it is created. These are list, dictionary and sets.
2. **Immutable Types** The values of immutable cannot be changed after it is created.These are integer, float, boolean, string and tuple.

9.6 Data Type Conversion

The process of converting the value of one data type (integer, string, float, etc.) to another data type is called type conversion.

The **type() function** is used to get the type of an object. It returns the type of the given object, which could be a builtin data type or a userdefined class. Python has two types of type conversion.

Implicit Type Conversion

For implicit type conversion, the python interpreter automatically assigns a data type to a variable once it is declared. For instance, if we have a variable x and we assign the value 10 to it, the variable x automatically becomes an integer datatype.

Example

```
# Python automatically converts
# a to int
a = 7
print(type(a))
```

In Implicit type conversion, Python automatically converts one data type to another data type. This process doesn't need any user involvement.

Explicit Type Conversion

In Explicit Type Conversion, users convert the data type of an object to required data type. We use the predefined functions like int(), float(), str(), etc to perform explicit type conversion.

This type of conversion is also called typecasting because the user casts (changes) the data type of the objects.

Syntax:

```
(required_datatype)(expression)
```

Typecasting can be done by assigning the required data type function to the expression.

9.7 Input and Output in Python

In computing, input/output or I/O is the communication between an information processing system (such as a computer) and the outside world, possibly a human or another information processing system.

Inputs are the data received by the system, and outputs are the data sent from it. In almost every computer program, the user has to input some data that will be stored in computer's memory and then subsequently processed.

The devices such as keyboard, mouse are input devices and are used to input data. The input data may be taken from a disk file or from another computer via a communication channel. The intermediate and final results of the computations are also stored in computer's memory. And finally, there is need to output the results of the computations. The output can be displayed on the computer screen, stored on a disk or transmitted *via* a communication channel to other computer. A program needs to interact with the user to accomplish the desired task, this is done using Input-Output facility

Input from User

A function is defined as a block of organised, reusable code used to perform a single, related action. Python has many built-in functions, you can also create your own. Python has an input function which lets you ask a user for some text input. You call this function to tell the program to stop and wait for the user to key in the data.

Python provides two built-in functions to read a line of text from standard input, which by default comes from the keyboard. These functions are as follows

(i) input( )

This function first takes the input from the user and then evaluates the expression, which means Python automatically identifies whether user entered a string or number or list. If the input provided is not correct, then either syntax error or exception is raised by Python. Before input( ) method was not capable of handling anything other than numbers.

But in Python 3, input( ) is capable of handing anything other than numbers like string.

Syntax

```
variable_name = input (< Message to be
displayed>)
```

e.g.

```
>>> a = input ("Enter a number : ")
Enter a number : 25
>>> print (a)
25
>>> name = input ("Enter your name : ")
Enter your name : Neha
>>> print (name)
Neha
```

(ii) print()

To output your data to the screen, use the print ( ) function. Print evaluates the expression before printing it on the monitor. Print statement gives output an entire (complete) line and then goes to next line for subsequent output. To print more than one item on a single line, comma (,) may be used.

Syntax

```
print (expression/ constant/ variable)
```

e.g.

```
>>> print ("Arihant")
Arihant
>>> print (5.65)
5.65
>>> print(10 * 3)
30
```

9.8 Comments

Comments are the entries in a computer program for the purpose of documentation or explanation. Comments are non-executable statements that are ignored by the interpreter or compiler and are not executed by the computer.

Types of Comments

There are two types of comments used in programs as follows.

(a) **Single line comment** A single line comment starts with # symbol.

e.g. # Here is define the function of addition # It helps to know the process of function

(b) **Multiline comment** A multiline comment starts with a '''symbol and ends with'''.

e.g. a = 20 '''Here we initialise the value of variable a as 20'''

9.9 Programs

1. Program to obtain length, breadth and height of a cuboid and calculate its volume.

```
l = int(input("Enter the length of the cuboid: "))
b = int(input("Enter the breadth of the cuboid: "))
h = int(input("Enter the height of the cuboid: "))
volume =l*b*h
print ("Length = ", l)
print ("Breadth = ", b)
print ("Height = ", h)
print ("The volume of cuboid = ", volume)
```

Output

Enter the length of the cuboid : 5
Enter the breadth of the cuboid : 4
Enter the height of the cuboid : 7
Length =5
Breadth =4
Height =7
The volume of cuboid =140

2. Program to convert kilometers to miles.

```
# To take kilometers from the user
kilometers = float (input ("Enter value in
                                    kilometers: " ))
# Conversion factor
conv_fac =  0.621371
# calculate miles
miles = kilometers * conv_fac
print ('% 0.3f kilometers is equal to %
0.3f miles' % (kilometers, miles))
```

Output

Enter value in kilometers : 5.5
5.500 kilometers is equal to 3.418 miles

3. Program to find simple interest for entered principal amount, time and rate of interest.

```
principal = int (input (" Enter principal
                                    amount:"))
time = int (input (" Enter time :"))
rate = int (input (" Enter rate of interest : "))
# calculate  simple interest
SI = (principal * time * rate)/100
print (" Simple interest is  " , SI )
```

Output

Enter principal amount : 5000
Enter time : 2
Enter rate of interest : 10
Simple interest is 1000.0

4. Program to convert Celsius to Fahrenheit using formula. F = C × 1.8 +32

```
Celsius = float (input ("Enter temp in
                                Celsius: "))
Fahrenheit = Celsius * 1.8 + 32
print ("Temperature in Celsius is : ", Celsius)
print ("Temperature in Fahrenheit is : ",
                                 Fahrenheit)
```

Output

Enter temp in Celsius : 25.4
Temperature in Celsius is : 25.4
Temperature in Fahrenheit is : 77.72

Try These 9.2

1. **What do you understand by sequence data type?**
2. **What is implicit conversion?**
3. **Name the operators used in comparison operator.**
4. **Explain the input () function.**

Glossary

Character Set It is a set of valid characters that a language can recognise.

Tokens A progarm consists of various statements and statement comprises a sequence of atomic units called tokens.

Identifiers They are the fundamental building blocks program which are used to give the name to data items included by the programmer.

Keywords They are predefined reserved words by the programming language that have some special or predefined meanings.

Operators They are those tokens that perform a specific task/computation when applied on variable or some other objects in an expression (known as operands).

Variable It is a container object that stores a meaningful value that can be used throughout the program.

Strings The sequence of character data.

List It is a sequence data type which is used to store the collection of data.

Tuple It is an ordered sequence of items same as list.

Set It is an unordered collection of unique elements.

Dictionaries lists of key: value pairs.

Type Coversion The process of converting the value of one data type (integer, string, float, etc.) to another data type is called type conversion.

REVIEW EXERCISE

Including Competency Based Questions

Part I

Multiple Choice Questions

1 Which of the following is a valid character in Python?

(a) @ (b) #
(c) $ (d) All of these

2 Which character is used to indicate the start of a string in Python?

(a) " (b) '
(c) Both (a) and (b) (d) None of these

3 How do you write a single line comment in Python?

(a) // (b) ##
(c) /* (d) #

4 Which of the following is used for multiline comments in Python?

(a) ' ' ' Comment ' ' ' (b) " " " Comment " " "
(c) Both (a) and (b) (d) None of these

5 Which of the following is not a keyword in Python?

(a) pass (b) eval
(c) assert (d) raise

6 What is the keyword used to define a function in Python?

(a) function (b) def
(c) func (d) define

7 Which of the following is a valid Python identifier?

(a) 123var (b) $var
(c) var123 (d) var 123

8 Which of the following is not allowed in a Python identifier?

(a) Numbers (b) Letters
(c) Underscore (_) (d) Hyphen

9 Which of the following is the correct way to declare a variable in Python?

(a) int x = 5 (b) x := 5
(c) x = 5 (d) declare x = 5

10 What will be the output of the following code snippet?

```
x = 10
y = 20
x, y = y, x
print(x, y)
```

(a) 10 20 (b) 20 10
(c) 10 10 (d) 20 20

11 Which of the following is an immutable data type in Python?

(a) List (b) Dictionary
(c) Set (d) Tuple

12 What is the datatype of the variable `x` in the following code?

```
x = 3.14
```

(a) int (b) float
(c) double (d) complex

13 Which function is used to convert a string to an integer in Python?

(a) str() (b) int()
(c) float() (d) eval()

14 What will be the output of the following code snippet?

```
x = "123"
y = int(x)
print(y + 1)
```

(a) 1231 (b) 124
(c) 123 (d) Error

15 Which of the following is the correct escape sequence for a newline character in Python?

(a) \n (b) \t
(c) \r (d) \b

16 What will be the output of the following code snippet?

```
print("Hello\tWorld")
```

(a) Hello World (b) Hello\tWorld
(c) Hello   World (d) Error

17 Which of the following is the correct operator for exponentiation in Python?

(a) ** (b) .
(c) * (d) Exp

18 What will be the output of the following code snippet?

```
x = 10
y = 3
print(x // y)
```

(a) 3.333 (b) 3.0
(c) 3 (d) 4

19 Which function is used to take input from the user in Python?

(a) input() (b) raw_input()
(c) scan() (d) get()

20 **What will be the output of the following code snippet?**

```
name = "John"
age = 30
print(f"My name is {name} and I am {age}
                              years old.")
```

(a) My name is John and I am 30 years old.
(b) My name is {name} and I am {age} years old.
(c) My name is John and I am years old.
(d) My name is and I am 30 years old.

21 **These operators are used to make a decision on two conditions.**

(a) Logical (b) Arithmetic
(c) Relational (d) Assignment

22 **Which data type contains only numeric value in Python?**

(a) Numbers (b) Strings
(c) Lists (d) Tuples

23 **Which of the following are sequence of character data?**

(a) Lists (b) Tuples
(c) Strings (d) Dictionaries

24 **In complex number, a + ib , where b represents as**

(a) real part
(b) imaginary part
(c) special part
(d) None of the above

25 **Which of the following is/are expression?**

(a) Arithmetic (b) Logical
(c) Relational (d) All of the above

Answers

1. (d)	2. (c)	3. (d)	4. (c)	5. (b)
6. (b)	7. (c)	8. (d)	9. (c)	10. (b)
11. (d)	12. (b)	13. (b)	14. (b)	15. (a)
16. (c)	17. (a)	18. (c)	19. (a)	20. (a)
21. (a)	22. (a)	23. (c)	24. (b)	25. (d)

Statement Based Questions

1 **Statement 1 Keywords in Python are case sensitive.**

Statement 2 The keyword "True" is used to represent a boolean value in Python.

(a) Both Statement 1 and Statement 2 are correct.
(b) Both Statement 1 and Statement 2 are incorrect.
(c) Statement 1 is correct but Statement 2 is incorrect.
(d) Statement 2 is correct but Statement 1 is incorrect.

2 **Statement 1 Identifiers can begin with a digit.**

Statement 2 Identifiers in Python are case sensitive.

(a) Both Statement 1 and Statement 2 are correct.
(b) Both Statement 1 and Statement 2 are incorrect.
(c) Statement 1 is correct but Statement 2 is incorrect.
(d) Statement 2 is correct but Statement 1 is incorrect.

3 **Statement 1 A variable in Python must be declared with a specific data type.**

Statement 2 The value of a variable can change during program execution.

(a) Both Statement 1 and Statement 2 are correct.
(b) Both Statement 1 and Statement 2 are incorrect.
(c) Statement 1 is correct but Statement 2 is incorrect.
(d) Statement 2 is correct but Statement 1 is incorrect.

4 **Statement 1 Operators are symbols that perform operations on variables and values.**

Statement 2 The assignment operator is denoted by the symbol "==".

(a) Both Statement 1 and Statement 2 are correct
(b) Both Statement 1 and Statement 2 are incorrect
(c) Statement 1 is correct but Statement 2 is incorrect
(d) Statement 2 is correct but Statement 1 is incorrect

5 **Statement 1 The print() function is used for output in Python programming.**

Statement 2 The input() function is used for input from user in Python programming.

(a) Both Statement 1 and Statement 2 are correct
(b) Both Statement 1 and Statement 2 are incorrect
(c) Statement 1 is correct but Statement 2 is incorrect
(d) Statement 2 is correct but Statement 1 is incorrect

Answers

1. (a)	2. (d)	3. (d)	4. (c)	5. (a)

Assertion & Reason Based Questions

1 **Assertion (A) The character set of a programming language determines the valid characters that can be used in source code.**

Reason (R) Character sets ensure that programming languages can handle different types of data, such as numbers, letters, and symbols.

(a) Both Assertion (A) and Reason (R) are true, and Reason (R) is the correct explanation of Assertion (A).
(b) Both Assertion (A) and Reason (R) are true, but Reason (R) is not the correct explanation of Assertion (A).
(c) Assertion (A) is true, but Reason (R) is false.
(d) Assertion (A) is false, but Reason (R) is true.

2 **Assertion (A) Comments in a program can affect the execution of the code.**

Reason (R) Comments are used to explain and clarify the code, making it easier for programmers to understand.

(a) Both Assertion (A) and Reason (R) are true, and Reason (R) is the correct explanation of Assertion (A).
(b) Both Assertion (A) and Reason (R) are true, but Reason (R) is not the correct explanation of Assertion (A).
(c) Assertion (A) is true, but Reason (R) is false.
(d) Assertion (A) is false, but Reason (R) is true.

3 **Assertion (A) Keywords are predefined reserved words in a programming language.**

Reason (R) Keywords can be used as variable names in a program.

(a) Both Assertion (A) and Reason (R) are true, and Reason (R) is the correct explanation of Assertion (A).

(b) Both Assertion (A) and Reason (R) are true, but Reason (R) is not the correct explanation of Assertion (A).

(c) Assertion (A) is true, but Reason (R) is false.

(d) Assertion (A) is false, but Reason (R) is true.

4 **Assertion (A) Datatypes specify the type of data that a variable can hold.**

Reason (R) Using the correct datatype is important for ensuring the efficient use of memory and proper data operations.

(a) Both Assertion (A) and Reason (R) are true, and Reason (R) is the correct explanation of Assertion (A).

(b) Both Assertion (A) and Reason (R) are true, but Reason (R) is not the correct explanation of Assertion (A).

(c) Assertion (A) is true, but Reason (R) is false.

(d) Assertion (A) is false, but Reason (R) is true.

Answers

1. (a) **2.** (d) **3.** (c) **4.** (a)

Part II

Very Short Answer Type Questions

1 **Define the term operator.**

Ans. Operators are symbols which take one or more operands to perform arithmetic or logical computations.

2 **What is data type?**

Ans. Data type is a term that is used to show the kind of data values or the type of data that is expected to be handled.

3 **Explain unary operator.**

Ans. A unary operator is an operator that performs its operation on only one operand.

4 **What is an expression?**

Ans. Combination of operands and operators form an expression.

5 **Differentiate between / and % operators.**

Ans. operator is used to find the quotient while % operator is used to find the remainder.

6 **Write the proper Python syntax for testing that value of A is between 2 and 9 inclusively.**

Ans. A > = 2 and A < = 9

7 **What is the use of relational operator?**

Ans. The relational operators are used for comparison between two or more operands.

8 **Differentiate between = and = = operators.**

Ans. = is an assignment operator whereas = = is a relational operator.

9 **Write the augmented assignment operators used in Python.**

Ans. + =, ? =, * =, / =, %=, // =, =

10 **What will be the output of following code?**

```
a = 7
b = - 7
print (" a = ", + a)
print ("b = ", + b)
```

Ans. Output

a = 7

b = – 7

11 **Name three logical operators.**

Ans. (i) AND operator (and)

(ii) OR operator (or)

(iii) NOT operator (not)

12 **What will be the result of following expression?**

– a <= 5

(i) if a = 5

(ii) if a = – 5

Ans. (i) True (ii) True

13 **Write the value stored in the variable Num by each of the following statements.**

(i) Num = 2 * 3 – 4

(ii) Num = 2 + 3 – 1 * 3

(iii) Num = (2 + 3) * 2

Ans. (i) Num = 2

(ii) Num = 2

(iii) Num = 10

Short Answer Type Questions

1 **Determine the output.**

(i)

```
x = -4
y = -x
print (" value of x =", x)
print (" value of  y =", y)
```

(ii)

```
x = 2
y = 3
z = x * *y + 3
x = y + 5
print("value of z = ", z)
print(" value of x = ", x)
```

Ans. (i) value of x = – 4

value of y = 4

(ii) value of z = 11

value of x = 8

2 Predict the output of the following code fragment.

```
b = 20
a = 90/b
print ("value of a is :", a )
```

Ans. value of a is : 4.5

3 Using the given values of x, y and z, evaluate the following:

```
(x >= y) and (not(z == y)) or (z < x))
```

(i) x = 5, y = 6, z = 20

(ii) x = 10, y = 4, z = 11

Ans. (i) False (ii) True

4 Predict the output of the following program.

```
a = 5
b = a = 15
c = (a < 15)
print ("a = ", a)
print ("b = ", b)
print ("c = ', c)
```

Ans. a = 15

b = 15

c = False

5 What will be the value of following if a = 2?

(i) (12/+a)%3

(ii) (21*+a)%9

(iii) (21//+a)%3

Ans. (i) 0.0 (ii) 6 (iii) 1

Long Answer Type Questions

1 Describe identifiers and keywords.

Ans. Refer from text on page no. 224 and 225 (Identifiers and keywords).

2 Explain various operators in Python.

Ans. Refer from text on page no. 225 (Operators).

3 Write a Python program which input the time in seconds and convert it into days. Also, display its output.

Ans.

```
time = float(input("Input time in seconds: "))
day = time // (24 * 3600)
time = time % (24 * 3600)
hour = time // 3600
time %= 3600
minutes = time // 60
time %= 60
seconds = time
print("Days : ",day)
print("Hours : ",hour)
print("Minutes : ",minutes)
print("Seconds : ",seconds)
```

Output

Input time in seconds: 360425060

Days : 4171.0

Hours : 14.0

Minutes : 4.0

Seconds : 20.0

4 Write a program which input three sides of triangle and calculate its perimeter, semi perimeter and area.

Ans.

```
a = float(input('Enter the First side of a
                                   Triangle: '))
b = float(input('Enter the Second side of a
                                   Triangle: '))
c = float(input('Enter the Third side of a
                                   Triangle: '))
# Calculate the perimeter
perimeter = a + b + c
# Calculate the semi-perimeter
s = (a + b + c) / 2
# Calculate the area using Heron's formula
area = (s * (s - a) * (s - b) * (s - c)) ** 0.5
print("\nThe Perimeter of the Triangle =
                              %.2f" % perimeter)
print("The Semi Perimeter of the Triangle =
                                      %.2f" % s)
print("The Area of the Triangle = %.2f" % area)
```

Output

Enter the First side of a Triangle: 13

Enter the Second side of a Triangle: 12

Enter the Third side of a Triangle: 5

The Perimeter of the Triangle = 30.00

The Semi Perimeter of the Triangle = 15.00

The Area of the Triangle = 30.00

5 The distance between two cities (in km) is input through the keyboard, write a Python program to convert this distance in meters.

Ans.

```
km = float (input("Enter the distance in km :"))
print("Distance in km :", km)
meters = km * 1000
print("Distance in meters :", meters)
```

Output

Enter the distance in km : 2.5

Distance in km : 2.5

Distance in meters : 2500.0

6 Write a Python program to find the perimeter of a rectangle.

Ans.

```
l = int (input ("Enter the length : "))
b = int (input ("Enter the breath : "))
```

```
print("Length : ", l)
print("Breath : ", b)
p = 2 * (l + b)
print("Perimeter of the rectangle : ", p)
```

Output

Enter the length : 6

Enter the breath : 4

Length : 6

Breath : 4

Perimeter of the rectangle : 20

7 Write a program to calculate the volume of sphere and hemisphere with using math modules. Also, display the appropriate output.

Volume of sphere = $4/3\pi r^3$

Volume of hemisphere = $2/3\ \pi r^3$

Ans.

```
print("Calculate the Volume of Sphere")
radius=int(input("Enter the radius of a
sphere : "))
print("Radius of Sphere : ",radius)
#volume of sphere
volume=(4/3)*3.14*(radius**3)
print("Volume of Sphere : ",volume)
print("\nCalculate the Volume of Hemisphere")
radius1=int(input("Enter the radius of a
hemisphere : "))
print("Radius of Hemisphere : ",radius1)
#volume of hemisphere
volume1=(2/3)*3.14*(radius1**3)
print("Volume of Hemisphere : ",volume1)
```

Output

Calculate the Volume of Sphere

Enter the radius of a sphere : 5

Radius of Sphere : 5

Volume of Sphere : 523.3333333333334

Calculate the Volume of Hemisphere

Enter the radius of a hemisphere : 4

Radius of Hemisphere : 4

Volume of Hemisphere : 133.97333333333333

8 Predict the output:

(i)
```
a = 3
b = a *2
print(a*3+6+b)
```

(ii)
```
a, b = 12, 10
c = a//b + 4 * 2
d = c — 10
print(d)
```

(iii)
```
a = 5
b = 6
((a and b)
or (a > b))
```

(iv)
```
a = 4
b = 6
c = 10
(a >= b)
or ((c = = b)
and (not(c < a)))
```

(v)
```
a = 4
b = 6
c = 10
(a <= b) and
((c == a)and
(not(c < b)))
```

(vi)
```
a = 60
b = 10
c = 85/b + a
print(c)
```

(vii)
```
a = 3
b = 4
c = a ** b + 5
print(c)
```

(viii)
```
b = 89
a = 78
c = (a <= b)
print(c)
```

Ans. (i) 21 (ii) –1

(iii) 6 (iv) False

(v) False (vi) 68.5

(vii) 86 (viii) True

ASSESSMENT EXERCISE

Multiple Choice Questions

1. These operators work on single operand
   (a) Binary (b) Unary (c) Ternary (d) None of these
2. Which of the following symbol is used for exponentiation?
   (a) // (b) ^ (c) * (d) ^ ^
3. Dictionary data types are created by using
   (a) { } (b) [ ] (c) ( ) (d) < >

Very Short Answer Type Questions

4. Which operator is used to connect relational expression?
5. What will be the value of z?
   z = 2 * 3 + 4 - 3/2 * 4
6. Convert the equation into corresponding Python statement a b 5c 3 2 + + .

Short Answer Type Questions

7. Define conditional operator with the help of an example.
8. Construct logical expression to represent the following condition
   (i) a is odd.
   (ii) age is less than 35 and greater than 18.
9. What will be the output of following program?

```
i = 4
j = -1
k = 0
w = i or j or k
x = i and j and k
print("w = ", w)
print("x = ", x)
```

10. Write the output of the following program:

```
x = 5
y = 3
z = ++ x + -- y
print ("z = ", - - z)
```

11. Evaluate the following expression and show their hierarchy

```
a = b * c/2 + 3/2 * c + 2 + d
(if b = 4, c = 1, d = 3.2)
```

Long Answer Type Questions

12. Any year is input through the keyboard. Write a program to determine whether the year is a leap year or not.
13. If a three digit number is input through the keyboard, write a program to reverse the number.
14. Write a Python program to input a number, if number is even print its cube otherwise print its square.
15. If the marks obtained by a student in five different subjects are input through the keyboard, find out the aggregate marks and percentage marks obtained by the student. Assume the maximum marks that can be obtained by a student in each subject is 100.
16. Ravish's basic salary is input through the keyboard. His dearness allowance is 40% of basic salary and house rent allowance is 20% of basic salary. Write a program to calculate his gross salary

Conditional and Looping Statements

CHAPTER 10

Python's conditional and looping statements are the building blocks for controlling the flow of your program. Conditional statements, like if, elif, and else, allow you to execute different code based on whether a condition is true or false. Looping statements, like for and while, let you repeat a block of code multiple times, either a set number of times (for loop) or until a certain condition is met (while loop). These statements working together give your programs the ability to make decisions and perform repetitive tasks efficiently.

10.1 Introduction

The two fundamental building blocks of Python programming: conditional statements and looping statements. These powerful tools allow your programs to make decisions and repeat actions.

Conditional statements in Python language decide the direction (Control Flow) of the flow of program execution. They evaluate a condition (often true or false) and execute different code blocks based on the outcome.

Looping statements are all about repetition. They allow you to execute a block of code multiple times, often iterating through a sequence of data like lists or strings.

10.2 Control Structure

A control structure is a programming language construct which affects the flow of the execution of program.

Various types of control structure are described below

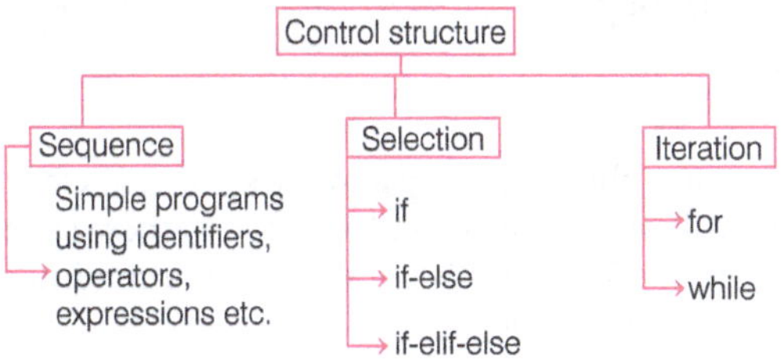

Sequence Statements

Sequence statements refers to the instructions that are executed in the sequence in which they are written in the program. When a program is run, the CPU begins execution, executes some number of statements and then terminates at the end.

The sequence of statements that the CPU executes is called the **program's path**. Many programs have been straight line programs. Straight line programs have sequential flow, i.e. they take the same path every time they are run.

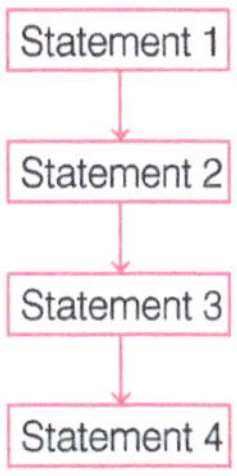

For example,

```
print("A program which adds two integers\n")
x = int(input("Enter first integer:"))
y  int(input("Enter second integer:"))
sum= x + y
print("Sum is : ", sum)
```

Output

A program which adds two integers
Enter first integer : 5
Enter second integer: 11
Sum is : 16

Selection Statements

These statements allow a program to execute a statement or a set of statements depending upon a given condition. These statements are also called conditional statements or decision statements. A selection statement is a control statement that allows choosing statement two or more execution paths in a program. Selection statements alter the sequential flow of instructions in a program. This is done using selection statements.

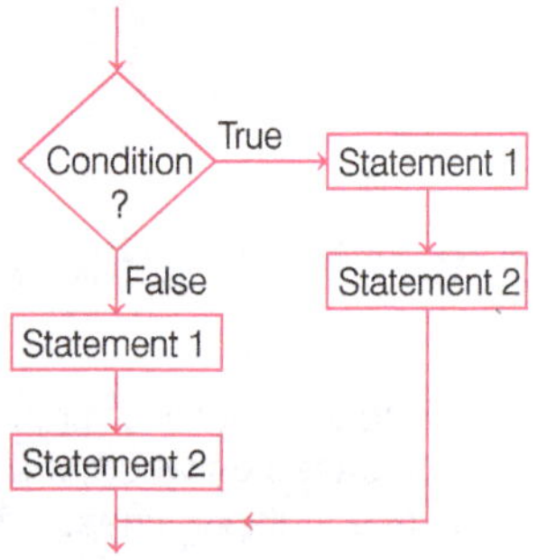

Python provides three types of selectors are described below

1. if statement

The simplest and most common selection structure is the if statement. The if statement allows branch depending upon the value or state of variables. If the condition evaluates true, an action is followed otherwise, the action is ignored.

Syntax

```
if(conditional expression):
    statement(s)
```

e.g.
```
x = 1
y = 3
x = x + y
if (x > y):
    print ("x is greater")
```

In the above example, the conditional statement under if( ) will be always evaluated as True because the value of x will become 4 before the comparison thus the expression (4>3) yields a True value letting the statement under if () to execute, i.e the output of the above code would be "x is greater".

Following flowchart illustrated if statement:

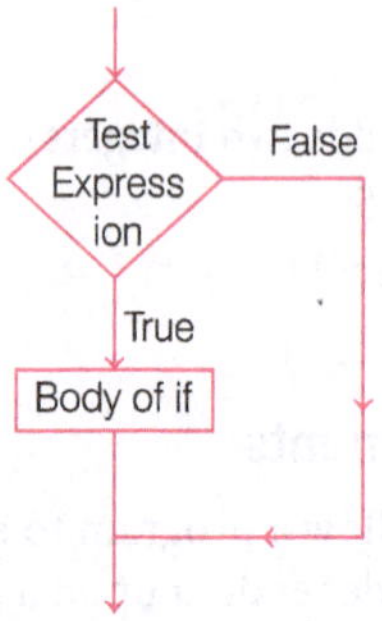

2. if-else statement

This statement also tests a conditional expression. If the condition is True, the entire block of statements following the if will be executed.

Otherwise, the entire block of statements following the else will be executed.

Syntax

```
if(conditional statement):
    statement(s)
else:
    statement(s)
```

Following flowchart illustrates if-else statement:

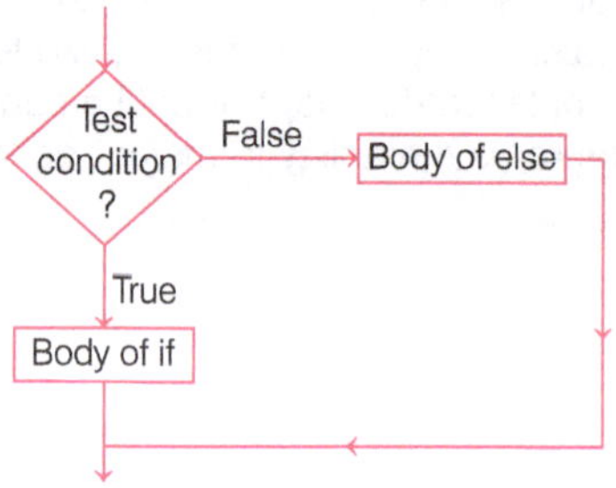

e.g.
```
x = 0
y = 3
x = x + y
if (x > y):
    print("x is greater")
else:
    print("we are in else part because x is not
                                                greater")
```

If the conditional statement under if( ) is evaluated to be True, then the statements under if( ) block will be executed otherwise the statements under else block will be executed. In an if-else statement, either if block or else block executes, never both.

The above code, produces an output as "we are in else part because x is not greater". Because the conditional statement under if( ) evaluates as False x is not greater than y, it is same as that of y.

e.g.
```
if(a == b):
    c = a
```

In above case, the if will stop and the statements following this line will not be considered a part of if, these statements will be executed irrespective of whether the condition a = = b is False or True.

3. if-elif-else statement

Sometimes, we need to execute different statement to perform in different conditions. It requires the evaluation of several conditions.

First of all, the first condition is evaluated, if it is true then respective statements are processed. Otherwise, the next condition is evaluated to process another say of statements.

This process is continued for several times.

Syntax
```
if (condition 1):
    statement 1
elif (condition 2):
    statement 2
else:
    statement 3
```

Or

```
if(condition 1):
    statement 1
elif(condition 2):
    statement 2
```

Expression is tested from the top towards the downside. As soon as the true condition is found, the associated set of statement is executed.

Following flowchart illustrates if-elif-else statement

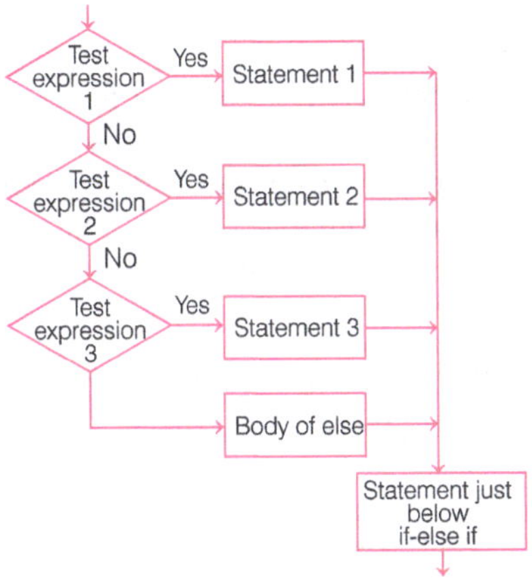

e.g.
```
if ((an x%5 ==0) and ( x%8 == 0)) :
    print("Divisible by both 5 and 8")
elif (x%8 == 0):
    print("Divisible by 8")
elif (x % 5 ==0):
    print("Divisible by 5")
else:
    print("Divisible by none")
```

4. Nested if statement

Nested means if statements or if-else statements are placed in the statement block of if statement or else statement.

Syntax
```
if(condition 1):
    if(condition 2):
        statement 1
    else:
        statement 2
else:
    statement 3
```

e.g.
```
if(a > b):
    if(a > c):
        result a
    else:
        result c
else:
    if(b>c):
        result b
    else:
        result c
```

The nested if can have one of the following four forms:

(i) if nested inside both, if part and else part
```
if(condition 1):
    if(condition 2):
        statement 1
    else:
        statement 2
else:
        if(condition 3):
            statement 3
        else:
            statement 4
```

(ii) if nested inside if part
```
if(condition 1):
    if(condition 2):
        statement 1
    else:
    statement 2
else :
    statement 3
```

(iii) if nested inside else part
```
if(condition 1):
    statement 1
else:
    if(condition 2):
        statement 2
    else:
        statement 3
```

(iv) One if inside another if statements
```
if(condition 1):
    statement 1
    if (condition 2):
        statement 2
```

Try These 10.1

1. **Give example of control statements.**
2. **Write a program to find the number which are divisible by 3 and 5.**
3. **Explain nested if statements.**

10.3 range( ) Function

The range( ) function is used to generate a sequence of numbers overtime. At its simplest, it accepts an integer and returns a range object (a type of iterable).

The range ( ) function has two sets of parameters, as follows

- **range (stop)**

  stop number of integers to generate, starting from zero.

- **range ([start,] stop [,step])**

  start starting number of the sequence.

  stop generate numbers upto, but not including this number.

  step difference between each number in the sequence.

Iterative Statements

Iterative statements or loops enable a program with a cyclic flow of logic. Each statement which is written under the scope of a looping statement gets executed the number of times the iteration/looping continues for.

There are two basic types of looping statements available in Python, they are as follows.

A looping statement enables repetition of tasks under its scope based on a particular condition called as loop-condition.

This loop condition evaluates to either True or False. A loop may be continued till a loop-condition is evaluated as True.

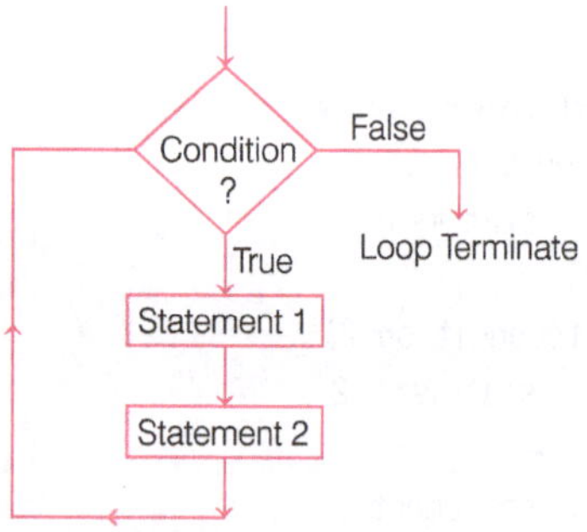

1. while loop

A while loop tests for its ending condition before executing the statements enclosed in the loop body even the first time. So, if the ending condition is met when the while loop beings, the lines of instructions its contains will never be carried out.

Syntax
```
while(loop-condition):
    statement(s)
```

Following flowchart illustrates while loop

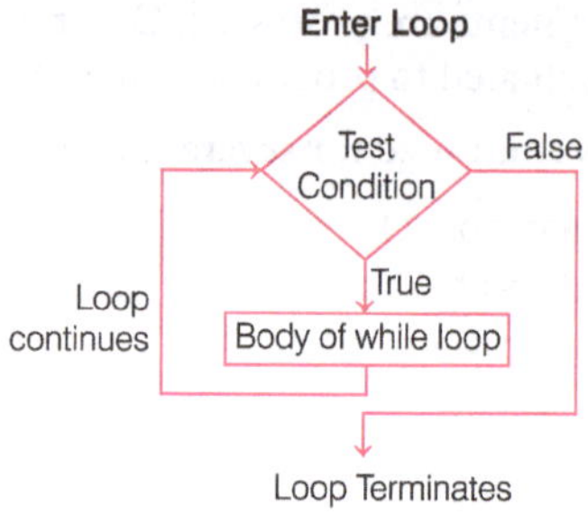

A while continues iteration cycle till its loop condition is evaluated as true. If the loop-condition is false for the first time iteration, then loop will not execute even once.

e.g.
```
x = 0
sum = 0
x = int(input("Enter a natural number:"))
while(x > 0):
    sum  = sum + x
    x = x - 1
print(" Sum is :" , sum)
```

The loop is executed till the x is greater than 0, as soon x becomes 0 the loop is terminated. We observe that within the scope of the loop the value of x is decremented, so that it approaches to its next previous value. Thus, with each iteration the value of x is added to a variable sum and is decremented by 1.

Let us assume that user inputs a value 4 for x then at

Initial	Condition	Sum	x
Initial	—	0	4 (input from user)
Ist Iteration	4 > 0 (True)	0 + 4 = 4	3
2nd Iteration	3 > 0 (True)	4 + 3 = 7	2
3rd Iteration	2 > 0 (True)	7 + 2 = 9	1
4th Iteration	1 > 0 (True)	9 + 1 = 10	0
5th Iteration	0 > 0 (False)		

In while loop, the looping condition is evaluated at the beginning of the loop's scope, i.e. prior to entering into the scope of loop. This type of checking is called "Entry control checking", if the condition fails this checking, then the entry into the scope of loop will not be allowed. So, while loops are often called as **Entry Control Loop.**

The while loop can accept expression and not just conditions, the following are all illegal expressions

(i) while(x = x + 1)

(ii) while (n– –)

(iii) while(count + =i)

When the result of x = x + 1, n – – or count + = i, evaluates to 0, then the while condition fails and the loop will exit.

2. for loop

The for statement encloses one or more statements that form the body of the loop, the statements in the loop repeat continuously a certain number of times.

This loop is also an entry control loop, as condition is checked before entering into the scope of the loop.

Syntax
```
for variable in <sequence>:
    statement(s)
```

e.g.
```
for i in range (1,5):
    print("A")
    print("B")
```

Output

A
B
A
B
A
B
A
B

Difference between 'for' loop and 'while' loop

Feature	'for' Loop	'while' Loop
Syntax	for (initialization; condition; increment/decrement)	while (condition)
Initialization	Initialization is done within the loop structure	Initialization is done before the loop structure
Condition	The loop continues iterating until the condition is false	The loop continues iterating until the condition is false
Increment/ Decrement	Increment or decrement is done within the loop structure	Increment or decrement must be done explicitly within the loop
Use Cases	Suitable for iterating over a known range or sequence	Suitable for indefinite iteration or when the number of iterations is unknown
Control	More control over the number of iterations	Less control over the number of iterations, but can handle more complex conditions
Examples	python for i in range(5):	python while x < 5:

Try These 10.2

1. **Explain entry control loops.**
2. **Why would you use a for loop in a programming language, and can you provide an example of its usage?**

10.4 Programs

1. For accepting an integer from user and checking if this integer is greater than 10.

```
a  = int(input ("Enter a number:"))
print ("Number is", a)
if (a>10):
    print (a, "is greater than 10")
```

Output

Enter a number: 56
Number is 56
56 is greater than 10

2. For adding a number to non-zero real number x.

```
Sum= 100.00
x  = float (input("Please enter a real number:"))
print("Real number is",x)
if(x ! =  0.0):
    sum=sum + x
    print("The sum is:", sum)
```

Output

Please enter a real number: 45.9
Real number is 45.9
The sum is: 145.9

3. For asking a user to answer Yes or No to a question such as "Are you ready to provide your credit card number"?

```
ans  = input ("Are you ready to provide your
        credit card number (1= Yes/0  =  No):")
print ("Your choice:", ans)
if(ans ==  '1'):
    print ("Now we will continue the processing
                                    of transaction")
elif(ans ==  '0'):
    print ("Now we will not continue the
                    processing of transaction")
```

Output

Are you ready to provide your credit card number (1 = Yes/0 = No):0
Your choice: 0
Now we will not continue the processing of transaction

4. To find the number is even or odd with compound statement.

```
n =  int(input("Enter a number:"))
print("The number is",n)
d =  n%2
if(d == 0):
```

```
        print ("Remainder on division by 2 is:" , d)
        print ("The number is an even number.")
    else:
        print("Remainder on division by 2 is:", d)
        print("The number is an odd number.")
```

Output

Enter a number:45

The number is 45

Remainder on division by 2 is: 1

The number is an odd number.

5. To accept a positive value from a user and prints the square of the number.

```
n = int(input(" Enter a number:"))
if (n<0):
    print ("Number is negative")
else:
    print (" The square of " ,n, "is" ,n ** 2)
```

Output

Enter a number : 6

The square of 6 is 36

6. To enter a character and print whether a given character is an alphabet, digit or any character.

```
ch = input ("Enter a character:")
if (((ch>='A') and (ch<='Z')) or ((ch>='a') and
                                   (ch=<'z'))):
    print ("You entered an alphabet")
elif(ch>='0' and ch=<'9'):
    print ("You entered a digit")
else:
    print ("You entered a character other than
                                alphabets and digits")
```

Output

Enter a character : a

You entered an alphabet

>>>

Enter a character:2

You entered a digit

7. To print the largest number out of 3 numbers.

```
i = int(input ("Enter first number:"))
j = int(input("Enter second number:"))
k =  int(input("Enter third number:"))
print("i =",i)
print("j=",j)
print("k=",k)
if ((i)and(j)and(k)):
    l=i
    if(j>l):
        l=j
    if(k>l):
        l=k
    print("The largest number is", l)
```

Output

Enter first number: 78

Enter second number: 54

Enter third number : 23

i =78

j = 54

k = 23

The largest number is 78

8. For fibonacci series using while loop.

```
n=int(input("Enter the limit:"))
i  = 1
a = 0
b = 1
while(i<=n):
    print(a)
        c = a + b
        a =  b
        b =  c
        i =  i +1  or  i += 1
```

Output

Enter the limit: 10

0
1
1
2
3
5
8
13
21

Glossary

Sequence Statements It refers to the instructions that are executed in the sequence in which they are written in the program.

Selection Statements These statements allow a program to execute a statement or a set of statements depending upon a given condition.

range( ) Function It is used to generate a sequence of numbers overtime.

REVIEW EXERCISE

Including Competency Based Questions

Part I

Multiple Choice Questions

1 **Which statement is a sequence of more than one statements?**

(a) Control statement (b) Compound statement
(c) Single statement (d) Sequence statement

2 **Which function is used to generate a sequence of numbers overtime?**

(a) range ( ) (b) len ( )
(c) limit ( ) (d) lim ( )

3 **These statements enable a program with a cyclic flow of logic.**

(a) Sequence (b) Compound
(c) Single (d) Iterative

4 **While loops are called as**

(a) entry control loops (b) exit control loops
(c) Both (a) and (b) (d) None of these

5 **A computer program is a set of instructions and are also known as**

(a) compounds (b) statements
(c) blocks (d) comments

6 **In Python programming, which statements are used for controlling the flow of a program? Choose the correct options.**

(i) Sequence statements
(ii) Selection statements
(iii) Iterative statements
(iv) Conditional statements

(a) Only (i) (b) Both (ii) and (iii)
(c) (ii), (iii) and (iv) (d) (i), (ii) and (iii)

Answers

1. (b) **2.** (a) **3.** (d) **4.** (a) **5.** (b) **6.** (c)

Statement Based Questions

1 **Statement 1 In Python, the "if" statement is used for making decisions based on a condition.**

Statement 2 The "if-else" statement allows for the execution of different code blocks based on a condition.

(a) Both Statement 1 and Statement 2 are correct
(b) Both Statement 1 and Statement 2 are incorrect
(c) Statement 1 is correct but Statement 1 is incorrect
(d) Statement 2 is correct but Statement 1 is incorrect

2 **Statement 1 Sequence statements in Python are executed in the order they appear in the code.**

Statement 2 The "elif" keyword is used for creating multiple conditions in a selection statement.

(a) Both Statement 1 and Statement 2 are correct
(b) Both Statement 1 and Statement 2 are incorrect
(c) Statement 1 is correct but Statement 2 is incorrect
(d) Statement 2 is correct but Statement 1 is incorrect

3 **Statement 1 The "for" loop in Python is used for iterative statements and executes a block of code a specific number of times.**

Statement 2 The "while" loop in Python is an example of a selection statement.

(a) Both Statement 1 and Statement 2 are correct
(b) Both Statement 1 and Statement 2 are incorrect
(c) Statement 1 is correct but Statement 2 is incorrect
(d) Statement 2 is correct but Statement 1 is incorrect

Answers

1. (a) **2.** (a) **3.** (c)

Assertion & Reason Based Questions

1 **Assertion The while loop in Python allows the execution of a block of code repeatedly as long as a specified condition is correct.**

Reason Iterative statements, like the while loop, are used for creating repetitive tasks and help in automating processes.

(a) Both Assertion and Reason are correct, and Reason is the correct explanation for Assertion.
(b) Both Assertion and Reason are correct, but Reason is not the correct explanation for Assertion.
(c) Assertion is correct, but Reason is incorrect.
(d) Assertion is incorrect, but Reason is correct.

2 **Assertion The "for" loop in Python is used for iterative statements, allowing a set of statements to be executed repeatedly.**

Reason The "for" loop is especially useful when the number of iterations is known beforehand.

(a) Both Assertion and Reason are correct, and Reason is the correct explanation of Assertion.
(b) Both Assertion and Reason are correct, but Reason is not the correct explanation of Assertion.
(c) Assertion is correct, but Reason is incorrect.
(d) Assertion is incorrect, but Reason is correct.

3 **Assertion In Python, the if statement is used for making decisions based on the evaluation of a condition.**

Reason Selection statements help in controlling the flow of a program by executing different code blocks depending on whether a condition is correct or incorrect.

(a) Both Assertion and Reason are correct, and Reason is the correct explanation for Assertion.

(b) Both Assertion and Reason are correct, but Reason is not the correct explanation for Assertion.

(c) Assertion is correct, but Reason is incorrect.

(d) Assertion is incorrect, but Reason is correct.

Answers

1. (a) **2.** (a) **3.** (b)

Part II

Very Short Answer Type Questions

1 **What is the minimum number of iterations that while loop could make?**

Ans. While loop could make minimum 0 iteration.

2 **Explain entry controlled loop.**

Ans. In an entry controlled loop, the loop control condition is evaluated at the entry point of the loop.

3 **Define iteration.**

Ans. Iteration is a process of executing a statement or a set of statements repeatedly, until some specific condition is specified.

4 **Define sequence statement.**

Ans. Sequence statements refer to the instructions that are executed in the sequence in which they are written in the program.

5 **What is looping?**

Ans. Looping is also iteration. It is the ability to perform the same set of operations repeatedly till a specific condition is met.

6 **Explain selection statement.**

Ans. The selection statement means the execution of statements depending upon a test condition.

7 **What is the body of loop and exit condition?**

Ans. The set of statements repeated again and again is called body of loop and the condition on which the exit of the loop depends, is known as exit condition.

8 **Write the purpose of for loop.**

Ans. The for loop is used for fixed number of iterations.

9 **Give the output for the following program segment given below.**

```
for i in range (-5, -7, -1):
    print(i+1)
```

Ans. The program segment does not produce any output.

10 **Find the output of the following code.**

```
i=1
while(i<5):
    print(i)
    i=i * 2
```

Ans. Output

1

2

4

11 **Write an appropriate loop for the condition-A loop is to be repeated 100 times.**

Ans. for i in range (0,100, 1):

12 **List the two looping structures.**

Ans (i) for loop (ii) while loop

Short Answer Type Questions

1 **Write two different forms of if statement.**

Ans. (i)
```
if (condition):
    statement(s)
```

(ii)
```
if (condition):
    statement 1
else:
    statement 2
```

2 **Find the syntax error in the following program and underline after correct them.**

```
w = 90 ;
while(w > 60)
    print(w)
    w = w - 50
```

Ans. Correct code is

```
w = 90
while(w>60):
    print(w)
    w = w - 50
```

3 **Construct logical expressions to represent the following conditions.**

(i) Weight is greater than or equal to 115 but less than 125.

(ii) Donation is in the range of 4000-5000 or Guest is 1.

Ans. (i) (weight > =115 and weight < 125)

(ii) ((Donation > = 4000 and Donation <= 5000) or Guest == 1)

4 Write a Python program to calculate simple interest and display it.

Ans.
```
p  = int(input("Enter the principal:"))
r =  int(input("Enter rate of interest:"))
t =  int(input("Enter time:"))
si = (p*r*t)/ 100
print("The simple interest is", si)
```

Output

Enter the principal : 5000

Enter rate of interest : 10

Enter time : 2

The simple interest is 1000.0

5 Write a program to input three angles and determine if they make a triangle or not.

Ans.
```
a = float(input("Enter first angle :"))
b = float(input("Enter second angle:"))
c = float(input("Enter third angle:"))
sum  = a+b+c
if(sum == 180):
 print ("These angles will make a triangle")
else:
 print ("These angles will not make a triangle")
```

Output

Enter first angle : 45.6

Enter second angle : 44.4

Enter third angle : 90.0

These angles will make a triangle

Long Answer Type Questions

1 Write a program to generate and print
(i) all odd numbers from 1 to 20.
(ii) numbers 5, 10, 15 and 50 only till 50.

Ans. (i)
```
print("The odd numbers from 1 to 20")
 for i in range (1,21,2):
   print('\t',i,end =" ")
```

Output

The odd number from 1 to 20

1 3 5 7 9 11 13 15 17 19

(ii)
```
num = 5
print("The numbers from 5 to 50 with 5
                                    intervals")
while(num < = 50):
  print('\t', num, end = " ")
  num  = num + 5
```

Output

The numbers from 5 to 50 with 5 intervals

5 10 15 20 25 30 35 40 45 50

2 Write a program to check whether a number is prime or not.

Ans.
```
n  = int (input("Enter the number:"))
print ("n=" , n)
if n>1:
   for i in range (2, n//2):
      if(n%i)  == 0:
         print(n, "is not a prime number")
         break
      else:
         print(n, "is a prime number")
else:
   print(n, " is not a prime number")
```

Output

Enter the number : 67

n = 67

67 is a prime number

3 Write a program to display a triangle of numbers using for loop within a while loop.

Ans.
```
x = 1
while (x< = 6):
   for y in range (1, x):
      print (x, end = " ")
   x = x +1
   print ("\n")
```

Output

2

33

444

5555

66666

4 An electricity board charges according to the following rules.

For the first 100 units - 40 P per unit

For the next 200 units - 50 P per unit

Beyond 300 units - 60 P per unit

All users have to pay meter charge also, which is ₹ 50. Write a program to read the number of units consumed and print out the charges.

Ans.
```
charges = 0.0;
units  = int (input ("Enter the number of units
                                   consumed:"))
if(units<=100):
   charges  = (units * 0.4)+50;
elif(units<=300):
   charges = ((units-100) * 0.5 + 40) + 50
```

```
elif(units>300):
    charges = ((units-300) * 0.6+140)+50
print("The charges is:", charges)
```

Output

Enter the number of units consumed: 125

The charges is : 102.5

5 Write a Python program to input the marks of 5 subjects and print their sum and average. Also, find the grade according to given conditions

Average	Grade
>=90 and <=100	A+
>=81 and <=90	A
>=71 and <=80	B+
>=61 and <=70	B
>=51 and <=60	C+
>=41 and <=50	C
>=0 and <=40	F

Ans.

```
print("Enter marks obtained in 5 subjects: ");
mark1 = input();
mark1 = int(mark1);
mark2 = int(input());
mark3 = int(input());
mark4 = int(input());
mark5 = int(input());
sum = mark1 + mark2 + mark3 + mark4 + mark5;
average = sum/5;
print("Total marks:",sum)
print("Average:",average)
if(average>=91 and average<=100):
    print("Your Grade is A+");
elif(average>=81 and average<=90):
    print("Your Grade is A");
elif(average>=71 and average<=80):
    print("Your Grade is B+");
elif(average>=61 and average<=70):
    print("Your Grade is B");
elif(average>=51 and average<=60):
    print("Your Grade is C+");
elif(average>=41 and average<=50):
    print("Your Grade is C");
elif(average>=0 and average<=40):
    print("Your Grade is F");
else:
    print("Strange Grade..!!");
```

ASSESSMENT EXERCISE

Multiple Choice Questions

1. for loop is also known as
   (a) entry control loop (b) exit control loop (c) Both (a) and (b) (d) None of these
2. Iterative statements evaluate the loop condition either.
   (a) True (b) False (c) Both (a) and (b) (d) None of these
3. Find the appropriate loop for the condition when a for loop is to be repeated 50 times.
   (a) for i in range (0, 50, 1) : (b) for i in range (1, 50, 1) :
   (c) for i in range (0, 51, 1) : (d) for i in range (0, 1, 50) :

Very Short Answer Type Questions

4. What is the smallest unit of execution in Python?
5. Write one difference between for loop and while loop.
6. The program execution starts with which statement?

Short Answer Type Questions

7. Find the syntax errors, if any, in the following program.

```
max = 0
a = int (input("Enter the value of a"))
b = int (input ("Enter the value of b"))
if (a>>b):
max = a
print (max):
```

8. What are the logical constructs used in for loop?
9. Write a program that accept a number and print cube of that number.
10. Write a program to find the sum of 3 numbers.
11. Is it necessary to write else with every if statement while writing nested if statements?

Long Answer Type Questions

12. Differentiate between if and if-else statements.
13. Give the purpose of iteration statement. What are the other names by which a iteration statement is referred to?
14. Describe a nested if statement.
15. Write a program that will allow an integer from 1 to 7 to be input and the name of the day of week corresponding to the integer to be output.
16. Write a program to input marks in five subjects. Find average and awards grades as per the following guidelines.

Percentage	Grade
90% and above	A
89% and 80%	B
79% and 70%	C
69% and 60%	D
59% and 50%	E
Less than 50%	Fail

17. Write Python program to sum the following series.
    Sum = 1+2+3+....... + n terms

CHAPTER 11

Lists in Python

In Python, a list is an ordered collection of items that allows you to store a group of elements together. These elements can be of any data type, like numbers, strings, or even other lists. Unlike strings, lists are mutable, meaning you can change their content after creation

11.1 Introduction

As we studied in the fundamental chapter, list is a type of container, which is used to store multiple data at the same time. List contains a sequence of heterogeneous elements which makes it powerful tool in Python. It can store integer, string as well as object in a single list. Lists are mutable which means they can be changed after creation. Each element of a list is assigned a number its position or index. The first index is zero, the second index is one, the third index is two and so on. List is one of the most frequently used and very versatile data type used in **Python**. A number of operations can be performed on the lists, which we will study as we go forward.

11.2 Creating a List

In Python, lists can be created to put the elements in square brackets [ ]. The elements in the list are separated by the comma (,).
For example,

```
a =[34, 76, 11, 98]
b = ['s', 3, 6, 't']
c =[34, 0.5, 75]
d =[ ]
```

Creating List From an Existing Sequence

In Python, list ( ) method is used to create list from an existing sequence.

Syntax `new_list_name = list (sequence/string)`

Here, sequence includes tuples, lists etc.

For example,

```
A = "PYTHON"
A1 = list(A)
print(A1)
```

Output

['P', 'Y', 'T', 'H', 'O', 'N']

```
A = list("PYTHON")
print(A)
```

Output

['P', 'Y', 'T', 'H', 'O', 'N']

```
l = ('P','Y','T','H','O','N')
l1 = list(l)
print(l1)
```

Output

['P', 'Y', 'T', 'H', 'O', 'N']

Or

list() method is also used to create list of characters and integers through keyboard.
For example,

```
a = list(input("Enter the elements :"))
print(a)
```

Output

Enter the elements :23456
['2', '3', '4', '5', '6']

```
b = list(input("Enter string:"))
print(b)
```

Output

Enter string:ARIHANT
['A', 'R', 'I', 'H', 'A', 'N', 'T']

We can create different types of list in python as follows

(i) Empty List

Empty list can be created in Python using [ ] . It takes the truth value as false.

Here is the two ways to create empty list as

```
a = []
print(a)
```

Output

[]

or

```
a = list()
print(a)
```

Output

[]

(ii) Mixed Data Type List

It can be created to place different data types such as integers, strings, double etc., into one list.

For example,

```
a = ['Neha','Sharma', 45, 34, 4]
print(a)
```

Output

['Neha', 'Sharma', 45, 34, 4]

(iii) Nested List

Nested lists are list objects where the elements in the lists can be lists themselves

For example,

```
A = ['Neha',4, 2, [5,23,4],65]
print(A)
```

Output

['Neha', 4, 2, [5, 23, 4], 65]

List A contains 5 elements while inner list contains 3 elements ([5, 23, 4]). List A is considered [5, 23, 4] as one element.

Accessing Lists

To access the list's elements, index number is used. Use the index operator [ ] to access the elements of a list. The index should be an integer. Index of 0 refers to first element, 1 refers to second element and so on. While the index of -1 refers to the last element, -2 refers to the second last element and so on.

For example,

```
l1 = [5, 7, 3, 4, 5, 6, 9, 0, 8]
```

It is called positive index

0	1	2	3	4	5	6	7	8
5	7	3	4	5	6	9	0	8
–9	–8	–7	–6	–5	–4	–3	–2	–1

↓

It is called negative index

```
l1 = [34,87,'Computer',12, 'Python', 11, 76, 'Option']
print(l1[0])
print(l1[6])
print(l1[-4])
print(l1[3])
print(l1[-3])
print(l1[8])
statement print (l1[8])
```

Output

34

76

Python

12

11

ERROR!

Traceback (most recent call last)

```
File "<main.py>", line 7, in <module>
```

IndexError: list index out of range

Statement print (l1[8]) will give Error as IndexError: list index out of range. Because it has 8 elements for which index are 0 to 7.

Traversing a List

Traversing a list is a technique to access an individual element of that list. It is also called **iterate over a list**. There are multiple ways to iterate over a list in Python.

These are as follows

(i) Using for loop

The most common and easy way to traverse a list is with for loop. for loop is used when you want to traverse each element of a list.

Syntax `for variable in list_name:`

For example,

```
a = ['P','R','O','G','A','M']
for i in a:
    print(i)
```

Output

P

R

O

G

A

M

(ii) Using for loop with range ( )

There is another method to traverse a list using for loop with range( ). This is also used len( ) function with range. This method is used when you want to traverse particular characters in a list.

Syntax `for variable in range (len(list_name)):`

For example,

```
a = ['P','R','O','G','A','M']
for i in range(len(a)):
    print(a[i])
```

Output

P

R

O

G

A

M

Program to display the elements of list

['P', 'Y', 'T', 'H', 'O', 'N'] in separate line with their index number.

For example,

```
list1 = ['P','R','O','G','A','M']
l1 = len(list1)
for i in range(l1):
    print("Element :", list1[i],"at index number",i)
```

Output

Element : P at index number 0

Element : R at index number 1

Element : O at index number 2

Element : G at index number 3

Element : A at index number 4

Element : M at index number 5

11.3 List Operations

We can perform various operations on list in Python, some of them are describe below.

(i) **Concatenate Lists** The most conventional method to perform on the list concatenaton, the use of (+) operator can easily add the whole of one list to other list and hence perform the concatenation.

Syntax list = list1+list2

For example,

```
l1 = [43, 56, 34]
l2 = [22, 34, 98]
l = l1+l2
print(l)
```

Output

[43, 56, 34, 22, 34, 98]

The (+) operator cannot add list with other type as number or string because this operator is used only with list types.

For example,

```
l1 = [2, 5, 7]
l = l1+5
print(l)
```

Output

ERROR!

Traceback (most recent call last):

File "<main.py>", line 2, in <module>

TypeError: can only concatenate list (not "int") to list

(ii) **Replicating List** You can repeat the elements of the list using (*) operator. This operator is used to replicate the list.

Syntax `list = list1 * digit`

For example,

```
l1 = [2, 5, 7]
l = l1 * 2
print(l)
```

Output

[2, 5, 7, 2, 5, 7]

(iii) **Slicing of a List** In Python list, there are multiple ways to print the whole list with all the elements, but to print a specific range of elements from the list, we use slice operation. Slice operation is performed on lists with the use of colon (:).

Syntax `s = list_name [Start:End]`

For example,

```
list1 = [4, 3, 7, 6, 4, 9, 5, 0, 3, 2]
s = list1 [2:5]
print(s)
```

Output

[7, 6, 4]

To print elements from beginning to a range use [: Index], to print elements from end use [: -Index] and to print elements from specific index till the end use [Index :].

For example,

```
list1 = [4, 3, 7, 6, 4, 9, 5, 0, 3, 2]
s = list1 [:5]
print(s)
s = list1[:-6]
print(s)
```

```
s = list1[3:]
print(s)
```

Output

[4, 3, 7, 6, 4]

[4, 3, 7, 6]

[6, 4, 9, 5, 0, 3, 2]

You can also print all elements of list in **reverse order** using [: : – 1].

For example,

```
list1 = [4, 3, 7, 6, 4, 9, 5, 0, 3, 2]
s = list1 [:: - 1]
print(s)
```

Output

[2, 3, 0, 5, 9, 4, 6, 7, 3, 4]

Lists are also provide slice steps which used to extract elements from list that are not consecutive.

Syntax `s = list_name [Start: Stop: Step]`

It takes three parameters which are as follows

- Start starting integer where the slicing of the object starts.
- Stop integer until which the slicing takes place. The slicing stops at index stop – 1.
- Step integer value which determines the increment between each index for slicing.

For example,

```
list1 = [4, 3, 7, 6, 4, 9, 5, 0, 3, 2]
l1 = list1 [1: 10 : 3]
print(l1)
l2 = list1 [2 : 12 : 2]
print(l2)
l3 = list1 [::4]
print(l3)
l4 = list1[::8]
print(l4)
l5 = list1 [3 : :]
print(l5)
```

Output

[3, 4, 0]

[7, 4, 5, 3]

[4, 4, 3]

[4, 3]

[6, 4, 9, 5, 0, 3, 2]

Try These 11.1

1. **What is the different types to create a list in Python?**
2. **How to iterate over a list in Python?**
3. **What are the operations in list?**

11.4 List Modification using Slicing

List can be modified after it created using slicing.

For example,

```
l1 = [2,4,'Try',54, 'Again']
l1 [0:1] = [34, "Hello"]
print(l1)
l1 [4] = ["World"]
print(l1)
l1[2] = "Hiiii"
print(l1)
```

Output

[34, 'Hello', 4, 'Try', 54, 'Again']

[34, 'Hello', 4, 'Try', ['World'], 'Again']

[34, 'Hello', 'Hiiii', 'Try', ['World'], 'Again']

11.5 Built-in Functions

Python has large number of built-in functions and methods that make programming easier. Some of them are as follows

(i) append ( )

This method is used for appending and adding elements to a list. It is used to add elements to the last position of a list.

Syntax `list_name.append (element)`

For example,

```
l1 = [34, 65, 23, 98]
l1.append (76)
print(l1)
```

Output

[34, 65, 23, 98, 76]

(ii) insert ( )

This method is used to insert an element at specified position in the list. This method takes two arguments : one for index number and second for element value.

Syntax `list_name insert (index, element)`

For example,

```
l1 = [34, 65, 23, 98]
l1.insert (3, 'New')
print(l1)
```

Output

[34, 65, 23, 'New', 98]

(iii) extend ( )

This method is used to add contents of list 2 to the end of list 1.

Syntax `listname1. extend (list_name2)`

For example,

```
l1 = [43, 'Hello', 56]
l2 = ['World', 'Try', 65,77]
l1.extend(l2)
print(l1)
```

Output

[43, 'Hello', 56, 'World', 'Try', 65, 77]

(iv) sum ( )

This method is used to calculate the sum of all the elements in the list.

Syntax `sum (list_name)`

For example,

```
l = [45, 23, 87, 5, 9]
print(sum (l))
```

Output

169

sum ( ) method is used for only numeric values otherwise it gives an error.

```
l = [45, 23, 87, 5, 'Hello']
print(sum (l))
```

Output

Trackback (most recent call last) :

File "<pyshell# 17>", line 1, in <module>

sum(l)

TypeError: unsupported operand type (s) for + : 'int' and 'str'

(v) count ( )

This method is used to calculate total occurrence of given element of list.

Syntax `list_name count (element)`

For example,

```
list1 = [4, 3, 5, 2, 54, 4, 2, 6, 4, 4, 5]
l = list1.count(4)
print(l)
```

Output

4

(vi) len ( )

This method is used to calculate the total length of list.

Syntax `len (list_name)`

For example,

```
list1 = [4, 3, 5, 2, 54, 4, 2, 6, 4, 4, 5]
l = len (list1)
print(l)
```

Output

11

(vii) index ()

It returns the index of first occurrence. Start and end index are not necessary parameters.

Syntax `list_name.index (element[, start [, end]])`

For example,

```
list1 = [3, 'New', 2, 6, 'Hello', 2]
l = list1.index ('Hello')
print(l)
```

Output

4

(viii) reverse ( )

Using the reverse ( ) method, we can reverse the contents of the list object in-place, i.e. we don't need to create a new list instead we just copy the existing elements to the original list in reverse order.

Syntax `list_name. reverse ( )`

For example,

```
list1 = [34, 76, 89, 33, 54, 65]
list1.reverse( )
print (list1)
l = ['Hii', 'Hello', 'Hey', 'Namesty']
l.reverse ( )
print (l)
```

Output

[65, 54, 33, 89, 76, 34]

['Namesty', 'Hey', 'Hello', 'Hii']

(ix) pop ( )

This function is used to remove the element and return last value from the list or the given index value.

Syntax `list_name.pop (index)`

For example,

```
l1 = [34, 65, 22, 90, 87, 61]
l1.pop (3)
print (l1)
```

If you do not give any index value, then it will remove last value from the list.

```
l1. pop ( )
print (l1)
```

Output

[34, 65, 22, 87, 61]

[34, 65, 22, 87]

(x) remove ( )

This method searches for the given element in the list and removes the first matching element. It takes a single element as an argument and remove it from the list.

Syntax `list_name. remove (element)`

For example,

```
list1 = [34, 76, 11, 98, 26, 20]
list1.remove (11)
print(list1)
```

Output

[34, 76, 98, 26, 20]

```
l1 = ['Maths', 'English', 'Hindi', 'History',
                                   'Science']
l1.remove('History')
print(l1)
```

Output

['Maths', 'English', 'Hindi', 'Science']

If the element (argument) passed to the remove ( ) method does not exist, ValueError exception is thrown.

l1. remove ( )

Trackback (most recent call last) :

File "<pyshell# 11>", line 1, in <module>

l1.remove ( )

TypeError : remove ( ) takes exactly one argument (0 given)

(xi) clear ( )

This function is used to remove all the items of a list. This method will empty the entire list.

Syntax `list_name. clear ( )`

For example,

```
l1 = [23, 45, 87, 12, 98]
l1.clear( )
print(l1)
```

Output

[ ]

(xii) sort ()

This function is used to sort the given list in ascending order.

Syntax `list _name. sort ( )`

For example,

```
list1 = [23, 65, 77, 23, 90, 99, 12]
list1. sort ( )
print (list1)
```

Output

[12, 23, 23, 65, 77, 90, 99]

```
list2 = ['abc' 'gdr', 'uyt', 'abc', 'nki']

list2. sort ( )
print (list2)
```

Output

['abc', 'abc', 'gdr', 'nki', 'uyt']

The sort function has an argument called

reverse = True. This allows us to sort the list elements in descending order.

Syntax `list _ name. sort (reverse = True)`

For example,

```
list1 = [23, 65, 77, 23, 90, 99, 12]
list1. sort (reverse = True)
print (list1)
```

Output

[99, 90, 77, 65, 23, 23, 12]

Try These 11.2

1. **Explain the different ways of slicing a list with a help of an example.**
2. **Mention the methods to remove elements from a list.**
3. **What is the method to remove an element from a list?**

11.6 Programs

1. Program to calculate the sum and mean of the elements which are entered by user.

```
list1 = list ()
sm = 0
num = int (input("Enter the size of the list :"))
print ("Enter the number:")
for i in range (int(num)):
    l = int (input(" "))
    list1. append (int(l))
    sm = sm + list1 [i]
```

```
mean = sm/num
print ("SUM =", sm)
print ("MEAN =", mean)
```

Output

Enter the size of the list : 6

Enter the number :

34

87

12

98

54

77

SUM = 362

MEAN = 60.333333333333336

2. Program to enter the elements of a list and reverse these elements.

```
list1 = list ( )
sm = 0
num = int (input("Enter the size of the list:"))
print ("Enter the number:")

for a in range (int(num)):
    l = int (input(" "))
    list1. append (int(l))
print ("Entered list:", list1)
revlst = [ ]
for i in reversed (list1) :
    revlst. append (i)
print ("Reversed list :" ,revlst)
```

Output

Enter the size of the list : 6

Enter the number :

34

76

23

98

67

23

Entered list : [34, 76, 23, 98, 67, 23]

Reversed list : [23, 67, 98, 23, 76, 34]

Glossary

List It is a type of container, which is used to store multiple data at the same time.

append() This method is used for appending and adding elements to a list. It is used to add elements to the last position of a list.

insert() This method is used to insert an element at specified position in the list.

extend() This method is used to add contents of list 2 to the end of list 1.

sum() This method is used to calculate the sum of all the elements in the list.

len() This method is used to calculate the total length of list.

pop() This function is used to remove the element and return last value from the list or the given index value.

remove() This method searches for the given element in the list and removes the first matching element.

REVIEW EXERCISE

Including Competency Based Questions

Multiple Choice Questions

1 **Which value is used to represent the first index of list?**

(a) 1 (b) 0 (c) -1 (d) a

2 **Choose the output of following Python code.**

```
l1=list ()
print (l1)
```

(a) [] (b) () (c) [,] (d) Empty

3 **Suppose list**

```
l1=[10, 20, 30, 40, 50, 60, 70]
print(l1[- 3])
```

(a) 30 (b) 50 (c) 40 (d) Error

4 **Choose the output from following code.**

```
list1 = ['A', 'R', 'I','H','A','N','T']
print (list1 [7])
```

(a) T (b) N (c) A (d) Error

5 **Which function is used to insert an element at specified position in the list?**

(a) extend () (b) append () (c) insert () (d) add ()

Answers

1. (b) 2. (a) 3. (b) 4. (d) 5. (c)

Statement Based Questions

1 **Statement 1 A list in Python can contain elements of different data types.**

Statement 2 Lists in Python are immutable.

(a) Both Statement 1 and Statement 2 are correct
(b) Both Statement 1 and Statement 2 are incorrect
(c) Statement 1 is correct but Statement 2 is incorrect
(d) Statement 2 is correct but Statement 1 is incorrect

2 **Statement 1 The index of the first element in a Python list is 1.**

Statement 2 You can use negative indices to access elements from the end of a list in Python.

(a) Both Statement 1 and Statement 2 are correct
(b) Both Statement 1 and Statement 2 are incorrect
(c) Statement 1 is correct but Statement 2 is incorrect
(d) Statement 2 is correct but Statement 1 is incorrect

3 **Statement 1 The append() method adds an element to the end of a list in Python.**

Statement 2 The remove() method deletes an element from a list by its index.

(a) Both Statement 1 and Statement 2 are correct
(b) Both Statement 1 and Statement 2 are incorrect
(c) Statement 1 is correct but Statement 2 is incorrect
(d) Statement 2 is correct but Statement 1 is incorrect

4 **Statement 1 Lists in Python can be nested, meaning a list can contain other lists.**

Statement 2 The len() function returns the number of elements in a list, including any nested lists as a single element.

(a) Both Statement 1 and Statement 2 are correct
(b) Both Statement 1 and Statement 2 are incorrect
(c) Statement 1 is correct but Statement 2 is incorrect
(d) Statement 2 is correct but Statement 1 is incorrect

5 **Statement 1 The slice operation in lists uses the syntax list[start:end] and includes the element at the end index.**

Statement 2 You can concatenate two lists in Python using the + operator.

(a) Both Statement 1 and Statement 2 are correct
(b) Both Statement 1 and Statement 2 are incorrect
(c) Statement 1 is correct but Statement 2 is incorrect
(d) Statement 2 is correct but Statement 1 is incorrect

Answers

1. (c) 2. (d) 3. (c) 4. (a) 5. (d)

Assertion & Reason Based Questions

1 **Assertion (A) A list in Python can contain elements of different data types.**

Reason (R) Lists in Python are mutable.

(a) Both A and R are true, and R is the correct explanation of A.
(b) Both A and R are true, but R is not the correct explanation of A.
(c) A is true, but R is false.
(d) A is false, but R is true.

2 **Assertion (A) You can add a new element to the end of a list using the append() method in Python.**

Reason (R) The append() method modifies the list in place.

(a) Both A and R are true, and R is the correct explanation of A.
(b) Both A and R are true, but R is not the correct explanation of A.
(c) A is true, but R is false.
(d) A is false, but R is true.

3 **Assertion (A) The len() function returns the total number of elements in a list.**

Reason (R) The len() function only works with lists that contain numeric data types.

(a) Both A and R are true, and R is the correct explanation of A.
(b) Both A and R are true, but R is not the correct explanation of A.
(c) A is true, but R is false.
(d) A is false, but R is true.

4 **Assertion (A) Lists in Python can be concatenated using the + operator.**

Reason (R) The + operator creates a new list that combines the elements of the original lists.

(a) Both A and R are true, and R is the correct explanation of A.
(b) Both A and R are true, but R is not the correct explanation of A.
(c) A is true, but R is false.
(d) A is false, but R is true.

Answers

1. (b) **2.** (a) **3.** (c) **4.** (a)

Very Short Answer Type Questions

1 What do you mean by list in Python ?

Ans. List is a type of container in data structures which is used to store multiple data at the same time.

2 Are lists mutable or immutable ?

Ans. Lists are mutable which means they can be changed after creation.

3 Which value is used to represent the first index of list?

Ans. Zero (0) is used to represent the first index of list.

4 Write the syntax to create the list from an existing sequence.

Ans. `new_list_name = list (Sequence/String)`

5 Write the output of below code.

```
>>>l1 = list ( )
>>>print (l1)
```

Ans. [ ]

6 What is traversing a list ?

Ans. Traversing a list is a technique to access an individual element of that list.

7 Find the output.

```
>>>l1 = [4, 3, 4, 5]
>>>l2 = [2, 6, 5, 4]
>>>l1 >= l2
```

Ans. True

8 Give the syntax for slicing a list's elements which are not consecutive.

Ans. `s = list_name [start : stop : step]`

9 What do you mean by insert ( ) method?

Ans. insert ( ) method is used to insert an element at specified position in the list.

10 How to count the element of a list?

Ans. `list.name.count (element)`

11 Which formula is used to sort the list in descending order.

Ans. list_name. sort (reverse = True)

12 What is the use of list ( ) method?

Ans. list ( ) method takes sequence types and converts them to lists. This is used to convert a given tuple into list.

Short Answer Type Questions

1 What is nested list ? Explain with an example.

Ans. Nested lists are list objects where the elements in the lists can be lists themselves.

For example,

```
list1 = [45, 43, 12, 'Math', 'Eng', [75, 34,
                                         'A'], 5]
```

list1 contains 7 elements while inner list contains 3 elements. list 1 is considered [75, 34, 'A'] as one element.

2 Observe the given list and find the answer of questions that follows .

```
list1 = [45, 77, 87, 'Next', 'Try', 33, 43]
```

(i) list1 [– 2] **(ii) list1 [2]**

Ans. (i) 33 (ii) 87

3 Distinguish between string and list.

Ans. Strings are immutable which means the values provided to them will not change in the program. While lists are mutable which means the values of list can be changed at any point of time in program.

4 What is the output of below questions?

```
l2 = [75, 43, 40, 36, 28, 82]
```

(i) l2.sort ( )
(ii) l2.sort (reverse = True)

Ans. (i) [28, 36, 40, 43, 75, 82]
(ii) [82, 75, 43, 40, 36, 28]

5 Find the errors.

```
L1 = [2, 4, 5, 9]
L2 = L1 * 3
L3 = L1  + 3
L4 = L1. pop (5)
```

Ans. Error 1 L3 = L1 + 3 because + operator cannot add list with other type as number or string.

Error 2 L1.pop (5) parentheses puts index value instead of element. In the given list, maximum index value is 3 and 5 is out of index range.

6 Predict the output.
L2 = [4, 5, 3, 1]
L3 = [3, 4, 11, 2]
(i) print (L2 + L3)
(ii) print (L2. count (0))
(iii) print (L3 [4])
(iv) print (L3. remove (11))

Ans. (i) [4, 5, 3, 1, 3, 4, 11, 2]
(ii) 0
(iii) IndexError
(iv) [3, 4, 2]

7 Find the output.
L = [3, 4, 53, 4, 0, 2, 4, 7, 29]
(i) L [2 : 5] **(ii) L [: 7]**
(iii) L [4 :] **(iv) [: : –1]**

Ans. (i) [53, 4, 0]
(ii) [3, 4, 53, 4, 0, 2, 4]
(iii) [0, 2, 4, 7, 29]
(iv) [29, 7, 4, 2, 0, 4, 53, 4, 3]

8 Find the output of the given code.
```
list2 = ['A', 'R', 'I', 'H', 'A', 'N', 'T']
for i in range (len (list2)):
    print (list2 [i])
```
Ans. A
R
I
H
A
N
T

9 Define the replicating lists with an example.

Ans. In Python, you can repeat the elements of the list using (*) operator. This operator is used to replicate the list.

For example,
```
>>>l1 = [4, 5, 7, 1]
>>>l2 = l1 * 2
>>>l2
[4, 5, 7, 1, 4, 5, 7, 1]
```

10 Consider the following list and answer the below questions:
l1 = [89, 45, "Taj", "Qutub", 93, 42, "Minar", "Delhi", "Agra"]
(i) l1 [5 :] **(ii) "Qutab" not in l1**
(iii) l1 [– 3] **(iv) l1 [9]**
(v) l1[2 : 5] **(vi) l1[-2 : 5]**

Ans. (i) [42, 'Minar', 'Delhi', 'Agra']
(ii) False
(iii) 'Minar'
(iv) It gives IndexError because there is index value 0 to 8.
(v) ['Taj', 'Qutub', 93]
(vi) [ ]

11 Predict the output.
```
L1 = [3, 4, 5, 9, 11, 2, 27]
print (L1. index (3))
print (len (L1))
```
Ans. Output
0
7

12 Write the suitable method's name for the below conditions.
(i) Adds an element in the end of list.
(ii) Returns the index of first occurrence.
(iii) Adds contents of list2 to the end of list1.

Ans. (i) append ( ) (ii) index ( )
(iii) extend ( )

Long Answer Type Questions

1 Write the best suited method's name for the following conditions.
(i) Insert an element at specified position.
(ii) Add contents from one list to other.
(iii) Calculate the total length of list.
(iv) Reverse the contents of the list object.

Ans. (i) insert ( ) (ii) extend ( )
(iii) len ( ) (iv) reverse ( )

2 Write a program to move all zeroes to the end of the list.

Ans.
```
list1 = [4, 7, 0, 9, 8, 0, 2, 0, 4, 9, 0]
n = len (list1)
count = 0
for i in range (n):
if list1[i] ! = 0:
        list1 [count] = list1[i]
        count + = 1
while count < n :
    list1 [count] = 0
    count + = 1
print ("List after pushing all zeroes to end of
                                          list:")
print (list1)
```
Output
List after pushing all zeroes to end of list
[4, 7, 9, 8, 2, 4, 9, 0, 0, 0, 0]

3 Observe the following list and answer the questions that follows.

```
l1 = [45, 65,"The", [65, "She", "He"], 90, 12,
                                      "This", 21]
```

(i) l1 [3 : 4] = ["That", 54] **(ii) [l1 [4]]**
(iii) l1 [:7] **(iv) l1 [1 : 2] + l1 [3 : 4]**

Ans. (i) [45, 65, 'The', 'That', 54, 90, 12, 'This', 21]

(ii) [54]

(iii) [45, 65, 'The', 'That', 54, 90, 12]

(iv) [65, 'That']

4 Write a python program to find the third largest number in a entered list.

Ans.
```
y = [ ]
num = int(input("Enter number of elements:"))
for i in range (1, num + 1):
    x = int (input ("Enter element:"))
    y.append(x)
y. sort ()
print("Third largest element is :", y[num-3])
```

Output

Enter number of elements : 5
Enter element : 76
Enter element : 45
Enter element : 98
Enter element : 90
Enter element : 23
Third largest element is : 76

5 Write a Python program to find the odd numbers and even numbers from entered list and display them in two different list.

Ans.
```
a = [ ]
num = int (input ("Enter number of elements:"))
for i in range (1, num +1):
    x = int (input ("Enter element:"))
    a. append (x)
even = [ ]
odd = [ ]
for y in a:
    if (y%2 = = 0):
        even.append (y)
    else :
        odd. append (y)
print ("The even list", even)
print ("The odd list", odd)
```

Output

Enter number of elements : 6
Enter element : 23
Enter element : 87
Enter element : 26
Enter element : 45
Enter element : 32
Enter element : 12
The even list [26, 32, 12]
The odd list [23, 87, 45]

6 Write a Python program to count a positive and negative numbers in a list.

Ans.
```
list1 = [ ]
num = int(input("Enter number of elements :"))
for i in range (1, num +1):
    x = int (input ("Enter element :"))
    list1. append (x)
pos_count, neg_count = 0, 0
for i in list1 :
    if i > = 0 :
        pos _ count + = 1
    else :
        neg_count + = 1
print ("Positive numbers in the list :",
                                  pos_count)
print ("Negative numbers in the list:",
                                  neg_count)
```

Output

Enter number of elements : 6
Enter element : 2
Enter element : – 5
Enter element : – 7
Enter element : 6
Enter element : 1
Enter element : 4
Positive numbers in the list : 4
Negative numbers in the list : 2

7 Suppose that L is the list

```
["These", ["are", "a"], ["few", "words"],
"that", "we", "will", "use"]
```

Based on the above code, answer the following questions.

(i) What is the value of len (L)?
(ii) What will be the output of L [2] [1 :]?
(iii) Find the output of L [1] + L [2].
(iv) What is the correct output of "few" in L [2 : 3]?

Ans. (i) 7

(ii) [“words”]

(iii) [“are”, “a”, “few”, “words”]

(iv) False

ASSESSMENT EXERCISE

Multiple Choice Questions

1. What is the output of following code?

```
list1=[4, 3, 7, 6, 4, 9, 5, 0, 3, 2]
l1=list1[1:10:3]
print(l1)
```

(a) [3, 7, 6] (b) [3, 4, 0] (c) [3, 6, 9] (d) [7, 9,2]

2. Identify the output of following Python statement.

```
a=[[0, 1, 2], [3, 4, 5, 6]]
b=a[1] [2]
print (b)
```

(a) 2 (b) 1 (c) 4 (d) 5

3. Identify the output of following code.

```
list1 = [2, 3, 9, 12, 4]
list1.insert(4, 17)
list1.insert(2, 23)
print(list1 [– 4])
```

(a) 4 (b) 9 (c) 12 (d) 23

Very Short Answer Type Questions

4. Which type of data can be store in list?
5. Write an example of mixed data type list.
6. How to compare a list in Python ?

Short Answer Type Questions

7. What is the use of (*) operator in list?
8. Explain the parameters of given syntax.

```
l = list_name [Start : Stop : Step]
```

9. Write a Python program to move all zeroes to the starting of the list.
10. Write a program to count the even numbers in a list.

Long answer Type Questions

11. Write the best suited method's name for the following conditions.
    (i) Remove the value from the list.
    (ii) Sort the elements in descending order.
    (iii) Calculate the sum of all the elements of list.
    (iv) Return the minimum element out of elements.
12. Write the program to print second largest number from the list.
13. Write a program to find maximum and minimum sum of elements of list in a list. Also, display its output.

Practical Work

Print

1. To print personal information like Name, Father's Name, Class, School Name.

```
# Personal information
print("Name: John Doe")
print("Father's Name: Robert Doe")
print("Class: 10th Grade")
print("School Name: XYZ High School")
```

2. To print the following patterns using multiple print commands-

```
*              * * * * *
* *            * * * *
* * *          * * *
* * * *        * *
* * * * *      *
```

(i)
```
# Number of rows in the triangle
num_rows = 5
# Loop through each row
for i in range(1, num_rows + 1):
    # Print stars for the current row
    print('*' * i)
```

(ii)
```
# Number of rows in the inverted triangle
rows = int(input("Enter the number of rows: "))
# Outer loop to iterate through rows in
reverse order
for i in range(rows, 0, -1):
    # Inner loop to print stars
    for j in range(0, i):
        print("* ", end="")
    print()
```

3. To find square of number 7.

```
# Finding square of number 7
number = 7
square = number * number
print("The square of", number, "is", square)
```

4. To find the sum of two numbers 15 and 20.

```
# Finding sum of two numbers
number1 = 15
number2 = 20
sum = number1 + number2
print("The sum of", number1, "and", number2,
"is", sum)
```

5. To convert length given in kilometers into meters.

```
# Converting kilometers into meters
kilometers = 5  # Example value
meters = kilometers * 1000
print(kilometers, "kilometers is equal to", meters,
"meters")
```

6. To print the table of 5 upto five terms.

```
# Printing the table of 5 up to five terms
number = 5
print(number, "* 1 =", number * 1)
print(number, "* 2 =", number * 2)
print(number, "* 3 =", number * 3)
print(number, "* 4 =", number * 4)
print(number, "* 5 =", number * 5)
```

7. To calculate Simple Interest if the principle_amount = 2000, rate_of_interest = 4.5, time = 10.

```
# Calculating Simple Interest
principle_amount = 2000
rate_of_interest = 4.5
time = 10
simple_interest = (principle_amount * rate_of_interest *
time) / 100
print("The Simple Interest is", simple_interest)
```

Input

1. To calculate Area and Perimeter of a rectangle.

```
# Program to calculate the area and perimeter of a
rectangle
# Taking input from the user
length = float(input("Enter the length of the rectangle: "))
width = float(input("Enter the width of the rectangle: "))
# Calculating area and perimeter
area = length * width
perimeter = 2 * (length + width)
# Displaying the results
print(f"The area of the rectangle is: {area}")
print(f"The perimeter of the rectangle is: {perimeter}")
```

2. To calculate Area of a triangle with Base and Height.

```
# Program to calculate the area of a triangle
# Taking input from the user
base = float(input("Enter the base of the triangle: "))
height = float(input("Enter the height of the triangle: "))
# Calculating area
area = 0.5 * base * height
```

```
# Displaying the result
print(f"The area of the triangle is: {area}")
```

3. To calculating average marks of 3 subjects.

```
# Program to calculate the average marks of 3 subjects
# Taking input from the user
mark1 = float(input("Enter the marks for subject 1: "))
mark2 = float(input("Enter the marks for subject 2: "))
mark3 = float(input("Enter the marks for subject 3: "))
# Calculating average
average = (mark1 + mark2 + mark3) / 3
# Displaying the result
print(f"The average marks are: {average}")
```

4. To calculate discounted amount with discount %.

```
# Program to calculate the discounted amount
# Taking input from the user
original_price = float(input("Enter the original price: "))
discount_percent = float(input("Enter the discount percentage: "))
# Calculating discounted amount
discount_amount = (discount_percent / 100) * original_price
final_price = original_price - discount_amount
# Displaying the result
print(f"The discounted amount is: {discount_amount}")
print(f"The final price after discount is: {final_price}")
```

5. To calculate Surface Area and Volume of a Cuboid.

```
# Program to calculate the surface area and volume of a cuboid
# Taking input from the user
length = float(input("Enter the length of the cuboid: "))
width = float(input("Enter the width of the cuboid: "))
height = float(input("Enter the height of the cuboid: "))
# Calculating surface area and volume
surface_area = 2 * (length * width + width * height + height * length)
volume = length * width * height
# Displaying the results
print(f"The surface area of the cuboid is: {surface_area}")
print(f"The volume of the cuboid is: {volume}")
```

List

1. Create a list in Python of children selected for science quiz with following names-
Arjun, Sonakshi, Vikram, Sandhya, Sonal, Isha, Kartik
Perform the following tasks on the list in sequence-
   - Print the whole list
   - Delete the name "Vikram" from the list
   - Add the name "Jay" at the end
   - Remove the item which is at the second position.

```
# Create the list of children selected for the science quiz
children = ["Arjun", "Sonakshi", "Vikram", "Sandhya", "Sonal", "Isha", "Kartik"]
# Print the whole list
print(children)
# Delete the name "Vikram" from the list
children.remove("Vikram")
# Print the list after deletion
print(children)
# Add the name "Jay" at the end
children.append("Jay")
# Print the list after adding the name
print(children)
# Remove the item which is at the second position (index 1)
del children[1]
# Print the list after removing the item at the second position
print(children)
```

2. Create a list num=[23,12,5,9,65,44]
   - print the length of the list
   - print the elements from second to fourth position using positive indexing
   - print the elements from position third to fifth using negative indexing

```
# Creating the list
num = [23, 12, 5, 9, 65, 44]
# Printing the length of the list
length = len(num)
print("Length of the list:", length)
# Printing the elements from the second to fourth position using positive indexing
elements = num[1:4]
print("Elements from second to fourth position using positive indexing:", elements)
# Printing the elements from the third to fifth position using negative indexing
elements = num[-4:-1]
print("Elements from third to fifth position using negative indexing:", elements)
```

3. Create a list of first 10 even numbers, add 1 to each list item and print the final list.

```
# Create a list of first 10 even numbers
even_numbers = [2, 4, 6, 8, 10, 12, 14, 16, 18, 20]
# Add 1 to each item in the list
for i in range(len(even_numbers)):
    even_numbers[i] += 1
# Print the final list
print(even_numbers)
```

4. Create a list List_1=[10,20,30,40]. Add the elements [14,15,12] using extend function. Now sort the final list in ascending order and print it.

```
# Create the initial list
List_1 = [10, 20, 30, 40]
# Extend the list with [14, 15, 12]
List_1.extend([14, 15, 12])
# Sort the final list in ascending order
List_1.sort()
# Print the final list
print(List_1)
```

If, For, While

1. Program to check if a person can vote.

```
age = int(input("Enter your age: "))
if age >= 18:
    print("You are eligible to vote.")
else:
    print("You are not eligible to vote.")
```

2. To check the grade of a student.

```
marks = int(input("Enter the marks: "))
if marks >= 90:
    grade = 'A'
elif marks >= 80:
    grade = 'B'
elif marks >= 70:
    grade = 'C'
elif marks >= 60:
    grade = 'D'
else:
    grade = 'F'
print("Your grade is:", grade)
```

3. Input a number and check if the number is positive, negative or zero and display an appropriate message.

```
number = float(input("Enter a number: "))
if number > 0:
    print("The number is positive.")
elif number < 0:
    print("The number is negative.")
else:
    print("The number is zero.")
```

4. To print first 10 natural numbers.

```
for i in range(1, 11):
    print(i)
```

5. To print first 10 even numbers.

```
count = 0
num = 2
while count < 10:
    print(num)
    num += 2
    count += 1
```

6. To print odd numbers from 1 to n.

```
n = int(input("Enter the value of n: "))
for i in range(1, n + 1):
    if i % 2 != 0:
        print(i)
```

7. To print sum of first 10 natural numbers.

```
sum = 0
for i in range(1, 11):
    sum += i
print("Sum of first 10 natural numbers is:", sum)
```

8. Program to find the sum of all numbers stored in a list.

```
numbers = [1, 2, 3, 4, 5, 6, 7, 8, 9, 10]
sum = 0
for number in numbers:
    sum += number
print("Sum of all numbers in the list is:", sum)
```

Sample Question Paper 1

Artificial Intelligence

Time : 2 hrs	M.M. : 50

1. Please read the instructions carefully.
2. This Question Paper consists of **21 questions** in two sections: Section A & Section B.
3. Section A has Objective type questions whereas Section B contains Subjective type questions.
4. **Out of the given (5 + 16 =) 21 questions, a candidate has to answer (5 + 10 =) 15 questions in the allotted (maximum) time of 2 hours.**
5. All questions of a particular section must be attempted in the correct order.
6. **SECTION A - OBJECTIVE TYPE QUESTIONS (24 MARKS):**
   i. This section has 05 questions.
   ii. Marks allotted are mentioned against each question/part.
   iii. There is no negative marking.
   iv. Do as per the instructions given.
7. **SECTION B – SUBJECTIVE TYPE QUESTIONS (26 MARKS):**
   i. This section has 16 questions.
   ii. A candidate has to do 10 questions.
   iii. Do as per the instructions given.
   iv. Marks allotted are mentioned against each question/part.

Section A : Objective Type Questions

1. Answer any 4 out of the given 6 questions on Employability Skills **(1 × 4 = 4 Marks)**

(i) Which is an example of a natural resource?
(a) Natural gas (b) Copper
(c) Fertile land (d) All of these

(ii) Businesses cater to the need of the
(a) area (b) society (c) market (d) village

(iii) "Ritu practiced yoga and meditation daily to manage her stress effectively. She also ensured a proper work-life balance by setting boundaries for her working hours."

Which self-management skill is clearly visible in the given statement?

(iv) .... includes computers, Internet, broadcasting technologies and telephony.
(a) ICT (b) Browser
(c) IT (d) None of these

(v) Communication skills are those skills which are needed to
(a) Speak properly
(b) Write properly
(c) Both (a) and (b)
(d) None of the above

(vi) Believing in yourself that you can do any task that is given to you is ....
(a) Self-control (b) Self-awareness
(c) Self-confidence (d) Positive thinking

2. Answer any 5 out of the given 6 questions **(1 × 5 =5 marks)**

(i) .... type of AI is designed to perform a specific task or solve a specific problem.

(ii) In ...., we need to address the problem and what the advantages will be for the stakeholders once the problem is solved.
(a) Who (b) What
(c) Where (d) Why

(iii) In the context of AI ethics, what are the key aspects covered under the term "Fairness"?

I. Treating everyone equally
II. Favoring specific groups
III. Considering historical biases
IV. Ensuring equal distribution of resources

(a) Both I and III (b) Only II
(c) Both I and IV (d) Only III

(iv) What advantage do businesses gain from data literacy?

(a) Increased confusion
(b) Decreased efficiency
(c) Improved innovation and competitive advantage
(d) Reduced customer satisfaction

(v) Which method involves collecting data by observing people's behaviour or the natural world?

(a) Surveys (b) Interviews
(c) Experiments (d) Observations

(vi) What mathematical technique is commonly used to adjust the parameters of AI models to minimize errors?

(a) Regression analysis
(b) Gradient descent
(c) Matrix factorization
(d) Monte Carlo simulation

3. Answer any 5 out of the given 6 questions **(1 × 5 = 5 marks)**

(i) Assertion Generative AI models can create new content, such as text, images, music, and videos, with some form of human input or prompt to generate content.

Reason These models are trained to understand patterns and structures within existing data and use that knowledge to generate new original data.

(a) Both the Assertion and Reason are true, and the Reason is the correct explanation of the assertion.
(b) Both the Assertion and Reason are true, but the Reason is not the correct explanation of the Assertion.
(c) The Assertion is true, but the Reason is false.
(d) Both the Assertion and Reason are false.

(ii) Python interpreters are available for operating system(s)

(a) Windows (b) MacOS
(c) Both (a) and (b) (d) None of these

(iii) What will be the output of the following code snippet?

```
print("Hello\tWorld")
```

(a) Hello World (b) Hello\tWorld
(c) Hello World (d) Error

(iv) .... statements enable a program with a cyclic flow of logic.

(v) Choose the output from following code.

```
list1 = ['A', 'R', 'I','H','A','N','T']
print (list1 [7])
```

(a) T (b) N (c) A (d) Error

(vi) Identify the given chatbot type:
This chatbot uses predefined rules and scripts to provide responses. It follows a decision tree and is unable to learn from new data or interactions.

4. Answer any 5 out of the given 6 questions **(1 × 5 = 5 marks)**

(i) When you explore the data and try to put it uniformly for a better understanding. It is called ....

(a) Data acquisition (b) Problem scoping
(c) Data exploration (d) Modelling

(ii) Aarav was studying different AI technologies and came across a system that can process and interpret human language, enabling computers to understand and respond. However, he couldn't recall its name. Can you help him?

(iii) What is one advantage of data literacy mentioned in the content?

(a) Information overload (b) Misleading data
(c) Smarter decisions (d) Lack of tech savvy

(iv) What is the primary goal of data used in the field of Computer Vision (CV)?

(a) To interpret and understand text data
(b) To extract meaningful information from images and videos
(c) To analyze numerical and categorical data
(d) To generate synthetic data

(v) Which measure of central tendency is the most common and is calculated as the sum of all values divided by the number of values?

(a) Mode (b) Median (c) Mean (d) Range

(vi) Statement 1 Generative AI can create new content such as text, images, music, and videos.

Statement 2 Generative AI models operate using machine learning, particularly deep learning.

(a) Both Statement 1 and Statement 2 are correct
(b) Both Statement 1 and Statement 2 are incorrect
(c) Statement 1 is correct but Statement 2 is incorrect
(d) Statement 2 is correct but Statement 1 is incorrect

5. Answer any 5 out of the given 6 questions **(1 × 5 = 5 marks)**

(i) When writing a computer program, which of the following are used to store information?

i. Variables
ii. Datatypes

iii. **Type conversion**

iv. **Comments**

(a) Only i (b) i and ii

(c) ii and iii (d) i, ii, and iii

(ii) In complex number, a + ib , where b represents as

(a) real part (b) imaginary part

(c) special part (d) None of these

(iii) Assertion The "for" loop in Python is used for iterative statements, allowing a set of statements to be executed repeatedly.

Reason The "for" loop is especially useful when the number of iterations is known beforehand.

(a) Both Assertion and Reason are correct, and Reason is the correct explanation of Assertion.

(b) Both Assertion and Reason are correct, but Reason is not the correct explanation of Assertion.

(c) Assertion is correct, but Reason is incorrect.

(d) Assertion is incorrect, but Reason is correct.

(iv) Choose the output of following Python code.

```
l1=list ()
print (l1)
```

(a) [] (b) () (c) [,] (d) Empty

(v) Mr. Dinesh Patel, a computer science teacher at kendriya vidyalya, has developed an educational humanoid namely Shalu, which can converse in 47 languages. Which AI technology helps Shalu, the robot, converse with us humans?

(a) NLP (b) CV

(c) ML (d) Data Science

(vi) Which phase of the AI project cycle involves identifying the problem and defining the goals clearly?

Section B Subjective Type Questions

Answer any 3 out of the given 5 questions in 20 - 32 words each on Employability Skills (2 × 3 = 6 marks)

6. What is the key to effective communication?

7. Define ICT in the workplace.

8. What is the primary purpose of entrepreneurship?

9. What are the three Rs in waste management, and how do they contribute to environmental conservation?

10. What does team work involve in self-management?

Answer any 4 out of the given 6 questions in 20-30 words each (2 × 4 = 8 marks)

11. Describe reason of AI bias.

12. Explain the Data Pyramid and its significance in data processing.

13. Enumerate three primary factors crucial for determining the usability of data, and briefly explain their significance.

14. What role does statistics play in preparing data for AI learning?

15. What are some examples of Generative AI models and their applications?

16. What is the difference between interactive mode and script mode in Python?

Answer any 3 out of the given 5 questions in 50-80 words each (4 × 3 = 12 marks)

17. Write a Python program which input the time in seconds and convert it into days. Also, display its output.

18. Write a program to check whether a number is prime or not.

19. Write a program to move all zeroes to the end of the list.

20. Akash wants to understand why people think Artificial Intelligence is beneficial. Can you explain some of the advantages of AI, especially in areas like healthcare, transportation, and education?

21. A wildlife conservation organization has gathered data on the population of endangered species in various national parks. The released statistics include 800 elephants, 600 rhinos, 400 tigers, and 300 pandas. What is the best visualization to represent this type of data in data visualization tools?

Sample Question Paper 2
Artificial Intelligence

Time : 2 hrs	M.M. : 50

1. Please read the instructions carefully.
2. This Question Paper consists of **21 questions** in two sections: Section A & Section B.
3. Section A has Objective type questions whereas Section B contains Subjective type questions.
4. **Out of the given (5 + 16 =) 21 questions, a candidate has to answer (5 + 10 =) 15 questions in the allotted (maximum) time of 2 hours.**
5. All questions of a particular section must be attempted in the correct order.
6. **SECTION A - OBJECTIVE TYPE QUESTIONS (24 MARKS):**
   i. This section has 05 questions.
   ii. Marks allotted are mentioned against each question/part.
   iii. There is no negative marking.
   iv. Do as per the instructions given.
7. **SECTION B – SUBJECTIVE TYPE QUESTIONS (26 MARKS):**
   i. This section has 16 questions.
   ii. A candidate has to do 10 questions.
   iii. Do as per the instructions given.
   iv. Marks allotted are mentioned against each question/part.

Section A : Objective Type Questions

1. Answer any 4 out of the given 6 questions on Employability Skills **(1 × 4 = 4 Marks)**

(i) With a .... you can only make calls and receive calls.

(a) Smartphone (b) Android phone
(c) Simple phone (d) Tablet

(ii) An entrepreneur is a self employed person and is willing to take a

(a) product and service (b) satisfying human need
(c) calculated risk (d) regular production

(iii) "Ananya always created a to-do list before starting her day, prioritized her tasks, and ensured that she completed them on time without procrastination."
Which self-management skill is clearly visible in the given statement?

(iv) Which type of resources can be replenished?

(a) Non-renewable resources
(b) Exhaustible resources
(c) Renewable resources
(d) Mineral resources

(v) The word 'Communication' came from the

(a) French word (b) Latin word
(c) Greek word (d) None of these

(vi) Ability to control your behaviour, discipline etc is regarded as

(a) Self-control
(b) Self-awareness
(c) Self-confidence
(d) Problem solving

2. Answer any 5 out of the given 6 questions **(1 × 5 =5 marks)**

(i) Which AI program defeated the world chess champion, Gassy Kasparov, in a highly-publicized match?

(a) Deep Blue (b) Watson
(c) Kismet (d) ELIZA

(ii) The AI Project Cycle is a .... that uses scientific methods to solve problems and draw conclusions.

(a) Step-by-step process
(b) Random process
(c) Reverse process
(d) None of the above

(iii) **A new AI-driven medical diagnosis system was introduced in a hospital. After a few months, it was discovered that the system occasionally provided incorrect diagnoses without any clear explanation. What AI ethical issue is highlighted in this situation?**

(a) Human rights and AI
(b) Accountability
(c) Unbiased
(d) Human-AI interaction

(iv) **........... is the fundamental building block of information.**

(v) **In a machine learning model to predict house prices, what would be considered an independent feature?**

(a) Sale price of the house
(b) Number of bedrooms
(c) Location
(d) Both (b) and (c)

(vi) **Which branch of mathematics is essential for optimizing the parameters of AI models?**

(a) Algebra (b) Geometry
(c) Calculus (d) Trigonometry

3. Answer any 5 out of the given 6 questions **(1 × 5 = 5 marks)**

(i) **Assertion** Generative Adversarial Networks (GANs) consist of two main components - a Generator Network and a Discriminator Network.

Reason The Generator network creates new data, while the Discriminator network tries to identify whether the data it sees is real or generated by the Generator.

(a) Both the Assertion and Reason are true, and the Reason is the correct explanation of the Assertion.
(b) Both the Assertion and Reason are true, but the Reason is not the correct explanation of the Assertion.
(c) The Assertion is true, but the Reason is false.
(d) Both the Assertion and Reason are false.

(ii) **In programming languages, which of the following are examples of data types?**

i. Integer **ii. Float**
iii. Character **iv. Loop**

(a) Only i and ii (b) i, ii, and iii
(c) ii, iii, and iv (d) Only iii

(iii) **Which of the following is used for multiline comments in Python?**

(a) ''' Comment ''' (b) """ Comment """
(c) Both (a) and (b) (d) None of these

(iv) **These statements enable a program with a cyclic flow of logic.**

(a) Sequence (b) Compound
(c) Single (d) Iterative

(v) **........... is used to represent the first index of list.**

(vi) **Identify the given chatbot type:**

This chatbot uses advanced algorithms and machine learning to understand natural language and provide human-like responses. It can improve over time based on data and user interactions.

4. Answer any 5 out of the given 6 questions **(1 × 5 = 5 marks)**

(i) **Refers to developing algorithms, also called models which can be trained to get intelligent.**

(a) Data acquisition
(b) Problem scoping
(c) Data exploration
(d) Modelling

(ii) **Priya heard about an AI system where computers learn from data without being explicitly programmed. She forgot the exact term for this process. Can you remind her?**

(iii) **What does data security aim to protect against?**

(a) Unwanted data collection
(b) Unauthorized access, corruption, or theft of digital information
(c) Data deletion
(d) Data miscommunication

(iv) **Which type of data interpretation focuses on understanding experiences, opinions, and reasons?**

(a) Quantitative Interpretation
(b) Statistical Interpretation
(c) Qualitative Interpretation
(d) Correlation Interpretation

(v) **Which measure of central tendency is the most common and is calculated as the sum of all values divided by the number of values?**

(a) Mode (b) Median
(c) Mean (d) Range

(vi) **Statement 1** VAEs (Variational Autoencoders) are used for generating new data by learning the underlying structure of a dataset.

Statement 2 GANs (Generative Adversarial Networks) use two neural networks, Generator and Discriminator, in an adversarial relationship to create new data.

(a) Both Statement 1 and Statement 2 are correct
(b) Both Statement 1 and Statement 2 are incorrect
(c) Statement 1 is correct but Statement 2 is incorrect
(d) Statement 2 is correct but Statement 1 is incorrect

5. Answer any 5 out of the given 6 questions
(1 × 5 = 5 marks)

(i) In Python programming, which is considered as keyword?
(a) var (b) data (c) time (d) and

(ii) What will be the output of the following code snippet?
```
x = 10
y = 20
x, y = y, x
print(x, y)
```
(a) 10 20 (b) 20 10
(c) 10 10 (d) 20 20

(iii) Which statement is a sequence of more than one statements?
(a) Control statement
(b) Compound statement
(c) Single statement
(d) Sequence statement

(iv) Suppose list

l1=[10, 20, 30, 40, 50, 60, 70]

print(l1[– 3])

(a) 30 (b) 50
(c) 40 (d) Error

(v) Which sector uses AI for weather forecasting and climate modeling?
(a) Environmental Sciences
(b) Manufacturing
(c) Aerospace
(d) Retail

(vi) In which phase of the AI Project Cycle do you collect and organize data required for training the AI model?

Section B : Subjective Type Questions

Answer any 3 out of the given 5 questions in 20 - 32 words each on Employability Skills (2 × 3 = 6 marks)

6. How does ICT benefit home life?

7. How does active listening improve communication?

8. How does entrepreneurship contribute to economic development?

9. How can you identify your strengths?

10. How do pollutants from human activities contribute to environmental pollution?

Answer any 4 out of the given 6 questions in 20-30 words each (2 × 4 = 8 marks)

11. What are Morals?

12. What is data literacy, and why is it important?

13. Explain the methods of data interpretation and give an example of each.

14. How does mathematics contribute to the foundation of AI?

15. How has Generative AI evolved over the years, and what are some significant milestones in its development?

16. What do you mean by IDLE in Python?

Answer any 3 out of the given 5 questions in 50-80 words each (4 × 3 = 12 marks)

17. Explain various operators in Python.

18. An electricity board charges according to the following rules.
For the first 100 units - 40 P per unit
For the next 200 units - 50 P per unit
Beyond 300 units - 60 P per unit

All users have to pay meter charge also, which is ₹ 50. Write a program to read the number of units consumed and print out the charges.

19. Write a python program to find the third largest number in a entered list.

20. How does AI enhance and advance our homes?

21. Wildlife India, an autonomous organization dedicated to the rehabilitation of injured wild animals, is keen on monitoring the treated animals by tracking details like their location and thermal information. Which method are most suitable for collecting this specific set of data?

Sample Question Paper 3

Artificial Intelligence

Time : 2 hrs	M.M. : 50

1. Please read the instructions carefully.
2. This Question Paper consists of **21 questions** in two sections: Section A & Section B.
3. Section A has Objective type questions whereas Section B contains Subjective type questions.
4. **Out of the given (5 + 16 =) 21 questions, a candidate has to answer (5 + 10 =) 15 questions in the allotted (maximum) time of 2 hours.**
5. All questions of a particular section must be attempted in the correct order.
6. **SECTION A - OBJECTIVE TYPE QUESTIONS (24 MARKS):**
   i. This section has 05 questions.
   ii. Marks allotted are mentioned against each question/part.
   iii. There is no negative marking.
   iv. Do as per the instructions given.
7. **SECTION B – SUBJECTIVE TYPE QUESTIONS (26 MARKS):**
   i. This section has 16 questions.
   ii. A candidate has to do 10 questions.
   iii. Do as per the instructions given.
   iv. Marks allotted are mentioned against each question/part.

Section A : Objective Type Questions

1. Answer any 4 out of the given 6 questions on Employability Skills **(1 × 4 = 4 Marks)**

(i) The information can be

(a) Drawings (b) Words
(c) Gestures (d) All of these

(ii) Which of the following statements about positive thinking is correct?

(a) Positive thinking results in positive circumstances.
(b) Positive thinking helps in focusing on the bright side of an individual's life.
(c) Positive people can easily overcome problems and achieve success.
(d) All of the above

(iii) Which of the following device is used to enter information into the computer?

(a) Output
(b) Input
(c) Computer
(d) Memory

(iv) Entrepreneurs uses optimal ways of using the resources to

(a) reduce cost (b) increase profit
(c) Both of these (d) None of these

(v) "Rohan constantly upgraded his skills by attending online courses and workshops, showing a strong desire to learn and improve continuously in his career."

Which self-management skill is clearly visible in the given statement?

(vi) If you are starting to use jute bags instead of plastic bags, then which 'R' you are doing?

(a) Reduce (b) Reuse (c) Recycle (d) All 3R

2. Answer any 5 out of the given 6 questions **(1 × 5 =5 marks)**

(i) You're a customer service manager for a growing tech startup. With an influx of inquiries, your team struggles to handle the volume efficiently. Clients often face delays in receiving support, impacting customer satisfaction.

To streamline customer support and enhance responsiveness, which AI tool should you integrate into your system?

(a) Robotics (b) Chatbots
(c) Natural Language Processing
(d) Computer Vision

(ii) .... **involves gathering and filtering data from various sources.**

(iii) Which ethical principle emphasizes the importance of ensuring that AI systems treat all individuals fairly and without bias?

(a) Autonomy (b) Beneficence
(c) Justice (d) Non-maleficence

(iv) What can data literacy empower individuals to do in their personal lives?

(a) Track finances and monitor health
(b) Become less responsible
(c) Rely solely on evidence for decision-making
(d) Ignore data completely

(v) What does data discovery involve in the context of data acquisition for AI models?

(a) Generating new data points
(b) Identifying and obtaining relevant datasets
(c) Augmenting existing data
(d) Cleaning and structuring data

(vi) How is variance calculated in a data set?

(a) By taking the sum of the data points
(b) By calculating the average of the data points
(c) By finding the average squared deviation from the mean
(d) By dividing the sum of the squares by the number of values

3. Answer any 5 out of the given 6 questions **(1 × 5 = 5 marks)**

(i) Which type of AI is most commonly used for tasks such as image and speech synthesis?

(a) Conventional AI (b) Generative AI
(c) Symbolic AI (d) Expert systems

(ii) When writing a program, which elements belong to the character set used in coding?

(a) Alphabets (A-Z, a-z)
(b) Digits (0-9)
(c) Special characters (!, @, #, etc.)
(d) All of the above

(iii) Which function is used to convert a string to an integer in Python?

(a) str() (b) int()
(c) float() (d) eval()

(iv) while loops are called as ....

(v) Assertion (A) You can add a new element to the end of a list using the append() method in Python.

Reason (R) The append() method modifies the list in place.

(a) Both A and R are true, and R is the correct explanation of A.
(b) Both A and R are true, but R is not the correct explanation of A.
(c) A is true, but R is false.
(d) A is false, but R is true.

(vi) Identify the given chatbot type:

This chatbot is specifically designed to perform a single task or solve a specific problem. It cannot handle tasks outside its defined scope or purpose.

4. Answer any 5 out of the given 6 questions **(1 × 5 = 5 marks)**

(i) Which visualization technique is best suited for illustrating the frequency of a particular occurrence?

(a) Scatter Plot
(b) Choropleth Map
(c) Word Cloud
(d) Histogram

(ii) Assertion Ethics plays a crucial role in guiding individuals' behaviour and decision-making, considering principles of fairness, justice, and moral acceptability.

Reason Ethics provides a set of principles or standards that help individuals determine what is right or wrong in various situations, influencing how people interact with others, make choices, and align their actions with societal values.

(a) Both Assertion and Reason are true, and Reason is the correct explanation of the Assertion.
(b) Both Assertion and Reason are true, but Reason is not the correct explanation of the Assertion.
(c) Assertion is true, but Reason is false.
(d) Assertion is false, but Reason is true.

(iii) Statement 1 Data privacy refers to your right to control your personal information, including who can access it and how it's used.

Statement 2 Data privacy is important for individuals, businesses and organizations.

(a) Both Statement 1 and Statement 2 are correct
(b) Both Statement 1 and Statement 2 are incorrect
(c) Statement 1 is correct but Statement 2 is incorrect
(d) Statement 2 is correct but Statement 1 is incorrect

(iv) Rahul learned about an AI concept where virtual or physical systems can perceive their environment and make decisions to maximize success. However, he can't remember its name. Can you tell him?

(v) Which field uses statistical analysis to evaluate player performance and predict game outcomes?

(a) Finance (b) Marketing
(c) Sports (d) Education

(vi) What was the first functioning generative AI created in 1964?

(a) GAN (b) LSTM
(c) ELIZA chatbot (d) Transformer

5. Answer any 5 out of the given 6 questions **(1 × 5 = 5 marks)**

(i) Which of the following is/are advantage(s) of Python?

(a) Easy to use
(b) Object oriented
(c) Portability
(d) All of the above

(ii) What will be the output of the following code snippet?

```
x = 10
y = 3
print(x // y)
```

(a) 3.333 (b) 3.0
(c) 3 (d) 4

(iii) In Python programming, which statements are used for controlling the flow of a program? Choose the correct options.

(i) Sequence statements
(ii) Selection statements
(iii) Iterative statements
(iv) Conditional statements

(a) Only (i) (b) Both (ii) and (iii)
(c) (ii), (iii) and (iv) (d) (i), (ii) and (iii)

(iv) Which function is used to insert an element at specified position in the list?

(a) extend () (b) append ()
(c) insert () (d) add ()

(v) Which AI application focuses on training machines to understand and interpret visual data?

(a) Machine Translation
(b) Natural Language Processing
(c) Computer Vision
(d) Speech Recognition

(vi) During which phase of the AI project cycle are patterns and insights discovered from the dataset using statistical and visualization techniques?

Section B : Subjective Type Questions

Answer any 3 out of the given 5 questions in 20 - 32 words each on Employability Skills (2 × 3 = 6 marks)

6. What does 'SMILE' stand for in cultivating a positive attitude?

7. How does entrepreneurship benefit society through competitive prices?

8. What is the impact of body language on communication?

9. How do smartphones enhance workplace productivity?

10. How can energy conservation contribute to saving fossil fuels?

Answer any 4 out of the given 6 questions in 20-30 words each (2 × 4 = 8 marks)

11. Give some examples of AI bias.

12. What are the key aspects and importance of data security?

13. What are the two main types of data and their defining characteristics?

14. In what ways does probability theory benefit AI systems?

15. How do Generative AI models contribute to innovation and problem-solving in various domains?

16. Python is free and open source, what is it mean?

Answer any 3 out of the given 5 questions in 50-80 words each (4 × 3 = 12 marks)

17. The distance between two cities (in km) is input through the keyboard, write a Python program to convert this distance in meters.

18. Write a program to display a triangle of numbers using for loop within a while loop.

19. Arjun is curious about the disadvantages of Artificial Intelligence (AI). Can you explain to him in simple terms, considering his class 9th level of understanding?

20. Write a Python program to count a positive and negative numbers in a list.

21. Write the problem approach in AI Problem Scoping.

Answers

Sample Question Paper 1

1. (i) (d) (ii) (c) (iii) Stress Management (iv) (a) (v) (c) (vi) (c)
2. (i) Artificial Narrow Intelligence (ANI) (ii) (d) (iii) (c) (iv) (c) (v) (d) (vi) (b)
3. (i) (a) (ii) (c) (iii) (c) (iv) Iterative (v) (d) (vi) Rule-based Chatbot
4. (i) (c) (ii) Natural Language Processing (NLP) (iii) (c) (iv) (b) (v) (c) (vi) (a)
5. (i) (a) (ii) (b) (iii) (a) (iv) (a) (v) (a) (vi) Problem scoping

Sample Question Paper 2

1. (i) (c) (ii) (c) (iii) Time Management (iv) (c) (v) (b) (vi) (a)
2. (i) (a) (ii) (a) (iii) (b) (iv) Data (v) (d) (vi) (c)
3. (i) (a) (ii) (b) (iii) (c) (iv) (d) (v) (0) (vi) AI-based Chatbot
4. (i) (d) (ii) Machine Learning (iii) (b) (iv) (c) (v) (c) (vi) (a)
5. (i) (d) (ii) (b) (iii) (b) (iv) (b) (v) (a) (vi) Data acquisition

Sample Question Paper 3

1. (i) (d) (ii) (d) (iii) (b) (iv) (c) (v) Self-motivation and Learning Skills (vi) (a)
2. (i) (b) (ii) Data Acquisition (iii) (c) (iv) (a) (v) (b) (vi) (c)
3. (i) (b) (ii) (d) (iii) (b) (iv) entry control loops (v) (a) (vi) Task-specific Chatbot
4. (i) (d) (ii) (a) (iii) (a) (iv) Intelligent Agent (v) (c) (vi) (c)
5. (i) (d) (ii) (c) (iii) (d) (iv) (c) (v) (c) (vi) Data exploration